Josiah Miller

Our Hymns

Their authors and origin, being biographical sketches of nearly two hundred of the principal Psalm and hymn-writers, with notes on their Psalms and hymns : a companion to the New Congregational hymn book

Josiah Miller

Our Hymns

Their authors and origin, being biographical sketches of nearly two hundred of the principal Psalm and hymn-writers, with notes on their Psalms and hymns : a companion to the New Congregational hymn book

ISBN/EAN: 9783337386467

Printed in Europe, USA, Canada, Australia, Japan

Cover: Foto ©Thomas Meinert / pixelio.de

More available books at **www.hansebooks.com**

OUR HYMNS:

Their Authors and Origin.

BEING

BIOGRAPHICAL SKETCHES OF NEARLY TWO HUNDRED OF THE
PRINCIPAL PSALM AND HYMN-WRITERS, WITH NOTES
ON THEIR PSALMS AND HYMNS.

A Companion to the New Congregational Hymn Book.

BY

JOSIAH MILLER, M.A.

London:
JACKSON, WALFORD, AND HODDER,
27, PATERNOSTER ROW.

MDCCCLXVI.

PREFACE.

No apology is needed for a new book on Hymnology. Some authors have difficulty in proving that there is really room for their work, but it is not so with those who write on this comparatively neglected subject. In saying this, we do not overlook the valuable articles on this subject that have appeared recently in newspapers and reviews; nor the useful labours of Montgomery, Creamer, Holland, Gadsby, Belcher, and Sir Roundell Palmer; nor the more learned works of such writers as Daniel, Archbishop Trench, Dr. Mason Neale, and Dr. Bonar; yet it remains true that this theme, which is rising into notice, and which is of practical importance because of its connection with our private and public devotion, has not yet received a thorough treatment.

This work is to be regarded only as a contribution to the subject. It is not an attempt to go over the whole field. The subject is so large that the writer found it necessary to fix some limit to his researches. He has confined himself to the authors whose psalms and hymns are contained in one of the most comprehensive and excellent of modern collections.* That collection was compiled by a competent committee in London, who were occupied from 1855 to 1859 in its preparation. They met frequently, and

---

* "The New Congregational Hymn Book."

had the assistance of numerous ministers and others in all parts of the country. It includes one thousand of the best psalms and hymns, of nearly two hundred writers of almost every country and religious denomination, and of various ages of the world, from the time of David to our own. It has not been prepared upon any narrow sectarian plan, but upon the broadest basis of Christian catholicity. A sale of more than half a million copies in a few years, has shown the favour with which it has been received, and besides the stimulus it gives to private devotion, it is from Sunday to Sunday ministering thought and life to the songs of numerous worshipping assemblies. The reader will find 'n this work biographies of the writers whose psalms and hymns are found in that collection, and a particular account of every hymn there given of which there was anything of interest to record. All the biographical sketches have been written on purpose for this work, and several living hymn-writers have most kindly supplied original autobiographical information that has never been published before.

Having to give the lives of so many eminent persons within the compass of one volume, it was necessary to pass rapidly over some parts of their history; but an attempt has been made to make the sketches as complete as possible. The best sources of information have been consulted; and in every case, the authors have been thought of as hymn-writers, and prominence has been given to what would inform us of them in that capacity. Each life is treated separately, and usually the biographical sketch is given first and the notes on the writer's hymns at the close of the sketch.

The necessary limits of the work did not allow of an attempt to trace the history of hymnology, but some light may be thrown upon that subject by the chronological order that has been adopted in the arrangement of the biographies. And it has been sought by means of two indexes, to assist the general reader as much as possible, and especially to render this work serviceable to those who will use it as a "Companion." There is first an alphabetical index of authors, and against each author's name a carefully prepared list of the psalms and hymns he has contributed to the collection to which this work is a companion. In that list, those that have been erroneously attributed in that collection to any author are omitted; and those that have been given without name are treated of under the heading "Anonymous." There is also an alphabetically arranged index of several hundred psalms and hymns. It contains only those of which this work gives some particular account; and against each hymn in that index there is the number of the page where that account can be found.

In our public assemblies prose compositions are usually given with the illustration they derive from our knowledge of the author. We know something of the speaker who addresses us; or he announces a well-known name as that of the author of what he reads; or if it be in a place of worship pre-informs us that he is going to read part of the Gospel of John, or of an epistle by Peter or Paul. And we very seldom put any prose composition to the disadvantage of being judged on its intrinsic merits and apart from our knowledge of its author (although, for special reasons, this is done in some departments of our literature). But our hymns usually suffer from this disadvantage. In many instances they embody the sentiments of a particular writer, and were born of the peculiar circumstances in which he wrote them, yet all that we know of them, beyond their internal testimony, is their number in a collection, or the page on which they are found. It is the object of this work to assist in the removal of that disadvantage and to lend new interest to our public praise by informing the worshipper of the lives of the authors whose hymns he sings, and of the origin and history of those hymns. To illustrate, every thoughtful reader or worshipper will see the new meaning and value that belong to such a psalm as—

"Out of the depths I cry to Thee,"—No. 215,

when he recognizes in its translator a Christian David, the storm-tossed Luther; and that—

"Lord, it belongs not to my care,"—No. 594,

is more than before, when received from much-suffering Richard Baxter, persecuted and afflicted, alike uncertain of his liberty and his life; and that—

"God moves in a mysterious way,"—No. 281,

has a new interest when accepted from the pen of Cowper, involved in thick clouds, yet not without some beams of light shining fitfully on him through their rifts. It is the object of this work to supply such illustrative information. The writer has felt the want of such a work, and finding it still unsupplied, he has made an humble attempt to supply it.

In judging of hymn-writers it may be desirable to carry in our minds a correct impression of what a Christian hymn ought to be. Nearly a century ago, the Rev. John Newton well said, "They should be hymns, not odes, if designed for public worship, and for the use of plain people. Perspicuity, simplicity, and ease, should be chiefly attended to; and the imagery and colouring of poetry, if admitted at all, should be indulged very sparingly and with great judgment." Sir Roundell Palmer says, along with other wise words about hymns—"Affectation or visible artifice is worse than excess of homeliness: a hymn is easily spoiled by a single falsetto note. Nor will the most exemplary soundness of doctrine atone for doggrel or redeem from failure a prosaic, didactic style." And one of the best definitions of a hymn is given in "The Contemporary Review" for March, 1866, in an article on "Church Hymn Books." It is as follows:—" An English hymn should be plain in diction, chastened in imagery, fervent in sentiment, humble in its approach to God. Its lines should be cunningly wrought, so that they may easily find their way to the ear of the simplest, and stay unbidden in his memory. It should be metrically faultless; so departing at times from perfect uniformity, as to render reason for the departure, and give a charm to its usual strictness." To these we need add only the words of one of our best hymn-writers, James Montgomery. He says, "A hymn must have a beginning, middle, and end. There should be a manifest gradation in the thoughts, and their mutual dependence should be so perceptible that they could not be transposed without injuring the unity of the piece; every line carrying forward the connection, and every verse adding a well-proportioned limb to a symmetrical body. The reader should know when the strain is complete, and be satisfied, as at the close of an air in music."

It is well where, as in the case of the collection this work illustrates, all hymns that manifestly transgress these wise rules are carefully excluded. The tasteful reader who has a true idea of what a hymn should be, is offended by such stilted sensational lines as—

> "Let this hardened heart of stone,
> Melt beneath the purple shower,
> From his body trickling down."

And the thoughtful worshipper feels that neither his taste nor his heart have received any benefit from such a mere jingle of words as the following (found in a modern collection)—

> "Toils and foes assailing, friends quailing, hearts failing,
>   Shall threat in vain;
> If He be providing, presiding, and guiding,
>   To Him again."

But in respect to those authors who have introduced an unusual amount of imagery into their hymns, and an elevation of manner of which the hymn was thought scarcely capable, perhaps it may be said in their vindication, that where their hymns have become favourites, their authors have at once advanced their art, and justified the new and splendid course they have taken. They have achieved what was possible to their sanctified genius, but what men of humbler capacities would in vain attempt to imitate.

Another subject that may demand a preliminary word is that of the alteration of hymns in modern collections. It has been usual to speak in terms of unmeasured censure of those who have ventured to alter the words of an author. But it should be borne in mind that the psalter or hymn-book used in public praise, is not to be judged merely on literary grounds. The first question to be asked is, how far it as a whole, and each hymn in particular, contributes to the high purposes of public Christian worship? Authors of genius have produced noble conceptions which they have not possessed taste, or in some cases have not given time, to clothe in the most appropriate language. They have left them diffuse or inaccurate, or unpleasing in expression, or with their meaning hidden from later generations by obsolete words. Men of taste coming after, have been able by the occasional alteration of a word, by skilful compression, and by sometimes even omitting an inferior stanza, to present the original productions in the serviceable form in which they now appear. To attempt such a thing while the author is still living, and without consulting him, would indeed be an impertinence. But the time comes when if such alteration be carried out judiciously, and in the spirit of the original author, and by those who are themselves hymn-writers, as it has been by the Wesleys, Montgomery, and others, it may be a positive advantage to the productions of the original author, and to all who use them ; just as an ancient cathedral, the magnificent design of some master builder of old, but whose details were not elaborated in his day, and whose lines of beauty are beginning to be effaced by the fingers of decay, may be successfully restored, and may at the same time put on a splendour the first designer never saw, by the toil and skill of humbler labourers of later times.

It only remains for the author of this work to express the deep obligation under which he lies to several living hymn-writers, and other competent helpers, for their most valuable co-operation, without which his toilsome labours and extended researches would have been in vain. To the following living hymn-writers, from whom he has received by private communication more or less of assistance, he tenders his grateful thanks:—Dr. W. L. Alexander, Rev. T. W. B. Aveling, William Bartholomew, Rev. Thomas Binney, Dr. H. Bonar, John Burton, James Edmeston, Charlotte Elliott, Rev. Christopher Elven, Rev. S. S. England, Rev. H. Mayo Gunn, Rev. H. March, Eliza F. Morris, G. R., A. C. Hobart Seymour, Dr. G. Smith, Dr. Spence, A. L. Waring, Dr. Wreford, and Miss Harriet Parr. It will be a matter of great regret to the author if he has in any case unintentionally made public what his correspondents did not communicate for public use. The pleasure of public usefulness may perhaps compensate for the pain of an undesired publicity. The author has also received very kind assistance from some of the relatives of deceased hymn-writers, and from others who by their official, or literary, or local position, had special facilities for obtaining information, and from others who have for years given attention to the subject of hymnology. He thankfully names the following :— Rev. Henry Allon, Mrs. Anstice, Revds. R. Ashton, Charles Bradley, J. Cawood, E. R. Conder, B. H. Cowper, J. A. Eberle, E. B. Elliott, H. Auber Harvey, James Martineau, T. Morell, Prof.

H. R. Reynolds, W. Robinson, G. L. Withers, Palmer Law, and C. D. Hardcastle, Henry Piggin, W. S. Rooker, and T. Stamford Raffles, Esqs. He must also present his special thanks to A. C. Hobart Seymour, Esq., who without regard to his own personal trouble has taken a deep interest in the preparation of this work and given him the benefit of his learned researches, and of his personal reminiscences of several distinguished hymn-writers of the last generation; and there are other helpers too numerous to name. The author also feels that it is due to Mr. Daniel Sedgwick, bookseller, of 81, Sun-street, Bishopsgate, to state that from the beginning of his researches he has had his valuable assistance. Indeed, without his rare collection of hymn-books, his "Index of Authors," his valuable "Reprints" and much more, his personal knowledge of this subject accumulated during many years, it would have been very difficult, if not impossible, to have produced this work.

Where so many thousands of facts are included, and some of them very difficult to verify, or at present the subject of literary dispute, and where it is already almost too late to rescue some of them from undeserved oblivion, the author can scarcely hope to have attained to the absolute accuracy he has aimed at. He therefore begs the co-operation of his readers that in a later edition (if the favour of the public should call for it) their corrections may be made, and the few remaining *lacunæ* may be satisfactorily filled up. He trusts that his work will encourage and assist the excellent modern plan of putting names and dates to the hymns in our collections; that it will supply useful materials to ministers and others, who will see it to be desirable to impart information about our hymns; and that it will be a serviceable contribution to the means that are being employed to enable men to sing "with the spirit and with the understanding also."

LIST OF AUTHORS.

	HYMNS.	PAGE
Addiscott, Rev. Henry, 650		376
Addison, Joseph, 20, 27, 166, 290, 739		68
Alexander, Rev. W. L., D.D., 886		378
Allen, Rev. James, 338, 871		210
Allen, G. N., 652		392
Alford, Rev. Henry, D.D., 607		383
Anonymous, 109, 110, 172, 235, 252, 352, 355, 376, 392, 399, 423, 438, 447, 452, 495, 504, 519, 552, 714, 740, 750, 762, 813, 821, 841, 882, 897, 904, 942, 948, 952, 987, 989, 990, 991, 997, 999		403
Anstice, Professor Joseph, M.A., 354, 593		377
Aquinas, Thomas, 878		10
Auber, Harriet, 110		285
Aveling, Rev. T. W. B., 626, 816, 976		389
Bakewell, John, 335		179
Barbauld, Anna L., 727		234
Bartholomew, William, 148, 931, 940		351
Barton, Bernard, 468, 682		306
Bathurst, Rev. W. H., M.A., 109, 432, 440, 836, 927		361
Baxter, Rev. Richard, 594		41
Beddome, Rev. Benjamin, M.A., 155, 502, 539, 819, 835, 843, 892		173
Bernard, 329, 405		7
Bernard of Cluny, 744		9
Binney, Rev. Thomas, 261		364
Boden, Rev. James, 513, 977		268
Bonar, Rev. H., D.D., 574, 814, 928		380
Bowdler, John, 207		300
Bowring, Sir John, LL.D., 349, 372		349
Bradley, Rev. Charles		367
Brady, Rev. Nicholas, D.D.		64
Bridges, Matthew, 413		373
Brontë, Anne, 525		392
Brown, W., 762		395
Browne, 812		73
Browne, Rev. Simon, 436, 534		71
Bruce, Michael, 104, 400, 725, 925		242

	PAGE
Bulmer, Rev. John, 770, 778	311
Burder, Rev. George, 786, 831	258
Burton, John, 464	284
Butcher, Rev. Edmund, 952	265
Cawood, Rev. John, M.A., 790	294
Carlisle	296
Carlyle, Rev. J. D., B.D., 810	296
Cennick, Rev. John, 310, 314, 334, 341, 396, 418, 630, 942	164
Charlemagne	7
Clayton, Rev. George, 969	306
Clemens, Alexandrinus, 975	3
Collyer, Rev. W. B., D.D., 520, 846, 857, 913	298
Conder, Josiah, 21, 26, 46, 49, 64, 121, 154, 178, 264, 277, 307, 348, 357, 407, 442, 450, 451, 459, 508, 512, 535, 559, 571, 591, 605, 636, 818, 856, 867, 905, 915	333
Conder, Mrs. Josiah, 949	362
Cooper, 447	363
Cotterill, Rev. Thomas, M.A., 352, 428, 821	289
Cowper, William, 100, 281, 284, 306, 474, 532, 537, 548, 588, 598, 640, 644, 651, 679, 686, 776, 805, 883	201
Darby	374
Davies, Rev. Samuel, M.A., 295	180
Decius, Rev. Nicholas, 291	12
Deck, James George, 600	374
De Courcy, Rev. Richard, 609	232
Dickson, Rev. David	5
Dobell, John, 495	269
Dober, Anna, 572	156
Doddridge, Rev. Philip, D.D., 62, 157, 278, 285, 292, 300, 302, 326, 347, 377, 386, 398, 443, 493, 562, 563, 573, 587, 613, 614, 617, 619, 675, 683, 691, 715, 719, 734, 736, 765, 767, 815, 844, 852, 861, 884, 891, 893, 896, 907, 916, 943, 954, 955, 956, 960, 966, 967, 978, 981, 983, 996	113
Dryden, John, 433	51
Duffield, Rev. George, 890	384
Dwight, J. S., 998	385
Dwight, Rev. T., D.D., 36, 828	253
Dyer	395
Edmeston, James, 840, 985	347
Elliott, Charlotte, 399, 517, 599	369
Elven, Rev. Cornelius, 530	363

HYMNS.

	PAGE
England, Rev. S. S., 6	385
Evans, Rev. Jonathan, 384, 788	249
Faber, Rev. Frederick W., D.D., 263, 965	387
Fanch, Rev. James	147
Fawcett, Rev. John, D.D., 273, 309, 466, 633, 832, 958, 968, 970	223
Fellows, John, 858	251
Fletcher, Samuel, 980, 982	312
Flowerdew, Anne, 950	301
Francis	249
Gellert, C. F., 388	159
Gerhard, Rev. Paul, 363, 374, 606	33
Gibbons, Rev. Thomas, D.D., 713, 908	176
Goode, Rev. William, M.A., 114	323
Grant, James, 610	153
Grant, Sir Robert, 162, 367, 369	317
Greene, Thomas, 602	264
Grigg, Rev. Joseph, 509, 622	149
Guest, Rev. Benjamin, 851	391
Gunn, Rev. H. Mayo, 903	391
Gurney, Rev. J. Hampden, M.A., 353	372
Guyon, Jeanne B. de la Motte, 681	59
Hammond, Rev. William, B.A., 339, 785	152
Harris, Rev. John, D.D., 882	369
Hart, Rev. Joseph, 435, 511, 615, 794, 849, 995	154
Hastings, Thomas, Mus. Doc., 494, 514, 521, 812	309
Haweis, Rev. Thomas, LL.B., M.D., 426, 506, 649	212
Heber, Bishop Reginald, 312, 332, 416, 417, 455, 733, 912	302
Heginbotham, Rev. Ottiwell, 957	236
Hemans, Felicia D., 721	356
Hervey, Rev. James, M.A., 282	157
Hill, Rev. Rowland, M.A., 504, 740	237
Homburg, Ernest C., 373	32
Hopkins, Rev. J.	23
Humphreys, Rev. Joseph, 557	169
Huntingdon, The Countess of, 423	126
Hurn, Rev. William, 826	326
Judson, Rev. Adoniram, D.D., 558	328
Keble, Rev. John, M.A., 276, 874, 888, 901, 933, 946	337
Kelly, Rev. Thomas, 387, 410, 411, 709, 710, 766, 789, 833, 919	273
Ken, Bishop Thomas, 458, 929, 938	56
Kippis, Rev. Andrew, D.D., 997	182

HYMNS.

	PAGE
Kirkham, 664	284
Langford, 365	188
Logan, John, 285	247
Luther, Dr. Martin, 66, 97, 215	13
Lyte, Rev. H. Francis, M.A., 10, 15, 32, 39, 65, 76, 89, 94, 116, 125, 126, 168, 230, 250, 289, 653, 758, 768, 827, 944	352
McCheyne, Rev. Robert Murray, 575	386
Madan	196
Mant, Bishop Richard, 245, 322, 637	287
March, Rev. Henry, 771	344
Marriott, Rev. John, 917	323
Mason, Rev. John, M.A., 986	46
Mason, Rev. William, M.A., 760	189
Medley, Rev. Samuel, 344, 366, 505	220
Merrick, Rev. James, M.A., 654, 757	175
Milman, Dean Henry Hart, D.D., 648, 808, 809	345
Milton, John, 123, 229	36
Montgomery, James, 8, 35, 58, 85, 107, 112, 167, 177, 182, 186, 206, 217, 220, 254, 343, 359, 382, 383, 427, 434, 454, 510, 529, 704, 735, 751, 772, 781, 784, 798, 800, 806, 829, 837, 845, 865, 872, 881, 889, 914, 922, 924, 926, 973	276
Morell, Rev. Thomas, 900	296
Morris, Eliza Fanny, 533	402
Needham, Rev. John, 951	148
Neumark, George, 720	50
Newton, Rev. James, M.A., 839	209
Newton, Rev. John, 287, 328, 419, 589, 608, 625, 642, 656, 692, 759, 795, 796, 801, 802, 807, 823, 838, 848, 885, 894, 947, 953, 959, 962	184
Nicolai, Dr. Philip, 749	25
Noel, Hon. and Rev. G. T., M.A., 877	298
Olivers, Rev. Thomas, 256	191
Onderdonk, Bishop H. U., 519	355
Palmer, Rev. Ray, D.D., 544	381
Park, Thomas, 249	285
Parr, Harriet, 945	401
Patrick	59
Perronet, Rev. Edward, 414	194
Pierpont, Rev. John, 779	315
Pope, Alexander, 728	75
Pyer, Rev. John, 803	343
Raffles, Rev. Thomas, D.D., 531, 747, 979, 988	330

LIST OF AUTHORS.

HYMNS.	PAGE
R——. G——, 438, 948, 987	396
Reed, Rev. Andrew, D.D., 441	318
Rinkart, Rev. Martin, 419	28
Ringwaldt, Rev. Bartholomew, 420	24
Rippon, Rev. John, D.D., 990	252
Robinson, Rev. Robert, 311, 666	214
Rothe, Rev. J. A., 611	73
Ryland, Rev. John, D.D., 355, 595, 685	262
Sandys, George, 91, 763	26
Scott, Elizabeth, 412	148
Scott, Rev. Thomas, 492	146
Seagrave, Rev. Robert, M.A., 703, 787	99
Seymour, A. C. Hobart, 920	339
Shirley, Hon. and Rev. Walter, 792	193
Shrubsole, Rev. William, 918	198
Smith, Rev. George, D.D., 333, 842	397
Smith, Rev. S. F., D.D., 813	395
Spence, Rev. James, D.D., 850	398
Steele, Anne, 331, 482, 518, 560, 601, 612, 635, 646, 971, 994	162
Stennett, Rev. Joseph, D.D., 753	65
Stennett, Rev. Samuel, D.D., 527, 741, 804	197
Sternhold, Thomas, 16	21
Stocker, John, 297	195
Straphan, Joseph, 974	269
Swain, Rev. Joseph, 584	271
Swaine, Edward, 902, 906	358
Tate, Nahum, 43, 45, 57, 93, 138, 141, 169, 203, 248, 456	63
Telesphorus	1
Tersteegen, Gerard, 561, 773	102
Toplady, Rev. Augustus M., 439, 526, 549, 632, 724, 937	226
Turner, Rev. Daniel, 389, 551	147
Voke, Mrs., 899, 909	283
Wardlaw, Rev. Ralph, D.D., 288, 756	291
Waring, Anna Lætitia, 590	399
Watts, Rev. Isaac, D.D., 1, 2, 3, 4, 5, 7, 9, 11, 12, 13, 14, 17, 18, 19, 22, 23, 24, 25, 29, 30, 31, 33, 34, 37, 38, 40, 41, 42, 44, 47, 48, 50, 51, 52, 53, 54, 55, 56, 60, 61, 63, 67, 68, 69, 70, 71, 72, 73, 74, 75, 77, 78, 79, 80, 82, 83, 84, 86, 87, 88, 90, 92, 95, 96, 98, 99, 101, 102, 103, 105, 106, 108, 111, 113, 115, 117, 118, 119, 120, 122, 124, 127, 128, 129, 130, 131, 132, 133, 134, 135, 136, 139, 140, 142, 143, 144, 145, 146, 147, 149, 150, 151, 152, 156,	

| | HYMNS. | PAGE |

Watts, Rev. Isaac, D.D., *continued*—
158, 159, 160, 161, 163, 164, 165, 170, 171, 173, 174, 175, 176, 179, 180, 181, 183, 184, 185, 187, 188, 189, 190, 191 192, 193, 194, 195, 196, 197, 198, 199, 200, 201, 202, 204, 205, 208, 209, 211, 212, 213, 214, 216, 218, 219, 221, 222, 223, 224, 225, 226, 227, 228, 231, 232, 233, 234, 236, 237, 238, 239, 240, 241, 242, 243, 244, 246, 247, 251, 257, 258, 260, 262, 265, 266, 267, 268, 269, 270, 271, 272, 274, 275, 279, 280, 283, 293, 294, 298, 299, 301, 303, 304, 305, 308, 315, 317, 318, 319, 320, 324, 337, 340, 342, 346, 350, 358, 360, 361, 368, 370, 371, 379, 380, 381, 390, 391, 393, 395, 397, 401, 402, 403, 408, 409, 415, 421, 425, 430, 431, 444, 446, 448, 453, 457, 460, 461, 462, 463, 465, 467, 470, 471, 472, 473, 475, 476, 477, 478, 479, 480, 481, 483, 484, 485, 486, 488, 489, 491, 496, 497, 498, 499, 500, 501, 507, 515, 516, 523, 524, 536, 538, 541, 542, 543, 545, 546, 553, 554, 555, 556, 565, 569, 576, 577, 578, 579, 580, 582, 583, 585, 586, 596, 597, 603, 604, 616, 618, 620, 621, 623, 628, 629, 634, 639, 641, 645, 647, 657, 658, 663, 667, 668, 669, 670, 671, 672, 673, 674, 676, 677, 678, 687, 688, 689, 690, 693, 694, 695, 696, 697, 699, 700, 701, 702, 705, 706, 707, 711, 712, 716, 717, 718, 722, 723, 729, 730, 731, 732, 737, 738, 742, 745, 746, 748, 752, 754, 755, 761, 769, 774, 775, 791, 797, 824, 825, 854, 855, 860, 862, 863, 864, 866, 868, 870, 873, 879, 880, 930, 932, 935, 936, 939, 941, 963, 964, 972, 993............ 78

Wesley, Rev. Charles, M.A., 28, 59, 81, 210, 259, 296, 313, 316, 321, 323, 327, 330, 336, 345, 356, 362, 364, 375, 385, 394, 406, 422, 424, 429, 437, 469, 487, 503, 522, 528, 540, 550, 564, 566, 567, 568, 570, 581, 592, 624, 638, 643, 655, 659, 661, 665, 680, 698, 708, 726, 777, 780, 782, 783, 799, 817, 820, 822, 830, 834, 841, 847, 853, 859, 869, 875, 876, 887, 895, 898, 921, 923, 934, 961, 992 132

Wesley, Rev. John, M.A., 517 123
Wesley, Rev. Samuel, 378 66
Wesley, Rev. Samuel, jun., M.A., 764 99
White, Henry Kirke, 627, 984 320
Wilks, Rev. Matthew, 910 245
Williams, Helen Maria, 286 272
Williams, Rev. William, 660, 911 170
Wither, George, 137, 255 29
Wreford, Rev. J. Reynell, D.D., 1000 367
Zinzendorf, Count N. L., 325, 662............ 105

OUR HYMNS:

THEIR AUTHORS AND ORIGIN.

TELESPHORUS.

"To God be glory, peace on earth."—No. 445.

THIS work is based on the assumption that a knowledge of the authors and origin of the hymns would add to the pleasure and profit of public worship. On the threshold, we have a good illustration. Hymn 445 might be sung without regard to its history, and valued only to the extent of its intrinsic excellence. But, on the other hand, if its history be known, what a halo of interest surrounds it! We justly rejoice that men who contend in argument, or remain apart in the coldness of sectarian separation, yet unite in song. This joyful doxology not only unites the living, it is an echo of scripture, an ancient testimony to fundamental doctrine, and a common expression of the devout thankfulness of Christians of every age since the time of the Apostles. As we sing this hymn, we feel that the church of Christ has a unity of doctrine and love which prevails over all diversity, and we see with emotion the great "cloud of witnesses" gathering out of every nation, and kindred, and people, and tongue.

The name "Telesphorus" is put in italics at the head of this chapter to show that, although it has been given as the name of the author of this hymn, there is no authority for its use. The mistake arose in the following way:—The prose translation of the Greek, of which hymn 445 is a free rendering, was given with music in some old music books, and a note added, "ascribed to Telesphorus." The Rev. Henry Allon, one of the compilers of the "New Congregational Hymn Book," adopted the name from that source. Telesphorus was bishop of Rome, where he was martyred, A.D. 139. Irenæus and Eusebius, who speak of him, make no reference to this hymn. Nor do writers who have given special attention to the "Lives of the Saints," such as Cave, Le Nain de Tillemont, and Alban Butler.

The Greek original of hymn 445 is the first twenty-nine lines of the ὑμνος ἑωθινος, placed after the Psalms in the Codex Alexandrinus. The learned editor of the "Journal of Sacred Literature," the Rev. B. H. Cowper, has given the whole of this Greek hymn in his introduction (page xxviii.) to his most valuable reprint of the New Testament portion of the Codex Alexandrinus (1860). Upon the first twenty-nine lines, he says, "Lines 1—3 are the angelic hymn from Luke ii. 14, and the next six lines appear to be a doxology, suggested by it. These are followed by a solemn invocation, forming a kind of introduction to what may be regarded as a Litany, ending with the word, Amen, at line twenty-nine." Most of the remaining part is taken from several psalms, and two lines of the remainder are in the "Te Deum." "Probably," he says, "it originally consisted only of the first twenty-nine lines, and even these may not be free from alterations. They differ repeatedly from the copy in the Apostolic Constitutions, and more or less from other relics to be found in several authors." Some of the modifications of the Greek hymn are known to have been made at a period prior to that when Mr. Cowper supposes the Alexandrine Codex was written, *i.e.*, about the middle of the fifth century.

The hymn in the form given in the "New Congregational" is found in a supplement to "Tate and Brady," 1703. The author's name is not given.

CLEMENS ALEXANDRINUS.

Died about a.d. 217.

This Clement, whose other names were Titus Flavius, and who was called Alexandrinus from his connection with Alexandria, was one of the first Christian hymn-writers of whom we have any record. He was born about the middle of the second century. He is said to have been an Athenian, and at first a stoic, but he afterwards joined the eclectic school. The bent of his mind as well as the necessities of his moral nature made Clement emphatically a seeker. Teachers of different countries and schools, Grecian, Assyrian, Egyptian, and Jewish taught him, but could not satisfy him.

As a "merchant-man seeking goodly pearls," he at length came to Alexandria, where, under the teaching of Pantænus, a Christian teacher, he found in Jesus the "one pearl of great price." Subsequently Pantænus went, as Eusebius informs us in his fifth book, as a missionary to India, and Clement succeeded his master in his catechetical office, and trained among his disciples Origen and Alexander, afterwards bishop of Jerusalem. Clement was also appointed presbyter of the church at Alexandria, about the year 190. Alban Butler, in his "Lives of the Saints," says, "that Clement died before the end of the reign of Caracalla, who was put to death a.d. 217."

In Clement's works we perceive the philosophizing tendency of his mind, his familiarity with the various systems of those times, his extensive range of knowledge, and sometimes his devoutness and spirituality. His writings were much commended by Eusebius and Jerome. Some are lost, including his "Commentaries on various parts of the Scriptures." Those which are extant are his "Exhortation to the Greeks," an appeal to them to turn from their false gods; "Pædagogus," a treatise on Christian education; and "Stromata," *i.e.*, "Patchwork," the name being chosen because of the multifarious contents of the work. This large work is to vindicate the claims of the Scriptures, and to teach Clement's philosophy as he built it on Christianity. Many quotations are given from the ancients, and along with much Christian truth there are traces of philosophic mysticism and Gnostic error. Eusebius also speaks of Clement's "Eight books of Institutions" as giving important information about the authorship, and other particulars, of several of the books of Scripture.

"Shepherd of tender youth."—No. 975.

This is a very free rendering of the hymn, handed down as the production of Clement. The original is a catalogue of epithets applied to Christ. That this rendering is not close to the original may be seen by comparing the translation of a recent author, who gives the first lines thus:—

> "Mouth of babes who cannot speak,
> Wing of nestlings who cannot fly,
> Sure guide of babes."

It is to be regretted that in our rendering we have departed from the archaic simplicity of the original.

Some forms of expression and thought in this hymn, especially in verse three, may be explained by the author's career as a philosopher, and by his Gnosticising tendencies. He mentions it in his works to the praise of the Gnostics, that they praised God both in their hearts and in frequent songs. But the hymn is chiefly to be valued as the poetic tribute of one who, disappointed elsewhere, found the "all" in Christ. The recent author, quoted above, truly says of this hymn—"Through all the images here so quaintly interwoven, like a stained window, of which the eye loses the design in the complication of colours, we may surely trace, as in quaint old letters on a scroll winding through all the mosaic of tints, "Christ all in all." The literary connection of this hymn is with Clement's "Pædagogus"—the guide or trainer of children. The warm sentiments of the prose essay find a suitable expression in this out-gush of Christian song.

DAVID DICKSON.

"Jerusalem my happy home."—No. 743.

This hymn of hymns is not, (in the form in which it appears in the " New Congregational Hymn Book)," the work of the Rev. David Dickson (1583—1662), to whom it is erroneously attributed. He is but one of the numerous poets who have found in the ancient Latin hymn, probably of the eighth century, a fount of Christian song. This form of the poem has not been traced back farther than the collection of Dr. Williams and Mr. Boden, 1801. It is there stated to be from " Eckinton Collection." The author's name and the original text of this rendering have not yet been discovered.

The early Latin hymn, as given by Daniel in his "Thesaurus Hymnologicus," consists of forty-eight lines, and begins—

> " Urbs beata Hierusalem,
> Dicta pacis visio."

The Latin writer, whose date and name have not been discovered, favoured by the language in which he wrote, has written with a compression and a force which we miss in the more diffuse productions of later times. Dr. Mason Neale, referring to the Latin form this hymn had taken in the beginning of the seventeenth century, says, "This grand hymn of the eighth century was modernised in the reform of Pope Urban VIII. into the 'Cœlestis urbs Jerusalem,' and lost half of its beauty in the process."

Archbishop Trench, in his " Sacred Latin Poetry," at page 313, says of the original Latin hymn, "It is most truly a hymn of degrees, ascending from things earthly to things heavenly, and making the first to be interpreters of the last. The prevailing intention in the building and the dedication of a church, with the rites thereto appertaining, was to carry up men's thoughts from that temple built with hands which they saw, to that other built of living stones in heaven, of which this was but a weak shadow."

It used to be customary to attribute the English form of this hymn to the Rev. David Dickson, because his biographer, Robert Wodrow, in his "Life of Dickson," 1726, speaks of having "seen in print" some short poems, on "pious and serious subects," published by Dickson, "such as the 'Christian Sacrifice,' 'O Mother, Dear Jerusalem,' and, on somewhat larger octavo, 1649, 'True Christian Love,' to be sung with the common tunes of the Psalms." Dickson was the author of "A brief explication of the Psalms." This was done in fifties, in the years 1653-4-5. Dickson's piece, taken from a broadside without date, but probably of the beginning of the last century, consists of 248 lines; it begins, "O mother dear, Jerusalem."

But the discovery of an earlier work containing this hymn has destroyed Dickson's claim. This work is a book of religious songs, in the British Museum, No. 15,225. Dr. Bonar, who has treated this subject very fully in his valuable contribution to hymnology, "The New Jerusalem," 1852, shows, from internal evidence that this book was probably not published prior to 1616, when Dickson had attained to manhood, so that the date does not destroy his claim. But the work consists of poems of a much earlier date; and the hymn is ascribed, not to Dickson, but it is entitled "A song made by F. B. P., to the tune of Diana." It is a different piece, consisting of only 104 lines, and beginning, "Hierusalem, my happy home!" It has traces of a Popish origin, while Dickson's appears to be an expansion of it with Presbyterian modifications. "Our Ladie singes Magnificat," in the original, becomes in Dickson's piece, "There Mary sings Magnificat."

It has been suggested that the initials "F. B. P." stand for "Francis Baker," "Pater," or priest.

The Rev. W. Burkitt, the expositor, in a work, dated 1693, gives this hymn in eight verses, in a form resembling that in which it is given in the "New Congregational Hymn Book," and with a few of the lines the same.

CHARLEMAGNE.

(742—814.) *Vide* under JOHN DRYDEN.

BERNARD.
1091—1153.

THE great Bernard, who is distinguished as Saint Bernard of Clairvaux, was born at Fontaine, in Burgundy. His father was a nobleman. Both his parents were pious, and he owed much to the piety of his mother, who died when he was young. After being educated at the University of Paris, he entered, at the age of twenty-two, the Cistercian monastery of Citeaux, near Dijon, in Burgundy. That which he was afterwards so distinguished for, his remarkable influence over the minds of others, already appeared. By means of it he induced his five brothers and several companions to accompany him into monastic life. The order was severe in its ascetic practices, and Bernard carried these so far as to injure his health. His austerity made him famous, and at the age of twenty-five he was appointed abbot of a new monastery at Clairvaux, in Champagne.

In this position, which he continued to retain, notwithstanding several offers of bishoprics, he obtained extraordinary power and reputation: even kings and popes received his advice. His eloquent preaching was everywhere welcomed. Convents and monasteries, after his model, sprang up in all parts of Europe. His works were read, and he was hailed as the champion of the orthodoxy of those times. Having been challenged by the rationalizing Abelard, Bernard met him for controversy, at Sens, in 1140; but after hearing Bernard's opening statement, Abelard lost all courage, and having appealed to the Pope, retired pusillanimously from the contest. It was Bernard also who persuaded the King of France to undertake the crusade of the year 1146.

Luther calls Bernard "the best monk that ever lived." He was a great theologian, a follower of Augustine in his doctrines, which he taught with definiteness and held with decision. Earnest in effort, self-denying in life, unsparing in censure of abuses and corruptions, full of zeal for what he believed to be Christian truth, he nevertheless erred in being carried by his fervour and success into extravagancies, especially in the claims he put forth for himself as the possessor of inspiration, and of the power to work miracles. Bernard is one of the principal saints in the Romish calendar, and has been styled the last of the Fathers.

His works include numerous "Epistles," "Sermons on the Song of Solomon," "Five Books on Consideration," with other sermons and treatises on religious and ecclesiastical subjects.

Bernard was also the author of some celebrated Latin hymns, "Jesus, the very thought of Thee" (No. 329); "O! Jesus, King most wonderful" (No. 405). These are parts of the translation of the same piece, "Jesu, dulcis memoria," a piece full of the ardent piety and missionary zeal of the illustrious author.

We are indebted to Edward Caswall for these beautiful renderings of Bernard. Hymn 329 is found at page 56 of "Lyra Catholica, containing all the breviary and missal hymns, with others from various sources, translated by Edward Caswall, M.A., 1849;" and hymn 405 is found at page 57 of the same work. Wackernagel in his "Das Deutsche Kirchenlied, 1862," has given the original Latin in fifty-six verses of four lines each. How near Mr. Caswall has kept to the original may be seen by taking verse four, with which "O! Jesus, King most wonderful" (No. 405) begins. The original Latin is as follows:—

"Jesu rex admirabilis
Et triumphator nobilis,
Dulcedo ineffabilis,
Totus desiderabilis."

Part of Bernard's piece—

"Salve, caput cruentatum."
"Hail! Thou Head, so bruised and wounded."

is freely given in Gerhard's—

"O! sacred Head, once wounded."—No. 374.
"O! haupt voll blut und wunden."

BERNARD OF CLUNY.

Twelfth Century.

This talented ecclesiastic must not be confounded with his still more celebrated fellow-countryman and cotemporary, Bernard, the Abbot of Clairvaux. He was born at Morlaix, in Brittany, and is said to have been the child of English parents. We know nothing of the incidents of his life. His poetry is his best memorial.

"To thee, O dear, dear country."—No. 744.

This is Dr. John Mason Neale's translation of part of a Latin poem of 3,000 lines, entitled, "De contemptu mundi." The translation is given in "The Rhythm of Bernard de Morlaix, Monk of Cluny, on the Celestial Country, 1862." The original poem was dedicated to Peter the Venerable, General of the order to which Bernard belonged. Cluny Abbey was the greatest in France, and Peter was at its head from 1122 to 1156.

The poetic form of the piece is strange to the reader, and most difficult to the writer. The hexameter terminates in a tailed rhyme, and it has also a feminine leonine rhyme between the two first clauses, each clause terminating in the same way, *e. g.*—

"Tunc nova gloria || pectora sobria || clarificabit:
Solvit enigmata || veraque sabbata || continuabit."

Although this form is not attractive, yet "no one," says Trench, "with a sense for the true passion of poetry, even when it manifests itself in forms the least to his liking, will deny the breath of a real inspiration to the author of these dactylic hexameters."

The subject of the poem is the wickedness of man; and the

vices of a corrupt age do not escape the poet's satire. "But," says Dr. Neale, "as a contrast to the misery and pollution of earth, the poem opens with a description of the peace and glory of heaven, of such rare beauty as not easily to be matched by any mediæval composition on the same subject."

This poem, as a whole, is open to the objection that throughout so many verses it still circles about the same subject without any marked progress of thought. But this favourite part is placed beyond the region of criticism by the dying commendation of those who have found in it the adequate expression of what Trench has happily called their "heavenly home-sickness."

Dr. Neale, whose opinion is second to none, says—"I have no hesitation in saying that I look on these verses of Bernard as the most lovely, in the same way that the "Dies Iræ" is the most sublime, and the "Stabat Mater" the most pathetic of mediæval poems."

THOMAS AQUINAS.

1227—1274.

THOMAS of Aquino, in Naples, was son of Landulf, count of Aquino, who was nephew of the emperor. At thirteen, he went to study at the University of Naples, and at the age of fifteen, without consulting his parents, he joined the order of Dominican preaching friars. When his mother endeavoured to prevent the completion of this arrangement, he hastened away to Rome, and then towards Paris. But on the way he was seized by his brothers and brought back. Interference and delay did not, however, prevent him from carrying out his cherished purpose. And at length, by the intercession of the emperor and the pope, his parents were prevailed upon to give their consent.

At the age of sixteen, he went to Cologne to hear the lectures of Albertus Magnus, and was recognized by his teacher as destined to accomplish great things. In 1253 Aquinas went to

Paris, where he wrote a work in defence of monastic life, and two years after he received from the University of Paris his degree of Doctor in Theology. In 1272 he returned to teach theology at Naples; and in 1274 he was about to set out for Lyons, whither he had been summoned by the Pope to endeavour to effect a union of the eastern and western Churches; but before going on this journey, he visited a relative, Frances of Aquino; and while at her castle, in Campania, he was overtaken by fatal fever, in his forty-eighth year.

Aquinas was celebrated especially for his dialectic skill. He followed Aristotle in method, and for the most part Augustine in doctrine. He was canonized by the Romish Church, and styled " the angelic doctor." His voluminous works are favourites with Roman Catholics. They find in them the argumentative advocacy of priestly efficacy and transubstantiation. Thomas Aquinas was the founder of the Thomists, who were arrayed against the Scotists, or followers of Duns Scotus, on the question concerning the efficacy of Divine grace.

The talents of Aquinas were various as well as great. His principal prose works were, his " Defence of the Monastic Life;" his " Summa Theologiæ;" his " Commentary on the Four Books of Peter Lombard;" and his " Commentaries on the Writings of Aristotle." He wrote in poetry as well as in prose.

"Sing, my tongue, the Saviour's glory."—No. 878.

This hymn is translated from one of his well known Latin hymns, " Pange, lingua gloriosi." One verse is omitted in the " New Congregational." Dr. Mason Neale, who gives another rendering of it, notes its high place in Latin poetry, and the difficulty of successfully translating it. Lines three and four in the first verse of the rendering in the "New Congregational Hymn Book" are different from Aquinas' original, but closely resemble two lines in a piece also commencing, " Pange, lingua gloriosi," by Venantius Fortunatus (530—609), the celebrated poet-bishop of Poitiers.

NICHOLAS DECIUS.
Died 1529.

This eminent German hymn-writer was a contemporary of Luther. His German name was Von Hofe. Like Luther, he was first a monk in connection with the Romish Church. He was prior of a monastery at Steterburg, in Wolfenbüttel, and afterwards joined in the Reformation. For a time, he occupied himself as a schoolmaster at Brunswick, and afterwards he became a Lutheran pastor at Stettin, where he died. His name lives as that of the author of well-known hymns, and of the favorite tunes to which they are sung. In the "New Congregational" there is a free rendering of the first stanza of his piece of four stanzas:—

> "To God on high be thanks and praise."—No. 291.
> "Allein Gott in der Höh', sei Ehr."

This is one of Decius' most celebrated hymns. It is said to be a free rendering of the old hymnus angelicus, "Gloria in excelsis Deo," which in its Greek version had very early come into use in the Eastern Church, and was introduced into the Latin Church about the year A.D. 360, by Hilary, Bishop of Poitiers. The German version was published in 1529. It was designed to take the place of the Latin "Gloria." The dying Christian has made it his parting song of triumph, and it has come into general use in Germany. The chorale, probably by Kugelmann, though others attribute it to Decius, has been introduced by Mendelssohn into his "St. Paul."

Decius is also the author of a celebrated hymn, not given in the "New Congregational Hymn Book"—

> "O, lamb of God, most stainless!"

It is founded on the ancient Latin hymn, "Agnus Dei, qui tollis peccata mundi, miserere nobis," which is used at mass. Luther introduced Decius' German rendering of it into the Protestant communion service.

Decius is also said to have been the author of the favorite tunes the Germans are accustomed to sing to these hymns.

MARTIN LUTHER, D.D.
1483—1546.

THE little town of Eisleben was the honoured birthplace of this prince of the Reformation. He was born there on the 10th November, 1483. A few months after his birth his parents removed to Mansfeldt, that his father, who was poor, might obtain work in the mines of that neighbourhood. There his father afterwards so far prospered as to establish smelting furnaces, and to obtain the means for Martin's education. From his pious parents, Martin received a careful, religious education; but too much severity left an unfavourable impression on the mind of the child, and his early religion was one of fear rather than of love. He learned what he could at the Latin school of Mansfeldt, and gave such promise as to awaken his father's highest expectations of his future course.

To further his education, Martin was sent, at the age of fourteen, to the Franciscan school at Magdeburg, where he used to sing in the streets for his bread, as his father was not yet able to support him. A year after he was removed to a celebrated school at Eisenach. He had relatives there, and hoped for their assistance, but they neglected him. It was there that Ursula, the wife of Conrad Cotta, took compassion on the singing boy, and, not only gave him temporary relief, but received him to her house, where for some years he enjoyed one of the most pleasant and profitable periods of his life. In that hospitable home young Martin greatly extended his knowledge of literature and science, and at the same time learned to play the flute and lute to please his kind benefactor, who was passionately fond of music; and thus became confirmed in him that love to music and song which afterwards bore such good fruits.

On reaching the age of eighteen, Luther went to the University of

Erfurth, where his father hoped he would pursue the study of the law. At Erfurth, Luther made great attainments, graduated M.A. and Doctor of Philosophy, and was admired for his genius by the whole University. There, too, he was much moved by meeting for the first time with the Bible. Books were rare in those days, and he had been content with the portions of Scripture he had heard read in public worship. But in the library at Erfurth he met with the whole Scriptures, and read them with deep thought and great wonder and delight. Providence also spoke to him by severe illness, by a dangerous wound received accidentally from his own sword, by the reported assassination of his companion Alexis, and by a violent storm in which his life seemed to be threatened. The effect of all these stirring events on the mind of Luther was, that before reaching the age of twenty-two, he disappointed the hopes of his father, and entered the monastery of St. Augustine, at Erfurth. There, during three years, Luther was passing through important spiritual conflicts, from which he at length emerged into evangelical rest and peace. In these struggles he was greatly assisted by Staupitz, the vicar-general of the Augustines, who knew and loved the evangelical doctrine, and was able to speak from his own experience of the way of deliverance.

In 1508, on the invitation of the Elector of Saxony, Luther undertook the office of Professor of Philosophy in Wittenberg University. And soon after he became Bachelor of Divinity, and was called to expound the Scriptures daily to the University. This work was engaged in by Luther with all his heart. Speaking, not in a cold and formal manner, but experimentally, and heeding Scripture for more than tradition, his lectures attracted crowds of hearers, and produced a great impression. He was invited to preach, and then appointed chaplain to the Council of Wittenberg. Thus he began to be the leader of the Reformation, though without as yet seeing all that was to follow.

Soon after, Luther was appointed to go on an important mission to Rome. Full of holy zeal, he anticipated his visit with the greatest interest; but what he heard there of the history of the Popes, and what he saw of the scepticism and levity of the priests and the immorality of the people, left an impression on his mind the opposite of what he expected. In 1512 Luther became Doctor of Divinity, and swore to "defend the evangelical truth with all his might,"—a work he set himself vigorously to do. Year by year he continued his various labours at Wittenberg, writing many letters, and fulfilling his duties as preacher and lecturer, and in other capacities. He also stirred the mind of the time by putting forth theological theses antagonistic to prevalent errors, and declarative of great Bible truths.

In order to supply Pope Leo X. with resources sufficient for the splendid life he then led, recourse was had to the sale of Indulgences. Pardon for sins, past or future, and speedy deliverance from purgatory, were offered in return for money. John Tetzel, prior of the Dominicans, was sent through Germany as the appointed dealer in these indulgences. This most unscrupulous imposture awakened indignation in the minds of the thoughtful. In 1516 Luther encountered it in the confessional. Some of his own hearers refused to forsake the sins they could so easily obtain indulgence for. Then Luther felt it to be his duty to warn his friends in private, and to preach and publish a sermon, in order to expose the pernicious error. And on the 3rd of October, 1517, as a further and still more decisive step, Luther posted upon the door of the Elector's Church, at Wittenberg, ninety-five theses against the doctrine of indulgences. This was done without previous intimation, and on a festival day, when crowds came to see the relics and to obtain such indulgences. Thus Luther openly broke with Rome. He soon found himself fully occupied in meeting the opponents his theses had raised against him. To aid the good work of Reformation, he also published his "Sermons on the Ten Commandments," and his "Explanation of the Lord's Prayer for simple and ignorant laymen."

In 1518 Luther thought it right to send a letter to the Pope, in order to explain his own position, and to deny the false reports that had been circulated to his injury. But, instead of receiving a favourable reply, he received a summons to Rome, which was at length exchanged for a command to appear before the Cardinal Legate, Cajetan, at Augsburg. This meeting, protracted through several interviews, led to no reconciliation, but only to the more thorough severance of Luther from Rome, though he still aimed to make what concessions he thought allowable. The legate begged the Elector to expel Luther from his dominions, or to send him to Rome; but the Elector refused. In the following year, another legate, a Saxon, named Militz, succeeded so far with Luther as to induce him to write an apologetic letter to the Pope. But the violent controversies into which Luther was drawn with Eckius rendered his own views more decided, and led him to declare openly against the doctrines of Popery; and his works on "Babylonian Captivity," and on "Christian Liberty" contained sentiments directly opposed to the teachings of the Romish Church. In consequence, the Pope issued a bull, threatening Luther with excommunication unless he retracted; and on the 10th of December, 1520, Luther finally and completely separated from Rome, by publicly burning this bull outside the walls of Wittenberg.

Then Frederic, Elector of Saxony, used his influence with the Emperor to have Luther's cause tried by a diet of the empire at Worms. This assembly took place in April, 1521. Before it Luther cleaved to his writings because of their Scriptural foundation, as he had done at Augsburg, and refused to retract. He was ordered to leave Worms, and a month after, an edict was issued putting him under the ban of the empire. But on his way from Worms, he was seized and carried to the castle of Wartburg. This was probably the act of a friend. Luther's place of concealment was kept secret; but in it he laboured most usefully, notwithstanding his bodily afflictions and spiritual trials. There he produced powerful treatises to aid the Reformation, and especially furthered it by translating the New Testament into the vernacular German. In all, his activity was sustained, as at other times in his life, by much communion with God. His New Testament was not completed till he had returned to Wittenberg, and availed himself of the assistance of his friend Melancthon. It was printed in 1522, and in Luther's forcible and idiomatic language was soon pouring forth by thousands from the presses of Wittenberg, for the newly-discovered power of the printing-press had come just in time to circulate Luther's stirring works throughout Germany and the world. Thus one strong hand sowed widely the fruitful seeds of the Reformation. He did not complete the whole Bible till 1530.

In 1524 Luther threw off his monastic dress, and in 1525 he married Catherine de Bora, a nun who had left her convent. In 1529 the reformed princes assembled at Spires, and separated from Rome by the "Protest" against the decree that was aimed at the Lutherans; and in 1530 the Lutherans presented their confession of faith at a diet at Augsburg.

Luther spent the remainder of his life in comparative quietude at Wittenberg, happy in his home, extensively useful by his writings, lectures, and letters, and cheered by seeing the Reformation extending into all parts of Europe. His internal sufferings were great during his later years, but his last illness continued only a few hours; and he was able to carry on his various labours almost till the day of his death. The calm Christian courage of his dying hour was in harmony with the confidence of his life. Along with other favourite passages, he thrice repeated the words, "Into Thy hands I commend my spirit, Thou hast redeemed me, O God of truth," and so fell asleep in Jesus. He died on the 18th February, 1546.

Besides the works already mentioned, Luther wrote many controversial works, one of the best known of which, is his reply to Henry VIII.'s "Defence of the Sacraments." His "Table Talk," and his "Commentary on the Galatians," are also prominent amongst his works. Besides these, he wrote commentaries on several books of the Bible, and his translation was accompanied with learned annotations. Nor should we omit his "Treatise on Good Works," published in 1520, in which he affirms the doctrine of "justification by faith only."

Luther was exceedingly fond of music and poetry. He ranked music next in place to theology. In the "concord of sweet sounds," he found solace in trouble and stimulus in his exhausting enterprises. He regarded it as a moral power for good, and an important element in good education. No teacher, he said, was worthy of the name who could not teach music; and he was most particular that his own son should be properly educated in it; and he took care to enlist this auxiliary in the service of the Reformation. At his own house he gathered a band of men skilled in music, with whose assistance he arranged to his own heart-stirring words the old and favorite melodies of Germany, taking care to adapt them to congregational worship, so that the people might resume that place in public praise of which their Romish guides had deprived them.

To provide the people with suitable psalms and hymns in their own tongue to be sung to these tunes, he translated some of the noblest of David's psalms. In writing to thank Eobanus Hesse for a copy of his translation of the psalms into Latin verse, Luther says, "I confess myself to be one of those who are more influenced and delighted by poetry, than by the most eloquent oration even of Cicero or Demosthenes. If I am thus affected by other subjects, you will believe how much more I am influenced by the Psalms. From my youth I have constantly studied them with much delight, and, blessed be God, not without considerable fruit. I will not speak of my gifts as preferable to those of others, but I glory in this, that, for all the thrones and kingdoms of the world, I would not relinquish what I have gained by meditating upon the psalms, through the blessing of the Holy Spirit. Nor would I be guilty of such foolish humility as to dissemble the gifts of God implanted in me. For of myself there is enough, and more than enough, which humbles me and teaches me I am nothing; but in God I may glory, and rejoice and triumph in his works. I do so with respect to my German psalter, and I will do so still more in yours, but giving the praise and glory to God, who is blessed for ever."

Luther also translated some of the best Latin hymns, improved some of the old German popular hymns, encouraged his friends to write, and wrote some himself, including metrical versions of some parts of the Bible. Some of his hymns were printed on single sheets, with the tunes, and circulated widely. In his own preface to his "Spiritual Songs," published in 1527, after showing that it is a scriptural practice to sing psalms and hymns, he says, "Accordingly to make a good beginning, and to encourage others who can do it better, I have myself, with some others, put together a few hymns, in order to bring into full play the blessed Gospel which by God's grace hath again risen."

Upon the minds of the people awakening to the new era, and already moved by reading Luther's noble translation of the New Testament, the singing of these evangelical psalms and hymns made a very deep impression. The masses sang Luther's tunes and Luther's words ; and the enemies of the Reformation said, "Luther has done us more harm by his songs than by his sermons." Coleridge says, "Luther did as much for the Reformation by his hymns as by his translation of the Bible." And another modern writer says, "These hymns made a bond of union among men who knew little of Creeds and Articles : while theologians were disputing about niceties of doctrine, every devout man could understand the blessedness of singing God's praises in good honest German, instead of gazing idly at the mass, or listening to a Latin Litany : the children learnt Luther's hymns in the cottage, and martyrs sang them on the scaffold."

Luther's psalms and hymns are not marked by their refined taste or their splendid imagery ; but we value in them their fulness of scripture truth, their plainness to the comprehension of all ; their simple beauty and homely strength : and they are not without traces of the boldness and sublimity of the genius of the writer. There are only three psalms by Luther in the "New Congregational Hymn Book," and no hymns.

"God is our refuge in distress."—No. 66.

The two verses given as a rendering of Luther's version of the 46th Psalm, are an inadequate representation of his well-known piece of four stanzas.

"Ein feste burg ist unser Gott."

They do not keep close to the German original, and lack its special force. Kübler says that D'Aubigné is in error in assigning this piece to the year 1530, because it had appeared in 1529, with the bold tune Luther had written for it in Joseph Klug's hymn book. This Protestant hymn, affirming that God was the defence of His people, was written in the year when the Evangelical princes delivered that protest at the diet of Spires, from which "Protestants" take their name. Luther used often to sing it in 1530, while the diet of Augsburg was sitting. It soon became a favourite psalm with the people. It was one of the watchwords of the Reformation, cheering armies to conflict, and sustaining believers in the hour of fiery trial. After Luther's death, when Melancthon was at Weimar with his banished friends, Jonas and Creuziger, he heard a little maid sing this psalm in the street, and said, " Sing on, my little girl, you don't know what famous people you comfort." The first line of this psalm is inscribed on Luther's tomb at Wittenberg. It has been called the national hymn of Protestant Germany.

"Let God arise, and let His foes."—No. 97.

Luther's rendering of Psalm lxviii.

"Out of the depths I cry to Thee."—No. 215.

Luther's rendering of Psalm cxxx. It was composed and published by him in 1524. In the same year he altered it and published it again. It is the second edition that is usually followed.

It was used by the Lutherans at funerals on Luther's own suggestion—and with much emotion at his own.

In the year 1530, during the diet of Augsburg, Luther's mental anxiety so overcame his bodily strength that he fainted. On recovering, he said, " Come, let us defy the devil, and praise God by singing the hymn, ' Out of the depths I cry to Thee.' " This hymn has often comforted the sick and dying. It is said to have been the last Protestant hymn sung in Strasburg Cathedral.

THOMAS STERNHOLD.

Died 1549.

The writings of Sternhold and Hopkins mark an era in the history of our sacred verse. The national muse had become at the Reformation puritanical and pious, but its piety was unattended by the power and genius of true poetry.

Sternhold was born in Hampshire, and educated at Oxford. He was Groom of the Robes to Henry VIII. and Edward VI. Along with John Hopkins, he produced the first English metrical version of the psalms attached to the "Book of Common Prayer." He completed only the first fifty-one; Hopkins and others composed the remainder. Thirty-seven of Sternhold's psalms were edited and published immediately after his death by his friend John Hopkins. Sternhold died, August, 1549. The work was entitled, "All such Psalms of David as Thomas Sternholde, late Groome of the King's Majestye's Robes, did in his Lyfe-time drawe into Englyshe Metre." The complete version annexed to the "Book of Common Prayer" did not appear till 1562. Of this version Montgomery says, "The merit of faithful adherence to the original has been claimed for this version, and need not to be denied, but it is the resemblance which the dead bear to the living." Wood, in his "Athenæ Oxonienses" (1691), vol. i. p. 62, has the following account of the origin of Sternhold's psalms.

"Being a most zealous reformer, and a very strict liver, he became so scandalized at the amorous and obscene songs used in the Court, that he, forsooth, turned into English metre fifty-one of David's psalms, and caused musical notes to be set to them, thinking thereby that the courtiers would sing them instead of their sonnets; but they did not, some few excepted. However, the poetry and music being admirable, and the best that was made and composed in these times, they were thought fit to be sung in all parochial churches."

The melodies to which the psalms were to be sung, many of them adopted from the German and French, were also given in this latter edition. Sternhold was also the author of "Certain Chapters of the Proverbs of Solomon, drawn into metre." Of Sternhold and Hopkins, old Thomas Fuller says, "They were men whose piety was better than their poetry, and they had drank more of Jordan than of Helicon:" and Thomas Campbell says, "with the best intentions and the worst taste, they degraded the spirit of Hebrew psalmody by flat and homely phraseology; and, mistaking vulgarity for simplicity, turned into bathos what they found sublime." Sternhold usually makes only the second and fourth lines rhyme, and not always those. Yet the great churchmen of those days maintained the unapproachable excellence of Sternhold and Hopkins. These writers may be taken as the representatives of the strong tendency to versify Scripture that came with the Reformation into England—a work men eagerly entered on without the talent requisite for its successful accomplishment. The tendency went so far that even the "Acts of the Apostles" was put into rhyme, and set to music by Dr. Christopher Tye.

"O God, my strength and fortitude."—No. 16.

Sternhold's rendering of Psalm xviii possesses poetic excellence, and is above his average style. The original piece extends to forty-nine stanzas.

J. HOPKINS.

Few of the incidents in the life of this psalm-writer are on record. He graduated B.A. at Oxford in 1544, and was afterwards a clergyman in Suffolk. His name is preserved as that of a coadjutor of Sternhold in the production of the first psalter attached to the "Book of Common Prayer." It appeared in 1562. Other writers supplied a few psalms. Amongst these were Whittingham, a friend of Calvin's; Norton, the translator of "Calvin's Institutes;" and Wisdome, Archdeacon of Ely.

Hopkins was editor of the Psalms, 1551. At first he translated fifty-eight of the psalms, forming the old version, but published only seven. He is thought to be somewhat superior as a poet to his coadjutor Sternhold. Some Latin stanzas prefixed to "Foxe's Martyrology" are attributed to him, and Bayle says of him that he was "Britannicorum Poetarum sui temporis non infimus."

"All people that on earth do dwell."—No. 153.

It has been customary to attribute this psalm to Hopkins, but not on good grounds. It is superior to his productions. Some have supposed that this psalm was by William Kethe, who was an exile with Knox, at Geneva, in 1555. He was chaplain to the English forces in Havre, in 1563, and last of all had the parish of Okeford, in Dorset. The old Psalter, of which a copy exists in the Library of St. Paul's Cathedral, London, had twenty-five psalms added to it in 1561, all of which, except the above 100th, had Kethe's initials, "W.K." That psalm had the initials "T.S.," for Thomas Sternhold, but as those initials were not afterwards repeated, it is supposed that that psalm was also by William Kethe; and it is said that in another edition of the same year, "W.K." was put to this rendering; and in the "Scottish Psalter" of 1564 this psalm has the initials "W.K." Internal evidence is also thought to support this view. In Dr. Williams's Library there is a sermon printed in black letter, preached at Blandford,

Dorset, Jan. 17, 1571, at the session held there, "By William Kethe, minister and preacher of God's Word."

"The whole Booke of Psalmes collected into Englyshe Meter, by Thomas Sternhold, J. Hopkins, and others, 1564," of which there is a copy, in the British Museum, contains sixty-two psalms by Hopkins, but the psalm given as the 100th is not that given as his in the "New Congregational," but an inferior production. In a later Psalter (1606), which gives the initials of the writers to the psalms, there are two renderings of this psalm, and each without initials. The latter of these is the rendering in the "New Congregational" exactly as it stands there. In this Psalter, "J. H." is put to Hopkins' psalms, and "W. K." to Kethe's, and as there is no name to this rendering, we conclude that the author cannot be ascertained with certainty. Perhaps we may venture to say the rendering is not Hopkins', but may be Kethe's.

BARTHOLOMEW RINGWALDT.

1530—1598.

RINGWALDT was born at Frankfort-on-the-Oder, in 1530, and was a faithful Lutheran pastor at Langfeld, in Prussia, where he died 1598. His hymns are of great excellence, and much resemble Luther's in their simplicity and power. Several of them were written to comfort himself and others in the sufferings they endured from famine, pestilence, fire, and floods. In 1581, he published "Hymns for the Sundays and Festivals of the whole Year." He also wrote two other works.

"Great God, what do I see and hear?"—No. 420.

This hymn, often erroneously attributed to Luther, was written in imitation of the well-known, oft-translated ancient Latin hymn, "Dies iræ, dies illa," which was written by the Franciscan, Thomas Celano, who died in 1253. Ringwaldt's hymn appeared in 1585.

Under Dr. Collyer, it is shown that half the hymn, as given in the "New Congregational Hymn Book," is by him. The hymn as it stands there resembles Ringwaldt's German original of seven stanzas, and beginning,—

"Es ist gewisslich an der zeit,"

but the resemblance is only in the first verse.

DR. PHILIP NICOLAI.
1556—1608.

That there have been writers who have produced only a few hymns, and those very good, is a curious fact for the psychologist. How such writers should arrive at great excellence without practice in their art, and why, having written so well, they should not write more, we must leave to him to determine. Nicolai is one of the class of writers referred to. He wrote three hymns, two of which are deservedly famous.

Dr. Philip Nicolai was born on the 10th August, 1556, at Mengeringhausen, in the principality of Waldeck, where his father was a Lutheran pastor. Philip followed his father in his profession, and commenced his ministry in 1576, as assistant to him in his native village. Thence he removed to Hardeck, whence he was expelled by the papists. Afterwards, he was in other places, and from 1596, at Unna, in Westphalia. In 1601, he removed to Hamburg, as pastor of St. Catherine's Church. He died at Hamburg on the 26th of October, 1608.

His two principal hymns—

"Awake, awake, for night is flying—"
(Wachet auf, ruft uns die Stimme,)

nd,

"O, Morning Star, how fair and bright—"
(Wie schön leucht uns der Morgernstern,)

were written in 1597, at Unna, during the raging of a dreadful pestilence, which carried off more than 1,400 persons. Nicolai could see their burials from his window, and his mind becoming much affected by the appalling events happening around him, he was led to think much of death, heaven, and eternity. His meditations cheered his own heart, and, in 1599, he published them for the benefit of others. The work is entitled, "Freudenspiegel des ewigen Lebens," or "Reflections of the joys of eternal life." To this work he appended the first-mentioned hymn, and entitled it, "Of the voice at midnight, and the wise virgins who met their heavenly bridegroom." This hymn has been translated into several foreign languages. The tune, introduced by Mendelssohn into his "Elijah," is said to have been composed by Nicolai, and harmonized by Jacob Pretorius, his organist, at Hamburg. The other hymn was given in the appendix to his "Freudenspiegel," and entitled, "A spiritual bridal song of the believing soul concerning Jesus Christ, her heavenly bridegroom, from Psalm xlv, of the Prophet David." The splendid chorale used for it was taken by Nicolai himself from a secular song. Nicolai wrote his third known hymn shortly before his death. His hymns found many imitators, and gave a new impetus to German religious poetry. Nicolai also wrote polemical works.

"Behold how glorious is yon sky,"—No. 749,

Is a translation of a piece attributed to Nicolai.

GEORGE SANDYS.

1577—1643.

POPE said that English poetry owed much to the translations of Sandys; Dryden styled him, "the best versifier of the former age," and Addison is believed to have benefited by the study of his style.

He was born at Bishopsthorpe, at the palace of his father, Dr. Edwin Sandys, then Archbishop of York, and he was brother of

Sir Edwin Sandys, author of "Speculum Europæ." The young poet studied at Oxford, at St. Mary's Hall, and afterwards, it is believed, at Corpus Christi College. At the age of thirty-three, he went on an extensive tour in Greece, Egypt, and the Holy Land. Of these travels he gave a poetic description in his piece entitled, "The Traveller's Thanksgiving." And he published, in 1615, a prose account entitled, "A relation of a journey begun in 1610, in 44 books, containing a description of the Turkish empire, of Egypt, of the Holy Land, and of the remote parts of Italy, and the islands adjoining." At the temple of Christ's Sepulchre, at Jerusalem, he had dedicated to the Redeemer his hymn, beginning, "Saviour of Mankind, Man, Emmanuel." After his travels in the East, he became treasurer of the English colony of Virginia, in America. During his residence there, he completed his translation of the "Metamorphosis of Ovid." This is claimed as one of the earliest American books. On returning to England, he was appointed one of the gentlemen to the privy chamber to the King, Charles I. In 1636, he published a "Paraphrase upon the Psalms of David, and upon the Hymns dispersed throughout the Old and New Testaments." Sir Thomas Herbert, in his "Memoirs of King Charles I.," says that this paraphrase was one of the books the King often read while confined at Carisbrooke Castle. At a later period he published paraphrases of several parts of the Old Testament. In 1639, he made a translation of Grotius' tragedy of "Christ's Passion." His last work was a poetical version of the "Song of Solomon," published in 1642. He died unmarried, March, 1643, at Bexley Abbey, Kent.

In the preface to his "Poetical Fragments," 1681, Baxter says, "It did me good when Mrs. Wyat invited me to see Bexley Abbey, in Kent, to see upon the old stone wall in the garden a summer-house, with this inscription in great golden letters, that, —In that place, Mr. G. Sandys, after his travels over the world, retired himself for his poetry and contemplations."

The two hymns given in the "New Congregational," Nos. 91 and

763, show his power of harmonious expression, and especially his skill in producing striking couplets, a gift of great value in translating the brief parallelisms of Hebrew poetry, and in providing psalms sometimes sung in portions of two or four lines.

"Sing the great Jehovah's praise."—No. 91.

This is a small portion of his rendering of Psalm lxvi. It is given in "A paraphrase upon the Divine Poems," by George Sandys, 1648, and begins in the original—

"Happy sons of Israel."

This work is dedicated by Sandys to King Charles. The first portion is a paraphrase on the Book of Job, and a brief preface to the Psalms explains that they were written before the paraphrase on Job, i. e. before 1648.

"Thou who art enthroned above."—No. 763.

Verse 1 of this hymn, as it is given in the "New Congregational," is the first portion of Sandys' rendering of the 92nd Psalm, in the work just referred to, given with slight alterations, but the other two stanzas bear no resemblance to the remaining portion as he has given it.

MARTIN RINKART.
1586—1649.

EILENBURG, in Saxony, was the birthplace of this German poet and pastor. His father was a cooper, and being unable to provide his son with the means of education, Martin supported himself by his musical skill while studying theology at Leipsic. In course of time, he became pastor in his native town, for whose good he laboured all through the "Thirty Years' War," and long after.

During the pestilence in 1637, and the famine in the following year, Rinkart was indefatigable in ministering to the necessities of his suffering congregation and neighbours. And in the year

1639, when the Swedish Lieutenant-Colonel Dörfling, demanded of Eilenburg no less a sum than 30,000 thalers, Rinkart first went out to intercede for his townsmen. And, failing in that, on his return, he invited them to assemble for prayer ; which God so answered that their seemingly overwhelming difficulty was removed, and the Swedish officer consented to terms which they were able to meet. Sometimes persecuted by those who were without, Rinkart always found a refuge of peace in his family, and happiness in his home ; and through good and evil report persevered in living a most pious and useful life.

The one hymn in the "New Congregational Hymn Book," by Rinkart, was written about the year 1644, in the prospect of the re-establishment of peace.

"Let all men praise the Lord."—No. 449.
(Nun danket alle Gott).

The original consists of four stanzas. The first two (the latter of which is not given in the "New Congregational Hymn Book)" are a metrical version of a passage in the Apocryphal Book of Ecclesiasticus, l. 22—24 :—

"Now therefore bless ye the God of all, which only doeth wondrous things everywhere, which exalteth our days from the womb, and dealeth with us according to his mercy. He grant us joyfulness of heart, and that peace may be in our days in Israel for ever. That he would confirm his mercy with us, and deliver us at his time!"

This noble hymn of praise has been called the popular "German Te Deum." It has sometimes been used by Christians to express their gratitude for special mercies ; and it has often been sung in Germany when great national blessings have been received.

GEORGE WITHER.
1588—1667.

THIS much-suffering poet was born at Bentworth, near Alton, in Hampshire. After studying at Oxford, he was sent to pursue his studies at the Inns of Law in London. But his genius leading him to poetry rather than to law, he gave himself to the muses, and became known as a poet. During his long life his pen was seldom idle. The list of his works fills about thirteen columns in Dr. Bliss's edition of the "Fasti Oxonienses!" Some of his pieces were political in their character, and brought him into serious troubles in the extended and eventful period during which he wrote—reaching as it did from the reign of James the First to that of Charles the Second.

In his twenty-fifth year, Wither published a poetical satire on the abuses of the times, entitled "Abuses Stript and Whipt." For this James's Government threw him into the Marshalsea, where his sufferings and privations were very great. During his imprisonment, he wrote his "Satire to the King." This production is believed to have assisted in obtaining his release. In 1619, he published "A Preparation to the Psalter," and in 1622, he had so far advanced in King James the First's favour, that he gave him a patent for his "Hymns and Songs of the Church," authorizing their insertion in the Psalter, during a period of fifty-one years. But his monopoly was resisted by those interested in the work of Sternhold and Hopkins. In 1632, he had his work "imprinted in the Netherlands," with the title, "The Psalms of David translated into Lyric Verse, according to the scope of the original, and illustrated with a short argument, and a brief prayer, or meditation before and after sermon." And the same contest was resumed when Chas. I. granted him an exclusive licence.

In 1639, Wither was captain of horse in the expedition against the Scots. But on the rise of the Commonwealth, the poet, who had already shown a leaning to the Puritans, sold his estate, and raised a troop of horse for the Parliament. "He was," says Wood, "made a captain, and soon after a major, having this motto on his colours, 'Pro Rege, Lege, Grege;' but being taken prisoner by the cavaliers, Sir John Denham, the poet (some of whose land at Egham, in Surrey, Wither had got into his clutches), desired his majesty not to hang him, 'because that so long as Wither lived, Denham would not be accounted the worst poet in England:'" and under Cromwell, Wither held several offices.

At the Restoration, he was thrown into prison, on the ground of a political pamphlet which was found amongst his papers. His imprisonment was again with severity. Being denied proper writing materials, he was reduced to the necessity of scrawling his verses with an "oker pencil" upon the trenchers. Some of his poems bear traces both of his suffering and of his divine consolation. One suggestive piece is devoted to the spiritual lessons an imprisonment may teach. It is entitled, "Meditations in Prison."

Wither's works are too numerous to mention; but there is one of too great historical interest to be overlooked. It is called "Britain's Remembrancer," and it was written to commemorate the Plague in London. To bear solemn testimony of this terrible calamity, he remained bravely at his residence on the bank of the Thames while some were fleeing, and many were falling around him. He wrote in prison one of the best of his pieces, "The Shepherds Hunting." In 1622, he published a collection of his poems, with the title, "Mistress of Philarete;" in 1635, his collection of "Emblems, Ancient and Modern;" and in 1638, eight separate poetical pieces, afterwards published together, under the title "Juvenilia." As a poet, he is classed with his contemporary, Francis Quarles (1592—1644), and it has been truly said of his poetry, "The vice of Wither, as it was generally of the literature of his age, was a passion for ingenious turns and unexpected conceits, which bear the same relation to really beautiful thoughts, that plays upon words do to true wit."

Wither's poetry was for a long period undervalued. It became usual to sneer at him. Pope, in the "Dunciad," calls him "Wretched Wither;" but impartial critics of later times, Hallam, Charles Lamb, Southey, and others, while acknowledging that he wrote too much to write always carefully, have found scattered in his writings many gems of poesy. Along with the warmth of a polemic, we find in his works the fervour of a pious Puritan, and sometimes the fire of true poetry.

Of his domestic union, he was able to say—

> "Now sing we will thy praise,
> For that thou dost as well prolong,
> Our loving as our days."

His political troubles appear to have arisen from his thoroughness in word and deed in favour of what he thought the right cause. It is consoling to know that, though he had again and again lived in prison, he did not die there, but was released four years before his death; and that, notwithstanding his various troubles, he was able to sing on nearly fourscore years in this suffering world.

This poet, patriot, and Christian, is represented in the "New Congregational Hymn Book" by only two hymns.

"The Lord is King, and weareth,"—No. 137,

Is his rendering of the brief 93rd Psalm. It will be seen to keep close to the original, and to possess much poetic force.

"Come, O come, with sacred lays." —No. 255.

This is extracted from his paraphrastic version of the 148th Psalm, and altered to adapt it to this collection.

ERNEST CHRISTOPHER HOMBURG.
1605—1681.

"Man of sorrows, and acquainted."—No. 373.

This ancient and most touching Christian hymn is No. 77 in the "Liturgy and Hymns for the Use of the Protestant Church of the United Brethren, 1836;" and Montgomery, in his "Christian

Psalmist, 1832," gives this hymn, with two additional verses of a similar character.

E. C. Homburg was born at Mühla, near Eisenach, in 1605. He practised as a lawyer at Naumburg, where he died on the 21st June, 1681. In his youth he composed secular songs, but affliction having come upon him, he turned his thoughts to sacred themes, and wrote many beautiful hymns.

PAUL GERHARD.

1606—1676.

THIS poet, whom the German people regard as emphatically their own, was born at Græfenhænichen, in Saxony, of which town his father was burgomaster, or chief magistrate. Studying during the time of the Thirty Years' War, he entered upon life in a period of suffering and distraction, and did not become a Christian pastor till the war was at an end. We have no record of his early course, but about the year 1648 we find him a private tutor at Berlin, in the family of the chancery-advocate, Andreas Bertholdt. His first pastorate was in a small village, Mittenwalde, whither he went in 1651. He married in 1655 his attached wife, who died the 5th March, 1668. In 1657 he removed to St. Nicholas' Church, Berlin. There he became known as a hymn-writer, and published his first collection in 1666. The Berlin citizens held him in high honour as a powerful preacher and an earnest Christian pastor; but, notwithstanding, he was in 1666 deposed from his spiritual office, because of his uncompromising adherence to the Lutheran doctrine. When he was informed of his deprivation, he said, "This is only a small Berlin affliction; but I am also willing and ready to seal with my blood the evangelical truth, and like my namesake, St. Paul, to offer my neck to the sword." The following year he was re-instated in his position; but on finding that it was with the understanding that he should give up that course of conduct in reference to the

Reformed faith, which he thought he ought to pursue, his tender conscience would not allow him to occupy a false position, and he was again superseded.

Deprived of his office, he was also afflicted with family bereavements. He had lost three children in their infancy, and in 1668 his affectionate wife, to whom he was devotedly attached, and who had proved a true help-meet for him, was, after much weakness and affliction, taken from him by death.

The same year, 1668, he was appointed to Lübben, in Saxony, where he became archdeacon. His portrait in the church there bears the inscription, "Theologus in cribro Satanæ versatus;" *i. e.*, " A divine sifted in Satan's sieve"—probably in reference to the detraction and unkindness he experienced at Lübben during the last seven years of his life. While thus maturing both by age and affliction, he wrote some of his most valued hymns.

Having charged his only remaining son to abide in the faith, he died on the 7th of June, 1676, repeating one of his own hymns—

" Wherefore should I grieve and pine."

And in the very act of repeating the words,

" him no
Death has power to kill,
But from many a dreaded ill
Bears his spirit safe away, &c."

In German sacred poetry of the older school, Gerhard ranks next to Luther, whom he in some respects resembles, and from whom he was separated by about a century. His hymns happily combine simplicity with depth and force. They are the heart-utterances of one who had a simple but sublime faith in God, and who recognized His fatherly presence in the operations of nature, the superintendence of Providence, and the daily bestowment of the surpassing gifts of redemption. They have reasonably been favourites with the German people, and are justly taking their place in our modern collections. Schiller's mother was one of many who taught their sons Gerhard's hymns; and the genius of the young poet was at once purified and nourished by these spiritual effusions, of which he became very fond.

> "Jesus, Thy boundless love to me."—No. 363.
> "O Jesu Christ, mein schönstes Licht."

John Wesley's translation (1739) is given. The original consists of sixteen stanzas.

> "O sacred head, once wounded."—No. 374.
> "O haupt voll blut und wunden."

The German original consists of ten stanzas. This was first published in 1659. It is an imitation of a Latin hymn, "Salve, caput cruentatum," by Bernard of Clairvaux, who lived in the twelfth century. The translation given in the "New Congregational" is that of James W. Alexander, 1849, altered. Several instances are on record of the comfort this hymn has been to Christians in death; especially interesting is the case of the missionary Swartz, whom the native Christians in India comforted by singing this hymn in their own Tamil, into which it had been translated.

> "Holy Lamb, who Thee receive."—No. 572.

This hymn is erroneously attributed to Gerhard. It is by Anna Dober (1735), *vide* under her name.

> "Give to the winds thy fears."—No. 606.

This is John Wesley's translation (1739) of part of Gerhard's most popular hymn—

> "Commit thou all thy griefs
> And ways into His hands."
> "Befiehl du deine Wege, &c."

It is said to have been written at the time when, owing to his views differing from those of the king, he was ordered to quit the country. He went, in reduced circumstances, with his wife on foot. One night, on seeking a refuge in a village inn, his wife, affected by their altered condition, burst into tears. Then the poet reminded her of the verse, "Commit thy way unto the Lord," Psalm xxxvii. 5; and, retiring to an arbour, wrote this hymn upon those words. The same night two gentlemen arrived who had come by order of Duke Christian, of Merseburg, to invite the poet to Merseburg, and to inform him that the Duke had settled a considerable pension on him as a compensation for the injustice of which he was a victim. Gerhard then gave his wife the hymn he had written in trouble but in faith, and said, "See how God provides! Did I not bid you to trust in God, and all would be well."

JOHN MILTON.
1608—1674.

Of the life of the celebrated author of the "Paradise Lost," Montgomery truly says, "His youth and his old age he devoted to himself and his fame, his middle life to his country. That Milton thus appropriated the different parts of his life will appear as we briefly recount his history.

His father, of the same name, was a man of good family, who had enjoyed educational advantages, and was especially skilled in music—a talent inherited by his greater son. The poet was born on the 9th of December, 1608, at a house in Bread Street, London, where his father carried on the profession of scrivener, or preparer of legal contracts. There was also a younger brother, who became a judge, Sir Christopher Milton; and a sister, whose children the poet afterwards educated. The young poet was educated at St. Paul's School, and afterwards at Cambridge, where he distinguished himself for the excellence of his Latin verses. There also he graduated M.A. in his twenty-fourth year. His father had intended to make him a minister of the State Church; but this was impossible with the views he already held, and especially at a time when Archbishop Laud was the ruling spirit of that Church. "If Milton had become a preacher, says Thomas Campbell, "he must have founded a Church of his own."

After leaving Cambridge, Milton spent five years with his father, who had gone to live on an estate he had purchased at Horton, near Windsor. This was a delightful and productive period of the poet's life. As a boy he had written some poetical versions of the Psalms. In his twenty-first year he had composed his "Hymn on the Nativity." He now wrote, in 1634, " Comus," a mask, " Lycidas," an elegy on the death of Sir John King; and about the same time he produced his " Arcades."

In 1638, he set out on a tour in France and Italy. During this journey he visited Grotius, Galileo, Manso, Tasso's patron, and many others, whose expressions of homage for his genius strengthened within him the inward prompting that he " might perhaps leave something so written to after-times as they should not willingly let die."

On his return he supplemented his scanty resources by the proceeds of a school, in which he instructed his nephews and a few other scholars. This school was carried on at a house in Aldersgate Street, London. At the same time he began to write important prose works, demanded by the political circumstances of the times, for the defence of Puritanism and the exposure of prelatical presumption.

At the age of thirty-four Milton married his first wife, Mary Powell, the daughter of a magistrate in Oxfordshire. But soon after, owing to uncongeniality of disposition, as it is supposed, she withdrew from her new home; and persisting in her absence, Milton published his views on divorce, and appeared to be about to act on them. This was prevented by the reconciliation which in a short time took place. This first wife was the mother of Milton's three daughters. She died nine years after the reconciliation.

In the year 1644 Milton published his noble " Speech for the liberty of unlicensed Printing." In this and some other of his prose writings, the writer, leaving the ordinary level, seems o rise to the high place of a prophet and lawgiver. In the same year appeared his tractate "On Education." About the same time a collection of his Latin and English poems appeared, including the "L'Allegro," and the "Il Penseroso." In 1649 he was appointed Latin Secretary to the Council of State, an office he held for ten years, till the time of the brief protectorate of Richard Cromwell. In his new office it devolved on him to reply to "Icon Basilike," or a "Portraiture of his sacred Majesty in his Solitude and his Sufferings," a work that was being generally read, and was lending some support to the royal cause. His reply was entitled "Iconoclastes," or the Image-breaker. Soon after he was appointed to rebut the "Defensio Regis" of Salmasius of Leyden, published in 1649. This he successfully accomplished in his "Defensio Populi Anglicani." This work was much read; and besides applause, he received as his payment the substantial sum of one thousand pounds. Excessive literary labour at length quite quenched his dim sight, which from his boyhood had been injured by unremitting application to studious pursuits, and as he says; so touchingly—

> "his light was spent
> Ere half his days, in this dark world and wide."

Milton's second wife, whom he married in 1656, the daughter of Captain Woodcock, of Hackney, was spared to him but one year. He has immortalized her memory in an unsurpassed sonnet, in which he calls her his "late espoused saint."

At the age of forty-seven Milton found himself free from official and political engagements, and able to turn his attention to his great literary projects. He made some preparation for a Latin Dictionary, and his manuscripts were afterwards used at Cambridge, in the production of a similar work. And he wrote part of a history of his country. But his blindness interfered with the progress of these works, and they were only commenced. The portion of history was published in 1670, entitled "Six Books of the History of England, reaching to the Norman Conquest." Now was the favoured time when he began seriously to set about his greatest poem, the "Paradise Lost;" for which his varied learning, and his native and acquired poetical skill, were suitable preparatives, and the plan of which had long been in his mind. He resided at that time at a house in the Artillery Walk, leading to Bunhill Fields. There he gave himself heartily to this work, seizing the intervals of his suffering from gout to compose his sublime epic, and availing himself of the assistance of friends, who wrote down what he had produced.

In 1663 Milton married his third wife, Elizabeth Minshul, daughter of a gentleman in Cheshire. He had not suffered at the Restoration in 1660 as we might have feared he would. This fact Dr. Johnson thus explains—"He was now poor and blind, and who would pursue with violence an illustrious enemy, depressed by fortune, and disarmed by nature."

During the Plague, in 1665, Milton took refuge at Chalfont, in Bucks, where one Elwood first saw a complete copy of "Paradise Lost," and said to the poet, "Thou hast said a great deal upon 'Paradise Lost!' what hast thou to say on 'Paradise Regained?'" This question led to the production of the "Paradise Regained," a work which, contrary to the general judgment, Milton himself preferred to the "Paradise Lost."

In the year 1667 the poet, having returned to London, obtained a licence to publish his great poem, and sold his copyright to Samuel Simmons for five pounds, with further payments according to the sale. Thus humble in the manner of its first appearance was that work of which Johnson says "it is not the greatest of heroic poems only because it was not the first." The sale was slow at first, for readers were few in those times, and the work was too learned in style for the majority of them. But Andrew Marvel and John Dryden welcomed it with generous but deserved praise; and later, Addison's papers on it, in the "Spectator," opened the way for it to take its lofty place of pre-eminence in our literature.

The "Paradise Regained" was published in 1667, and in the

same year his "Samson Agonistes." Milton was also the author of several political works, besides those already mentioned, and of works on "Logic," and "Grammar." His "Treatise on True Religion" was printed in 1673. He wrote also a "Treatise on Theology," the manuscript of which was discovered in the State Paper Office, in 1823. This work shows that late in life Milton had adopted Arian views of the person of Christ, though he still believed in His atoning sacrifice. Joseph Warton styles him "the most learned of our poets." His learning in various tongues and in almost all branches of knowledge was scarcely second to his incomparable genius, and his nobility of soul not inferior to either. His sonnets include some of universal celebrity. One of the most affecting and beautiful is that already referred to on his own blindness. Returning again to the subject of the loss of the use of his eyes, he speaks in another sonnet thus nobly:—

> "What supports me, dost thou ask?
> The conscience, friend, to have lost them overplied
>   In liberty's defence, my noble task,
> Of which all Europe rings from side to side.
>   This thought might lead me through the world's vain mask,
> Content, though blind, had I no better guide."

For translations of some of his Latin poems we are indebted to Cowper. In addition to the painful privation of sight, the illustrious poet suffered much bodily affliction towards the end; but at length, at the age of sixty-six, he sank peacefully in death, on Sunday, the 8th of November, 1674. He was buried in St. Giles's, Cripplegate.

Such is a brief account of the life and labours of our greatest epic poet—the equal of Dante and Homer, and at the same time the brightest star of Independency—the poet of Puritanism when Cromwell was its prince.

Milton did not write many pieces suitable for use in ordinary public worship, but he made poetical translations of some of the Psalms—

"The Lord will come and not be slow."— No 123,

is made up of verses taken from his version of Psalms lxxxii, lxxxv, and lxxxvi. His renderings of the Psalms, from which these verses are taken, are remarkable for their closeness to the original. They are thus headed, "Psalms done into metre; wherein all but what is in a different character, are the very words of the text, translated from the original." And in some verses there is not a word which is not found in the original. These Psalms were written in the year 1648, Milton's fortieth year. He paraphrased nine of the Psalms thus, at one time, and eight at another.

"Let us with a gladsome mind."—No. 229,

is a part of his version of Psalm cxxxvi, and was written in his fifteenth year. The complete poem consists of twenty-four verses. Those omitted here show the richness of his youthful imagination as those retained reveal its promise of future poetic power. The whole is worthy of study as the production of one, who, more than thirty years after, and not till then, wrote the "Paradise Lost."

RICHARD BAXTER.
1615—1691.

THE eminent author of the "Call to the Unconverted," and the "Saints' Everlasting Rest," was born at Rowton, in Shropshire, where he lived with his maternal grandfather, till at ten years of age he was taken home to his parents at Eaton Constantine, in the same county. His father had but recently become a Christian, and chiefly through the reading of the Scriptures. Hence he especially enjoined this duty upon his son, for whose religious welfare he laboured and prayed. The petty persecutions his father was exposed to on account of his Christian profession, and the way he met them, opened the eyes of young Baxter to the true character of the Christian religion; and at about the age of fifteen, several books that he read, including "Bunny's Resolutions," and "Sibbs' Bruised Reed," were of much spiritual benefit to him. "Thus," he says, "without any means but books, was God pleased to resolve me for Himself." Baxter's education was carried on by tutors, from whose neglect he sometimes suffered, and he did not enter either of the Universities; yet he gave early promise of future eminence.

When he was in his nineteenth year, he was induced to try his success as an attendant at Court. But the Court of Charles I. was no place for a man of Baxter's religious training and tendencies, and he soon left it. At the age of twenty-three, he became head master of the Grammar School at Dudley, Worcestershire. He had previously occupied for a short time a similar position at Wroxeter. He also received a theological training; and having at that time no scruples about Conformity, was episcopally ordained. When he had been three-quarters of a year at Dudley, he went to be assistant minister at Bridgnorth, in Shropshire. There he remained one year and nine months, and then removed to Kidderminster, in Worcestershire. This town had petitioned the Long Parliament against its minister, who, knowing the weakness of his case, compromised it by receiving Baxter as his curate. It was in 1640 that, after one day's preaching, Baxter was unanimously chosen. When the civil war broke out he withdrew for a time to Gloucester, and then to Coventry; but at length, for purposes of Christian usefulness, he accepted the appointment of chaplain to one of Cromwell's regiments. In this capacity his labours were unremitting.

After a time, the sickness from which he had sometimes suffered increased upon him so much that he was obliged to desist from his duties as a military chaplain, and remain for months resting at the houses of his friends. During this period he wrote his world-renowned work, the "Saints' Everlasting Rest." The design was formed at the house of Sir John Cook, Melbourne, Derbyshire, and a great part of it was executed at the seat of Sir Thomas Rous, at Rous Lench, in Worcestershire. The author was very ill, and had few books at hand, but he found "that the transcript of the heart hath the greatest force on the hearts of others," and he says, " it pleased God so far to bless this book to the profit of many, that it encouraged me to be guilty of all those writings which afterwards followed."

After his illness, Baxter returned to Kidderminster; and then followed one of the most active and successful periods of ministerial service the world has ever seen. Baxter's preaching was intensely earnest, and as practical as it was spiritual; and his own prayerful and self-denying life bore witness to what he preached. To his preaching he added private catechetical meetings for the instruction and moral benefit of his people, and he exercised a special care over the young. Now and again he prepared for his people heart-stirring tracts and addresses; and having himself experienced the great value of good books, he took care to circulate such amongst them. During his long pastorate at Kidderminster he himself wrote about sixty works. Of these the most extensively known was his "Call to the Unconverted." This book was written in consequence of a conversation with Bishop Usher, in which he urged Baxter to the production of such works. Some of the great spiritual blessings that have attended the reading of this book are known, others, we may safely predict, will be revealed in eternity. The effect of such labours upon Baxter's congregation, and upon the inhabitants of Kidderminster generally, was surprising and delightful. Ceasing to be a people notorious for their impiety and profanity, they became known for their sobriety and godliness.

At the end of nearly twenty years of ministerial labour at Kidderminster, Baxter went in 1660 to London, where, on the Restoration, he was appointed one of the chaplains to Charles II. Afterwards, being offered a bishopric, he declined it; only asking to be allowed to return to his flock at Kidderminster. But arrangements could not be made with the old vicar, who, though incompetent, retained his place.

Previously to the Act of Uniformity, passed in 1662, Baxter had preached in several parts of London, part of the time at St. Dunstan's and St. Bride's, Fleet Street. But after that Act came into operation he retired to Acton, near London, where he held service in his house, and continued to produce his voluminous works. His preaching at Acton led to his suffering six months' imprisonment at Clerkenwell. It grieved him to be thus prevented from any longer ministering to the people who came to him at Acton, and also to be separated from his neighbour and companion, Lord Chief Justice Hale. But his imprisonment was not accompanied with hardship, and it was cheered by the society of his wife, whom he had married a few months before. She proved to be then and always a true helpmeet for him.

Afterwards, having taken a licence as a Nonconformist minister, Baxter began, in 1673, to give lectures on Tuesdays and Fridays in London; and he continued to produce useful books for different classes. He had written his "Reformed Pastor" for ministers. He now wrote for the labouring classes "The Poor Man's Family Book." Subsequently Baxter built a chapel in Bloomsbury, but not permitted to occupy it, preached in Swallow-street.

Baxter was often harassed by threats and fines, and, at length, in 1685, he was brought to trial before the notorious Jefferies for his "Paraphrase on the New Testament;" and after much brow-beating, and the mere form of a trial, without justice, he was condemned to pay 500 marks.

Being unable to pay this sum he remained in prison, but no longer solaced by the society of his beloved wife, for she had died four years before. Yet he was not without human sympathy. Matthew Henry, and other eminent friends, Onesiphorus-like, sought out, and found this "prisoner of the Lord."

After this imprisonment, Baxter assisted Mr. Sylvester in the ministry for four years and a half; and when he could no longer preach he still laboured with his pen. Nearly all his life he suffered from a complication of disorders, yet his written works form a library, and his other labours were most abundant and successful.

Baxter held a conspicuous and honourable position in the age in which he lived. In his intercourse with Cromwell and Charles

II., he showed himself superior to the undue influence of office and name; and by his calm courage in the presence of Jefferies, he proved that he possessed the martyr-spirit; and he was as zealous for union as he was ready to suffer for what he believed to be the truth. In the "Savoy Conference" he laboured, though unsuccessfully, to accomplish a plan of "Comprehension," which was to include the ministers of all denominations. He was also an earnest advocate of the missionary cause at a time when few had begun to favour it; and he pleaded successfully for the North American Indians when their missionary society would otherwise have been broken up.

Baxter's end was calm and triumphant. In the year 1691 he fell asleep in Jesus." When asked, during his last illness, "How he did?" his reply was, "Almost well."

Baxter gave their name to those who hold the doctrines called Baxterian. Their views, though usually stated differently, differ but little from those of the moderate Calvinists of the present day.

He was the author of a metrical version of the Psalms. It was left ready at his death, and his friend Sylvester published it in 1692. Baxter also published two volumes of poetry. His poetic compositions sometimes lack finish, as he begrudged them the time necessary for their perfection, but they contain some fine passages.

One characteristic hymn of Baxter's is found in the "New Congregational Hymn Book;" his sole contribution.

"Lord, it belongs not to my care."—No. 594.

It is part of a piece found at page 81 of his "Poetical Fragments," 1681, and beginning—

"My whole, though broken heart, O Lord!
From henceforth shall be thine."

The piece consists of eight eight-line stanzas. Of these the fourth, seventh, and eighth are given in the "New Congregational," the fourth being slightly altered. The original piece is entitled, "The Covenant and Confidence of Faith," and there is the following note at the end :—" This covenant, my dear wife, in her former sickness, subscribed with a cheerful will."

The piece is evidently the composition of an afflicted, persecuted man, uncertain of life, yet leaning on God, and hoping for heaven. This is seen especially in verse v.—

> "Then I shall end my sad complaints,
> And weary, sinful days;
> And join with the triumphant saints,
> Who sing Jehovah's praise."

And the last words of the hymn declare his strength and his hope—

> "But 'tis enough that Christ knows all,
> And I shall be with Him."

Baxter's "Poetical Fragments" consist of poetical accounts of his religious experiences, and are entitled, "The Complaint," "The Resolution," &c. They were sent forth on the death of his wife, after nineteen years' marriage, and contain some references to her. They are dated, "London, at the door of eternity, Richard Baxter, August 7, 1681." The second edition appeared in 1689, and there was a new edition in 1822. The work bears the quaint title, "Poetical Fragments. Heart Imployment with God and itself. The concordant discord of a broken-healed heart." Baxter had a plan of making certain words in his lines capable of being omitted or retained, so that the hymn might be sung as long or common metre, and he claimed to be the inventor of that plan.

JOHN MASON, M.A.
Died 1694.

The name "John Mason" is best known as that of the author of "A Treatise on Self Knowledge," and of other popular works.

He was an eminent dissenting minister, and son of a dissenting minister. The John Mason, the hymn-writer, the subject of this sketch, was the grandfather of the first-mentioned John Mason. He attended school at Strixton, in Northamptonshire, and removed thence to Clare Hall, Cambridge. He was at first curate to the Rev. Mr. Sawyer, at Isham, in Northamptonshire. Afterwards, on October 31st, 1668, he was presented to the vicarage of Stanton-Bury, and in January, 28th, 1674, to the rectory of Water Stratford, Buckingham, where he remained till his death in 1694. During this twenty years of faithful service he was much beloved by his parishioners. He spent much time in prayer. In the pulpit his words were with power, and in the pastorate his labours were useful and acceptable. Mr. Baxter calls him "the glory of the Church of England," and says, "the frame of his spirit was so heavenly, his deportment so humble and obliging, his discourse of spiritual things—and little else could we hear from him—so weighty, with such apt words and delightful air, that it charmed all that had any spiritual relish, and was not burdensome to others, as discourses of that nature have been from other ministers." As Mr. Mason approached his end, his views on the personal reign of Christ on earth and the resurrection of the dead were tinged with an exaggerated enthusiasm. He professed that he had seen the Lord; and so spoke in a discourse delivered at Water Stratford, in 1694, and entitled "The Midnight Cry," as to lead some there to expect the immediate coming of Christ. Mr. Mason's last words were, "I am full of the loving-kindness of the Lord."

Mr. Mason was the author of "Spiritual Songs, or Songs of Praise to Almighty God, upon several occasions, together with the Song of Songs, which is Solomon's," first edition, 1683. Also of "Dives and Lazarus, a Sacred Poem, incorporated with the former in 1685." To the later editions of the first-mentioned work, from the year 1692, the "Penitential Cries" were added. They were written chiefly by the Rev. Thomas Shepherd, of Braintree (1665—1739), a Congregational minister; but Mr. Mason wrote six of them. Mr. Daniel Sedgwick has published

(1859) a reprint of the "Songs of Praise" and "Penitential Cries." There are by Mason thirty-four songs of praise, six penitential hymns, and a rendering of the 86th Psalm, consisting of twenty-one verses.

Mr. Mason was also the author of "A little Catechism, with verses and sayings for little children." Two sermons of his were published by the Rev. T. Shepherd, and entitled, "Mr. Mason's Remains:" and his letters and sayings were published with the title, "Select Remains of the Rev. John Mason, M.A." The letters were much commended by Dr. Watts. An account of Mr. Mason's life was written by John Dunton, in 1694, and another, in 1695, by the Rev. Henry Maurice, Rector of Tyringham, Bucks.

Of Mason's hymns, which were used in Congregational worship before Watts had written, Montgomery says, "The style is a middle tint between the raw colouring of Quarles, and the daylight clearness of Watts. His talent is equally poised between both, having more vigour, but less versatility than that of either his forerunner or his successor." Quarles (1624—1665) was his contemporary, but Mason's poetry seems to have been more influenced by George Herbert (1593—1632), of Bemerton, who had flourished just before. Without reaching the unique depth and beauty of Herbert, there are yet verses which might have been written by the elder poet; and we notice similar expressions, as if Mason were intentionally following the great master,—as, for instance, in his Sunday piece, beginning—

"Blest day of God, most calm, most bright."

Resembling Herbert's well known piece, which begins—

"O! day most calm, most bright."

It has been justly remarked of Mason's hymns that they "are often quaint and harsh in diction, but compact with thought, and luminous with imagery." And it has been justly said of him that "his name is amongst the honoured few who wrote good hymns prior to the time when Watts made an era in the history of the hymn-writing art."

"Now, from the altar of our hearts." (No. 986.)

This is one of Mason's "Songs of Praise." It is entitled "A Song of Praise for the Evening." A stanza of eight lines is omitted. The stanza omitted is the quaintest and most Herbert-like, beginning—

> "Man's life's a book of history,
> The leaves therof are days,
> The letters mercies closely joined,
> The title is Thy praise."

David Creamer, in his "Methodist Hymnology," 1848, says of this hymn :—

"Excepting the third verse, this certainly is one of the best specimens of sacred devotional poetry in the English language, whether regard be had to the thoughts contained in it, or to the manner of their expression. The poem has not the polish of a Pope, nor the elegance of a Wesley, both of whom our author preceded: but its diction is far before the prevailing style of the age; its sentiments are lofty, original, and uncommon; and the poem ends with a perfect epigram. The volume from which it was taken evidently furnished Watts and Wesley with some of their best thoughts; while in the third stanza of the above hymn is found the germ from which Dr. Franklin extracted the conception of his well-known epitaph upon himself, wherein he compares his body to "the cover of an old book, the contents torn out, and stripped of its lettering and gilding," &c.

John Mason was one of the few earlier hymn-writers to whom Dr. Watts was indebted. The lines—

> "What shall I render to my God
> For all His gifts to me?"

found in one of Watts' divine songs, are taken without alteration from one of Mason's "Songs of Praise," which begins with these words.

GEORGE NEUMARK.
1621—1681.

If it puts honour upon human nature when the hard struggle with poverty is not allowed to subdue the nobler exercises and aspirations of the soul, then we must give his due meed of praise to George Neumark. He was born of poor parents at Thüringen, on the 16th March, 1621. He studied law at the University of Königsberg, where Simon Dach, (1605-1659,) the centre of the Königsberg school of poetry, was Professor of Poetry and Poet Laureate. Dach was also a great musician. Under his influence the young law-student became, like his Professor, a musician and a poet. As a student he had to suffer privations, and he continued to be a sufferer when he went to obtain a precarious living at Dantzic and at Thorn. In 1651, he went to live at Hamburg. There his poverty was so great that he was obliged to part with his viol-di-gamba, a six-stringed instrument then in use, and upon which he played very skilfully. Notwithstanding his sufferings he refused every unworthy method of seeking a livelihood, and preserved his simplicity of life and his trust in God.

Just at the time of his greatest distress he found an unexpected friend in need in an attendant of the Swedish Ambassador, Bawn von Rosenkranz. This servant made bold to relate to his master Neumark's romantic story of suffering genius. The story was well received, and the young poet was appointed secretary to the Ambassador. His first act on receiving the joyful news of his appointment was to purchase back his viol, which he had parted with most unwillingly. And then, as expressive of the way in which his faith had been justified by the issue, he composed his most famous hymn, (1653)—

"Leave God to order all thy ways."
(Wer nur den lieben Gott lässt walten,)

which he played on his viol with tears of gratitude. The tune also is said to be by him, as it is now given in Mendelssohn's "St. Paul." Soon after, he was appointed by Duke William IV., Librarian of the Archives at Weimar. He made Weimar the place of his permanent residence, living a life of cheerful confidence in God, and often giving expression to his pious sentiments in Christian hymns. But it has been noticed that the hymns made in his earlier years of trial are better than those he wrote in his later years of prosperity. The war of life revealed the brave soldier; his arms, if they did not rust, yet lost their keen edge in the time of peace. He died at Weimar, on the 8th of July, 1681.

"To Thee, O Lord, I yield my spirit."—No. 720.

This has been taken as part of a translation of the above celebrated hymn; but it bears no resemblance to that German original. The verse might better be taken as a free rendering of part of his—

"Ich bin müde mehr zu leben,"

a piece of ten stanzas, 1655.

JOHN DRYDEN.

1632—1700.

The principal incidents recorded of the life of Dryden are of a literary nature, illustrating his position as a writer rather than his character as a man. He was the grandson of Sir Erasmus Dryden, Bart., of Canons Ashby, Northamptonshire, in which county the poet is said to have been born. His education was carried on at first at Westminster School, where he was instructed as one of the King's Scholars by Dr. Busby, and in 1650 he was elected to one of the Westminster Scholarships at Cambridge, where he graduated M.A., in 1657. At school he wrote poems, but at College he appears to have confined his attention to his studies. While at Cambridge he received a small fortune at the death of his father, and on leaving there he entered upon a subordinate public office.

On the death of Cromwell, in 1658, he published "Heroic Stanzas on the late Lord Protector." But two years after, when the King was restored, Dryden had so far changed his political views as to be able to write "Astrea Redux, a Poem on the happy Restoration and Return of his most sacred Majesty King Charles the Second." A still greater change took place when, on the accession of James, Dryden declared himself a convert to Popery.

From 1663 to the end of his life, Dryden was occupied, with occasional intervals, in writing for the stage. Several of his pieces were of a character against which fundamental objections lie. They were heroic dramas in rhyme, after the style of the French school. It is justly objected to this class of dramas that the heroic element removes from our sympathies those characters that, according to the requirements of the drama, should enlist those sympathies. After the celebrated attack on heroic dramas made in the "Rehearsal," in 1671, Dryden exchanged tragedy for comedy, though he afterwards returned to tragedy; and a few years after he gave up his preference for rhyme, in which he had greatly excelled, and wrote in blank verse. His "Annus Mirabilis" had appeared in 1667.

Some of his plays were alterations and expansions of Shakspere's, and others were taken from the classics. And he did not take any pains to meet the charge of plagiarism, which was often brought against him; but showed himself a master in using the materials of others and in uniting with them his own. Some of his pieces had a political meaning. "Absalom and Achitophel," produced in 1681, was of this class. This satire, written against the faction which, by Lord Shaftesbury's incitement, set the Duke of Monmouth at its head, met with a large and ready sale. In it Monmouth, Shaftesbury, and Buckingham, are held up to ridicule and scorn. And when a medal was struck to celebrate the refusal of the jury to find a true bill for high treason against Shaftesbury, Dryden wrote another severe satire on Shaftesbury, entitled, "The Medal." "The satirical powers of Dryden," says Sir Walter Scott, "were of the highest order. He draws his arrow to the head, and dismisses it straight upon his object of aim."

One of Dryden's pieces is of a religious nature, "The Hind and the Panther," in which "The Hind" represents the Church of Rome, and "The Panther" the Church of England. Of this production, Dr. Johnson justly says, "A fable which exhibits two beasts talking theology appears at once full of absurdity." Dryden's plays are too numerous to mention, and some flowed from his productive pen with extraordinary rapidity.

In 1668 Dryden was made poet-laureate, an office he retained till 1688, when, on account of the accession of William, it was not possible for a Papist any longer to hold the position. The appointment in his place of his old enemy Shadwell was so offensive to Dryden, that he celebrated his inauguration by a satirical poem, entitled "Mac Flecknoe," a work imitated by Pope, as he acknowledges, in his celebrated "Dunciad."

At the age of thirty-one, Dryden married Lady Elizabeth Howard, daughter of the Earl of Berkshire. Of their sons, Charles and John assisted their father in his translation of "Juvenal." Dryden's private fortune and his official income were not together sufficient to meet his expenses, so that he sometimes wrote under the pressure of pecuniary necessity.

Several prose works were written by Dryden. His "Essay on Dramatic Poetry," an elegant and instructive dialogue, is valued as the earliest work of the kind in the English language, and as marking an era in the history of our poesy. Of this essay, Dr. Johnson says: "It will not be easy to find, in all the opulence of our language, a treatise so artfully variegated with successive representations of opposite probabilities, so enlivened with imagery, so brightened with illustrations." He also published a translation of Maimbourg's "History of the League," a work undertaken to promote Popery: and by his various works in prose and poetry, he at length came to possess so high a position amongst writers that his assistance was eagerly sought in all important literary enterprises.

But it is as a translator of the classics that Dryden's fame stands highest. He seized the true idea of the work of a translator, and had genius enough to carry out his own correct estimate of his chosen work. In his capacity as a translator he wrote lives of Polybius, Lucian, and Plutarch, to be prefixed to versions of their works, and he supplied a treatise on translation in a preface to the Epistles of Ovid. He also wrote poetical translations of Persius, and of part of Juvenal and Tacitus, and he was the author of a complete translation of the poems of Virgil, his most laborious work.

Other poems of Dryden's were his "Religio Laici," his "Ode for Cecilia's Day," and his "Poem on the Death of Mrs. Killigrew, "the noblest ode," says Dr. Johnson, "that our language ever has produced." He also reproduced part of Chaucer, but not with perfect success; better success attended his rendering of Boccacio. His last work was his "Fables," including the first "Iliad" of Homer in English, intended as a specimen of the whole.

Dryden was not a learned poet, yet in the rich and varied imagery employed in his poems we trace an acquaintance with almost every branch of knowledge. In this he resembled his great predecessor, Shakspere, whom he was one of the first to hail as the prince of poets and to welcome to the high place that men have since learned by common consent to assign to him.

Of Dryden's works Pope said "he could select from them better specimens of every mode of poetry than any other English writer could supply." And Johnson adds, "What was said of Rome, adorned by Augustus, may be applied by an easy metaphor to English poetry embellished by Dryden; *lateritiam invenit, marmoream reliquit.* He found it brick, and he left it marble."

But Dr. Johnson must have forgotten Milton, Shakspere, and others, and their prior poetical achievements, when he spoke of

English poetry not relapsing after the time of Dryden into "its former savageness." He is, however, correct in attributing to Dryden the praise of having made the rhyming couplet what it has become, and says truly: "Dryden knew how to choose the flowing and the sonorous words; to vary the pauses, and adjust the accents; to diversify the cadence, and yet preserve the smoothness of his metre."

The tendency to immorality, which is a blemish in some of Dryden's poems, was a matter of regret to him in his later years, and he gave expression to that regret. The excessive adulation of his dedications to titled patrons, and the bitterness and scurrility of his attacks on Settle and other rival poets needed, though they did not obtain, a similar acknowledgment of regret. "Dryden," says Wordsworth, "had neither a tender heart nor a lofty sense of moral dignity," and the same poet speaks in not less disparaging terms of his powers of imagination. Sir Walter Scott, who wrote a life of Dryden, says, "The distinguishing characteristic of Dryden's genius seems to have been the power of reasoning, and of expressing the result in appropriate language." And Thomas Campbell considers that Dryden is justly deserving of commendation for his course of improvement carried on persistently to the end. None can deny to this poet the praise of those gems of poesy that adorn his works, nor the grateful acknowledgments due to one who revealed in the art of poetry a capacity of cultivation before almost unknown.

> "Waller was smooth; but Dryden taught to join,
> The varying verse, the full resounding line,
> The long majestic march, and energy divine."—POPE.

"Creator Spirit! by whose aid."—133.

In the "New Congregational Hymn Book," this hymn is erroneously attributed to Charlemagne. It is the work of Dryden, and consists of twenty-four lines of a piece of thirty-nine lines, entitled, "Veni, Creator Spiritus, paraphrased." It is believed to have been written by Dryden, late in life, when he had become a Romanist. Of the old Latin hymn, the "Veni, Creator Spiritus," Trench says: "This hymn, of which the authorship is popularly ascribed to Charlemagne, but which is certainly older, has had always attributed to it more than an ordinary worth and dignity. Such our Church has recognized and allowed, when, dismissing every other hymn, she has yet retained this in the offices for the ordering of priests and the consecrating of bishops. It was in old time habitually used, and the use in great part still survives, on all other occasions of a more than common solemnity, as at the coronation of kings, the celebration of synods, and, in the Romish Church, at the creation of Popes, and the translation of the relics of saints." A modern writer has sufficiently vindicated Charlemagne from the charge of being unable to write this piece because of his ignorance of Latin. He could have been the author, but internal evidence may prove it to have been written before his time. Others have thought it was the work of Ambrose of Milan, who flourished in the fourth century. And it is said that in primitive times, the day being divided into eight parts of three hours each, and a service being held at the end of each period, this hymn was sung at nine o'clock in the morning, at which hour the Holy Spirit descended on the Day of Pentecost, according to the words of Peter, who said, "It is but the third hour of the day." The Rev. J. Chandler, in his "Hymns of the Primitive Church," maintains this view.

Dryden also wrote a paraphrase of the "Te Deum."

THOMAS KEN, D.D.
1637—1711.

This bard-bishop was born at Berkhampstead, in Hertfordshire. His eldest sister was the wife of the celebrated Izaak Walton. After receiving a pious education at home, he went to Winchester to study, and afterwards to Oxford. He took his bachelor's degree in 1661, and in 1666 he was elected to a vacant fellowship in the College at Winchester, where he went to reside. There he became domestic chaplain to the bishop, and it was for the benefit of the Winchester scholars that he produced his "Manual of Prayers," the work to the third edition (1697), of which were added the "Morning," "Evening," and "Midnight Hymns," a book that was useful to Whitefield in the early period of his college life. The "Morning Hymn,"

"Awake my soul and with the sun,"—No. 929,

so generally a favourite now, was very dear to its author, who used often to sing it in the early morning to the accompaniment of his lute.

In 1675 Ken travelled in Italy, and in 1679 he was chaplain to the Princess of Orange at the Hague, where he resided for a year. In 1683 he accompanied the expedition of Lord Dartmouth against Tangier, and on the voyage wrote a poem, entitled "Edmond." After being chaplain to Charles II., Ken was raised in 1684 to the see of Bath and Wells. In his new capacity he attended his royal master in his last illness, but his pious words appear to have been unheeded by the dying monarch. As we might suppose from his hymns, Ken was a pious, earnest, and laborious bishop. His "Exposition of the Church Catechism" was intended to lessen the prevailing darkness of those times.

Ken was a political sufferer. His inflexibility in maintaining what he believed to be right, and his courage in reproving kings where it was necessary, made him many and powerful enemies. In May, 1688, he was committed to the Tower for refusing to read the "Declaration of Indulgence,"—a declaration introduced by James II. to favour his Roman Catholic friends. For this refusal he suffered two months' imprisonment, and in 1691, as a non-juror, he was deprived of his episcopal emoluments. Having made his protest, he retired to Longleate, where, after years of suffering, he died. It is said that, after burying him, his attendants saluted the opening day with the strains of his "Morning Hymn."

During ten years of severe affliction the poet wrote his "Anodynes" to relieve the tedium of his sufferings. Another of his poems is called "Hymnotheo, or the Penitent." It is a piece founded on a story of apostolic times, given in Eusebius' Ecclesiastical History. His hymns and poems have been published in four small volumes. Ken was also the author of some prose works.

"Bishop Ken," says Montgomery, "has laid the Church of Christ under abiding obligations by his three hymns, 'Morning,' 'Evening,' and 'Midnight.' Had he endowed three hospitals he might have been less a benefactor to posterity."

The "Morning Hymn" is given in the "New Congregational Hymn Book" (No. 929), with six verses omitted. The "Evening Hymn" is No. 938—

"Glory to Thee my God this night."

It is given with the omission of five verses.*

The Doxology, No. 458—

"Praise God from whom all blessings flow,"

is also the last verse of the Morning and Evening hymns. The author at first wrote the third line—

"Praise Him above, ye angelic host."

Of this verse Montgomery says: "The well-known doxology,

"'Praise God from whom all blessings flow,' &c.,

"is a master-piece at once of amplification and compression: amplification, on the burthen, 'Praise God,' repeated in each line; compression, by exhibiting God as the object of praise in every view in which we can imagine praise due to Him; praise,

---

* Sir Roundell Palmer has in his possession an edition of Ken's work (1709), with the Bishop's latest corrections, which proves the genuineness of the text of the three hymns as it is now given.

for all His blessings, yea, [for '*all* blessings,' none coming from any other source,—praise, by every creature, specifically invoked, 'here below,' and in heaven 'above;' praise to Him in each of the characters wherein He has revealed Himself in His Word, 'Father, Son, and Holy Ghost.'" Probably there is no other verse in existence that is so often sung by Christians of all denominations. With this glad utterance of praise to the Triune Jehovah, they have, times without number, brought to a conclusion their most solemn and most delightful assemblies.

PATRICK.

"O God, we praise Thee, and confess."—No. 253.

THIS hymn has been erroneously attributed in the "New Congregational" to Dr. John Patrick, author of the "Century of Select Psalms, 1679." It resembles his rendering, but is not the same. It is the first portion of the Prayer Book version of the "Te Deum Laudamus," whose date and author are as yet undetermined, but to which a very high antiquity is by common consent assigned.

JEANNE BOUVIER DE LA MOTTE GUYON.

1648—1717.

THIS eminent quietist poetess was born at Montargis, and educated at two of the convents of her native city. At the early age of sixteen she entered upon an uncongenial marriage with M. Guyon, a man of wealth, twenty-two years her senior. Twelve years after, her husband died, leaving her with a family. Previous to this time she had met with severe trials. Her mother-in-law treated her with unkindness; her favourite son was snatched away at the engaging age of four; and she herself was prostrated by illness at a time when the state of her husband's health prevented him from ministering to her wants. In this illness, which happened to her at the age of twenty-two, her beauty was taken away by small-pox, and she was left disfigured.

These trials brought with them those deep religious experiences which resulted in her becoming a prominent advocate of quietism—a mystic system characterized by the importance it attaches to the peaceful prosperity of the personal spiritual life, and by the meditative means it takes to promote that prosperity. In order to propagate her views, Madame Guyon travelled for some years, and to aid in her missionary work she wrote books explanatory of her new doctrines and new methods. One of her works was entitled, "A short and easy method of Prayer." It contains her account of the "prayer of silence," in which not only is there no utterance by the voice, but even the mind, instead of turning from one request to another, willingly concentrates its whole energy in the one desire, "Thy will be done." This work was feared by the Romanists, who collected it by hundreds, and burnt it. Another of her principal works was "The Song of Songs, interpreted according to the mystic meaning." She treats the Scripture Book as a conversation between the truly sanctified soul and Christ, and uses it for the unfolding of her own peculiar religious views. Words in the French Bible describing the torrents rising in the hills, suggested to her the title of one of her most characteristic works. She called it "The Torrents." It is believed to be partly autobiographical, and describes the long and devious course of the soul in its progress towards God.

On her return to Paris in 1686, Madame Guyon's views excited the opposition of the dignitaries of the Romish Church. She was put into a convent, and her confessor, La Combe, was sent to the Bastile. Bossuet especially opposed the new doctrine, seeing in it only a revival of Gnostic heresy. Upham, in his invaluable memoir of Madame Guyon, has preserved a detailed record of the intensely interesting controversial interviews of the pious enthusiast and the powerful logician.

But the Abbé de Fenelon, instead of opposing the new doctrine became a convert to it, and spoke and wrote in defence of it, and of his new friend; and thus brought upon himself banishment, and upon his book papal censure.

Madame Guyon's first imprisonment was in 1688, on the ground of her Protestant tendencies. It was in a convent, in Paris, and was continued for eight months. Her second imprisonment was in the Castle of Vincennes, in 1695, after Bossuet had failed alike by argument, persuasion, and threatening, to turn her from her new doctrine and life. Thence she was removed to Vaugirard, and in 1698 to the Bastile, where she was imprisoned for four years. From this gloomy dungeon she was taken in 1702, to be banished to Blois. During the remainder of her life she resided with her son at Diziers, near Blois. Her constitution was too much wasted by protracted imprisonment to allow of her still engaging in active effort, but she continued to enjoy to the end that happy "fixed" state which she had prescribed for others, the state in which the soul, under all circumstances and in all places, is satisfied in God. She departed in peaceful triumph on the 9th of June, 1717, in her seventieth year.

Madame Guyon's works were numerous and extensive. In addition to those already mentioned, she was the author of "Commentaries on the Old and New Testament," in twenty volumes; and her memoir, published soon after her death, is believed to have been taken chiefly from her own testimony. She was also the author of a work entitled "Spiritual Songs, or Emblems upon Divine love."

Her hymns were published in 1689, in Amsterdam. They are the expression of her religious belief, and of the varied phases of her interior life. They are intensely spiritual, and sometimes mystic. Their sentiment is warm and impassioned, their diction elegant, and their flights of fancy sometimes bold and striking; but the expressions made use of in reference to the Divine being appear in some instances extravagant, presumptuous, and almost profane. She seldom refers in her hymns to the outward events of her life; but the following verses possess a peculiar interest when taken with the remembrance of her protracted imprisonment:—

> "Nor exile I, nor prison fear;
> Love makes my courage great;
> I find a Saviour everywhere,
> His grace in ev'ry state.
>
> "Nor castle walls, nor dungeons deep,
> Exclude His quick'ning beams;
> There I can sit, and sing, and weep,
> And dwell on heavenly themes."

They are found in a piece entitled, "Love increased by Suffering." To Cowper, who found some resemblance between the tried life of Madame Guyon and his own, we are indebted for admirable translations of some of the best of her hymns and religious poems.

> "All scenes alike engaging prove."—No. 681.

This is part of Cowper's translation of a piece entitled, "The soul that loves God finds Him everywhere." Five verses of nine are given, and the last is altered to avoid an expression of familiarity in respect to the Divine being, which would be unsuitable for public worship, and in all cases of doubtful propriety. Upham thinks it highly probable that this hymn was written when, at the age of thirty-four, she was leaving Paris, not knowing what was in store for her of toil or persecution, but bent on evangelical work, experienced in the Christian life, and determined to see God everywhere. This is the only hymn by Madame Guyon in the "New Congregational Hymn Book," but it is very characteristic. We see in it her mysticism and extravagance, and the traces of the habit she carried so far, that of applying the warm expressions of human love to the Divine affection; at the same time, we admire in it the marks of her spiritual life, her almost angelic piety, her unreserved acquiescence in the Divine will, and her peaceful resting in the love of God.

NAHUM TATE.
1652—1715.

This psalm-writer was born in Dublin, and educated there at Trinity College. His father, Faithful Teate, D.D., was a clergyman in Ireland, and a poet. After completing his education, Tate (his name having taken an English form), came to live in London. Intemperance and improvidence, its frequent companion, were blemishes in his life.

Tate was the author of several pieces for the stage, and of "Memorials for the Learned, collected out of eminent Authors in History," 1686. In his capacity as poet-laureate, which position he held from 1690 to his death, he wrote several odes, and an "Elegy on the death of Queen Mary." He also wrote "Characters of Virtue and Vice, &c., in verse," 1691; "Miscellanea Sacra, or Poems on Divine and Moral Subjects," 1696, and "Panacea, a Poem on Tea," 1700; "The Triumph," 1705, and some other short poems.

But it is chiefly by his metrical version of the Psalms, which he executed in conjunction with Dr. Nicholas Brady, that Tate is known. This version has taken the place of the earlier Psalter, by Sternhold and Hopkins, and is now commonly printed in the "Book of Common Prayer." Sternhold's version was published in 1562, Tate's was authorized by King William in 1696. Of this later version, Montgomery truly says, "It is nearly as inanimate as the former, though a little more refined." Twenty Psalms were published in 1695. The whole Psalter was authorized in 1696. The whole of the Psalms, fitted to the tunes, appeared in 1698, and a supplement of Church Hymns in 1703.

A few of the best of their renderings of the Psalms are given in the "New Congregational Hymn Book." With little claim to be called poetry, they have the merit of being simple, suitable for public worship, and of keeping close to the words of Scripture. The nine Psalms by Tate and Brady, given in the "New Congregational Hymn Book," are all slightly altered and reduced to about one half their original length, except No. 138, their rendering of Psalm xciii., which is given in full, and it is shown under Telesphorus that the first known rendering into English verse of the ancient hymn—

"To God be glory, peace on earth,"—No. 445,

is found in "Tate and Brady's Appendix," 1703. It is not known which Psalms are by Tate and which by Brady.

NICHOLAS BRADY, D.D.
1659—1726.

BRADY, the co-worker with Tate, was the son of an officer in the Royalist army, and was born at Brandon, a town in Ireland. He studied at Westminster school, and at Christ Church College, Oxford, and graduated at Trinity College, Dublin, whence he subsequently received his degree of Doctor of Divinity. He was chaplain to a bishop, and prebend of the cathedral of Cork. As a zealous partizan of the Prince of Orange, he saved his native place, Brandon, several times from the destruction threatened by King James; and on the accession of William and Mary, he was sent to London with a petition claiming redress of grievances. During his stay, he became minister of the Church of St. Catherine Cree, and lecturer of St. Michael's, Wood-street. Afterwards he became chaplain to the King, and received other appointments.

But being like Tate, his companion in labour, a bad economist, he found it necessary to commence a school at Richmond, Surrey. Here in one of the pleasant retreats of that charming neighbourhood, where he held a living, he made a translation of the Psalms. He published several volumes of his sermons, and some smaller works; and, in the year of his death, a "Translation of the Æneid of Virgil," a work now little known. His name remains as the fellow-labourer with Tate in the production of the authorised version of the Psalms in use in the Church of England, a work of little poetic merit, and of which more is said under the name of Tate. The Right Hon. Maziere Brady, Lord Chancellor of Ireland, is a descendant of the above writer.

JOSEPH STENNETT, D.D.
1663—1713.

Born of pious parents at Abingdon, Berks, Mr. Joseph Stennett profited by his religious training, and under his father's ministry was early converted to Christ, and became the most eminent member of a family remarkable for their talent and piety. After receiving some education at the public grammar school at Wallingford, young Mr. Stennett pursued his studies in almost every branch, including philosophy, divinity, and the Oriental languages.

At the age of twenty-two he went to London, where for five years he was engaged in the work of tuition. During this period he increased his store of knowledge, and made the acquaintance of some persons of eminence, to whom he commended himself by his clever productions in prose and verse as well as by his brilliant conversation. In the year 1688, he was married to Susanna, daughter of George Gill, Esq., a French merchant, his wife's elder sister being married to the celebrated Dr. Daniel Williams. About this time he began to preach, and he gave an evening lecture in Devonshire-square, by which he became known. On the 4th of March, 1690, he was ordained the pastor of the congregation there. They were Baptists, and observed the seventh day, and afterwards held their meetings at Pinner's Hall. He continued to be their pastor till his death, and he preached to other congregations on the first day. His family was large, and his remuneration small, but he refused all offers of lucrative preferment in the Church. During his later years he received a few young men into his house to be trained for the ministry. Dr. Stennett died on the 11th of July, 1713, in his forty-ninth year. At the last he was calm and confident, giving his children his counsel and his blessing. Amongst his last words were, "I rejoice in the God of my salvation, who is my strength and God."

Dr. Joseph Stennett was the author of a reply to Mr. David Russen's work, "Fundamentals without a Foundation; or, a True Picture of the Anabaptists," and of some sermons, and of some useful translations of works from the French. He was also the author of a poetical piece of some pretension—a commendatory poem on the Rev. Samuel Wesley's "Ingenious Poem, entitled the Life of Christ, &c., published anno 1693." His "Hymns for the Lord Supper" appeared in 1697. In the first edition they were thirty-seven in number, in the third, 1709, they had been increased to fifty. His "Version of Solomon's Song with the 47th Psalm" was published in 1700, and the second edition in 1709. His twelve hymns on "Believers' Baptism" were sent forth in 1712. The whole of his hymns, poems, sermons, and letters, with an account of his life, were published in four volumes, in 1732, several years after his death.

"Another six days' work is done."—No. 753.

This is the only hymn by Dr. Joseph Stennett in the "New Congregational Hymn Book." It is found in his collected works. Four of the verses are taken from a Sabbath hymn of fourteen verses. Verse two is not in the original; it has been added by some other author.

SAMUEL WESLEY.

Born about 1688. Died 1735.

This Wesley, who was rector of Epworth, Lincolnshire, was the father of the celebrated John and Charles, and son of John Wesley, a nonconformist minister, who had been ejected from the living of Winterbourne Whitchurch, near Blandford, Dorset, by the Act of Uniformity, in 1662. Samuel Wesley was also further connected with nonconformists by his marriage to the youngest daughter of the Rev. Dr. Samuel Annesley, an eminent nonconformist minister. She was the mother of nineteen children, of whom Samuel, John, and Charles rose to eminence.

Samuel Wesley was the author of several prose works, of which the principal was a Latin Commentary on the book of Job. Some of his works in verse were the following:—In 1693, " The Life of Christ," an heroic poem; in 1695, " Elegies on Queen Mary and Archbishop Tillotson;" in 1701, " The History of the New Testament attempted in verse;" in 1704, " The History of the Old Testament in verse;" and in 1705, a poem on the Battle of Blenheim, for which the Duke of Marlborough made him chaplain to a regiment. His translation of the " Hymn to the Creator," by Eupolis, who flourished B.C. 420, is justly praised; and he was the composer of the famous speech delivered before the House of Lords, by Dr. Sacheverel, in the reign of Queen Anne. In writing to Swift, Pope says of this Wesley, " I call him what he is, a learned man, and I engage you will approve his prose more than you formerly did his poetry."

The dying words of this worthy father of greater sons were remarkably fulfilled in the time, and by the Christian labours of his family. "He often laid his hand upon my head," said Charles, and said, ' Be steady. The Christian faith will surely revive in this kingdom; you shall see it, though I shall not.' " And to his daughter Emily, he said, " Do not be concerned at my death. God will then begin to manifest himself to my family."

There is one admirable hymn by him in the " New Congregational Hymn Book"—

" Behold the Saviour of mankind."—No. 378.

This hymn was found upon a piece of music which was saved, though not without bearing marks of the flames, when its author's parsonage was consumed by fire the second time, August 24,

1709, when John, his son, was saved from death almost by miracle. It is stated on the music that "the words are by the Rev. Samuel Wesley, rector of Epworth." Two additional verses —Nos. 2 and 6—were given. John Wesley gave this hymn in "A collection of moral and sacred poems from the most celebrated English authors, 1744."

JOSEPH ADDISON.
1672—1719.

JOSEPH ADDISON was born at Milston, near Amesbury, in Wiltshire. His father was rector of Milston, and afterwards dean of Lichfield. After enjoying the advantage of instruction from his father, Addison was sent to school at Amesbury and Salisbury, and afterwards to the Charterhouse, London, where he made the acquaintance of his great literary compeer, Richard Steele. Addison afterwards graduated at Oxford, where the excellence of his Latin verses attracted attention and brought him honour.

After producing some minor pieces, he wrote in 1695 a poem to King William, with an introduction addressed to Lord Somers; and in 1697 appeared his Latin poem on the peace of Ryswick. These productions procured him a pension of £300 a year. Availing himself of this pecuniary assistance he travelled on the Continent, gathering facts for future use, and extending his knowledge of men and manners in other lands. During his travels he found leisure to write his "Dialogue on Medals," and part of his tragedy, "Cato;" and, while in Italy, he sent to Lord Halifax his celebrated "Poetical Letter" on that classic land. On his return, he published his travels; and in 1704 he celebrated the battle of Blenheim in a poem called "The Campaign." It is in this poem that his well-known comparison is found, in which Marlborough, leading the battle, is compared to an angel directing a storm. For this poem he was rewarded with the appointment of Commissioner of Appeals; and, after holding other offices, he rose in 1717 to the responsible position of Secretary of State, a place he held but for a short time, as his diffidence unfitted him for public debate, and his fastidiousness stood in the way of the dispatch necessary in the business of his office.

His other poetical works were—his English opera, "Rosamond, a comedy;" "The Drummer, or the Haunted House;" and in 1713 his principal work, the tragedy of "Cato." Upon this last chiefly rested his fame in his own day. It was a piece in conformity with the artificial tastes of those times, and it was for political reasons welcomed by the plaudits of his party. Addison was also the author of several political pamphlets, and of an unfinished work on the evidences of Christianity.

But his fame now rests on the part he took in the production of the daily essays that were begun in his time. The "Tatler" was commenced by Steele in 1709, and was succeeded by the "Spectator" in 1711. This was followed by the "Guardian" in 1713; and Addison again lent his assistance when the "Spectator" was revived for a short time in 1714. These papers, although ephemeral in form, and continued but for a short period, contain works that will never die, and have given for all time a place in our literature to the periodical essay: and the moral tendency of the essays was good; suited to raise the general taste and to produce an improved tone of feeling in regard to the duties and associations of ordinary life. Addison's contributions are the best, especially those on the imagination; his criticism on Milton, and his religious pieces, which usually appeared on Saturday. In these last appeared for the first time some of his hymns. They have taken a permanent place as favourites. They are of the highest excellence, written in the maturity of his powers, and wanting only a stronger infusion of definitely Christian sentiment to make them superior to every attack of adverse criticism.

In 1716, Addison married the Countess Dowager of Warwick. It is to be lamented that the unhappiness of this marriage drove him from his home to seek pleasure in convivialities that were sometimes carried to excess. Addison left one daughter. He died June 17, 1719.

Dr. Johnson speaks of it as to the lasting praise of this poet, that by the pleasing character of his criticisms on the "Paradise Lost" he has made Milton a universal favourite, with whom readers of every class think it necessary to be pleased. Of Addison's poetry, Johnson says, "It is polished and pure; the product of a mind too judicious to commit faults, but not sufficiently vigorous to attain excellence." There are five of Addison's hymns in the "New Congregational Hymn Book." They were all written in 1712, when his powers had reached the greatest height of cultivation and development.

"The spacious firmament on high."—No. 20. (Psalm xix.),

appeared at the close of an article by Addison on "The right means to strengthen Faith," in the "Spectator," No. 465, August 23, 1712.

"The Lord my pasture shall prepare."—No. 27. (Psalm xxiii.),

first appeared at the close of an essay on "Trust in God," in the "Spectator," No. 441, July 26, 1712. Verses 3 and 4 are transposed in this collection. The essay that is introductory to this translation contains the following appropriate and beautiful words by Addison, the author of it and of the hymn:—"The person who has a firm trust on the Supreme Being is powerful in *His* power, wise by *His* wisdom, happy by *His* happiness. He reaps the benefit of every Divine attribute, and loses his own insufficiency in the fulness of infinite perfection."

"How are thy servants blest, O Lord."—No. 166.

This is given with No. 489 (Saturday, Sept. 20, 1712) of the "Spectator"—a paper on "The Sea" as affecting the imagination by its greatness. The hymn is entitled, "The Traveller's Hymn." The original piece consists of ten verses. It was written by "A Gentleman upon the Conclusion of his Travels."

One omitted verse is of great beauty. It is as follows: —

> "Thy mercy sweeten'd every soil,
> Made every region please;
> The hoary Alpine hills it warm'd,
> And smooth'd the Tyrrhene seas."

"When all thy mercies, O my God."—No. 290,

is appended to an article on "Praise to God" in the "Spectator," No. 453, August 9, 1712. There are four more verses in the original. Addison commenced, but did not complete a version of the Psalms.

"When rising from the bed of death."—No. 739.

This is given with an article in No. 513 of the "Spectator," Saturday, Oct. 18, 1712, with two verses that are omitted in the "New Congregational." The article contains these words—"Among all the reflections which usually arise in the mind of a sick man, who has time and inclination to consider his approaching end, there is none more natural than that of his going to appear naked and unbodied before Him who made him." Addison's hymns have been found fault with for their omission of evangelical doctrine. This charge does not hold against this hymn. Every Christian heart will rejoice in the testimony borne in the fourth verse. If indeed the way in which Addison has prefaced the letter of which the article consists does not make it uncertain whether he wrote it, he says:—"The following letter has come to me from that excellent man in holy orders, whom I have mentioned more than once as one of that society who assist me in my speculations." It may be that Addison only wrote the hymn.

The claim to two of Addison's hymns for Andrew Marvell, put forth by Captain Thompson, in an edition of Marvell's works, in 1776, cannot be sustained.

SIMON BROWNE.
1680—1732.

This early hymn-writer, a contemporary with Dr. Watts, was

born at Shepton Mallet, Somersetshire, about 1680. He studied under the Rev. John Moore, of Bridgewater. He began to preach before he was twenty years of age, and was soon settled as the minister of a good congregation at Portsmouth. In 1716, he became pastor of the Independent Church in Old Jewry, London.

Seven years from that time he was afflicted with a singular malady. He imagined that God had in a gradual manner annihilated in him the thinking substance, and utterly divested him of consciousness. It was supposed by some that this condition of mental aberration had its origin in the distress he experienced on finding that he had been unwittingly the cause of the death of a highwayman. Being attacked by one of these ruffians, a struggle ensued in which he overcame his adversary, but on relinquishing his grasp and rising from the ground, he found to his great distress that the highwayman was dead. He was also greatly distressed by the loss of his wife and only son in the same year, 1723. In his mental distress Mr. Browne felt a strong propensity to destroy himself; and strange as his notion was concerning himself, he felt it peculiarly painful to be contradicted with regard to it. While in this state, he wrote a work in defence of Christianity, and a work on the Trinity, compiled a dictionary, and prepared the exposition on the first epistle to the Corinthians in the continuation of Matthew Henry's Commentary; yet he still maintained that he had no power to think. He died in 1732. The "Protestant Dissenters' Magazine" of 1797 names twenty-three separate publications from his pen.

His hymn-book was entitled, "Hymns and Spiritual Songs, in three books, designed as a supplement to Dr. Watts."

The preface is interesting in the history of hymnology. It gives some account of the earlier hymn writers.

The first edition was published in 1720, the second in 1741, and the third in 1760. He also wrote some of the tunes prefixed to his book. His hymns have not much poetical beauty, but they are free from blemishes, and are never below respectable mediocrity.

"Come, gracious Spirit, heavenly dove."—No. 436.

This is part of his No. 131 (second edition). It is headed "The soul giving itself up to the conduct and influence of the Holy Spirit."

"Lord, at Thy feet we sinners lie."—No. 534.

This is No. 15 in his collection, but his third verse is omitted.

"O Lord, Thy work revive."—No. 812.

This is erroneously attributed to Browne. It is by Thomas Hastings, 1857. Vide under his name.

JOHN ANDREW ROTHE.
1688—1758.

Rothe was born at Lissa, in Silesia, where his father was pastor. He studied theology in Leipsic, and was for some time private tutor in the family of Schweinitz. Upon coming of age, Count Zinzendorf, who had bought the estate of Berthelsdorf, had to appoint a pastor to the cure. His choice fell on Rothe, who was chosen as a man of earnest piety and an excellent preacher. In his letter of invitation, bearing date the 19th of May, 1722, the count says :—" You will find in me a faithful helper and an affectionate brother, rather than a patron. Rothe was ordained at Berthelsdorf by Mr. Schæffer, August 30, 1722. And when Herrnhut was founded immediately after, Rothe undertook a pastor's work there also. He co-operated heartily with the count in his various enterprises, and was one of four who met frequently to concert plans of religious action. The four were Zinzendorf, Baron Watteville, Schæffer, also a Christian pastor, and Rothe. The count had a high regard for Rothe, but they did not always work well together. Rothe was in favour of using some authority; the count, though the patron, would hear of no authority but power of argument and the suasion of love. At length one special cause of disagreement arose. In the absence of the count, the brethren agitated the subject of leaving the old Moravian church, and joining the Lutheran church, in order to be safer from persecution. The count was deeply grieved by this confession of unworthy fear, and made a strong and successful protest. Thus the breach was widened between him and Rothe, and at length, in 1737, Rothe resigned, and took another charge as Lutheran pastor in a village of Silesia, where he died July 6, 1758. Though sometimes differing from him, Zinzendorf treated Rothe with continual kindness, and always held him in honour. Of him he spoke in the following generous and admiring terms:— "Rothe was profoundly learned, and possessed in a high degree the talent of teaching; he so clearly comprehended everything which he discussed, that he preached without the slightest hesitation, and in the most systematic manner, as the notes taken while he was delivering his discourses show. For an extemporaneous preacher, he had a wonderful precision, and although he spoke rather like a professor giving his lectures, he was never dry, nor did he ever appear long and tedious. This might arise partly from the rapidity of his utterance, but more from the extraordinary gift of eloquence which he possessed; the talents of Luther, Spener, Francke, and Schwedler, were united in him. The lowest peasant understood him, and the greatest philosopher heard him with attention and respect. He was admired even by his enemies, and the brethren acknowledged that of all the apostolic discourses which were ever delivered among them at that time, none were to be compared for solidity of thought, spiritual unction, or wise admonition with those of Rothe." "On Lord's-day morning, Rothe preached with great power; he seemed as if he would exhaust every subject, and collect together a treasure of comfort against the evil times which were coming upon the church. If three or four festivals occurred in succession, it was not too much either for the preacher or the church; on the contrary, the last day was generally the most glorious, and the minister seemed to possess in a high degree the gift of presenting the doctrine of salvation in a fresh aspect, and with a grace and savour ever new; no one was weary."

Some of the count's poems were dedicated to Rothe, and he in return dedicated to Zinzendorf on his birthday, in 1728, the well-known hymn :—

"Now I have found the ground wherein."—No. 611.

"Ich habe nun den Grund gefunden."

The original extends to ten stanzas.

This hymn was written just when the count and Rothe were at the height of the happiness and usefulness of their Christian association. It was in the year when the religious system that had worked so well at Herrnhut was extended to Bethelsdorf. Wesley's translation (1740) is here given. Rothe wrote about forty-five hymns, many of which are very beautiful. In the "New Congregational Hymn Book" this hymn is erroneously attributed to Zinzendorf.

In the "Records of Wesleyan Life," we read of the lines in verse 2—

"While Jesus' blood, through earth and skies,
Mercy, free, boundless mercy, cries!"

"These were almost the last words of Mr. Fletcher, of Madeley, whose impression in the hour of death of the truths they contain was so strong, that his feeble voice re-echoed the word 'boundless,' 'boundless,' with surprising energy."

Rothe published, in 1727, a learned work on the Hebrew Bible.

ALEXANDER POPE.

1688—1744.

THE incidents of Pope's life were few and unimportant. His father was in business in London, and retired during the poet's childhood to Binfield, in Windsor Forest. At the age of thirty, Pope found himself in a position to purchase his celebrated villa at Twickenham, where he resided till his death on the 30th of May, 1744. He had previously spent two years at Chiswick, where he published his collected works. He was deformed and afflicted, and attained only to the age of fifty-six. But he gathered around him the greatest celebrities of his time, and stood first amongst them for his criticism and poetry.

Pope says of himself: " I lisped in numbers, for the numbers came ;" yet in almost all his works he is either the imitator or translator of the productions of others, and he is the last man to whom we should apply the dictum of the old Latin poet, "*poeta nascitur, non fit.*" Some of his principal works are the following: —His " Pastorals," published in 1709 ; the " Essay on Criticism," highly praised by Dr. Johnson, 1711 ; the " Rape of the Lock," a mock-heroic poem on the stealing of a lock of a lady's hair by Lord Petre ; the " Temple of Fame," 1715 ; " Windsor Forest," the " Dunciad" (his severe satire on some of the literary men of his day), in 1728 ; the " Essay on Man," in 1733 ; and " Characters of Men and Moral Essays," in 1734. Without producing striking characters or skilful plots in his poems, Pope succeeded in writing lines that will never be lost, and his words are quoted by many who never read his works.

Pope's fame rests in part on his poetical translation of the Iliad (1720), and Odyssey (1725) of Homer. This work is valued for its poetic taste and skill rather than as a translation. It often departs from he original, and is written in a style having its acknowledged excellencies, but felt to be unsuitable for the reproduction, in another language, of the force and grand simplicity of the original. Pope's style has been commended by some and condemned by others, and probably part of the disfavour it has met with has arisen from the tame and tedious imitations of those who had not genius enough to equal its excellencies. Of it Thomas Campbell says —" Pope has a gracefully peculiar manner, though it is not calculated to be an universal one. . . . His pauses have little variety, and his phrases are too much weighed in the balance of antithesis. But let us look to the spirit that points his antithesis, and the rapid precision of his thoughts, and we shall forgive him for being too antithetic and sententious." He also says: "Pope gave our heroic couplet its strictest melody and tersest expression."

Pope was more successful in his imitation of Horace (1739) than he had been in his translation of Homer. The similarity of the style of the Latin poet and his not less distinguished translator made the work of translation delightful, and Pope gave his whole strength to his new undertaking. Another of his poetical productions was a sacred eclogue the "Messiah," which appeared in the "Spectator" for May 14, 1712, with an introductory word of commendation by Addison. But Pope afterwards lost the friendship of Addison, whom he resembled in being distinguished for the possession of genius, without producing its greatest and most enduring works.

There is one hymn by Pope in the "New Congregational Hymn Book"—

"Vital spark of heavenly flame."—(No. 728).

Like Pope's other works, it is an imitation. The original of this hymn is to be found in a poem composed by the illustrious Roman emperor, Adrian, who dying (A.D. 138) thus gave expression to his mingled doubts and fears. His poem begins thus—

"Animula vagula blandula,
Hospes comesque corporis," &c.

"Sweet spirit, ready to depart,
Guest and companion of the body," &c.

It is afterwards found freely rendered in a piece by a poet of some name in his own day, Thomas Flatman, of London—a barrister, poet, and painter. Flatman's piece is called "A Thought of Death;" and as he died in the year Pope was born, and the poems are very similar, there can be little doubt that Pope has imitated his predecessor. The emperor wrote in dim and timid uncertainty. Flatman only rises to the thought of liberty by death, and of a life beyond that may be better, and cannot be worse, than this; but

Pope, in a more Christian strain, speaks definitely of heaven, and concludes with the Scripture questions of defiant confidence—

"O grave, where is thy victory?
O death, where is thy sting?"

In a letter written at the time, the author acknowledges his indebtedness to his classic predecessors. He says: "You have it, as Cowley calls it, just warm from the brain; it came to me the first moment I waked this morning. Yet you'll see it was not so absolutely inspiration, but that I had in my head not only the verses of Adrian, but also the fine fragment of Sappho."

From Pope's correspondence we learn that on Nov. 7, 1712, he sent a letter to Mr. Steele for insertion in the "Spectator" on the subject of Adrian's last words. This letter contained a translation in two four-line verses of those words. The ver begin:

"All fleeting Spirit! wandering fire," &c.

They are very inferior to the piece, "Vital Spark," &c., but contain the germ of it. On December 4 of the same year, Steele wrote to Pope asking him to make of those words an ode in two or three stanzas for music. He replied immediately, saying that he had done as required, and sent the piece, "Vital Spark," &c., as the result.

ISAAC WATTS.
1674—1748.

This most popular of English hymn-writers was the son of a respectable schoolmaster at Southampton, and the eldest of eight children. He was born July 17, 1674. His parents were eminently pious, and suffered much in the persecution during Charles II.'s reign, his father being more than once imprisoned for his nonconformity. In a pocket book MSS., headed "Memorable Affairs in my Life," there is this note:—"1683, My father persecuted and imprisoned for nonconformity six months. After that forced to leave his family, and live privately for two years." Isaac was a precocious child, and made such progress in his classical studies under the care of a clergyman, the Rev. Mr. Pinhorne, at that time rector of All Saints, Southampton, as to awaken the delight and expectation of his friends. At the age of sixteen, he declined a proposition to support him at the university, and declared his resolution of taking his lot with the Dissenters. He went to London to study in the academy of the Rev. Thomas Rowe, an Independent minister. "Such he was," says Dr. Johnson, "as every Christian church would rejoice to have adopted." There he made progress in his studies, and became decided in his Christian character. At the age of nineteen, he joined the church then meeting at Girdlers' Hall, under the pastoral care of his tutor. To both these preceptors Watts has inscribed odes in his "Horæ Lyricæ." During his stay in London, the young student injured his constitution for life by excessive study. Leaving London for a time, Watts returned, at the age of twenty, to his father's house, to spend two years in more extended preparatory studies. During this time he wrote many of his hymns, and continued the poetic pursuits he had begun in his boyhood. Having complained to his father of the compositions ordinarily used by the congregation with which they worshipped at Southampton, his father, who was a deacon of the church and a man of taste, suggested that he should try his hand, and these hymns were the result. The first composed is said to have been—

"Behold the glories of the Lamb"—(No. 303)

in the "New Congregational Hymn Book," where it is given with the omission of two verses.

From 1696 to 1702 Watts resided with Sir John Hartopp, Bart., at Stoke Newington, in order to be tutor to his son. This was a most valuable seedtime for future harvests, and Watts gladly prolonged his stay after he had commenced his pastoral work.

Sir John was a staunch Nonconformist, and heavy fines were inflicted on him because of his adherence to his principles. He was also a man of deep sympathy with almost every department of literature and science. Hence, Watts could learn while he taught. And though in comparative seclusion, his knowledge was expanded and his principles were firmly grounded so as to fit him for the public duties of his long and active life. It was during this period that he formed the outline of his work on "Logic."

Watts began to preach on his birthday, 1698, and was chosen the same year as assistant minister to the Rev. Dr. Isaac Chauncy, pastor of the Independent Church, Berry-street, London. His services were acceptable, but they were interrupted by illness. In 1702, he succeeded Dr. Chauncy in the pastoral office, notwithstanding the discouragement to Nonconformists, arising from the death of King William, which happened at that time. But subsequently Watts's uncertain health made it necessary to associate with him an assistant minister. The appointment fell on the Rev. Samuel Price, who some years later became co-pastor with him, and with whom Watts spent, as he says, "many harmonious years of fellowship in the work of the Gospel."

In 1712, Watts went to visit Sir Thomas Abney, at his seat at Theobalds, in Hertfordshire. By the request of his kind entertainer this visit became a permanent residence; and for the remainder of his life—thirty-six years—the poet preacher found with Sir Thomas, and afterwards with Lady Abney, a rural home just suited to his delicate state of health, and very favourable for the prosecution of his laborious literary pursuits. Sir Thomas had been knighted by King William, and was Lord Mayor in 1700. He had been brought up as a Dissenter, and married a daughter of the celebrated Caryl. Watts not only found at Theobalds a congenial place of residence, but had also there the advantage of being within an easy distance of his congregation, to whom he preached as often as his health permitted. His attacks of illness were very severe, and from 1712 to 1716 he was obliged to desist altogether from his ministerial work.

Watts' collected works were first published by him in 1720, in six quarto volumes. They consist for the most part of sermons (to some of which suitable hymns are appended), and treatises on great theological subjects; and while comprehensive and scholarly in their character, and in some places marked by the boldness of their speculations, they are notwithstanding of a very practical nature.

Southey, in his life of Watts, has pointed out that the poet acknowledges that in his later years his speculations were content with a lower flight. For in a note appended to his sermons on the Trinity, which were published years after they were written, Watts says they were "warmer efforts of imagination than riper years could indulge on a theme so sublime and abstruse." And he adds, " Since I have searched more studiously into the mystery of late, I have learned more of my own ignorance ; so that when I speak of these unsearchables, I abate much of my younger assurance, nor do my later thoughts venture so far into the particular modes of explaining the sacred distinctions in the Godhead."

His sole aim in his prose works, as in his psalms and hymns, was Christian usefulness. In addition to his theological treatises his works include that already mentioned on " Logic." This had reached a seventh edition in 1740; one on " Astronomy ;" one on the " Improvement of the Mind ;" his " Art of Reading and Writing English ;" an " Essay to encourage Charity Schools ;" a " Guide to Prayer" (1716), containing the substance of what he had addressed to the younger members of his church in a society for prayer and religious conference he formed for their benefit (sixth edition, 1735); his " Improvement of the Mind" (second edition, 1743); his " World to Come" (second edition, 1745); his " Humble Attempt towards the Revival of Religion" (third edition, 1742), and some others.

Dr. Watts did not claim to be a poet. He says : " I make no

pretences to the name of a poet, or a polite writer, in an age wherein so many superior souls shine in their works through the nation." He did not produce any great poetic work, yet he thought it wise to publish his "Lyric Poems" as his introduction to the public before he ventured on the publication of his hymns. His work "Horæ Lyricæ" was sent forth in December, 1705. In his MSS. we read, "Published my Poems, 1705." In it there are several imitations of a modern Latin poet, Matthias Casimir (Sarbiewski), who was a favourite with the young poet. To his own copy of that poet's works, which he purchased in 1696, Watts has prefixed an index in his own handwriting. M. C. Sarbiewski (1595—1640) was a learned and talented Pole. He had become a Jesuit, and was a professor and preacher in high repute. He was an enthusiastic admirer and imitator of the classics. Dr. Watts, in his preface to the "Lyrics," speaks of his poems in the most glowing terms. This undesirable model rather encouraged than checked Watts' early defects of style But some of the "Lyrics" are to be commended, and some make good hymns, and are found in the "New Congregational Hymn Book." His "Lyrics" met with favour, and prepared the way for his "Hymns," which appeared in July, 1707. We give the date from his own memoranda. And, in 1709, their number was increased by the publication of additional hymns in a second edition.

It is as a writer of psalms and hymns that Dr. Watts is known everywhere, and justly held in high admiration. Some of his hymns were written to be sung after his sermons, the hymn in each case giving expression to the meaning of the text upon which he had been discoursing. Produced as they were wanted, and for a practical purpose, some of these hymns lack the fire and genius of poetry, and the same must be admitted of some of his other productions. He apologizes for the absence of poetic form and display on the ground of his desire to write to the level of ordinary worshippers, and says he expected to be often censured for a too religious observance of the words of scripture, whereby the verse is weakened and debased according to the judgment of critics," yet all will admit that many of his hymns are of unparalleled excellence. Montgomery justly styles Watts "the greatest name among hymn-writers."

To Dr. Watts must be assigned the praise of beginning in our language a class of productions which have taken a decided hold upon the universal religious mind. On this account, Christian worshippers of every denomination and of every English speaking land owe him an incalculable debt of gratitude. Mason, Baxter, and others, had preceded Watts as hymn-writers, but their hymns were not used in public worship. Prejudice prevented the use of anything beyond the Psalms, and those not yet in their Christian rendering. But Watts made the Christian hymn part of modern public worship. "He was," says Montgomery, "almost the inventor of hymns in our language, so greatly did he improve upon his few almost forgotten predecessors in the composition of sacred song." His aim was usefulness in public worship. He says, "The most frequent tempers and changes of our spirit, and conditions of our life, are here copied, and the breathings of our piety expressed according to the variety of our passions, our love, our fear, our hope, our desire, our sorrow, our wonder, and our joy, as they are refined into devotion, and act under the influence and conduct of the blessed Spirit, all conversing with God the Father by the new and living way of access to the throne, even the person and the mediation of our Lord Jesus Christ. To Him also, even to the Lamb that was slain and now lives, I have addressed many a song, for thus doth the holy Scripture instruct and teach us to worship in the various short patterns of Christian psalmody described in the Revelation. I have avoided the more obscure and controverted points of Christianity, that we might all obey the direction of the Word of God, and sing His praises with understanding (Psalm xlvii. 7). The contentions and distinguishing words of sects and parties are excluded, that whole assemblies might assist at the harmony, and different churches join in the same worship. without offence."

That Watts is in some cases tame and prosaic; that his rhymes are sometimes poor, and sometimes omitted where they are needed; that his expressions are sometimes unguarded and objectionable; that his doctrines are sometimes drawn rather from system than from scripture; and that he has not always escaped the defects that disfigure the early Latin Christian hymns—must be admitted with regret. Yet Watts must always stand high for the comprehensiveness and catholicity of his hymns, for their fulness of gospel doctrine; and for the numerous instances in which they fulfil all that can be required in a Christian hymn, and in which criticism is forgotten in the joyful consent of the Christian reader's heart.

In his Preface to his Psalms, and in his "Essay towards the Improvement of Psalmody," he has explained the special service he rendered in producing a Christian version of the Psalms. He gives it as his view that the Psalms "ought to be translated in such a manner as we have reason to believe David would have composed them if he had lived in our day." And in contrast with the practice of his predecessors, he says, "What need is there that I should wrap up the shining honours of my Redeemer in the dark and shadowy language of a religion that is now for ever abolished; especially when Christians are so vehemently warned, in the epistles of St. Paul, against a Judaizing spirit in their worship as well as doctrine?" And of his own work, he says, "I think I may assume this pleasure of being the first who hath brought down the royal author unto the common affairs of the Christian life, and led the Psalmist of Israel into the church of Christ, without anything of a Jew about him." Hence the author of the "Poet of the Sanctuary" justly says, "Whatever Dr. Watts might borrow from his predecessors, he stands alone as the evangelical psalmist." Dr. Watts carried out his design by omitting whatever was so peculiar to David, whether personally or in his official capacity, as to render it unfit for congregational use. He also left out whatever was unsuitable to the advanced dispensation under which we live, and either omitted names of persons and places that are now little known, or substituted known names and persons for them. And where prophecy has become history, he spoke of it as such. In the quarto edition of his works notes, between the Psalms, with references to New Testament passages, explain how he has carried out his design. This design was carried out in the face of some opposition. Romaine and Adam Clarke condemned Watts for thinking he could improve on the Psalms of David. The full title of the work was, "The Psalms of David, imitated in the language of the New Testament, and applied to the Christian state and worship," 1719. In his preface, he acknowledges that he was occasionally indebted to the labours of his predecessors in the same work, Sir John Denham, Mr. Milbourn, Mr. Tate, Dr. Brady, and Dr. John Patrick, and says that to the last-mentioned writer he owes the most. Dr. Watts laboured at his Psalter from 1712 to 1716, during his cessation from public duties in consequence of illness. The complete work was published in 1719, after the sixth edition of the hymns, and met with a very ready sale.

Dr. Watts was beloved and useful as a Christian pastor and preacher, and his written works had an extensive circulation. In addition to those already spoken of as actually published, he sketched out the plan of the "Rise and Progress of Religion in the Soul." But growing infirmities having prevented him from writing it, he handed the work over to Dr. Doddridge, took deep interest in its progress, and expressed his approval of the manner of its execution. In a letter, bearing date Sept. 13, 1744, four years before his death, he says: "I wish my health had been so far established that I could have read over every line with the attention it merits, but I am not ashamed by what I have read to recommend it as the best treatise on practical religion which is to be found in our language." Dr. Watts never married, but he was very fond of children, and proved himself their friend by writing many simple books for them. His far-famed "Catechisms" and "Divine Songs" were written at the request of Sir Thomas and Lady Abney, and evince the adaptive power of the writer, who could teach alike young or old, in poetry or prose, by the pulpit or the press. Dr. Watts received his Doctor's degree in 1728, from the Universities of Edinburgh and Aberdeen, both of which had, without his knowledge, conferred it upon him with every mark of respect.

As we might judge from his hymns, Dr. Watts' Christian character was of the highest order. His humility and generosity were particularly conspicuous. During thirty-six years, he constantly devoted a fixed part of his income to charitable purposes; and he was not less noted for his liberality of sentiment towards Christians of other denominations, with many of whom he enjoyed Christian friendship. Nor is it necessary to say how zealous he was for the truths of the Gospel and for the cause of Christ, since this shines out in all his productions.

Dr. Johnson, the celebrated lexicographer, will not be suspected of partiality to a Dissenter, yet he gives in his "Lives of the Poets" the following high yet just estimate of Dr. Watts. "Few men," he says, "have left behind such purity of character, or such monuments of laborious piety. He has provided instruction for all ages, from those who are lisping their first lessons, to the enlightened readers of Malebranche and Locke; he has left neither corporeal nor spiritual nature unexamined; he has taught the art of reasoning, and the science of the stars. His character, therefore, must be formed from the multiplicity and diversity of his attainments, rather than from any single performance; for it would not be safe to claim for him the highest rank in any single denomination of literary dignity; yet perhaps there was nothing in which he would not have excelled, if he had not divided his powers to different pursuits."

For his own sake we must regret the weakness and suffering of Dr. Watts' life; yet since thereby opportunities for retirement and composition were afforded him, and his deep experiences became the riches of the church, we cannot but recognise therein the wisdom and goodness of a superintending Providence. When the venerable poet, at the age of seventy-five, approached his end, he expressed himself as "waiting God's leave to die," and thus he entered into his rest. Dr. Watts died Nov. 25, 1748, at the residence of Lady Abney, who survived him, at Stoke Newington, where he had resided many years.

In a letter, dated Stoke Newington, Nov. 24, 1748, Mr. Parker sends Dr. Doddridge the following words, as just noted down from Dr. Watts' dying lips. The dying divine said: "I would be waiting to see what God will do with me; it is good to say as Mr. Baxter, 'what, when, and where God pleases.' The business of a Christian is to do and hear the will of God, and if I was in health I could but be doing that, and that I may be now. If God should raise me up again, I may finish some more of my papers, or God can make use of me to save a soul, and that will be worth living for. If God has no more service for me to do, through grace, 'I am ready.' It is a great mercy to me that I have no manner of fear or dread of death; I could, if God please, lay my head back and die without alarm this afternoon or night." At another time, he said: "My chief supports are from my view of eternal things, and the interest I have in them; I trust all my sins are pardoned through the blood of Christ."

Dr. Watts' evangelical psalms and hymns are believed to have done much during the eighteenth century to preserve the Congregational Churches from the frigid formalism of those times. And now, having found their way into Episcopalian, Wesleyan, and other collections, they are carrying on their Gospel mission in many communities and in many lands.

From among many who have expressed their indebtedness to Dr. Watts, we select that celebrated convert to Christ, Colonel Gardiner, whose testimony is strong and decided. In a letter to Dr. Doddridge, he expresses his fear lest the poet should die before he had an opportunity of thanking him,—a fear not fulfilled, as Dr. Watts lived to acknowledge Dr. Doddridge's letter conveying the thanks. The pious Colonel writes: "Well am I acquainted with his works, especially with his Psalms, Hymns, and Lyrics. How often, by singing some of them when by myself, on horseback, and elsewhere, has the evil spirit been made to fly away.

> "Whene'er my heart in tune was found,
> Like David's harp of solemn sound."

Dr. Gibbons, in his "Life of Watts," has shown that his Psalms and Hymns, though showing art by veiling art, are yet rich in rhetorical figures.

Thus, in

> "The heavens declare thy glory, Lord."—No. 17.

How happy the moment and the manner in which the *apostrophe* of the fifth verse is introduced,

> "Great Sun of Righteousness arise."

In

> "What sinners value I resign,"—No. 13,

the *exclamations* of the third verse,

> "O glorious hour! O blest abode!"

are at once most natural and most expressive. No circumlocution of words could produce the same effect. In

> "God is the refuge of His saints,"—No. 63,

the words are most admirably adapted to the various scenes pictured. They are not merely the names of the things described, but their "sounds are an echo to the sense" conveyed. If we did not know the meaning of the words used in verse two, we should yet know that it spoke of what was abrupt and terrible. And we could be equally sure that verse four spoke of what was flowing and delightful.

And in the favourite hymn,

> "There is a land of pure delight,"—No. 742,

where the poet was obliged to introduce death in the midst of the most pleasing objects, he does so by a *periphrasis* that disarms it of its terrors:

> "Death, like a narrow sea, divides
> This heavenly land from ours."

And there are many other similar beauties. More is said of the excellencies of Dr. Watts' Hymns, in a comparison of the claims of Dr. Watts and Charles Wesley, which has been attempted under "CHARLES WESLEY."

In Dr. Watts' Psalms and Hymns, including "parts" and doxologies, there were six hundred and ninety-seven separate pieces. In the "New Congregational Hymn Book," in order to make room for numerous other writers, and to keep the whole book of a moderate size, it was necessary to make a great reduction from this number. But not less than three hundred and ninety-one of Watts' are retained; the next largest contributor, Charles Wesley, supplying only seventy-four. And good service is done not only by omitting those of Watts' that were least used and least valuable, but also by introducing a few good hymns found in his works though not included in his collection.

As an illustration of the kind of notes Dr. Watts has sometimes appended to his Psalms, we give the following, given at the foot of his rendering of Psalm xxxii.—

"Blest is the man, for ever blest."—No. 41.

He says "These two first verses of this psalm being cited by the Apostle, in the fourth chapter of Romans, to show the freedom of our pardon, and justification by grace without works, I have, in this version of it, enlarged the sense by mention of the blood of Christ, and faith, and repentance; and because the Psalmist adds, 'A spirit in which is no guile,' I have inserted that sincere obedience, which is a scriptural evidence of our faith and justification." These notes illustrate the poet's method, but are not of sufficient importance to deserve reproduction. The hymns have no notes.

"Show pity, Lord; O Lord, forgive."—No. 71.

For the first three lines of this psalm, Watts is indebted to the "Psalmodia Germanica," a translation by John Christian Jacobi, 1722, a work of which he occasionally made use.

Dr. Belcher gives an anecdote of a young man, who complaining of the hardening effect on himself of a severe sermon on sin, was further asked to read this psalm, and, attempting to do so, his feelings overcame him, and he could proceed no further than the words—" I am condemned," v. 4. He then burst into tears, and rushed out of the room. From that day his life began to be changed.

"Before Jehovah's awful throne,
Ye nations bow, with sacred joy."—No. 152.

These words are by John Wesley (1741), Dr. Watts (1719) wrote instead :—

"Nations, attend before His throne,
With solemn fear, with sacred joy."

"My soul thy great Creator praise."—No. 161.

Watts' rendering of Psalm civ.; the original piece consists of twenty-eight verses. It takes its first verses from the version of Sir John Denham, (1615—1688), whom Pope styles "majestic Denham." Dr. Johnson says, "he is one of the writers that improved our taste, and advanced our language." He is best known as the author of "Cooper's Hill." In the history of English versification, it was his part, in conjunction with Waller, to cultivate the rhyming couplet, till it became almost perfect in the hands of Dryden.

"When Israel, freed from Pharaoh's hand."—No. 179.

Dr. Watts' rendering of Psalm cxiv. has a peculiar interest from having been first printed in the "Spectator," August 19th, 1712, accompanied with a letter, in which the writer says that he had observed what had escaped the notice of several other poetical translators, that the force and beauty of the psalm are preserved only by keeping the name of Jehovah till the end. This he has done with good effect in his rendering, while they have marred the rhetorical arrangement of the psalm by introducing the name of God at the beginning.

"I'll praise my Maker with my breath."—No. 242.

Dr. Watts' version of Psalm cxlvi. has a special interest as the last psalm used by John Wesley—when very weak he suddenly broke forth in these most appropriate words. It is given in the "New Congregational Hymn Book," with the 2nd verse omitted:—

"Eternal Power—whose high abode."—No. 257.

This is the last piece in Book I. of Watts' "Horæ Lyricæ" (1706). It is headed "God exalted above all praise," verses two and three of the original are, in the "New Congregational Hymn Book," compressed into one verse.

"Keep silence, all created things."—No. 267.

This is part of a piece of twelve verses, headed "God's dominion and decrees," and found in Book I. of Watts' "Horæ Lyricæ," (1706.)

"The Lord—how fearful is His name."—No. 268.

This is a piece in Watts' "Horæ Lyricæ," Book I., headed "Sovereignty and Grace." A verse has been omitted before verse four, and verse four has been improved by alteration.

"Almighty Maker, God."—No. 271.

This is part of a piece of eleven stanzas in Watts' "Horæ Lyricæ," (1706), Book I. It is headed "Sincere Praise."

"Eternal wisdom, Thee we praise."—No. 275.

This consists of the first verse and the last three verses of a piece of eighteen stanzas, and divided into five parts, in Watts' "Horæ Lyricæ," Book I. (1706). It is headed "A Song to Creating Wisdom."

"Blest be the wisdom and the power."—No. 298.

This is song 3 of Watts' "Divine Songs for Children." It is headed "Praise to God for our Redemption;" one verse is omitted.

"Father, how wide Thy glory shines!"—No. 299.

This is part of a piece in Watts' "Horæ Lyricæ, (1706), Book I. It is headed "God glorious and sinners saved."

"When I survey the wondrous Cross."—No. 371.

A writer of one of the "Oxford Essays" (1858) fixes on this as Watts' finest hymn. It is given in the "New Congregational Hymn Book" without abbreviation or alteration. The same writer regards the poet's rendering of the 90th Psalm:—

"Our God, our help in ages past,"—No. 130,

as his finest paraphrase. It is given in the "New Congregational Hymn Book," with the omission of two verses.

"He dies, the Friend of sinners dies:
Lo! Salem's daughters weep around:
A solemn darkness veils the skies:
A sudden trembling shakes the ground."—No. 380.

This verse, in its improved form, is by John Wesley. Dr. Watts wrote it thus:—

"He dies, the heavenly Lover dies;
The tidings strike a doleful sound
On my poor heart-strings: deep He lies
In the cold caverns of the ground."

It appeared in his "Lyrics," first book, (1706), and is entitled "Christ Dying, Rising, and Reigning."

"Jesus, Thou everlasting King!"—No. 403.

This is part of Watts' hymn 72, first book. It begins:—

"Daughters of Sion, come, behold!"

And is headed "The Coronation of Christ, and Espousals of the Church."—Sol. Song iii. 11.

"Questions and doubts be heard no more."—No. 463.

This is one of two hymns given at the close of three sermons on "The Inward Witness to Christianity," on the text 1 John

v. 10, "He that believeth on the Son of God hath the witness in himself." The other hymn is not in the "New Congregational Hymn Book."

"Great God, with wonder and with praise."—No. 465.

This is part of Song 7 of Watts' "Divine Songs for Children." It is headed "The Excellency of the Bible."

"How is our nature spoiled by sin!"—No. 477.

This hymn is given by Dr. Watts at the close of his Sermon xxxiv., on "The Atonement of Christ," on the text "Whom God hath set forth to be a propitiation."—Rom. iii. 25.

"What shall the dying Sinner do?"—No. 481.

This is given after Sermons xvi. and xvii., on "A Rational Defence of the Gospel; or, Courage in Professing Christianity." The hymn is headed "The Gospel—the power of God to salvation," on the text Rom. i. 16, "I am not ashamed of the gospel of Christ," &c.

"And is this life prolonged to me?"—No. 488.

This is the hymn to Sermon xxxix., on "The Right Improvement of Life," on the text "Whether life or death—all are yours."—1 Cor. iii. 22.

"Sinner, O why so thoughtless grown?"—No. 491.

This is taken from a curious piece in Watts' "Lyrics," headed "The Hardy Soldier," and dedicated to the Right Honourable John Lord Cutts (at the siege of Namure). Watts' piece begins—

"O why is man so thoughtless grown?"

and the second verse—

"Are lives but worth a soldier's pay?"

There are six stanzas. Who gave the piece its present striking form is not ascertained; but it appears as we have it in "Rippon's Collection," 1787.

"Not all the blood of beasts."—No. 546.

The note book of a London City Missionary contains the narrative of a Jewess, who seeing part of this hymn on a piece of paper round some butter, read it, and could not shake off the impression produced. She was led thereby to read the Bible, and thence to find in the despised Nazarene her true Messiah. In consequence of this religious change, her husband found means to obtain a divorce. He went to India, married again, and died. She lived in poverty, but was rich in Christ, to whom she remained faithful to the end.

"Mighty Redeemer, set me free."—No. 554.

This is part of Watts' 130th hymn, second book, beginning:—

"Attend, while God's exalted Son."

"Blessed Redeemer, how divine!"—No. 582.

This is the hymn for Sermon xxxiii., on "The Universal Rule of Equity," on text, Matt. vii. 12—"All things whatsoever ye would," &c. Three verses are omitted, and the last verse is altered.

"Let bitter words no more be known."—No. 585.

This is Watts' 130th hymn, first book, beginning—

"Now by the bowels of my God."

The hymn is improved by the omission of this first verse.

"Happy the heart where graces reign."—No. 586.

Part of this hymn is found in Watts' "Lyric Poems," Book I., in a piece beginning—

"'Tis pure delight without alloy."

"Awake my zeal, awake my love."—No. 618.

This is the hymn to Sermon xl., on "The privilege of the

Living above the Dead," on the text 1 Cor. iii. 22, "Whether life or death—all are yours." One verse is omitted.

"Are we the soldiers of the cross?"—No. 623.

This is part of a hymn beginning—

"Do I believe what Jesus saith?"

Part of which is No. 620, the hymn for Sermon xxx, on "Christian Morality, viz., Courage and Honour," on the text "If there be any virtue," &c.—Phil. iv. 8.

"With heavenly weapons I have fought."—No. 629.

This is part of Watts' 27th hymn, first book, beginning—

"Death may dissolve my body now."

"O that I knew the secret place."—No. 641.

This is given at the end of No. 6 of "Sermons on Miscellaneous Subjects." The subject is "Sins and Sorrows spread before God," and the text, "O that I knew where I might find him," &c.—Job xxiii. 3, 4. One verse is omitted.

"Now to the hands of Christ our King."—No. 667.

This is part of Watts' 113th hymn, second book, a hymn of eight verses, beginning—

"The majesty of Solomon."

"Immortal principles forbid."—No. 676.

This is the latter part of Watts' hymn cxliii, first book, a hymn of ten verses, beginning—

"So new-born babes desire the breast."

"How vast the treasure we possess."—No. 687.

The first verse of this hymn is the first verse of the hymn to Sermon xxxvii., on "The Christian's Treasure," on the text "All things are yours."—1 Cor. iii. 21. The last four verses are part of the hymn to Sermon xxxviii., on "All things working together for good," on the same text. The hymn begins—

"My soul survey thy happiness."

"Oh happy soul that lives on high."—No. 695.

This is the hymn for Sermons ix. and x., on "The Hidden Life of a Christian, on the text "For ye are dead and your life is hid with Christ in God."—Col. iii. 3. Two verses are omitted.

"My God, the spring of all my joys."—No. 697.

Some critics struck by the excellencies of this hymn, have declared it his best production.

"Do flesh and nature dread to die?"—No. 716.

This is the hymn to Sermon xliii, on "Death, a Blessing to the Saints," on the text given under No. 718.

"Must friends and kindred droop and die?"—No. 718.

This is the hymn for Sermon xlii., on "Death of Kindred Improved," on the text 1 Cor. iii. 22., "Whether life or death—all are yours."

"There is a land of pure delight."—No. 742.

Local tradition connects this hymn with the neighbourhood of Southampton, and says that it was, while "looking out upon the beautiful scenery of the harbour and river, and the green glades of the New Forest on its farther bank, that the idea suggested itself to Dr. Watts of 'a land of pure delight,' and of 'sweet fields beyond the swelling flood, dressed in living green,' as an image of the heavenly 'Canaan.'"

The imagery of the verse—

"There shall I bathe my weary soul
In seas of heavenly rest,
And not a wave of trouble roll
Across my peaceful breast."—No. 705.

may also be reasonably attributed to the associations of the neighbourhood in which he wrote.

> "When I can read my title clear
> To mansions in the skies."—No. 705.

It has been remarked that Cowper has used these lines in his poem on "Truth," in the comparison of the lot of Voltaire and that of the poor but believing cottager, who

> "Just knows, and knows no more, her Bible true—
> A truth the brilliant Frenchman never knew:
> And in that charter *reads with sparkling eyes*
> *Her title to a treasure in the skies.*"

> "Our journey is a thorny maze."—No. 706.

This is the last five verses of a hymn of twelve verses, the 53rd, second book, beginning—

> "Lord, what a wretched land is this!"

> "Absent from flesh! O blissful thought!"—No. 723.

This is one of five lyric odes on "Death and Heaven," given by Dr. Watts in his "Miscellaneous Thoughts" in prose and verse, at page 554 of the fourth volume of his collected works. These odes were sent to a friend to solace him in bereavement. The letter that accompanied them explained that they had all been written about the same time, and had afterwards lain in silence. The preface to the "Miscellaneous Thoughts" bears date 1734. Another of these odes is—

> "Unveil thy bosom, faithful tomb!"—No. 732.

and another, not given in the "New Congregational," begins—

> "And is this heav'n? and am I there!"

In these odes Dr. Watts takes a very high flight, and they are of great poetic excellence.

> "How bright these glorious spirits shine!"—No. 750.

This is given without name in the "New Congregational Hymn Book." It is Dr. Watts' 41st hymn, first book—

"These glorious minds, how bright they shine?"

greatly altered by the Rev. William Cameron (1751—1811), minister of Kirknewton, in Mid-Lothian, Scotland. Mr. Cameron was associated with Logan and others in producing "The Psalms of David, in metre, according to the version approved by the Church of Scotland." At the end of this work there were sixty-six translations, in paraphrases in verse, of several passages of the sacred Scriptures. This was one of a small number contributed by Cameron.

"Give me the wings of faith to rise."—No. 752.

Dr. Doddridge mentions the powerful effect of singing this hymn, after a sermon by him on Heb. vi. 12, "Followers of them who through faith and patience inherit the promises." The hymn so successfully gave expression to the sentiments of the text and the sermon, that many were too much moved to sing, and others sang with tears.

"This is the day when Christ arose."—No. 754.

This is song xxvii. of Watts' "Divine Songs for Children," published about 1720. This hymn is headed "For the Lord's-day Morning."

"Lord, how delightful 'tis to see."—No. 797.

This is song xxviii. of Watts' "Divine Songs for Children," 1720. It is headed "For the Lord's-day Evening."

"Now let the children of the saints."—No. 854.

This is part of Watts' 114th hymn, first book. It begins—

"Gentiles by nature, we belong."

"How glorious is our heavenly King."—No. 963.

This is song i. of Watts' "Divine Songs for Children." It is headed "A General Song of Praise to God."

"The praises of my tongue."—No. 964.

This is part of song viii. of Watts' "Divine songs for Children." It is headed "Praise to God for learning to read."

SAMUEL WESLEY JUN., M.A.
1690—1739.

Like his father, Samuel the elder, and like his younger brothers John and Charles, Samuel Wesley, jun., was a hymn-writer. Even in childhood he showed a taste for poetry. He was sent to Westminster School in 1704, was admitted a King's scholar in 1707, and in 1711 was elected to Christ's Church, Oxford, where he remained till he had taken his M.A. degree. Being a man of great classical attainments, he was appointed one of the ushers at Westminster School. He held this position for twenty years, and in 1732 was appointed head master of the Free School at Tiverton. There he remained till his death, in 1739. He took orders in the Church of England, and was considered a good preacher, but he did not receive any preferment. He was not in sympathy with the religious views of John and Charles, but, trained in high-church principles, used his best efforts to turn his brothers from what he called their "new faith." He was the author of "Poems on Several Occasions," published in 1736, and a second edition in 1743. Some of his pieces evince much poetical talent, and some of his hymns are very good. There is only one by him in the "New Congregational Hymn Book," a good Sabbath hymn:

"The Lord of Sabbath let us praise."—No. 764.

ROBERT SEAGRAVE, M.A.
Born 1693.

An honourable place amongst hymn-writers belongs to Robert Seagrave, some of whose hymns will probably yet be better known. How fine, for instance, are the following verses, taken from a funeral hymn of seven similar verses! Verses 4 and 5:

> " Death, thou that spoil'st the human race,
>   And boastest in thy reign,
> Know, thy own ruin hastes apace,
>   Thou dy'st, we live again.
>
> " Not amongst evils now, but friends,
>   We rank the stingless foe;
> Our passage into life it stands,
>   Our greatest friend below."

Robert Seagrave was born Nov. 22nd, 1693, at Twyford, in Leicestershire, where his father, of the same name, was vicar from 1687 to 1720. When the younger Robert had almost completed his seventeenth year, he was admitted, Nov. 8th, 1710, subsizar of Clare Hall, Cambridge, where he graduated B.A. in 1714, and M.A. in 1718.

His public life as a Christian minister had one special object to rouse the Church of England and the people in general from the religious lethargy into which they had sunk. He traced their unhappy condition to the merely moral preaching which prevailed. It was his aim to replace this by thoroughly Gospel preaching. In furtherance of this object he published several tracts and pamphlets. The first about the year 1736, " A letter to the people of England, occasioned by the falling away of the Clergy from the doctrines of the Reformation, by Paulinus. London, printed for A. Cruden." Mr. Seagrave gave his name to this in place of the assumed name of Paulinus, in the fourth edition. This letter he followed up by a sermon on Gal. iii. 24, entitled, " A draught of the justification of man, different from the present language of our pulpits." He had previously, in 1731, sent forth anonymously, " A Remonstrance addressed to the Clergy," &c. In 1737, he published " Six Sermons upon the manner of Salvation, being the substance of Christianity, as preached at the time of the Reformation;" and, in 1738, " Observations upon the conduct of the Clergy, in relation to the Thirty-nine Articles, wherein is showed that the Church of England, properly so called, is not now existing: with an Essay towards a real Protestant Establishment." And in the year 1746, he wrote "The True Protestant," a book of a similar character to those mentioned before. And at the time of his becoming connected with Mr. Whitefield, in 1739, he wrote in his vindication, "An Answer to Dr. Trapp's Four Sermons against Mr. Whitefield," and "Remarks upon the Bishop of London's Pastoral Letter."

Finding much discouragement in his good work of reformation within the Church, Mr. Seagrave saw it, as it appeared also to Wesley and Whitefield, more advantageous to work outside her pale. Hence, in 1739, he was appointed Sunday Evening Lecturer at Lorimers' Hall, in Cripplegate. This place of meeting had been in the hands of the General Baptists, and afterwards of the Independents, but at that time it was used by the early Methodists. The building is now taken down. There Mr. Seagrave preached till 1750, and during the same period he preached frequently at the Tabernacle. We have no particulars of his last years, but one John Griffiths, in his "experience," speaks of having heard Mr. Seagrave in a Nonconformist Chapel in 1759, and of the spiritual benefit he received. So that as late as his sixty-sixth year, Mr. Seagrave was still successfully preaching the Gospel. His hymns show his high appreciation of the distinctive doctrines of the atonement, and the pains he took to proclaim them. He had learned them in his own experience. He says of himself,

"Moral my hope, my saviour self,
Till mighty grace the cheat display'd."

And then adds, in a verse commended by Whitefield, in his letter 420, bearing date 1742:

"Glad, I forsook my righteous pride,
My tarnish'd, filthy, sinful dress;
Exchang'd my loss away for Christ,
And found a robe of righteousness"

Mr. Seagrave prepared his Hymn-book for his congregation at Lorimers' Hall, in 1742. It is entitled "Hymns for Christian Worship, partly composed and partly collected from various authors." The third edition followed in 1744, and the fourth in 1748. Mr. Daniel Sedgwick has published all Mr. Seagrave's Hymns (1860), with a biographical sketch of the author. The hymns are fifty in number. As hymns, they are all good, and some are of great excellence. They are rich in Christian experience, and full of scriptural and spiritual meaning.

"Rise, my soul, and stretch thy wings,"—No. 703,

erroneously attributed in the "New Congregational Hymn Book" to Madan. This remarkably fine hymn, which Seagrave calls "The Pilgrim's Song," is given with the omission of a third verse—a similar verse that we regret to spare.

"Now may the Spirit's holy fire."—No. 787.

This is four verses of a piece of nine verses designed to be sung "at the opening of worship." It is erroneously attributed in the "New Congregational Hymn Book" to Toplady. The omitted verses are not less excellent than those that are given.

GERARD TERSTEEGEN.
1697—1769.

Tersteegen has been called the greatest poet of the mystical school of the 17th and 18th centuries. This school was founded by Angelus (1624—1677) of Silesia, who was an enthusiastic mystic, and whose works are in direct contrast to those of Luther, substituting as they do sentiment for strength.

Gerhard and several of the early German hymn-writers, following Luther in doctrine as well as in poetic skill, were of the Lutheran church, but Tersteegen belonged to the Reformed. A philanthropist as well as a poet, he devoted himself unreservedly to those works of Christian usefulness which his single life left him free to pursue. Known to posterity as a Christian poet, he was best known by many in his own time as their faithful adviser in the hour of spiritual need.

He was born in the town of Mörs, in Westphalia; and his father, a godly tradesman, died soon after his birth. As his mother's circumstances rendered it necessary, young Tersteegen went into business, in his fifteenth year, at Mühlheim on the Ruhr. There he experienced a great spiritual work. But, finding his business unfavourable to the progress of his religious life, he entered upon another—the manufacture of silk ribbons. This business could be carried on without the assistance of other workmen, and did not interfere with meditation; hence it suited the mystic tendencies of his mind, and he found much happiness while engaged in it. After enjoying his retirement for some time, he still further lightened his business cares by associating with himself one Sommer as a partner.

Tersteegen's religious experience was remarkable. While an apprentice at Mühlheim, his faith was strengthened by what happened to him while on a journey to Duisburg. On his way, and when in a forest and alone, he was overtaken by violent spasms that threatened his life. He prayed earnestly that he might be spared in order that he might better prepare himself for eternity. His prayer was immediately answered, and he at once dedicated himself entirely to Christ. But he did not escape the snares of self-righteousness. Austerities were tried, but in vain, and he passed through the experience he writes of when he says, making use of Augustine's well-known saying,

> " My heart is pained, nor can it be
> At rest, till it finds rest in Thee."

At length he could gratefully write, " He took me by the hand, He drew me away from perdition's yawning gulf, directed my eye to Himself, and instead of the well-deserved pit of hell, opened to me the unfathomable abyss of His loving heart." At the age of twenty-seven, he wrote in his own blood a form of dedication of himself to Jesus. He writes, " God graciously called me out of the world, and granted me the desire to belong to Him, and to be willing to follow Him. I long for an eternity that I may suitably glorify Him for it." His subsequent life of devotion to Christ may be expressed in his own words—

> "Is there a thing beneath the sun,
>   That strives with Thee my heart to share ?
> Ah ! tear it thence, and reign alone,
>   The Lord of every motion there."

Three years after his act of dedication a spiritual awakening was experienced at Mühlheim, and Tersteegen was prevailed upon to overcome his aversion to publicity, and to address the people on Christian themes. Beginning with meetings in private houses, his sphere at length so widened, and so many were drawn to him, that he found it necessary to give up his ribbon-making in order to attend to his writings, his public addresses, and his work of caring for the sick and poor. His house, which received the name of "The Pilgrims' Cottage," became the resort of multitudes from his own and other countries. They came to him for medicine alike for body and mind. Many claims were made upon him, and he managed to meet them from the savings of his own abstemiousness and the kind gifts of his friends. Often absorbed in communion with God, and constantly seeking to be unknown to men, he yet found his fame extending on every hand.

He sometimes made journeys to fulfil his Christian mission, but at the age of sixty, having overtasked his energies by addressing large multitudes, he found it necessary to lessen and limit his labours. Like many other eminent Christians, Tersteegen was a great sufferer, and he had also to bear the calumnies of men; but by simplicity of character and humble submission to the will of God, he proved himself superior to hostile circumstances; and, after bearing with patience his last affliction, an attack of dropsy, he peacefully fell asleep in Jesus.

Besides other poetical productions, Tersteegen wrote more than one hundred hymns. Those in the "New Congregational Hymn Book" show the spiritual and God-seeking character of his mind.

"Thou hidden love of God, whose height."—(No. 561).
"Lo! God is here; let us adore."—(No. 773).
"Gott ist gegenwärtig, lasset uns anbeten."

These are parts of John Wesley's translations—given in his "Hymns and Sacred Poems, 1739"—of two of Tersteegen's best-known hymns.

"In his "Plain Account of Christian Perfection," Mr. Wesley says he translated hymn 561 while at Savannah, Georgia, in the year 1736, finding verse 3 in particular expressive of his feelings at that time.

NICHOLAS LOUIS ZINZENDORF.
1700—1760.

Not the least in the noble army of hymn-writers was Count Zinzendorf, the founder of Herrnhut, and the champion of the United Moravian Brethren. He was born in Dresden on the 26th of May, 1700, and was the son of Count Zinzendorf, who held high office under the Elector of Saxony. His father died when he was only six weeks old, and his mother, who was a woman of great piety and talent, and for whom he had great reverence, having married again, his education was entrusted to his maternal grandmother, the widow of Baron Gersdorf, a pious and learned lady, and a writer of hymns and religious books. Her chief friend was the celebrated Jacob Spener, the founder of the "Pietists," and himself the author of some hymns.

No doubt these early associations helped to make Zinzendorf what he became as a hymn-writer and religious reformer. He had been taught also to hold in honourable remembrance the count, his grandfather, who had become a voluntary exile rather than renounce his Lutheran principles. Zinzendorf was remarkable for his early piety. As a child, he used to gather children to pray with him, and he even wrote letters to his beloved Saviour. Referring back to his childhood, he writes thus in 1740 :—" It is more than thirty years since I received a deep impression of Divine grace, through the preaching of the cross. The desire to bring souls to Jesus took possession of me, and my heart became fixed on the Lamb. It is true that I have not always taken the same road to come to Him, for at Halle I went to Him directly, at Wittemberg through morality, at Dresden through philosophy, and after that through an endeavour to follow His steps. It was not till after the happy establishment of the community at Herrnhut, and since the affair with Dippel, that I came to Him through the simple doctrine of His sufferings and His death." He then goes on to say, "I have uniformly acted from love to Jesus, and without any secondary motive," and he urges others to spare themselves the needless fears he had allowed to trouble him in his spiritual course.

From his eleventh to his sixteenth year, Zinzendorf studied at Halle under A. H. Franke, the celebrated pietist, and the founder of the world-renowned orphan school. At Halle the same love to Jesus ruled in the young count's heart, and he formed himself and his companions into a religious order, with its mottoes and insignia; and, while still a youth, he began writing those hymns which afterwards formed so important a part in the spiritual agency he employed. In 1716, his uncle, General Zinzendorf, who was his guardian, sent him to Wittemberg University, where Lutheran orthodoxy was preferred to pietism. There the young count was to study law, but the change of place and purpose did not turn him from his religious pursuits. He continued to hold religious meetings, and resolved to be a Christian minister. At first he went to extremes in the practice of the ascetic pietism of the school he had been compelled to leave, but at length he learned that there was good at Wittemberg also, and he took the good of each aspect of truth without blindly giving the preference to either. In 1719, Zinzendorf quitted Wittemberg to enjoy the advantages of travel. He spent a short time in Holland, and then resided for a few months in Paris, meeting with several eminent persons, and especially with Cardinal Noailles, Archbishop of Paris, with whom he had much religious intercourse, and to whom he dedicated his translation of Arndt's work on " True Christianity." In his subsequent journeying he was detained by illness at Oberbirg, where he formed a strong attachment to his cousin Theodora, the daughter of the Countess of Castell. But subsequently, under a strong sense of duty, he resigned his place in her affections to his friend Henry XXIX., the reigning Count of Reuss-Ebersdorf, a young man of similar religious sentiments. Of this surrender he said to Charles Wesley, "From that moment I was freed from all self-seeking, so that for ten years I have not done my own will in anything, great or small. My own will is hell to me."

On attaining his majority, in 1721, Zinzendorf yielded to the wish of his relatives, and entered upon his duties as a judge and member of the Aulic Council in the electorate of Saxony. But his heart was still devoted to Christian work; and at Dresden he took every opportunity of pleading for Christ with his courtier companions, and he held religious meetings in his own house, at which he delivered addresses to all who would come. In 1722, he bought the estate of Bethelsdorf, rebuilt the mansion, and appointed as the pastor, Rothe, a man of earnest piety, and, like his patron, a good hymn-writer. In the same year Zinzendorf married Erdmuth Dorothy, a sister of his friend Count Reuss. She was a woman of great talent and piety, a true helpmeet for him. Of her he wrote, in 1747, "An experience of twenty-five years has taught me that the help I have had is the only kind of help that touches my vocation at every point." They had twelve children—several of them died in infancy, two of them bore a beautiful Christian testimony. The loss of his son, Christian René, at the age of twenty-four, in 1752, was a great grief to the count. Three daughters survived their father, and many of the descendants of one, Benigna, who married John Watteville, are found now in America. On his marriage, Zinzendorf transferred his property to his wife, that, free from every trammel, he might give himself wholly to the service of Christ.

About the time of his marriage, Zinzendorf heard from David Christian an account of the sufferings the Moravian brethren endured under the Austrian government. The count expressed his readiness to receive the persecuted refugees on his estate. They were followers of John Huss, in Moravia, descendants of the faithful few who had never altogether yielded either to the Greek or Roman churches. On the 17th of June, 1722, David Christian and a few companions commenced building their dwelling at the foot of the Hutberg, or "pasture hill," near Bethelsdorf. The settlement was called "Herrnhut"—*i. e.*, under the protection of the Lord, the word "hut" meaning protection and pasture. To this settlement, which grew by the arrival of fresh emigrants, and at length sent out missionaries to heathen lands, Zinzendorf gave much of his property, and of the energies of his life. With great forbearance he bore with them in their strifes, and again and again saved them from dissolution by division. He would never consent to their being anything but a free spiritual community; and he succeeded in maintaining their ancient constitution as "United Brethren," including in their number members of the Moravian, Lutheran, and Reformed churches. He defended them from misrepresentation, aspersion, and persecution. In all parts of the world he vindicated the claims of the Moravians, and when the community was almost insolvent, he undertook the burden of their debt, and at his death he owed more than a quarter of a million of money on their account.

In 1731, Zinzendorf resigned his public duties in order to devote himself to Christian work. His religious duties had been growing upon him. He had been elected president of Herrnhut, and devoted himself heartily to its spiritual interests. Of one of the means employed, Felix Bovet says in his recent very interesting memoir, "Singing was another of the means of religious improvement to which he attached great importance, and, with the assistance of his secretary, Tobias Frederick, who was a good musician, he organized meetings for psalmody. His stock of hymns, which he could at any time recall, was as wonderful as his power of extemporaneous composition. Sometimes he would sing a number of verses taken from various hymns, and interspersed with others composed at the moment, thus producing a kind of lyric discourse—an echo to the voice of the Hebrew prophets—which seems to have produced a profound impression."

In the year 1732, Zinzendorf received an order to sell his estates and quit the country. This arose from the mismanagement by his aunt, at Hennersdorf, of her Bohemian settlement. The settlers, weary of her restraint, removed to Herrnhut, and could not be prevailed upon by the count to return to his relative. They wandered about, and some were imprisoned, and they became a cause of annoyance and anxiety to the government, and most unreasonably the count was made to suffer for this unhappy state of things. In 1734, Zinzendorf went to Stralsund, and without revealing his title, passed an examination, and obtained a certificate of orthodoxy. Afterwards, he had recourse to the Faculty of Theology at Tübingen, and at last obtained the requisite authorization to act as assistant pastor at Herrnhut. After this, he went on his evangelical errand to Denmark, Holland, Prussia, and England; and on the 20th of May, 1737, he received episcopal consecration at Berlin, but not finding admission to the pulpits there, he opened his own house, where he gave addresses daily for four months. These were subsequently published by the name of the "Berlin Discourses." They went through many editions, and were translated into several languages.

In 1729, Zinzendorf paid a short visit to St. Thomas, and in 1741 he paid a missionary visit to America, where he remained more than a year doing a good work in Pennsylvania, and attempting something for the North American Indians. After fourteen years of banishment the count was recalled to Saxony, by the king, in 1748. Between that year and 1755, he spent much time in London, where the affairs of the brethren needed his presence; and in 1756 the sermons he had preached there from 1751 to 1755 were collected and printed in two volumes, forming a kind of sequel to his "Discourses in Berlin."

Soon after the count had left London, the countess died, on the 19th of June, 1756. In June of the following year he married Anne Nitschmann, who for thirty years held the office of elder among the Sisters. Zinzendorf's last years were devoted without any reservation to the spiritual good of Herrnhut, and he came into intimate association with every member of the community. His last writing was a collection of "Texts" for the year following. Two days before his death he composed an ode of thirty-six stanzas in commemoration of a special service held among the unmarried sisters, and in the evening he attended an agape. He was very full of joy in the love that prevailed amongst the brethren, and at the success beyond expectation which had attended their labours in the world. Among his last words were, "I am going to the Saviour. If He does not wish to employ me any longer here below, I am quite ready to go to Him, for I have nothing else to keep me here." He died on the 9th of May, 1760.

Zinzendorf had to bear with the mis-interpretation of friends as well as the opposition of enemies. One of the worthiest of men, he was yet continually spoken against. Even the Wesleys, after intimate association with him, and after receiving lasting spiritual benefits from Moravian teachers, parted company with the count because of their divergence of doctrine. And Whitefield, though differing in doctrine from the Wesleys, was found arrayed against Zinzendorf. To the men of sects, Zinzendorf, owing to his charity to men of all religions, and his readiness for truth from every quarter, seemed to be a latitudinarian. To men of expediency, his simplicity of life and his freedom from worldliness seemed strange and unreasonable, though he was not without skill in ruling men by reason and love, and in negotiating with kings and governments when it was necessary. And to men of weak faith and superficial spirituality, his familiarity with Christ and his professed knowledge of the working of Divine providence seemed to border on fanaticism; and perhaps he was not altogether free from it. To his honour in all time it must be recorded that, having devoted his life to a great spiritual enterprise, he was singularly free from personal ostentation and self-assertion in its accomplishment.

Zinzendorf's prose works were very numerous. In addition to those mentioned, in 1725 he published a weekly review, called the "Dresden Socrates." It was continued in the following year, and reprinted in 1732 under the name of the "German Socrates." It was a satirical philosophical work, intended to correct abuses and lead men to Christianity. One of his principal works was his "Reflections Naturelles," written in twelve parts, between the years 1746 and 1749. It explains his views and the reasons for his course of action. He also published, about the year 1740, "Conversations on various Religious Truths," and a work entitled "Jeremiah, the Preacher of Righteousness," a stirring word to preachers. He also gave much time to a translation of the New Testament, the corrected edition of which appeared in 1744; and he published translations of other parts of the Scriptures. While in America, in 1742, he wrote, amongst other works, an "Introduction to Spiritual Direction," and a Latin letter, "To Free Thinkers;" and to defend the position of the church at Herrnhut against Bengel and others, he wrote his work on "The Present State of the Kingdom of the Cross of Christ;" and, in 1757, he published a harmony of the gospels, entitled "The History of the Days of the Son of man." Spangenberg, his biographer, gives a list of his published works, amounting to a hundred and eight.

Among his poetical works were—in 1725, "A Paraphrase, in verse, of the Last Discourse of Jesus before His Crucifixion," and the same year "A Collection of Hymns for the parish of Berthelsdorf;" and, in 1727, for the spiritual benefit of the German Catholics, he published "A Selection of Prayers and Hymns from Angelus Silesius, an eminent German mystic poet." All his life he was writing hymns—as a child, and in old age—amid the excitement of Paris, and when in the quietude of Berthelsdorf. Some of his best were written on his voyage to America, in 1741. There was a period in the history of his hymn-writing—between 1740 and 1750—when they gave expression to compassion and gratitude for Christ's physical sufferings rather than to the Scripture view of the meaning and value of the Atonement. These he afterwards suppressed. He wrote in all about two thousand hymns—128 are in the "English Hymn Book" used by the United Brethren. Many of the hymns were produced extemporaneously. The Brethren took them down and preserved them. Zinzendorf says of them, in speaking of his services at Berlin:—"After the discourse, I generally announce another hymn appropriate to the subject. When I cannot find one, I compose one; I say, in the Saviour's name, what comes into my heart. I am, as ever, a poor sinner, a captive of eternal love, running by the side of His triumphal chariot, and have no desire to be anything else as long as I live."

The two hymns by Zinzendorf in the "New Congregational" represent, the one, No. 662, his simplicity and life-trust; and the other, No. 825, his hearty acceptance of the great doctrine of justification by Jesus. They were written during what is regarded as his best time of hymn-writing.

"Jesus, still lead on." (No. 662),

"Jesu geh voran,"

was written in 1741, when as a young man he was preferring suffering with Christ to state honours and worldly rewards. The translation in the "New Congregational" is that given in "Hymns from the Land of Luther," 1853.

And the well-known hymn—

"Jesus, Thy robe of righteousness." (No. 325.)

"Christi Blut und Gerechtigkeit,"

was written in 1739, when he had been for years an earnest preacher of the Gospel. It is said to have been written during his voyage to visit the missionaries who had gone forth from Herrnhut to the West Indies. Wesley's translation (1740) is given. The original consisted of thirty-three stanzas. Wesley's first line was—

"Jesus, Thy blood and righteousness."

"Now I have found the ground wherein." (No 611.)

This is erroneously attributed to Zinzendorf. It is the production of his companion Rothe. *Vide* Life of Rothe.

Besides the collections already named, Zinzendorf published a collection of German poems in 1735. In 1739, he published a small collection containing the substance of sermons preached at Wurtemberg that year, and in 1741 another collection. In 1753, he finished his large collection of German hymns, containing 2,169, at Lindsey House, Chelsea, where he printed it at his own press. In 1754, he completed his "English Hymn Book," and in the following year the Appendix to it.

PHILIP DODDRIDGE, D.D.
1702—1751.

GREAT as hymn-writers, and great in so many other respects, Doddridge and Watts flourished together, making an era in the history of the denomination whose ministry they adorned. Doddridge, as the younger, continued in his vigour when Watts' strength was failing; but as Doddridge's course was disappointingly brief, he did not long survive his celebrated compeer. They were in deep and delightful sympathy, and co-operated together in the production of one of their principal works.

Philip Doddridge was born in London. His father was in

business there as an oilman. His mother, to whom he owed much, and from whom he learned the well-stored teachings of the Dutch tiles, was the daughter of an exile, a Bohemian clergyman, who was master of the Free School at Kingston-on-Thames. Philip was the twentieth child, and at birth seemed too feeble to live; and he had the misfortune to lose both his parents in his childhood. After studying at Kingston Grammar School, he went, at the age of fifteen, to be instructed by the Rev. Nathaniel Wood, at St. Alban's. There the orphan found a "friend in need" in the Rev. Samuel Clark, an excellent Presbyterian minister, and the author of "Scripture Promises."

At the age of seventeen, Doddridge, having given evidence of earnest piety and promise of aptitude for the ministry, went to study at the Academy at Kibworth, Leicestershire, presided over by the Rev. John Jennings. It was not for convenience, but on conscientious grounds, that Doddridge thus connected himself with Dissenters. The Duchess of Bedford offered to maintain him at Cambridge, but he declined. After three years, the academy removed with its tutor to Hinckley; and thither Doddridge went to complete his studies. At the termination of his studies, he accepted an invitation to become the Congregational pastor at Kibworth, the quiet village where his tutor had ministered. Three years after, he joined with this charge the duties of assistant-minister to Mr. Some, of Market Harborough.

In the year 1729, at the age of twenty-seven, and when his former tutor had died, Doddridge, yielding to the solicitations of Dr. Watts and others, who saw that he was qualified for such a work, opened an "academy" for the training of young men for the ministry, at Market Harborough. In the following year, he became pastor of the Church assembling in Castle-Hill Meeting House, Northampton; and having removed his academy to Northampton, he carried it on there till the end of his life. About 200 students received their training from him, of whom about 120 entered the ministry. While fulfilling his collegiate duties, he produced his voluminous works, and continued to meet his various claims as a stated minister, and the pastor of a large Christian Church.

Dr. Doddridge's written works were numerous and valuable, and some of them have a world-wide celebrity. In 1730, he published "Free Thoughts on the Best Means of reviving the Dissenting Interest;" Dr. Watts wrote on a similar subject in the following year. In 1732, he published his "Sermons on the Education of Children," and in 1735, his "Sermons to Young People." Other sermons and volumes of sermons followed in 1736 and 1741. He was also the author of "Memoirs of Colonel Gardiner," and of a "Life of the Rev. Thomas Steffe," one of his pupils.

The "Rise and Progress of Religion in the Soul" was written by Doddridge at the suggestion of Dr. Watts, whose enfeebled health did not admit of his carrying out his own design, but who was spared to revise a part of what Doddridge had written. This book was of the greatest spiritual service to William Wilberforce, prompting him to write his scarcely less useful work; it has been widely circulated and translated into several languages, and it is singled out as the most useful Christian book of the eighteenth century. Doddridge was also the author of the "Principles of the Christian Religion in Plain and Easy Verse." This work was written at the suggestion of Mr. Clark, of St. Alban's, and was a favourite of Geo. III. when in his boyhood. It was very popular, and did much to convey evangelical principles to the minds of the young.

The "Family Expositor," Doddridge's greatest work, was published in 1739, after many years of study, during which his early hours in the morning, and all the moments he could snatch from his numerous occupations, were devoted to it. His premature death prevented the accomplishment of the similar work he had planned for the Old Testament. His letters in reply to "Christianity not founded on Argument," and his professorial lectures, are also found in his works.

Dr. Doddridge was a man of extensive personal influence, and enjoyed the friendship of Bishop Warburton, the Countess of Huntingdon, the Wesleys, Whitefield, Hervey, Dr. Watts, and of many other of the celebrities of those times. His name will be always remembered in connection with the cause of modern missions, a cause he heartily befriended when it was looked upon with comparative indifference. His name will also always be honoured in connection with the history of the founding of Dissenting Colleges. He warmly advocated such institutions, himself taught in several departments, not shrinking from the learned toil it involved ; and it is said, that to his influence we owe the munificence of Mr. Coward for College purposes.

The comparatively early death of one so endeared to his family and beloved by his people and students, was felt as a severe shock, and produced general and unfeigned regret. Doddridge's over-wrought life was brought to a too early end by pulmonary disease, against which no means availed. For the benefit of warmer air, he had journeyed to Lisbon, where, soon after his arrival, and at the age of fifty, he fell asleep in Jesus.

According to the custom of the times, and to meet a want then felt, Doddridge wrote hymns, presenting in a brief and striking manner the principal teachings of his sermons, and designed to be sung at the close of them. They have been compared to "spiritual amber fetched up and floated off from sermons long since lost in the depths of bygone time." These hymns were not printed during the author's life-time ; but they were read in MSS. An account of his MSS. is given at the end of this sketch.

Lady Frances Gardiner, wife of Col. Gardiner, writing (1740) to Doddridge, speaks of having read his " charming hymns," and says that she has been requested to urge him to publish them. And in 1742, the poet, Robert Blair, writing to submit to Doddridge's opinion his work, "The Grave," which Dr. Watts had already praised, expresses himself as delighted with Doddridge's hymns. The collected hymns were published after the author's death. Dr. Doddridge had intended to publish them himself, but, on the failure of his health, he committed the work to his faithful biographer, Job Orton. The collection is entitled, "Hymns founded on various Texts in the Holy Scriptures, 1755." The book was designed as a supplement to Dr. Watts'. The hymns are 364 in number, and are arranged in the Biblical order of the texts. In the year 1838, some additional hymns were published, taken from Doddridge's MSS., in a book with the title, "Doddridge's Scripture Hymn Book," by John Doddridge Humphreys.

Of the hymns of Doddridge, Montgomery says, "They shine in the beauty of holiness ; these offsprings of his mind are arrayed in 'the fine linen, pure and white, which is the righteousness of saints;" and, like the saints, they are lovely and acceptable, not for their human merit (for in poetry and eloquence they are frequently deficient), but for that fervent unaffected love to God, His service, and His people, which distinguishes them.'"

In the number of hymns contributed, Doddridge stands third in the list of contributors to the "New Congregational Hymn Book," having supplied fifty hymns. Like all his other works, they are marked by their self-forgetful devotion to the high cause he served. As hymns, many of them are not above mediocrity, but some are of a high order, and others have some special excellencies. As one thoroughly familiar with the various public occasions in the history of Congregational Churches, Doddridge provided several very useful hymns for such occasions. For instance, he has supplied hymns 891, 893, and 896, to be sung at the "Ordination of Pastors," hymn 893 containing the characteristic verse :—

> "'Tis not a cause of small import
> The pastor's care demands ;
> But what might fill an angel's heart,
> And filled a Saviour's hands."

We also owe to him three good New-year Hymns (Nos. 954,

955, 956,) and two excellent Hymns for the Young, in whom he took a deep interest (Nos. 966, 967), the first commencing:

> "Ye hearts with youthful vigour warm,
> In smiling crowds draw near;
> And turn from every mortal charm,
> A Saviour's voice to hear."

And the second, containing the fine verse:—

> "Then let the wildest storms arise:
> Let tempests mingle earth and skies;
> No fatal shipwreck shall I fear;
> But all my treasures with me bear."

And to Doddridge we are indebted for one of our very best missionary hymns:—

> "Arise, my tenderest thoughts, arise."—No. 907.

In this hymn the most affecting considerations are gathered together into one dark picture, over which the agony of the writer sheds a still deeper gloom. Moved himself, the author moves the hearts of his readers; and stony must be the heart of the reader who, on reaching verse four, where the author reviews the whole scene, and turns what he sees into motives for Christian activity, should yet remain unaffected. His well-known words are:—

> "My God, I feel the mournful scene;
> And my heart bleeds for dying men;
> While fain my pity would reclaim,
> And snatch the firebrands from the flame."

The above hymn has in Doddridge's autograph MSS. the title, "Of beholding Transgressors with Grief," from Psalm cxix. 158. June 10, 1739."

To Doddridge, also, we owe one of our favourite Sunday hymns:

> "Lord of the Sabbath! hear our vows."—No. 765.

"The Eternal Sabbath," from Heb. iv. 9. Jan. 2, 1736-7.

One of Dr. Doddridge's best hymns,

> "While on the verge of life I stand,"

is not found in the "New Congregational Hymn Book." It is the poetic expression of a dream in which he seemed to meet with Christ, and to receive especial favours from Him, and to taste for a moment of the joys of the glorified.

Hymn 62 :

> "Gird on Thy conquering sword."

This begins with a different verse in Doddridge's Collection :

> "Loud to the Prince of Heaven."

> "O God of Bethel, by whose hand."—No. 285.

This has been erroneously attributed to Logan. It bears date in Doddridge's own manuscript, Jan. 16th, 1736-7. The text is given thus: "Jacob's Vow; from Gen. xxviii. 20—22." It was in Doddridge's Collection when Logan was a child, but Logan claimed it in its altered form as his own, in his "Poems, 1781." It is not certain whether even the alterations were his. These, also, were probably appropriated from Michael Bruce.

> "Grace! 'tis a charming sound."—No. 292.

This hymn resembles, and may have been taken from one by the Moravian hymn-writer, Esther Grünbeck, who was born at Gotha, 1717. Her hymn is No. 327 of the "Hymn Book of the United Brethren," and begins :—

> "Grace, grace, oh, that's a joyful sound!"

> "God of my life, through all its days."—No. 302.

This hymn may be read autobiographically, especially verse three, in reference to the peaceful thankfulness in his heart when the last wave of his life was ebbing out at Lisbon. The words are :—

> "When death o'er nature shall prevail,
> And all its powers of language fail,
> Joy through my swimming eyes shall break,
> And mean the thanks I cannot speak."

"Jesus, I love Thy charming name."—No. 326.

This was written to be sung after a sermon on, "Unto you that believe he is precious." (1 Pet. ii. 7.) The second verse begins:

> "Yes, Thou art precious to my soul."

"Hark! the glad sound, the Saviour comes."—No. 347.

"Christ's Message" from Luke iv. 18, 19. Dec. 28, 1735.

> "Behold the amazing sight." —No. 377.

"The soul attracted to a Crucified Saviour," from John xii. 32. May 8, 1737.

> "Now let our cheerful eyes survey."—No. 398.

"Christ bearing the names of his people on his heart," from Exod. xxviii. 29. No date in the MS.

> "O happy day, that fixed my choice."—No. 563.

This is mentioned as a favourite, and as an excellent hymn for any occasion of personal dedication.

> "Now let the feeble all be strong."—No. 614.

"Temptation moderated by the divine fidelity, power, and grace." (1 Cor. x. 13.) June 24, 1739.

> "Ye servants of the Lord."—No. 619.

This hymn deserves a separate notice as a favourite, and as distinguished for its force, unity, and closeness to Scripture.

> "Now let our mourning hearts revive."—No. 736.

This was composed on the "death of a minister," at Kettering, Aug. 22, 1736. The title is, "Comfort in God under the removal of ministers or other useful persons by death." (Joshua i. 2, 4, 5.)

> "Lord of the Sabbath! hear our vows."—No. 765.

This was written (1737) to be sung after a sermon on "There remaineth therefore a rest to the people of God."

"My God, and is Thy table spread?"—No. 861.

This is inserted as a Communion Hymn in the "Prayer Book of the Church of England." It was introduced by a University printer about half a century ago. He was a Dissenter, and filled up the blank leaves at the end of the Prayer Book with hymns he thought would be acceptable. The authorities did not interfere, and the hymns thus took their place. In some books there are two hymns by Doddridge, one probably by Wesley, one by Sternhold or J. Mardley, and Bishop Ken's Morning and Evening Hymns, altered and abridged. The other hymn by Doddridge in the Prayer Book is:

"High let us swell our tuneful notes."

It is not in the "New Congregational Hymn Book."

"Shepherd of Israel, bend Thine ear."—No. 844.

This was composed "at a Meeting of Ministers at Bedworth during their long vacancy, April 10, 1735."

"And will the great eternal God."—No. 884,

is headed, "On the Opening of a new Meeting-place at Oakham," from Psalm lxxxvii. 4.

"Let Zion's watchmen all awake."—No. 893.

This was written when the poet was from home—the name of the place cannot be deciphered—on the occasion of an ordination, October 21, 1736.

"Interval of grateful shade."—No. 943.

This hymn consists of twenty lines, taken from a piece of seventy lines, and entitled, "An Evening Hymn, to be used when composing one's self to sleep."

"Thou glorious Sovereign of the skies."—No. 916.

This is part of a hymn of ten stanzas, "For a Day of Public Humiliation; or, a Day of Prayer for the Revival of Religion." It begins in the original,

"Indulgent Sovereign of the skies."

"Thrice happy souls, who, born from heaven."—No. 983.

"Of spending the day with God," from Prov. xxiii. 17. March 27, 1737.

"Great God of heaven and earth, arise.—No. 996.

This is entitled in Doddridge's manuscript, "A Hymn for the Fast-day." January 9, 1739-40.

For several of the above notes on Dr. Doddridge's hymns the author of this work is indebted to W. S. Rooker, Esq., of Bideford, who has supplied them from an autograph MS., containing 100 hymns, and headed "Hymns written by P. D." The hymns are in some cases slightly different from the form in which they are given by Orton. The MS. is believed to be older than Orton's collection, but it is possible that Dr. Doddridge may have supplied Mr. Orton with variations that were not inserted in the MS. It is not difficult to trace the history of the MS. to its present possessor. Dr. Doddridge resided for a time in the house of a Mr. Shepherd, at Northampton, and took an interest in his son James, who was one of his students. When this young man died early in his ministry, a few of his sermons were printed, together with a funeral sermon by Dr. Doddridge, who composed expressly for the funeral occasion a hymn, beginning, "Jesus, we own Thy sovereign hand." A sister of this James Shepherd was Mrs. Lavington, the wife of the late Rev. Samuel Lavington, of Bideford, and grandmother of Mr. Rooker, the present possessor of the MS. The precious document is justly valued as an heirloom in the family.

JOHN WESLEY, M.A.

1703—1791.

The father of the Wesleys, the Rev. Samuel Wesley, rector of Epworth, Lincolnshire, was the son and grandson of ministers ejected from the Established Church in 1662; and the mother of the Wesleys was the daughter of the Rev. Dr. Annesley, the eminent Nonconformist divine. And to his mother's superior judgment John deferred in so important a matter as the employment of lay-agency in preaching the Gospel.

John was five years older than Charles. They were both born at Epworth. John was educated at the Charter House, London, and afterwards at Christ Church, Oxford. He became a fellow of Lincoln College, Oxford, and graduated M.A. in 1726. Of a serious disposition from his childhood, the religious element was developed in him by reading such works as the "De imitatione Christi," and Jeremy Taylor's "Holy Living and Dying."

During his time of study at Oxford, a small circle of young men became distinguished for their devoted piety and active usefulness. Of their number were George Whitefield, James Hervey, author of the "Meditations," Charles Wesley, the poet, and some others. They were called in derision "Methodists." Not the least promising member of this band was John Wesley. For the sake of enjoying the advantage of such religious association, he preferred to remain at Oxford instead of seeking, as his father recommended, the next presentation to the rectory at Epworth. He had previously assisted his father as a curate, but had returned to Oxford to fulfil the duties of his fellowship.

Impelled by missionary zeal, he went in company with his brother Charles, in 1735, on a mission to Georgia, to preach to the settlers and Indians. But, owing to personal differences, this mission was not successful. But, though unsuccessful, it was attended with most important results to the Wesleys, through the spiritual benefits they derived from the Moravian Christians, who sailed with them in the same ship. Thus they were brought under the influence of Spangenberg, Zinzendorf, whom they afterwards met, and especially Peter Böhler. Jackson, in his life of Charles Wesley, says, "The Wesleyan connexion owes to the Moravian Brethren a debt of respect and grateful affection which can never be repaid. Mr. John and Mr. Charles Wesley, with all their excellencies, were neither holy nor happy till they were taught by Peter Böhler that men are saved from sin, its guilt, dominion, and misery, by faith in Christ."

On his return to England, in 1738, John Wesley experienced a great religious change. This he attributed to God's blessing on his association with the Moravian brethren he met with in London, and the immediate cause of it was the reading of Luther's "Preface to the Epistle to the Romans." He had gone unwillingly on the 24th May to a meeting in London, where this was being read, and in that hour his heart was fully opened to the Gospel of Christ. The same year, he formed, in conjunction with Whitefield and others, the first Methodist society, at the Moravian Chapel, in Fetter Lane, London.

From that period to the end of his long and laborious life, he was constantly engaged in going from place to place to preach the Gospel. He met with much opposition and sometimes with personal violence, but this did not deter him from prosecuting his great work. He also spent much time in preparing his commentaries on the Bible, and his other theological works. But his chief work was the founding and organizing of the great and growing denomination that bears his name, and the provision he made for its introduction to other lands. His principal preaching places were London and Bristol. The ordinary course of his life was sometimes varied by occasional visits for religious purposes to Ireland, Scotland, the Channel Isles, and Holland. He also visited Zinzendorf, and the Moravian settlement at Herrnhut, in Upper Lusatia.

His separation from the Church of England arose from the force of circumstances, and not from choice. His whole system, with its lay-preaching, its services in rooms and in the open air, its separate societies, and its elaborate arrangements for discipline—was eschewed by the adherents of the Establishment as irregular, so that he had no alternative but to work separately. John Wesley was a good writer and preacher, and possessed extensive learning. He was a man of unfailing perseverance, great self-denial, large liberality, singular devotedness to the Master's service, and eminent piety. But perhaps his most remarkable gift was the power he possessed of making men willing to fall in with his purposes, and of organizing systematic action for the benefit of his followers.

About the year 1750, Wesley married Mrs. Vizelle, a widow with four children. But the union was not congenial, and after leaving her husband again and again, Mrs. Wesley left him in 1771 not to return. She died in 1781. Wesley left no children. He died in London, after a short illness, on the 2nd of March, 1791, in the eighty-eighth year of his age.

His prose works are too numerous to name. They appeared soon after his death in a collected edition of thirty-two vols. They include "A Translation of Thomas-à-Kempis;" "A Collection of Moral and Sacred Poems, from the most celebrated English authors, 1744," in three vols.; some "Histories;" and his own "Journal;" but they are chiefly theological. Mr. Wesley also established, in 1780, the "Arminian Magazine," afterwards called the "Methodist Magazine," and continued to edit it till his death.

Mr. Wesley regarded singing as an important part of public worship. He published a collection of tunes for the use of his followers, and did much by his own personal efforts to encourage psalmody.

He made the first Wesleyan "Collection of Psalms and Hymns," in 1738, and translated for it some German hymns. Several of these translations are used in the "New Congregational Hymn Book;" his name and the date of his translations are given under the names of the authors of the original pieces.

Most of the hymns in the first "Wesleyan Collection" were by Charles, who had a greater gift for hymn-writing, and to whom John left this part of the work. John also published some later collections, and his name was associated with his brother's in the production of some other collections.

In his college days, John gave promise of being a poet, but his subsequent absorbing pursuits called off his attention from poesy. He, however, wrote a few useful hymns. One of these is in the "New Congregational Hymn Book."

"Ho! every one that thirsts draw nigh."—No. 517.

It bears date 1740, only the first part of his hymn is given.

That we are indebted to John Wesley, and not to Charles, for the translations from the German is now generally admitted. There is no proof that Charles knew German; and in his sermon, "On knowing Christ after the flesh," John, speaking of the Moravians, twenty-six in number, whom he met with in his voyage to America, says, "We not only contracted much esteem, but a strong affection for them on all occasions. *I translated many of their hymns* for the use of our own congregations." It is justly argued, that if Charles had taken any part in the work of translation, John, who always acted with fairness and generosity to his brother, would have given him his share of the credit.

THE COUNTESS OF HUNTINGDON.
1707—1791.

THE great religious movement of the eighteenth century owed scarcely less to the labours and liberality of the Countess of Huntingdon than to the preaching and itinerancy of the great evangelical leaders themselves. Every faithful minister found in her an influential friend; her purse was open when money was required to erect chapels or to found colleges, and to train students for the ministry. Her wise counsels were as valuable as her piety and liberality, and she formed an important bond of union between the leaders of the new religious life and the higher ranks of society to which she by birth and family belonged. Even royalty itself was open to her; and George III., captivated by her piety and zeal, said to a complaining bishop : " I wish there was a Lady Huntingdon in every diocese in the kingdom.

Lady Huntingdon has enjoyed the advantage of having her memoir written by a member of the houses of Shirley and Seymour. From his extensive work we glean many of the following particulars. Selina Shirley was the second daughter of Washington, Earl Ferrars. She was born August 24th, 1707. At the age of nine, she received serious impressions while attending the funeral of a child. Some years after she was struck by a remark of her sister-in-law, Lady Margaret Hastings, "That since she had known and believed in the Lord Jesus Christ for life and salvation, she had been as happy as an angel." She was a stranger to such happiness. During a dangerous illness, which overtook her soon after, she sank into great depression of mind, and then rose in triumph and joy through prayer and faith in Jesus Christ.

In June, 1728, and before she had attained to her twenty-first year, the countess received the title by which she is known, by marrying Theophilus Hastings, Earl of Huntingdon. He was in sympathy with her in her religious pursuits, and they often went together to hear Whitefield, and other similar preachers, at the Moravian Chapel, Neville's-court, Fetter-lane, where the first Methodist Society was founded by Wesley, Whitefield, Ingham, and others, in 1738. This chapel was afterwards returned to the Moravians. The first Methodist Conference was held in Lady Huntingdon's house, in June, 1744, and Lady Huntingdon herself was a member of the first Methodist Society in Fetter-lane. Deeply impressed with the value of true religion, and feeling sure that she had received it from such men as Whitefield and Wesley, she willingly bore the obloquy that came upon her when she pleaded the cause of the despised Methodists. She encouraged Mr. Maxwell to expound the Scriptures before he was ordained, and thus opened the way for lay-agency. She threw open her house at Chelsea for the preaching of Whitefield; and there Lords Bolingbroke and Chesterfield, and many others of the aristocracy, heard him. When Doddridge, sinking in consumption, found it necessary to go to Lisbon, the countess gladly gave and collected the requisite funds.

The celebrated Romaine, turned out of St. George's, Hanover-square, was invited by the countess to preach at her house in Park-street. He became her chaplain, and her adviser in her work of chapel building and itinerancy of ministers for the preaching of the Gospel. She herself made tours with Whitefield, Romaine, and others, and accompanied them in their field-preaching and other works of usefulness. Mr. Romaine's success encouraged the countess to establish chapels in different parts of England, where they seemed to be needed. Some of the principal were those at Brighton, Bath, Bristol, Swansea, Chichester, Guildford, Basingstoke, Oathall, and there were others besides what was done in London. On the death of the Earl of Huntingdon, in 1746, she had the entire command of her fortune, which she employed without stint for religious purposes.

When the breach between Wesley and Whitefield took place, the Tabernacle, Moorfields, was used by the party of the latter. There Whitefield, Cennick, Ingham, and others of the Calvinistic school preached, and there the countess attended; and afterwards at Tottenham Court Chapel, which was opened in 1756, and at Long Acre Chapel. On the 24th August, 1768, the sixty-first anniversary of the countess's birthday, Mr. Whitefield preached at the opening of Trevecca College, South Wales, an institution for the training of ministers, which she had founded at her own expense. Many useful ministers were sent forth from this institution, and their ministry was especially blessed in Yorkshire, whither they had been invited. In 1792, after her death, this institution was removed to Cheshunt, where it has ever since been successfully carried on. And not long before her death, in order to assist her in her widely extended work, the " Connexion" was founded which continues to bear her name. It had not been the intention of the countess to leave the Established Church, but the ecclesiastical proceedings taken against her ministers rendered it necessary. The countess died as she had lived. Almost her last words were : " My work is done : I have nothing to do but to go to my Father." She died on the 17th of June, 1791, in her eighty-fourth year, at her house in Spa-fields, next to the chapel. The number of eminent ministers she associated with and assisted during her long life was remarkable. Several of them were hymn-writers In the list we find Watts, Wesley, Whitefield, Haweis, Rowland Hill and Hervey, Doddridge, Toplady and Romaine, Berridge, Ingham, Shirley, Perronet, De Courcy, and Fletcher of Madeley. At the time of her death there were more than sixty chapels in her "Connexion." Its legal form is a trust-deed bequeathing the chapels. The first four trustees were Dr. and Mrs. Haweis, Lady Ann Erskine, and Mr. Lloyd.

In 1764, the countess published her first collection of hymns. It is taken from the works of others, and consists of one hundred and seventy-nine hymns We give a part of the preface as illustrative of her earnestness and force of character. She says :—

"And now, reader, it is neither your approbation of these hymns nor the objections you can make to them that is the material point ; you are a creature of a day, and your heart, with trembling, often tells you this truth. Look well, then, for a refuge from the sins of your life past, and from the just fears of death and judgment fast approaching. This is the grand point which lieth altogether between God and thy own soul. And be assured that nothing can bring comfort in life or death to thee a sinner (and such thou now standest before God), but a Saviour so full and complete as Jesus is found to be.

" Bring Him, then, thy heart, miserable and evil as it is. He will make it happy ; He will keep it so ; and, by a loving constraint on all thy actions, make thee delight in His most holy ways. A title to the joys of an eternal world is purchased for thee by His obedience in life and death, and is that righteousness He will freely give here, which, whilst I am writing this, my heart importunately prays Him to give thee, reader, as the inestimable merit of His death."

This collection, after receiving previous additions, had reached three hundred and seventeen hymns in the fourth edition; the probable date of which is 1772. It was in this fourth edition that there appeared, for the first time, the striking and well-known hymn by the countess—

"Oh! when my righteous Judge shall come."

This, slightly altered, is given as No. 428 in the "New Congregational Hymn Book." The name of the authoress is omitted. It is part second of a piece on the Judgment-day, which has a first part of five verses, beginning :—

"We soon shall hear the midnight cry."

About the year 1774, her collection underwent a final revision by her brother-in-law, the Hon. and Rev. Walter Shirley, also one of our hymn-writers.

Although the countess was not much known as a hymn-writer, yet it is proved beyond doubt that she was the author of a few hymns of great excellence. Her biographer acknowledges this, although he has not spoken of it in his work, and it is known that a list of her own hymns existed, but was unfortunately lost. Dr. Doddridge, writing to his wife in 1748, speaks of preaching in her family, and hearing her sing, and adds: "I have stolen a hymn, which I steadfastly believe to be written by good Lady Huntingdon, and which I shall not fail to communicate to you." The countess had remarked the religious value of hymns to the Methodists in their work of revival, and she gave attention to the subject of psalmody, and obtained the services of an eminent Italian, Giardini, to make some suitable tunes. Horace Walpole says: "It will be a great acquisition to the Methodist sect to have their hymns set by Giardini."

Mr. Daniel Sedgwick, to whom hymnology owes so much, has recently shown, on what he believes to be good evidence, that the countess is the author of the hymn erroneously attributed to Robinson:—

"Come, thou fount of every blessing."—No. 666.

The evidence is as follows:—On some fly-leaves in a volume of "Hymns and Sacred Poems," by the Wesleys, 1747, there are some hymns written, including this, which the writer attributes to the Countess of Huntingdon. The writer is Diana Vandeleur, afterwards Diana Bindon. On a ticket of the Wesleyan Society that was in use about 1760, the maiden name of Vandeleur is found. This ticket is pasted over the writing, which appears to be of the same date as the hymns, and of course earlier than the ticket. The MS. of the hymns also appears to be written earlier than the autograph on the title-page, "Diana Bindon, 1759." Miss Vandeleur was a personal friend of the countess, and claims the hymn for her. Over against this evidence, we have the distinct claim made by Robinson himself, that he published this hymn in 1758. Mr. Sedgwick has also found a similar hymn by Robinson:—

"Hail! Thou source of every blessing,"

which he supposes accounts for the other being attributed to him by mistake. Two other verses are given in some collections, of which one is thought to be by the countess, or by Miss Vandeleur, and the last of these two verses is by Charles Wesley. It is in his fifty-first hymn, in his second volume of "Hymns and Sacred Poems," 1749.

Vide a fuller discussion of this question under *Robinson*.

CHARLES WESLEY, M.A.
1708—1788.

This eminent member of the Wesley family, to whom by common consent has been assigned the appellation of "the bard of Methodism," was the third son of Samuel Wesley, sen., and five years younger than his brother John, the founder of the Wesleyan denomination. He was at first educated at Westminster School, under his eldest brother Samuel; and afterwards proceeded to Oxford, where he graduated M.A.

His purpose was to remain in the capacity of a tutor at Oxford; but in 1735 he was prevailed upon to take orders and accompany his brother John as a missionary to Georgia. This was a colony in North America, intended for prisoners in this country who, having completed their time of imprisonment, found on their liberation no prospect in life. It was founded by General Oglethorpe, who took a deep interest in that class of sufferers. John and Charles Wesley went to the new colony as the missionaries of the Society for the Propagation of the Gospel in Foreign parts, and Charles became also secretary to the General. But, as he could not work harmoniously with him, he returned to England in the year 1736.

Up to this time he does not appear to have been personally in the possession of what he afterwards saw to be vital godliness. Writing in his diary in 1760, he says, "Just twenty-two years ago, I received the first grain of faith," *i.e.*, in the year 1738. The reading of Luther's "Commentary on the Epistle to the Galatians" was of the greatest spiritual service to him. Leaving the unsatisfying methods of self-righteousness, he found the better way of justification by faith. It was during an illness that he thus found "saving health." The pious conversation of Peter Böhler, a Moravian minister, of whom he speaks in his diary, April 19, 1738, and who went to visit him during his illness at Oxford, was very helpful to him. And he speaks of the benefit he received from a Mr. Bray, whom he describes as "a poor ignorant mechanic, who knows nothing but Christ."

In 1738, he mentions in his diary that he corrected George Whitefield's diary for the press. And in the same year he had to appear before the Bishop of London to answer for certain alleged irregularities in the fulfilment of his official duties. His zeal for Christ led him to overstep the restraints of system; and his earnest labours and evangelical doctrines awakened remark and aroused opposition.

For several years Charles united with his brother in the great work of preaching the Gospel to a dormant generation. His diary records the opposition he met with in his preaching tours, the perseverance with which he continued in his work, the rich blessing that sometimes attended his eloquent discourses, and the way in which the good cause took root in different parts of the country.

In the year 1749, he was united in marriage to Miss Sarah Gwynne, a lady of a good family in Brecknockshire; and after that time, he confined his preaching labours almost entirely to Bristol and London. Two of his sons, Charles and Samuel, had a remarkable talent for music, and became celebrated, the first as a performer from his early childhood, and the other as an eminent composer.

Leaving administrative arrangements and the advocacy of a system to John, who found in them congenial work, and willingly resigning to him the Calvin-like firmness that seems necessary to every great reformer, Charles, naturally cheerful in his piety, gladly became the hymn-writer of Wesleyanism. And it is in this capacity that his name lives, and will live amongst posterity. In respect to hymn-writing, John willingly assigned the palm to his more poetical brother; while, on his part, Charles benefited by the co-operation of John, who, with severer taste, pruned away the luxuriance of his brother's productions to the advantage of what remained. There was one respect in which John had the advantage of Charles, he was familiar with German; and this knowledge enabled him to enrich his collection with translations from Gerhard, Tersteegen, and Zinzendorf. The prominence of Charles in the department of hymn-writing may be judged by the fact that in the "Wesleyan Hymn Book," of 770 hymns—623 are by Charles Wesley, and the contributor next in respect to number, is not John, but Dr. Watts, who supplies 66 hymns.

The following is a list of the principal poetical works written by Charles or produced by him in conjunction with his brother, with the dates in most cases of the first edition of each work, marking its place in the life of the writer. We have taken pains to make the following list of works as accurate as possible. It is, in itself, a literary curiosity, and perhaps unparalleled in the history of hymn-making:—

"A Collection of Psalms and Hymns," by John Wesley, London, 1738, the first collection of all; "Hymns and Sacred Poems," different volumes in 1739, 1740, and 1742, and two additional volumes, with the same title, in 1749; "Hymns on God's Everlasting Love," by C. Wesley, 1741; "Elegy on the Death of Robert Jones, Esq.," by C. Wesley, 1742; a poem of about six hundred lines. Mr. Jones was a fellow-collegian with Charles Wesley, and a convert to Christ through the labours of the Methodists. "A Collection of Psalms and Hymns," first published by John Wesley, in 1741, and in later editions added to by Charles. " Hymns for the Watch Nights," by C. Wesley, about 1744; "Hymns on the Lord's Supper," by C. Wesley, 1745. To this work was prefixed a Spiritual treatise by a clergyman, Dr. Brevint, on " The Christian Sacrament and Sacrifice." The hymns are a kind of paraphrase of the treatise. This work had a great sale. "Hymns for Times of Trouble and Persecution," by C. Wesley, 1744; "Hymns for the Nativity of our Lord," by C. Wesley, second edition, 1745; "Hymns for those that seek and those that have found Redemption in the blood of Jesus Christ," by C. Wesley, 1746; "Hymns for our Lord's Ascension," by J. and C. Wesley, 1746; "Hymns for our Lord's

Resurrection," by C. Wesley, 1746; "Hymns of Petition and Thanksgiving for the promise of the Father," J. and C. Wesley, 1746; "Hymns for the Public Thanksgiving Day, October 9th, 1746," by C. Wesley; "Hymn to the Trinity," by C. Wesley, 1746; "Graces before and after Meat," by C. Wesley, about 1746; "Hymns for New Year's Day," J. and C. Wesley, 1750, and several other years to 1788; "Hymns occasioned by the Earthquake in 1750," by C. Wesley; "Hymns and Spiritual Songs for the use of real Christians of every denomination," by J. and C. Wesley, 1753; "Hymns of Intercession for all mankind," by C. Wesley, 1758; "Hymns on the Expected Invasion," by C. Wesley, 1759; "Funeral Hymns," by C. Wesley, 1759; "Hymns for those to whom Christ is All in All," by C. Wesley, 1761; "Hymns to be used on the Thanksgiving day, November 29th, 1759," by C. Wesley; "Hymns for the use of the Methodist Preachers," by C. Wesley, given in J. Wesley's "Reasons against a Separation from the Church of England," 1760; "Short Hymns on select passages of the Holy Scriptures," by C. Wesley, 1762. This is an extensive work. In the first edition there were 2,145 hymns, and some of considerable length, though the majority are in accordance with the title of the work. This work is said to have been revised by the author eight times after it was finished. "Hymns for Children and others of riper years," by J. and C. Wesley, 1763; "Elegy on the late Rev. George Whitefield," by C. Wesley, 1771; "Preparation for Death," by C. Wesley, 1772; "Hymns for Families," by C. Wesley; "Hymns written in the time of the Tumults," June, 1780, by C. Wesley: "Hymns for the Nation, in 1782;" "Prayers for Condemned Malefactors," 1785,—this was the last work he sent from the press,—the prayers are given in hymns; and also, a "Poetical Version of nearly the whole of the Psalms of David," by C. Wesley, recently discovered, and re-published in 1854.

Some of the above works consist of only a few pages, others of several hundred. They show that the poet was continually producing new works, and it is recorded that he died almost in the act of poetical composition. Of some of the above works several editions appeared during the author's life, and other editions were published afterwards.

In the preface to his collection, which consisted for the most part of Charles's hymns, John says, "In these hymns there is no doggerel, no botches, nothing put in to patch up the rhyme: no feeble expletives. Here is nothing turgid or bombast, on the one hand; or low and creeping, on the other. Here are no cant expressions, no words without meaning. Here are (allow me to say) both the purity, the strength, and the elegance of the English language, and at the same time the utmost simplicity and plainness, suited to every capacity!" And this statement is not exaggeration, but the simple truth.

As a hymn-writer, Charles Wesley takes his place by the side of Dr. Watts; and it is an open question to which the preference should be given. Wesley certainly surpassed Watts in the number and average excellence of his hymns. In these respects Wesley stands first in the whole history of Christian literature. Of Dr. Watts's numerous hymns, many must be rejected as poor and altogether below the average. There is nothing to choose between the two writers in respect to their adherence to Scripture and their knowledge of Christian experience: in these respects both leave nothing to desire. But each writer shows some traces of the influence of the system he maintained; Wesley speaking more of the active effort and perfectibility of man, and Watts more of the helplessness of man and the sovereign will of God.

And if we occasionally meet with a verse in the hymns of the Wesleys that does not commend itself to our judgments, nor seem exactly in harmony with Scripture, the following note given in the preface to the "Hymns and Sacred Poems," 1739, may remove our astonishment. It shows that some of the hymns were produced before the authors were rooted and grounded in the faith. It is as follows:—"Some verses, it may be observed, in the following collection were wrote upon the scheme of the mystic divines; and these, it is owned, we once had in great veneration, as the best explainers of the gospel of Christ. But we are now convinced that we therein greatly erred, not knowing the Scriptures, neither the power of God."

In Charles Wesley's verses we trace the influence of his careful classical training, though this is less manifest than we might have expected. Hymn 570—

" O, Thou who camest from above,"

may be taken as an illustration. It is a hymn worthy of Addison, but with a more decidedly Christian character than he would have given it. We notice in it for commendation, the unity of the whole, and the varied and appropriate imagery employed to illustrate the different aspects of thought introduced. There is a classical finish in this and other pieces, wanting in the hymns of Dr. Watts. Wesley also owed something to the influence of the Moravian Christians, with whom he had much spiritual intercourse. They are thought to have influenced John's system; they certainly influenced Charles's spiritual songs. For proof of this, we may refer to Hymns 503 and 528, but we will especially refer to No. 362—

" O, Love Divine, how sweet thou art!"

This is one of Wesley's best hymns. For its delight in interior spiritual blessedness, and its warm impassioned expressions of desire after the love of God, it may be compared with the best productions of Saint Bernard. Aided by his spiritual German friends, Wesley has here reached a strain of thought and expression we should in vain search for in the writings of Watts. And Wesley is free from the minor blemishes of Dr. Watts—bad rhymes or rhymes omitted where they are required. Nor would our view of Charles Wesley as a hymn-writer be complete if we did not recognize in some of his hymns the presence of decided genius, giving them a place amongst the best productions of the muses. Hymn 631—

" Come on, my partners in distress,"

is a favourable example. All must feel the force and poetry of such lines as—

> "On faith's strong eagle-pinions rise,
> And force your passage to the skies,
> And scale the mount of God."

Neither Wesley nor Watts have left any one great poem. Wesley will, perhaps, be judged to have best maintained his claim to the name of poet, but the question of which is the better hymn-writer must still, we think, be left undecided. Even the greatest admirers of Charles Wesley admit that Watts excels him in the sweeter flow of his numbers, and in those of his hymns which are designed to administer comfort to the afflicted. Watts is certainly very happy in describing the safety and happiness of God's people, as we may see in hymns 132 and 213, and in many others. We also observe in him, along with unaffected simplicity, a manifestation of conscious strength that is very pleasing. Free from exaggeration and painful effort, nature itself speaks to us.

Take for instance, (No. 17)—

> "The heavens declare Thy glory, Lord,"

his rendering of the 19th Psalm. Notice its happy presentation of the original, its Christian application, its practical aim, the noble apostrophe of the fifth verse—

> "Great Sun of Righteousness, arise;"

and the strength, beauty, and sublimity of the whole. By such productions Watts has taken a position of peerless excellence. As a further illustration, take Watts's admirable hymn—

> "Blest morning, whose young dawning rays."—No. 755.

Charles Wesley did not stand alone as a hymn-writer. Besides the relation in which he stood to his brother John in this respect, his diary shows the association he had with John Cennick, Edward Perronet, Count Zinzendorf, and other hymn-writers of his day.

Next to Dr. Watts, Charles Wesley is the largest contributor to the "New Congregational Hymn-Book." Watts supplies 391 hymns, Wesley, 74. In the old "Congregational Hymn-Book" there were only 34 by Charles Wesley. Several of his hymns are shortened, and some are slightly altered.

The greater proportion of his hymns are taken from the volumes entitled "Hymns and Sacred Poems," and published in 1739, and in several later years; but some are from the hymns written at different times on special subjects.

For example: Hymn 313—

"Ye servants of God,"

is from "Hymns for Times of Trouble, &c." Hymn 323—

"Light of those, whose dreary dwelling,"

is from "Hymns for the Nativity, &c." Hymns 820, 869, 876, are from "Hymns on the Lord's Supper." Hymns 296, 564, 566, 570, 822, 898, are from "Short Hymns on Select Passages of Scripture." Hymns 364, 661, 780, are from "Hymns for those that seek, and those that have found, &c." Hymn 394—

"God is gone up on high,"

is from "Hymns for our Lord's Ascension." Hymn 437 is from "Hymns of Petition, &c., for the Promise of the Father." It is in the original—

"Spirit of Faith, come down."

Hymn 487 is from "Hymns for Children, &c." Hymn 503—

"Would Jesus have the sinner die?"

is from "Hymns on God's Everlasting Love."

"Head of the Church triumphant!"—No. 316.

This noble hymn, worthy of the pen of Luther, derives interest from the circumstances in which it was written. It appeared in "Hymns for Times of Trouble and Persecution," 1745. England was at war with France and Spain. Many outrages were taking place throughout the country, and the Wesleyan preachers were often the victims of false charges and persecution.

"Jesus, the name to sinners dear."—No. 327.

This is part of a hymn (1749) beginning—

"Jesus, the Name high over all."

"O, for a thousand tongues to sing."—No. 330.

The original hymn extended to eighteen verses. The first verse here was the seventh. Burgess says, "This is part of a hymn written originally *for the anniversary day of one's conversion. It was probably composed about May, 1739, just a year after the period when the two brothers were first brought into the enjoyment of Christian liberty.*" It appeared in "Hymns and Sacred Poems," 1739. It began with the words—

"Glory to God and praise and love."

"Hark! the herald angels sing,
Glory to the new-born King."—No. 345.

This is entitled a "Hymn for Christmas Day." Two verses are omitted. Charles wrote it (1739)—

"Hark! how all the welkin rings,
Glory to the King of kings."

John Wesley altered it to its present form.

"All ye that pass by."—No. 375.

This is the first hymn in Mr. Wesley's celebrated "Pocket Hymn Book for the use of Christians of all Denominations," 1785. That work included numerous additional hymns, and some that might not be readily understood in a congregation, but were useful for private reading, and for the "still hour" of thought.

"Rejoice, the Lord is King."—No. 406.

This is from a tract containing sixteen hymns, and entitled "Hymns for our Lord's Resurrection, 1746."

"Lo! He comes with clouds descending."—No. 418.

The part C. Wesley had in the production of this hymn is stated in the article "John Cennick." The hymn was given by C. Wesley in his "Hymns of Intercession for all Mankind," 1758. At that time England, as well as nearly the whole of Europe, was at war. The tract contains forty hymns suited to the circumstances of the country, including hymns for the fleet and army, for prisoners and enemies, as well as hymns for the King and the authorities.

"Ye virgin souls, arise."—No. 422.

This is one of the "Hymns for the Watchnight," about 1744. The last verse—

"Then let us wait to hear,
The trumpet's welcome sound," &c.,

gave a true expression to the feeling of religious excitement and expectation felt by the midnight worshippers. Crowther, in his "Portraiture of Methodism," says on this subject, "A.D. 1742. The first watchnight was held in London. The custom originated with the colliers of Kingswood, near Bristol, who had been in the habit, when slaves to sin, of spending every Saturday night at the alehouse. They now devoted that night to prayer and singing of hymns. Mr. Wesley, hearing of this, and of the good that was done, resolved to make it general. At first he ordered watchnights to be kept once a month, when the moon was at the full, and afterwards fixed them for once a quarter."

"Thou God of glorious Majesty."—No. 424.

Charles Wesley visited the Land's-end, in July, 1743, about the time this piece was written; and it has been supposed that the peculiar nature of the scenery there, where a neck of land stretches out between the Bristol and English channels, suggested the imagery of verse two—

"Lo! on a narrow neck of land,
'Twixt two unbounded seas I stand."

Jackson, in his life of Charles Wesley, says that this account rests only on tradition, but that it is on record that the following hymn was written by Charles Wesley on the occasion of his visit to the Land's End, and sung there—

> "Come, Divine Immanuel, come,
> Take possession of Thy home;
> Now Thy mercy's wings expand,
> Stretch throughout the happy land," &c.

The verses are founded on the words of Isaiah viii. 8 :—"He shall reach even to the neck, and the stretching out of his wings shall fill the breadth of thy land, O Immanuel." Hymn 424 is headed, "A Hymn of Seriousness." It may have referred to the visit, but the author has not connected it therewith.

> "Come, Holy Ghost, our hearts inspire."—No. 429.

This is a hymn to be used "Before reading the Scriptures." The second verse is sometimes sung in Wesleyan chapels just before the sermon.

> "Father of all, in whom alone."—No. 469.

This also is a hymn to be used "Before reading the Scriptures." These two (429 and 469) first appeared in "Hymns and Sacred Poems," 1740.

> "Come, O Thou all-victorious Lord."—No. 522.

This was composed by Charles Wesley, in June, 1746, before preaching at Portland, in Dorsetshire, where the people were mostly employed in the stone quarries. Hence perhaps the lines—

> "Strike with the hammer of Thy word,
> And break these hearts of stone."

They are almost an exact rendering of Jeremiah xxiii. 29—"Is not my word . . . like a hammer that breaketh the rock in pieces?"

> "Depth of mercy! can there be
> Mercy still reserved for me."—No. 528.

An actress, in a provincial town, overhearing this hymn being given out by one of a small company assembled in a cottage for worship, was struck by it, and entered and joined in their worship. She obtained the book containing the words, and by reading it, under God's blessing, her heart was changed. This led her to leave the stage; but on one occasion being prevailed on for once to act a part she had often acted, she could utter only these words, which she did to the astonishment of the audience. She afterwards led a Christian life, and became the wife of a Christian minister.

"Author of faith, eternal Word."—No. 540.

This is part of a paraphrase and amplification of the eleventh chapter of the Epistle of the Hebrews, entitled "The Life of Faith Exemplified," and consisting of eighty-eight stanzas.

"Jesus, refuge of my soul."—No. 550.

Wesley wrote it, 1740—
"Jesus, *lover* of my soul."

"Lord, if Thou the grace impart."—No. 581.

This is erroneously attributed in the "New Congregational" to Madan. It is by Charles Wesley, 1741.

"Soldiers of Christ, arise."—No. 624.

This is part of a piece consisting of sixteen double stanzas, and forming a spirited paraphrase and versification of Ephesians vi. 11—18:—"Put on the whole armour of God," &c. It appeared first in "Hymns and Sacred Poems," 1749.

"Stay, thou insulted Spirit, stay."—No. 643.

This hymn, bearing date 1749, is of an autobiographical character; and in the original the fourth line of the second stanza was—

"For *forty* long rebellious years."

"God of my life, whose gracious power."—No. 665.

The original has fifteen stanzas, and is entitled, "At the Approach of Temptation." It refers to incidents in the author's life; his deliverance from shipwreck, sickness, and death. The last line of verse four stood in the original—

"*The fever* own'd Thy touch and fled!"

This hymn appeared in "Hymns and Sacred Poems," 1740.

"Come, let us join our friends above."—No. 708.

This soul-moving hymn is found in an anonymous tract containing forty-three hymns, and entitled, "Funeral Hymns, London. Printed in the year 1759." John Wesley concurred with those who gave a first place to his brother's "Funeral Hymns."

"Come, Thou Almighty King."—No. 782.

This is an imitation of our National Anthem. It appeared in one of Charles Wesley's halfpenny leaflets, 1757, and is believed to be by him. The date and author of the National Anthem have not yet been discovered. It first appeared in print in the "Gentleman's Magazine" for 1745, where it is called "A Song for Two Voices." The insertion of the above-mentioned hymn in the Appendix to "Madan's Collection," third edition, 1764, led to its being erroneously attributed to Madan.

"Lord, I believe a rest remains."—No. 799.

The original (1740) extends to seventeen stanzas.

"See how great a flame aspires."—No. 817.

This animated and jubilant hymn was written in the time of the author's success amongst the Newcastle colliers, and it is thought that the imagery of the first verse was suggested by the large fires burning there by night. It appeared in "Hymns and Sacred Poems," 1739.

"Brother in Christ and well-beloved."—No. 841.

This is part of a long hymn by C. Wesley, 1740, beginning, "Brethren in Christ and well-beloved," and headed "Admission of Members."

"Blest be the dear uniting love."—No. 847.

Three stanzas are omitted. The last line in verse 2 was originally—

"And *do His work* below."

This hymn appeared in "Hymns and Sacred Poems," 1742.

"Lamb of God, whose bleeding love."—No. 869.

This hymn appeared in 1745 in the "Hymns for the Lord's Supper."

"Come, Father, Son, and Holy Ghost."—No. 859.

In the original (1749) this hymn appears to countenance the unprofitable doctrine of "apostolical succession." In the "New Congregational" it is much altered to avoid that error.

"For ever here my rest shall be."—No. 875.

This is part of a hymn (1740) beginning

"Jesus, Thou art my righteousness."

"Give me the faith which can remove."—No. 887.

One of C. Wesley's excellent hymns, "For a Preacher of the Gospel."

"Blow ye the trumpet, blow!"—No. 923.

This hymn, sometimes erroneously attributed to Toplady, was one of seven—six of which appeared for the first time—contained in a tract entitled "Hymns for New Year's Day," and published in 1755.

"The Lord of earth and sky."—No. 961.

One of C. Wesley's "New Year Hymns"—an improvement and application of the Scripture parable of the "barren fig-tree," bearing date 1749.

THOMAS SCOTT.

Died about 1776.

"Hasten, O sinner, to be wise."—No. 492.

This writer must not be confounded with the well-known commentator who flourished a generation later. The subject of this sketch was the son of a dissenting minister at Norwich, and a nephew of Dr. Daniel Scott, an eminent minister and author. He was born at Norwich, where he received his early education. In the early part of his ministerial life he resided at Wartmell, near Harleston, in Norfolk, and kept a boarding-school, preaching once a month at Harleston. About 1733 he settled in the ministry at Lowestoft, in Suffolk. But finding the air too keen for his delicate constitution, he removed in 1737 to be co-pastor with Mr. Baxter, minister of the Presbyterian congregation at Ipswich, and in the year 1740 he succeeded to the sole pastorate on the death of Mr. Baxter. This he continued till 1761, and then with assistance held his position till 1774. At that time his health became so enfeebled that he found it necessary to resign his position at Ipswich. But he still exercised his ministry at Hupton, in Norfolk, till the time of his death about two years after.

Mr. Scott was the author of "A Father's Instructions to his Son, 1748," a pleasing and affectionate poem, full of wise and weighty advice to his son; also of "The Table of Cebes; or, the Picture of Human Life, in English verse, with notes, 1754." This is a poem full of high-toned morality, describing in a graphic manner the snares and mistaken principles of life, and suggesting the true principle and way. He also published some sermons and "Lyric Poems and Hymns, devotional and moral, 1773." His largest work is "The Book of Job, in English verse; translated from the original Hebrew, with remarks historical, critical, and explanatory, 1771;" second edition, 1774, a work valued more for its learning than for its poetic merit. For some of these particulars we are indebted to Walter Wilson's valuable MS. record, deposited at Dr. Williams's Library.

JAMES FANCH,
1764.

Vide under the following name.

DANIEL TURNER, M.A.
1710—1798.

DANIEL TURNER was born March 1st, 1710. He was originally a schoolmaster, but in 1748 he became pastor of the Baptist Church at Abingdon, Berkshire. He was the author of a work on the subject of full Christian communion among the churches of his own denomination, and of a work entitled " A Compendium of Social Religion." His "Divine Songs, Hymns, and other Poems" bears date 1747. And his work "Poems Devotional and Moral" was privately printed in 1794.

" Jesus, full of all compassion,"—No. 551,

is an ardent, impassionate Bernard-like hymn. It is altered from the original. And there is another hymn by Turner in the " New Congregational Hymn Book," sufficient by itself to establish a reputation—

" Beyond the glittering starry skies.—No. 389.

It is somewhat altered, and erroneously attributed to Grigg. The authorship is proved in a note dated February 22nd, 1791, and inserted in the " Baptist Register." It is from Mr. Turner to Dr. Rippon, the editor, and is as follows:—" As to your inquiry concerning the hymn, ' Jesus seen of Angels,' it is true, as you were told by our good brother Medley, that one part of it was made by my dear friend, the Rev. James Fanch, of Rumsey, and the other part by me." The original hymn consists of twenty-eight verses, and is given in full in the "Baptist Memorial" for 1849. Turner wrote by far the larger portion of the twenty-eight verses, and they appeared in his "Poems," 1794. The hymn as it given in the "New Congregational" appears with the addition of one verse in the "Gospel Magazine," June, 1776, with the signature "F," and it is believed that Fanch wrote the first part of the piece.

Rev. James Fanch was the author of a "Paraphrase on a select number of the Psalms of David, done from the Latin of Buchanan, to which are added some occasional pieces," 1764. "Free Thoughts on Practical Religion," &c., 1768, and of "Ten Sermons on Practical Subjects," 1768.

ELIZABETH SCOTT.
Lived about 1764.

In Dr. Dodd's "Christian Magazine" for 1764, there are a few hymns by this authoress, who is believed to have been the daughter of a dissenting minister.

"All hail, incarnate God!"—No. 412.

This is hymn 386 in "Dobell's Collection," 1806, where it has the name "Scott." The second verse beginning—

"To Thee the hoary head,"

has this note—"Composed on seeing an Aged Saint and a Youth taken into Church communion together." It is to be regretted that we have no more particulars of Miss Scott. Her hymns are very good.

JOHN NEEDHAM.

John Needham was a Baptist minister. He was for some years pastor of the Baptist church at Hitchin, Hertfordshire. Thence he removed, in the year 1746, to become co-pastor with the Rev. John Beddome, at the chapel in the Pithay, Bristol. In 1752, being violently cast out of his position (a controversy having arisen on the subject of having two pastors), he removed with a part of the congregation to Callowhill, another part of Bristol, where he remained till 1787. In 1768, his " Hymns Devotional and Moral" were printed at Bristol. They are 263 in number. They are pleasing in character, and full of scriptural and spiritual thought, but the versification is slovenly. The first and third lines of the four-line verses do not rhyme.

"Fountain of mercy, God of love."—No. 950.

This is erroneously attributed to Needham in the " New Congregational Hymn Book." The versification is superior to his. It is by Anne Flowerdew, *vide* under her name.

"To praise the ever-bounteous Lord,"—No. 951,

is No. 56 in the above-mentioned collection. It is a pleasing harvest hymn, but verse 3 may be said to be entirely devoid of rhyme. There is an additional verse in the original hymn.

JOSEPH GRIGG.
Died 1768.

We have but little on record concerning this hymn-writer, whose few but well-known hymns encircle his name with interest. He seems to have justified the Latin poet's saying, "*poeta nascitur non fit!*" for he wrote one of his best hymns at the age of ten. He was at first in humble circumstances. Dr. Belcher speaks of him as "a labouring mechanic." Afterwards he entered the ministry. From 1743 to 1747 he was assistant minister to the Rev. Thomas Bures, pastor of the Presbyterian Church, Silver Street, London. During this period Mr. Grigg wrote some of his hymns. Two of his hymns are dated March, 1744, and one February, 1745. In the year 1747 Mr. Bures died, after carrying on a successful ministry at Silver Street for twenty-five years; and at his death Mr. Grigg retired from the pastorate, married the widow of Colonel Drew, a lady of considerable property, and went to St. Albans. There he continued to write and preach. In 1756, some of his compositions in prose and poetry appeared in " Miscellanies on Moral and Religious Subjects, &c., published by and for Elizabeth Harrison." And, in the same year, he published a Fast Sermon "On the Threatened Invasion of 1756." At the end there is a fine forcible hymn, beginning—

" Shake, Britain, like an aspen shake! "

and ending—

" Britons shall feel and feeling own,
God is her shield and God alone ;
And heart and voice, and life shall sing,
To God the Universal King."

Mr. Grigg also contributed twelve hymns to the " Christian's Magazine " for 1765 and 1766. And in 1765, three years before the author's death, a small anonymous tract was published with the following title :—" Four Hymns on Divine Subjects, wherein the Patience and Love of our Divine Saviour is displayed." Two of these four were Nos. 509 and 622 in the " New Congregational Hymn Book," of which the latter had been written many years before. In 1806, a posthumous tract was published, entitled " Hymns by the late Rev. Joseph Grigg, Stourbridge ;" and Mr. Daniel Sedgwick has published what he believes to be a complete collection of Mr. Grigg's poetical productions. It is entitled " Hymns on Divine Subjects," &c., 1861, and consists of forty hymns, many of them founded on passages of scripture ; and seventeen short moral pieces called " Serious Poems." Most of the hymns want the special excellence of those by which Mr. Grigg is known. They do not reveal any of the personal experiences of the author. They are all poetical in form and diction, free from special faults, full of scriptural sentiment and doctrine, and here and there the author seems to be on the point of entering the higher rank of hymn-writers.

Mr. Thomas Greene, of Ware, also one of our hymn-writers,

wrote an "Elegy on the death of the Rev. Joseph Grigg," in which he speaks of him as the friend of the poor, the charm of the social circle, and the attractive and useful preacher. He says—

> "The pious Grigg has bid our world adieu!
> Who long dispensed delight and profit too.
> Death has in silence seal'd th' instructive tongue,
> That used to captivate the list'ning throng :
> No more he stands to plead a Saviour's name,
> And these cold hearts of ours with love inflame ;
> No more he shows the path where duty lies,
> That path of pleasure leading to the skies."

"Beyond the glittering starry skies,"—No. 389,

attributed in the "New Congregational" to Grigg is not by him, but by Daniel Turner and James Fanch, *vide* page 147.

"Behold a stranger at the door."—No. 509.

Five verses not inferior in excellence are omitted from this hymn. Slight alterations are made in other verses, and in what stands here as the 5th verse, an important alteration, and we think, an improvement, is made.

The original is—

> "Admit Him ; for you can't expel ;
> Where'er He comes, He comes to dwell."

The altered reading is—

> "No mortal tongue their joys can tell,
> With whom He condescends to dwell."

"Jesus, and can it ever be?"—No. 622.

This was composed when the author was ten years of age. As a marvel of precocious talent it takes its place along with Milton's psalm—

"Let us with a gladsome mind,"—No. 229,

written at the age of fifteen. It was first altered from the original by the Rev. Benjamin Francis. He is said to have supplied a copy to the "Gospel Magazine," and to have given the name and age of the author. The hymn appears in the "Gospel Magazine" for April, 1774, with the title " Shame of Jesus conquered by Love, by a child of ten years." Five verses are given, but there is no author's name mentioned. Two verses of slightly inferior merit are omitted here, the other verses are not materially altered.

WILLIAM HAMMOND, B.A.
Died 1783.

William Hammond was of St. John's College, Cambridge, and graduated B.A., and in 1744 he published "Médulla Ecclesiæ: the doctrines of original sin, &c., stated and demonstrated from the homilies of the Church of England." This reached a second edition, and was reprinted in America. He is said to have afterwards been one of the early Calvinistic Methodist preachers, and, subsequently, with his friend Cennick, he joined the Moravian Brethren. He was interred in their burying-ground at Chelsea, London. He also published some discourses, and left in manuscript an autobiography, written in Greek. His "Psalms, Hymns, and Spiritual Songs, and Discourses," were published in 1745.

We are indebted to him for the vigorous heart-stirring hymn—

"Awake, and sing the song."—No. 339.

The original is found at page 84 of the work of 1745 just referred to. In the original the hymn consists of 14 stanzas, and headed, "Before singing of hymns, by way of introduction."

"Lord, we come before Thee now."—No. 785.

This is part of a piece of eight stanzas of eight lines given at page 32 of the same work. Hammond's hymns are full of Scripture truth, and of the experience of the Christian. He says in the preface, "In the following pages are a number of hymns suited to the various states and capacities of the children of God."

JAMES GRANT.
Died 1785.

The date of James Grant's birth is not ascertained. His parents, after giving him a sound religious education, apprenticed him to an ironmonger in Edinburgh, where he afterwards carried on a business on his own account during the greater part of his life. In 1731 he married his first wife. This union continued till her death, in 1771, and during this period several children were born. In 1779 Mr. Grant married his second wife, who survived him. She was a daughter of the Rev. Mr. Plenderleath, one of the ministers of the Tolbooth Church, Edinburgh.

Mr. Grant's high character as a man of business talent, unswerving integrity, and Christian benevolence, commended him to the notice of his fellow-citizens, and he was repeatedly appointed a member of the Town Council. In 1746 and 1747 he held the office of Treasurer to the Town Council of Edinburgh; in 1749 and 1752 he was elected to the Magistracy, and during 1754 and 1755 he served as Dean of Guild. He was a member of the Established Church of Scotland, and belonged to the congregation of the Tolbooth Church; and his religious principles were so decided that he paid a fine rather than attend the services of a city church, where, as he believed, the Gospel was not preached. If he had accepted the office of Lord Provost, or Chief Magistrate, he would have been obliged to have attended that church regularly. Hence he declined those highest offices when they were open to him.

Mr. Grant was a friend of good men, and an advocate and supporter of pious and benevolent institutions. In particular, he took a deep interest in the Orphan Hospital in Edinburgh—an institution established in 1733, and subsequently much increased by the exertions of the Rev. George Whitefield. To this institution Mr. Grant devoted the profits of the first and second editions of his poems. For many years he was a great sufferer, and during the latter part of his life his sufferings were very severe; but he bore all with patience, and at the close spoke of himself as one looking back with gratitude on the blessings God had given him, and waiting to be for ever with the Lord. He died on the 1st of January, 1785.

His hymns and poems were written to provide Christian words for the Scotch melodies, of which he was very fond. These words were to be used instead of the objectionable terms ordinarily used. His pieces were not intended to be printed, but were published, at the request of friends, first in 1784, with the title, "Original Hymns and Poems, written by a private Christian for his own use." The second edition was posthumous in 1820, and Mr. Daniel Sedgwick published a reprint of the work in 1862, with a biographical sketch of the author. The work consists of sixteen hymns and six poems, all full of scriptural thoughts, and some of them rich in Christian experience. The versification is easy, and the sentiment always good; but there is little manifestation of poetical talent. One hymn and a poem, "On the reviving of Religion, in the year 1741-2," were first published in the Rev. George Whitefield's "Christian History," in 1742.

"O Zion, afflicted with wave upon wave.'—No. 610.

This is, we think, Grant's best piece. It was written to the air of the "Yellow-haired Laddie." In the "New Congregational Hymn Book," one inferior verse is omitted, and the other verses are slightly altered.

JOSEPH HART.

1712—1768.

For the particulars of the history of this sacred poet we are indebted to his own "Experience," as it is given in his preface to his collection of hymns. He was born of pious parents in London, in 1712. He received a good education, and was occupied at first as a teacher of languages. At the time when he was arriving at the age of manhood, he felt anxiety with regard to his spiritual interests. But, for several years, he was satisfied with a course in which repentance was again and again followed by a return to sin.

At length, a great domestic affliction was made the occasion of his obtaining an affecting sense of the sinfulness of his state. Then followed a strange condition of spiritual perversion, in which he even gloried in his supposed liberty of sinning. He says: "In this abominable state I continued—a loose backslider—an audacious apostate—a bold-faced rebel—for nine or ten years, not only committing acts of lewdness myself, but infecting others with the poison of my delusions. I published several pieces on different subjects, chiefly translations of the ancient heathens, to which I prefixed prefaces, and subjoined notes of a pernicious tendency, and indulged a freedom of thought far unbecoming a Christian." His work on "The Unreasonableness of Religion" is dated 1741.

Subsequently, he became the subject of compunctions of conscience, which led to reformation of conduct. But he was still self-righteous and morally dead, and at times, in pride of heart, even denied the necessity for an atonement. In 1757, after a period in which feelings of despondency alternated with feelings of hope, he had an "amazing view of the agony of Christ in the garden," and received an impression too deep ever to be obliterated. This was followed by great distress for having so culpably misused his Gospel privileges. At this stage in his history, he sometimes found comfort in attending the ministry at the "Tabernacle in Moorfields, and sometimes at the chapel at Tottenham Court." And at length he entered into the fulness of the blessing of the Gospel of peace, while listening to a sermon at the Moravian Chapel, Fetter Lane, on the text Rev. 3, v. 10,—"Because thou hast kept the word of my patience, &c." The details of the history of his religious course are remarkable, and deserving of thoughtful perusal. In addition to the prose account given of them in his preface to his Hymns, he has given a poetical narration of them in a hymn of twenty-three verses—No. 27 in his collection. In 1759 he commenced preaching and hymn-writing, and soon after became minister of Jewin Street Independent Chapel. He died May 24th, 1768. The first edition of his "Hymns composed on various subjects," bears date 1759; the second edition, with a large supplement, 1762: many other editions have been published.

"Come, Holy Spirit, come."—No. 435.

The original piece contains four more verses. It was probably suggested by the old Latin hymn "Veni Sancti Spiritus."

"Come, ye sinners, poor and wretched."—No. 511.

In Hart's collection this is headed, "Come and welcome to Jesus."

"This God is the God we adore."—No. 615.

This is the last verse of a piece of seven verses, beginning, "No prophet or dreamer of dreams," Hymn 73 in Hart's collection.

"Lord, look on all assembled here."—No. 995.

This was written "for a Public Fast." Five verses are omitted in the "New Congregational Hymn Book;" and verse 2, which is not in the original, gives the sense of the omitted verses. 794 and 849 are also by Hart.

ANNA DOBER.

1713—1739.

"Holy Lamb, who Thee receive."—No. 572.

This is part of John Wesley's translation (1740) of a piece of ten stanzas, written by Anna Dober, in the year 1735. Her hymn is No. 1046 in the "German Hymn Book of 1735;" and Wesley's translation is found on page 93 of his "Hymns and Sacred Poems," 1740. Wesley omitted stanzas 8 and 9, and his fifth and sixth are omitted in the "New Congregational." The hymn was written to be sung at a children's school feast.

Anna Dober, whose maiden name was Schindler, was born at Kunewalde, in Moravia, April 9, 1713. Her brief life was not too short to include in it useful Christian service. While still in youth we find her at the interesting settlement of Herrnhut, whose history we ordinarily associate with the name of Count Zinzendorf. There she shone in talent and piety, and in the faithful fulfilment of her Christian work.

On July 13, 1737, she married John Leonard Dober, with whom she was associated in Christian labours until her early death. Her husband was for two years (from 1732 to 1734) engaged in a difficult and perilous mission at St. Thomas in the West Indies. In 1734 he was recalled to undertake the general eldership, a position of great responsibility, in which he had to superintend the whole work of the brethren at home and abroad. He held this office till 1740. She did not publish any work, but she composed many fine hymns, of which several are inserted in the brethren's collection. Her hymns are proofs of the influence of Zinzendorf at Herrnhut. They have the same thirsting for holy love, and the same personal devotion to Jesus as the Crucified One, and we can have no doubt that with his spiritual susceptibilities, he felt the presence of Anna Dober, and marked her pathway of light when she ascended to be so early crowned.

JAMES HERVEY, M.A.

1714—1758.

James Hervey had for his college tutor at Oxford John Wesley, and was one of the small band of godly young men at the University who were in derision called "Methodists." He was born at Hardingstone, near Northampton. His father was a clergyman. He studied at Lincoln College, and graduated M.A. He was a good scholar, a man of great benevolence, and an earnest evangelical minister. All his available means, together with the profits of his popular works, which were great, were devoted to purposes of charity. In 1736 he became curate of Dummer, in Hampshire, where he remained a year. He then went to reside at Stoke Abbey, in Devonshire. In 1740 he became curate of Bideford, where he was much beloved; but in 1742 he was deprived of his position by a new rector. In 1743 he became curate to his father, who was rector of Weston Favel and Collingtree, in Northamptonshire. He succeeded his father in both livings in 1752. His early death, by consumption, is said to have been hastened by his laborious devotedness to the duties of his sacred calling.

His view of himself was humble, but probably just. He said to his biographer, John Ryland, sen., "My friend, I have not a strong mind; I have not powers fitted for ardent researches, but I think I have a power of writing in somewhat of a striking manner, so far as to please mankind, and recommend my dear Redeemer." His works, which were all on religious subjects, were in the form of dialogues and letters. They were written in a florid and familiar style, and with an amount of graphic picturing and reference to natural scenery, quite peculiar to themselves. His style pleased the public of that day, and was imitated by some writers and preachers; but it has now by common consent been laid aside. In 1746-7 he published "Meditations among the Tombs," "Reflections on a Flower Garden," "Contemplations on the Night," &c. The "Meditations among the Tombs" is said to have been suggested by a visit to the churchyard of Kilhampton, in Cornwall, during his residence in Devonshire: and one of his principal works was "Theron and Aspasio; or, a series of Dialogues and Letters upon the most important and interesting subjects." From some letters published in the "Gospel Magazine" for 1774, and written by Hervey in 1753, we learn that he was then at work at this book: it appeared in January, 1755. It treats of several scriptural doctrines in the dialogues and letters of two imaginary characters, "Theron" and "Aspasio," but "the grand article," as he says in his preface, "that which makes the principal figure, is the imputed righteousness of our divine Lord." This work brought him into controversy with Wesley on Calvinism. It had a very large sale, and had reached a ninth edition in 1811. He was also the author of " Remarks on Lord Bolingbroke's Letters on the Study and Use of History."

Hervey is not known as a hymn-writer, but we have in the " New Congregational Hymn Book " one good hymn by him—

"Since all the downward tracks of time."—No. 282.

It appeared in Dr. Dodd's " Christian Magazine," June, 1765. It was headed " Humble Acquiescence."' The second verse of the original begins—

"Since none can doubt His equal love."

The hymn ends with the oft-quoted lines—

" E'en crosses from His sovereign hand,
Are blessings in disguise."

CHRISTIAN FÜRCHTEGOTT GELLERT.

1715—1769.

KÜBLER, in his "Historical Notes to the Lyra Germanica," says that Gellert "may be called the head of a new school of German hymn-writers, during the middle and latter half of the last century, in whose hymns the didactic element prevails, since they mostly enforce lessons of Christian duty, and inculcate religious doctrines."

Gellert was born at Haynichen, in Saxony, where his father was minister for fifty years. To his pious mother he owed very much. He valued her approval more than the praise of posterity, and congratulated himself on having received his life from her. His father was a poet, and young Gellert early showed his poetical tastes by writing a poem, " On his Father's Birthday." His first studies were pursued at Meissen, but in 1734 he entered the University of Leipsic, where he studied philosophy and theology. He tried his powers by sometimes speaking from his father's pulpit, but his excessive modesty and timidity prevented him from undertaking the work of a preacher.

After four years at Leipsic, the expenses of the University proved too great for his father's narrow means, and Gellert was recalled to his home. For a time he occupied himself advantageously in that which was to form an important part of his life-work—in teaching others. But in 1741 he again went to Leipsic, taking with him his nephew. This second period of study was turned to good account by the acquirement of French and English, by an extended study of the classics, and by the formation of a style of writing. His verses and pieces, contributed to periodicals, soon attracted attention by their simplicity and beauty; and he formed the acquaintance of J. E. Schlegel, and other men of genius, by associating with whom his aspiring genius was encouraged and helped.

But his aim was not merely literary. For a long time his piety had been of a high order. He wished to live to some good purpose, and longed to occupy some position of public usefulness. With a view to this, he took a degree in the faculty of *belles lettres*, sustained theses according to custom, and acquired the right of giving public lessons in the year 1745-6. His lectures on poetry and eloquence were very popular with the students, and Goethe was at one time among his pupils. He also lectured on philosophy, of which he became professor at Leipsic.

As an author, he published his " Tales and Fables," which were very popular in Germany, and were translated into French. He also composed comedies, " The Devotee" and " The Lottery Ticket ;" and having suffered much from melancholy and from a bad state of health, he wrote a book entitled " Consolations for Valetudinarians." This was published in 1747, and met with success. He subsequently wrote more " Fables;" published his " Moral Poems," and his " Letters," which were literary productions for which he chose an epistolary form. And in 1754 he sent forth his "Didactic Poems." Year by year he continued writing, teaching, and lecturing, with only such intermission as his attacks of melancholy rendered necessary.

In the year 1757 the calamities of war led him to wish to leave Leipsic, and he retired for a time to Bonau, and afterwards to Eisenberg. At length, his services were publicly recognized by the bestowment on him of a pension, which served to recruit his resources, so often reduced by his benefactions. In the year of his death, 1769, he occupied himself with revising his moral lessons, which are entitled "Thoughts on Religion," but it was left to others to publish them. After much affliction, he at length died in prayer, an appropriate ending of his holy life. His biographer says, "Perhaps no grave has ever been watered with so many and such sincere tears."

His "Sacred Odes and Hymns" bear date 1757. Of these his biographer says : " These sacred songs bear the faithful impression of Gellert's character ; they show how deeply his mind was penetrated with the precepts of religion, how readily he acquiesced in its mysteries, how much he desired to be as good as this heavenly guide invites us to become ; they show his unfeigned humility, the moderation of his wishes, his love for his fellow-creatures, his efforts to promote their happiness, and to subdue them to the benevolent empire of virtue and true piety. He frequently uses the language of Scripture. He prefers to metaphorical expressions those which address themselves directly to the heart. The same choice appears in his hymns, which contain more reasoning than warmth, and are more intended to instruct, than to display sentiment."

Gellert's hymns were not mere literary performances. He preceded their composition by prayer and careful heart-preparation ; and if he felt that his heart was not in tune, he refrained from composition. He says on one occasion, "I will for a time lay aside this work ; perhaps God of His grace will inspire my mind with new vigour, and improve my present dispositions." Gellert lived near to God. He was a great Bible reader, and a firm believer in Providence. In a pamphlet, entitled "The Adventures of a Hymn," published in London, 1862, there is a graphic description of the way in which Providence put it into the hearts of those already favourably disposed towards Gellert, to assist him in his hour of need, and how faith justified uttered itself in new songs. The hymns of Gellert do not equal in grandeur and simple strength those of earlier writers, such as Luther, Ringwaldt, and Gerhard. Gellert felt this, and said that he would give up all his own hymns for one of theirs; but Gellert's hymns are heart utterances, and reach the heart. With the simplicity of the author, they convey the strength of his convictions, and the clear teaching of the truths he firmly believed. His sole contribution to the "New Congregational Hymn Book" illustrates this view—

"Jesus lives, no longer now."—No. 388.

"Jesus lebt, mit Ihm auch ich."

The translation is by Frances Elizabeth Cox, 1841.

ANNE STEELE.

1716—1778.

Miss Steele was the daughter of the Rev. Wm. Steele, a Baptist minister at Broughton, in Hampshire. The Steeles were for several generations possessed of good talents and means, which they devoted unreservedly to the cause of Christ. Anne was a member of the Church under her father's care, and a person eminent for her piety and useful Christian activity. She was the authoress of "Poems on subjects chiefly devotional," in three vols. (1780), with the signature "Theodosia;" and of a version of the Psalms. Her hymns in the "New Congregational Hymn Book" are free from the defects which mar some others, good in their versification, pious in their spirit, and scriptural in their teaching, without any special excellencies or any manifestation of genius on the part of the writer. They are ten in number, 331, 482, 518, 560, 601, 612, 635, 646, 971, 994. Some of them are given with verses omitted.

"Almighty Maker of my frame."—No. 482.

This is four verses of her psalm 39, consisting of thirteen verses, and beginning—

"When I resolv'd to watch my thoughts."

"Father, whate'er of earthly bliss."—No. 601.

This is the last three verses of her hymn, bearing date 1760, on "Desiring Resignation and Thankfulness," and beginning—

"When I survey life's varied scene."

Miss Steele was a great sufferer. A few hours before the time of her wedding, the object of her affections was drowned while bathing. She carried with her through life a weak and afflicted body, and she never recovered the shock of her father's death. He died September 10, 1769. But she bore all with resignation, and before her peaceful departure, uttered the triumphant words, "I know that my Redeemer liveth." She died in 1778, at the age of sixty-one.

Mr. Daniel Sedgwick has published (1863) the collected poetical works of Anne Steele, entitled "Hymns, Psalms, and Poems, by Anne Steele, with memoir by John Sheppard:" it includes 144 hymns on various subjects, thirty-four of the principal of David's Psalms in verse, and about fifty poems on moral subjects. One piece, on the death of the Rev. James Hervey, "O Hervey, honoured name, forgive the tear," is said to be the original of the epitaph, "Forgive, blest shade," &c. The profits of Miss Steele's works were devoted by her to charitable objects. Her poems were reprinted in America in 1808.

JOHN CENNICK.
1717—1755.

Prefixed to a volume of Cennick's sermons, published in 1803, there is a life by the Rev. Matthew Wilks. He had received some information from Cennick's daughter, and was probably familiar with the poet's own account of his " Life and Call to the Ministry," as it is given in the preface to his hymns, published in 1741. To Mr. Wilks' sketch we are indebted for some of the following facts.

John Cennick was born at Reading, where his grandparents, who were Quakers, had been persecuted and imprisoned. But his parents brought him up in connection with the Established Church. As a youth, he delighted in attending dances, playing at cards, and going to the theatre. But in 1735, while walking hastily along in Cheapside, London, he experienced deep convictions of sin. These convictions were strengthened by his association with pious companions. He was greatly depressed in mind, and so far reformed his outward life as to give up his gay practices. But he did not as yet possess the true Christian peace. On the contrary, he went, step by step, down into the dark depths of spiritual despair. Beginning with neglect, he went on to infidelity and open sin.

For three years this distressing condition of character continued. All kinds of errors troubled his agitated mind; he was daily pressed down with convictions of sin and fear of God's wrath. He was weary of life, and often prayed for death. Sometimes he thought of fleeing from his distress by retiring into the country to some place where he was unknown, and there working as a labourer; and he even went on journeys for this purpose. He also vainly tried austerity as a cure for his misery. He says, " I even ate acorns, leaves of trees, crabs and grass, and wished often heartily that I could bring myself to live only upon roots and herbs."

Subsequently, he became a land measurer at Reading. And in 1787 we find him reading "Hugo's Emblems" with profit, and beginning to fall into the hands of God. In the following year he found great pleasure in reading Whitefield's journal, and his Christian light increased. At the time when he was conscious of needing sympathy and help, he heard of one Kinchin, who was despised at Oxford because he was a Methodist, and justly concluded he was such a friend as he needed. Forthwith he set out for Oxford, and was welcomed and helped by his new friend. The new friendship was fruitful in important results to Cennick. It brought him into the circle of John and Charles Wesley, George Whitefield, and other kindred spirits.

In the following year, 1789, Cennick went to be a teacher in the school for colliers' children, which Mr. John Wesley had established at Kingswood. Circumstances soon called him out as a preacher. On his arrival, a large assembly in the open air was disappointed of a preacher. Cennick was persuaded to address them, and did so with success. Subsequently he assisted Mr. Wesley in his preaching labours. But in 1740, in consequence of divergence of doctrine, he separated from the Wesleys, and went on preaching journeys without having any connection with their societies. Charles Wesley, in his diary (October 31, 1740), says, "while I was testifying Christ died for all, in the hearing of many, Mr. Cennick gave me the lie."

In 1741, on the return of Whitefield from America, he invited Mr. Cennick to assist him in his various labours. To this he consented, and often went on preaching tours, meeting with the persecution to which ministers of the Gospel were exposed in those times. In 1745, Mr. Cennick went over to the Moravian Brethren, and thus caused a division in Whitefield's congregation at the Tabernacle, London. Being connected with the Moravians, the poet on two occasions visited Germany, their principal seat. We also find him preaching in the North of Ireland. In the year 1755, having come to London, he was taken ill of a fever, which caused his death. He was married to a lady, Jane Bryant, of Clack, Wiltshire, and had a family of three children. His friend John Gambold, a bishop of the Moravian Church, wrote a poem in honour of his memory. Cennick wrote some volumes of "Village Discourses," and was the author of the "Graces" which are so often sung on public religious occasions. Before meat:—

"Be present at our table, Lord," &c.

After meat:—

"We bless thee, Lord, for this our food," &c.

The latter has four additional lines that have ceased to be used:—

"Praise shall our grateful lips employ,
While life and plenty we enjoy,
Till worthy we adore thy name,
While banqueting with Christ, the Lamb."

Other works by him were, "His Life, written by himself," 1745; "An Account of the late Riot in Exeter," 1745; "A Letter to the little Children; especially to those who want to know how to go to heaven," fifth edition, 1782; "Nunc Dimittis, lines written by John Cennick," 1757; "An account of the Conversion of G. Lee, who was executed." One of his poems is a piece of thirty-six verses, describing elaborately his remarkable religious experience.

In it he says:—

"Dangers were always in my path,
And fears of death, and endless wrath:
While pale dejection in me reign'd,
I often wept, by grief constrain'd.
* * * *
Through every day I wailed my fall—
Three years of grief exceeded all!
No rest I knew! a slave to sin!
With scarce a spark of hope between."

After his death, a poem was found in his pocket-book, headed "Nunc dimittis." It expresses submission to the Divine will, but at the same time "a desire to depart."
In it he says :—

> "O Lamb! I languish till that day I see,
> When Thou wilt say, come up and be with me.
> Now twice seven years have I Thy servant been;
> Now let me end my service and my sin."

Some of Cennick's hymns are printed after his sermons. They were probably written to be sung with them. His first hymns were published while he was at Kingswood. Under date July, 1739, C. Wesley says in his Diary, "I corrected Mr. Cennick's hymns for the press." His work is entitled, "Sacred Hymns for the Children of God in the Days of their Pilgrimage," 1741; also two more parts in 1742. He also wrote "Hymns for Children," 1754, and a "Collection of Sacred Hymns," 1752; and the Rev. Sweetner, Cennick's son-in-law, published from MSS. some of his father-in-law's hymns in the Moravian collection, of which he was editor, in 1789. Several of his hymns in the "New Congregational Hymn Book" are from his work entitled, "Sacred Hymns for the Use of Religious Societies, in three parts" (1743—5). In his preface to the second part, he says, "Our Saviour has again given me freedom to give into your hands another little parcel of hymns. I pray they may be sanctified to your dear souls through His blood and wounds to whose honour they are composed. Let love cover every fault you meet with, and if the Lamb of God blesses these hymns at all to any of God's dear societies, let them praise the Lamb only for them."

"We sing to Thee, Thou Son of God."—No. 310.

This is an altered form of part of Cennick's second hymn in his "Hymns, 1743"—his rendering of the "Te Deum" in twelve verses.

"Brethren, let us join to bless."—No. 314.

This is Cennick's (1742), somewhat altered.

The well-known hymn—

"Jesus, my all, to heaven is gone,"—No. 334,

expressive of the poet's own experience, is No. 64 in the last-mentioned collection. It is headed in the original—

"Following Christ, the sinner's way to God,"

and consists of nine stanzas. Hymns 341 and 396 are also in the same collection. The compilers have wisely dispensed with several inferior verses. There is little poetry in Cennick's hymns, and the favourite words, phrases, and doctrines of the writer's particular school appear with unpleasant frequency. Here and there we are offended by such couplets as—

"Louder we than any ought
Jesus and His grace to shout;"

but they are full of Christian fervour, and of the lessons of the writer's singular experience. They are generally written in the form of dialogues; each pair of lines being complete in itself, and the last two of the four printed in italics, as if to be repeated in response.

"Children of the Heavenly King."—No. 630.

This is also by Cennick, and bears date 1743. Of the same date also is hymn 896.

To Cennick also we are indebted for

"Lo! He comes with clouds descending,"—No. 418;

one of the finest hymns ever written. His hymn begins—

"Lo! He cometh; countless trumpets."

It first appeared in a Dublin collection, entitled "A Collection of Sacred Hymns," 1752. To it belongs the credit of being the first attempt to render the thoughts and sentiments of the "Dies iræ" in this fine appropriate measure: the flowing majestic lines first, then the first trumpet note of the chorus, then the full sounding line at the close; upon which, to change the figure, the whole verse rests gracefully, but firmly. There were many pieces written afterwards upon the same subject, in the same metre. As the hymn stands in the "New Congregational Hymn Book," stanzas 1, 2, and 5 are by Charles Wesley, given in his "Hymns of Intercession for all Mankind," 1758, and stanzas 3 and 4 by John Cennick, 1752. Sir Roundell Palmer attributes the selection of stanzas and some variations to Martin Madan. The hymn is in the "New Congregational Hymn Book" erroneously attributed to Thomas Olivers. He made the tune Helmsley, to which it is often sung, from a street-tune, and probably this may have led to the mistake. He also wrote a hymn in the same metre, and beginning with the same line, which might easily be confounded with that by Wesley and Cennick.

"Ere I sleep, for every favour."—No. 942.

This, which is given without name in the "New Congregational Hymn Book," is also by John Cennick. It is in "Sacred Hymns for the Children of God in the days of their Pilgrimage," 1741. It is his admired evening hymn, with two stanzas omitted. The morning hymn that is printed with it—

"Rise, my soul, adore thy Maker,"

is not in the "New Congregational."

JOSEPH HUMPHREYS.

LITTLE is known of this hymn-writer. He was one of the early Calvinistic Methodist preachers of the last century. He died in London, and was buried in the Moravian cemetery at Chelsea. Six of his hymns were published at the end of Cennick's "Sacred Hymns for the use of Religious Societies," 1743. A note is placed before them, "These were done by Mr. Joseph Humphreys." His sole contribution to the "New Congregational Hymn Book" is—

"Blessed are the sons of God."—No. 557.

It is erroneously attributed to Hammond in the "New Congregational." In the original it is given in eight stanzas of four lines each; but in the "New Congregational" only four stanzas are given, and each is lengthened by the addition of the last two lines of the hymn. It is headed in the original, "The Privileges of God's children."

WILLIAM WILLIAMS.
1717—1791.

WILLIAMS, of Pantycelyn, who may be called the Watts of Wales, was born in 1717 at Cefnycoed, in the parish of Llanfair-ar-y-bryn, near Llandovery, Carmarthenshire. After receiving a good education, he began to study for the medical profession; but before completing his medical studies, an event happened to him that changed the current of his life. While listening to the burning words of Howell Harris, in Talgarth churchyard, his soul was stirred, and he was won to Christ. With the first fervour of the new life, he resolved to give himself to the work of the Christian ministry, and in his twenty-third year he was ordained deacon, and began his ministry at Llanwrtyd and Llanddewi Abergwesin. About the age of thirty-two he married Miss Mary Francis, in whom he found a worthy helpmeet. Being opposed in the Established Church, and refused priest's orders, he became an itinerant preacher in the Welsh Calvinistic Methodist connexion. In this capacity he laboured unceasingly for half a century, incessantly hastening from place to place in every part of the Principality, to preach the Gospel to listening thousands. His sermons, warm with his own fervour, bright with the vivid picturing of his lively imagination, and always radiant with the presence of his Divine master, produced a most powerful effect upon his impressible fellow-countrymen; and Williams, working with such men as Rowlands and Harris, was felt as a power in the "Association" meetings of the connexion to which he belonged. He was also a great power for good in the *private society* or church-meetings, held weekly, in which there was opportunity for conversation upon religious experience, and for sympathy and counsel.

Williams wrote in prose as well as in poetry. In 1768 he published in Welsh " Three men from Sodom and Egypt," and " The Crocodile of the River of Egypt," and some other treatises.

After a period of suffering he ended his holy, laborious, and successful course at Pantycelyn, near Llandovery, January 11th, 1791, aged 74.

Williams was as much celebrated for his poetry in his native tongue as he was for his talent and usefulness in preaching the Gospel. The popularity of the preacher opened the way for the reception of his poems, and the excellence of the pieces themselves made them retain their place when once received. They are now generally used by all denominations of Christians in the Principality, and held in the highest veneration by the people. They originated in a challenge given by Harris at an " Association " meeting to the brethren to try their hands at producing a few stanzas, to be read at the next meeting. Williams's perspicuity of expression and richness of imagination at once declared him "*facile primus;*" and, thus encouraged, he began to write for the service of Christ. His first Welsh book of hymns was his " Alleluia," which went through three editions about 1750. In 1762 he sent forth his next book of hymns, " The Sea of Glass." This soon passed through five editions. Then followed a third volume, " Visible Farewell; Welcome to Invisible Things." And yet another, called " Alleluia again." His Welsh hymns are now collected in one volume. Soon after his first " Alleluia," Williams published a work rich in Christian theology, " A View of the Kingdom of Christ." He translated " Erskine on the Assurance of Faith." He also produced " Pantheologia," and a work resembling Bunyan's " Pilgrim's Progress," entitled " Theomemphus " (1781). He also wrote a large number of elegies, including one of considerable length on the death of Whitefield. This was published in 1771, and dedicated to the Countess of Huntingdon.

Many of Williams's hymns have appeared in English, in the use of which he was not so much at home as in his native tongue. One of his works is entitled, "Hosannah to the Son of David; or, Hymns of Praise to God for our glorious Redemption by Christ. Some few translated from the Welsh Hymn Book, but mostly composed on new subjects." The reprint of this work, published by Mr. Daniel Sedgwick, bears date 1759. It contains 51 hymns. His other principal English hymn-book was entitled, "Gloria in Excelsis; or, Hymns of Praise to God and the Lamb," 1772. This book consists of 71 pieces, the last on "The Passion" extending to 7 parts and 89 verses. The Rev. E. Morgan, A.M., Mr. Williams's biographer, says that Lady Huntingdon having seen the "Hosannah to the Son of David," persuaded Williams to prepare the "Gloria in Excelsis," to be sent to Whitefield's Orphan House in America. In the latter work there is a marked advance in style and taste upon the former, and it is from it that his most prized pieces are taken. His fervour of sentiment and vigour of imagination always please, his versification is sometimes very pleasing, and where he offends it is by sacrificing refinement to force.

"While Thee I seek, Almighty Power."—No. 286.

This is not by W. Williams, but by Helen Maria Williams, 1786, *vide* under her name.

"Guide me, O Thou Great Jehovah."—No. 660.

This hymn was taken from the Welsh of W. Williams. It appeared in Mr. Whitefield's collection, 1774, two years after the publication of "Gloria in Excelsis." It is uncertain whether it was translated by the author or by W. Evans. It is given in the "New Congregational Hymn Book," with slight verbal alterations. But in the original there is the following additional verse:

"Musing on my habitation,
  Musing on my heav'nly home,
Fills my soul with holy longing,
  Come, my Jesus, quickly come.
    Vanity is all I see,
    Lord, I long to be with Thee!"

"O'er the gloomy hills of darkness."—No. 911.

This is hymn 38 in "Gloria in Excelsis," 1772. It is given with slight verbal alterations, and with the omission of two verses. It is especially interesting as being a noble missionary hymn, composed before the founding of the modern missionary societies.

BENJAMIN BEDDOME, M.A.
1717—1795.

This Christian pastor and poet was born at Henley-in-Arden, Warwickshire, January 23rd, 1717; but at the age of seven, he removed to Bristol with his father, the Rev. John Beddome, who had undertaken a co-pastorate at the Pithay church. At a suitable age he was apprenticed to a surgeon in Bristol, and afterwards removed to London.

John Beddome, his father, was a Baptist minister, and when at the age of twenty Benjamin had received deep religious impressions; he used often to weep as he listened to his father's faithful discourses, though in his earlier years he had heard with indifference. In 1739 he became a member of Mr. Wilson's church, in Goodman's Fields, London. Having studied at the Baptist College, Bristol, and also at an Independent Academy, in Tenter Alley, Moorfields, London, he went, in 1740, to supply the Baptist congregation at Bourton-on-the-Water, Gloucestershire; and in 1743 became their pastor. In December, 1749, he married Miss Elizabeth Boswell. On the death of Mr. Wilson, he was invited to become pastor of the church in Goodman's Fields, but he declined, and continued faithfully labouring for his flock at Bourton, to whom he preached till the time of his death in 1795. In 1770 he was made M.A. by Providence College, Rhode Island. In his hymns on affliction, he could draw on his own experience, having lost a son, an accomplished medical doctor, in 1770, and a son by drowning, and also his own wife, in the year 1784. He was composing a hymn a few hours before he died, September 3, 1795.

He was the author of an "Exposition on the Baptist Catechism, 1752." "Twenty short Discourses from his MSS." were published in 1805, and his work, "Hymns Adapted to Public Worship or Family Devotion" was published in 1818. In 1835 there was published a work entitled, "Sermons Printed from the MSS. of the late Rev. B. Beddome, M.A., with a brief Memoir of the Author." It contains sixty-seven sermons on practical subjects.

Montgomery speaks of him as a "writer worthy of honour, both for the quantity and the quality of his hymns." And says, "His compositions are calculated to be far more useful than attractive, though, on closer acquaintance, they become very agreeable, as well as impressive, being for the most part brief and pithy. A single idea, always important, often striking, and sometimes ingeniously brought out, not with a mere point at the end, but with the terseness and simplicity of the Greek epigram —constitutes the basis of each piece." Many of Beddome's hymns were written to be sung after his sermons, and to serve as applications of their principal lessons.

Robert Hall, in his introduction to Beddome's "Hymns Adapted to Public Worship or Family Devotion," 1818, says— "The man of taste will be gratified with the beautiful and original thoughts which many of them exhibit, while the experimental Christian will often perceive the most sweet movements of his soul strikingly delineated, and sentiments portrayed which will find their echo in every heart." He also commends the erudition, wit, talent, and piety of the author.

Beddome's hymns were written at various times. They were not written for the general public, and he did not collect them himself, but he allowed some to appear in a general collection prepared for the Baptist denomination.

The posthumous collection of 1818 contains 830 pieces. The seven hymns by Beddome, in the "New Congregational Hymn Book," are in it.

"In all my ways, O God."—No. 155.

This is his 568th.

> "Did Christ o'er sinners weep."—No. 502.

This is his 587th. The original has only the first three verses. Some later writer has ventured to add the fourth.

> "Faith! 'tis a precious grace."—No. 539.

This is his 165th.

> "Let party names no more."—No. 819.

This is his 638th. It is given with slight alterations. Like the others, it shows the author's main excellence to be his skill in preserving the unity of each hymn, grouping all the ideas around one central subject. The hymn also shows the excellent spirit of the writer.

> "Witness ye men and angels; now!"—No. 835.

This is his 647th.

> "Each other we have owned."—No. 843.

This is given with the omission of one verse. It is his 665th.

> "Father of mercies, bow Thine ear."—No. 892.

This admirable ordination hymn is his 700th.

JAMES MERRICK, M.A.
1720—1769.

THIS sacred poet, coming after Tate and Brady, prepared a new version of the Psalms, for which royal sanction was sought, but not obtained. It contained some excellent pieces, but was spoiled by its excess of verbiage. It was entitled, "The Psalms Translated, or Paraphrased, in English Verse, 1765." In 1797 the Rev. W. D. Tattersall published an edition "divided into stanzas for parochial use." In some instances he found it necessary to alter the author's language. Merrick was a great classical scholar, and a fellow of Trinity College, Oxford. Lord

North was one of his pupils. The poet took orders as a clergyman, but his delicate health prevented him from undertaking parochial duties. Bishop Lowth characterized him as one of the best of men, and most eminent of scholars. He was the author of "The Destruction of Troy, Translated from the Greek of Tryphiodorus into English Verse, with Notes, &c., 1742."

His poem, "The Chameleon," is well-known, and his "Song of Simeon" is justly admired.

"Eternal God! we look to Thee."—No. 654.

This is somewhat altered from the original, and one verse is omitted. The line—

"That fear, all fear beside"

resembles, it has been observed, a line in Racine's "Athalie"—

"Je crains Dieu, cher Abner, et n'ai point d'autre crainte."

"The festal morn, my God, is come."—No. 757.

This is the first four stanzas of Merrick's rendering of Psalm 122—

"I was glad when they said unto me, &c."

They are altered from the original, which consists of seven stanzas. Dr. Collyer so highly esteemed Merrick that he has put fifty-one of his Psalms and Hymns in his collection of 1812.

THOMAS GIBBONS, D.D.
1720—1785.

WHEN the great lexicographer, Dr. Johnson, was writing his "Lives of the Poets," and was seeking for the necessary material for the life of "Dr. Watts," he was directed to one of his biographers, Dr. Gibbons, the subject of this sketch, one of the ablest Congregational ministers of his day; and, Tory though he was, Dr. Johnson felt that his heart was won by the talented sectary, whom he afterwards numbered amongst his friends.

Thomas Gibbons was born at Reak, in the parish of Swaffham Prior, near Newmarket, May 31, 1720. His father, of the same name, was pastor first at Olney, and then at Royston. Young Gibbons received his early education in Cambridgeshire, and, in 1735, was placed under the care of Dr. Taylor, at Deptford. In 1742, he was ordained, and became assistant preacher to the Rev. Mr. Bures, at Silver Street Chapel; and, in 1743, he became pastor of the Independent Church assembling at Haberdashers' Hall, in which position he continued to the end of his life. In 1744, he married Hannah, daughter of the Rev. John Shuttlewood. His family consisted of four sons.

In 1754, he became tutor of the Dissenting Academy at Mile End, where he taught logic, metaphysics, ethics, and rhetoric. In the year 1759, he further added to his duties by becoming Sunday evening lecturer at Monkwell Street. The degree of M.A. was conferred on him in 1760, by the college of New Jersey, America; and in 1764, he received the diploma of Doctor of Divinity from Aberdeen. Dr. Gibbons was intimate with the Countess of Huntingdon and other religious celebrities of his day, and especially with Dr. Watts, in whose honour he wrote, in 1749, an elegiac poem. He also wrote a " Memoir of Dr. Watts," in 1780. He died of apoplexy, February 22, 1785.

Amongst Dr. Gibbons' works were " Calvinism and Nonconformity Defended, &c.," 1740. " Rhetoric," 1767. " Female Worthies," in 2 vols., 1777. " Sermons on Various Subjects," 1762; and after his death, three volumes of his sermons were published by subscription.

It was a weak point with Dr. Gibbons, that he rated his poetical powers beyond their real worth. He translated Dr. Watts' Latin poems, and wrote several elegies, which are more remarkable for their grandiloquence than for any poetic excellence they possess. In 1750 he published " Juvenilia: Poems on Various Subjects of Devotion and Virtue." His first collection of hymns, in two books, appeared in 1769; and the second, in two books, in 1784. The sermons published in 1762 were entitled, " Sermons on Various Subjects, with an Hymn adapted to each Subject." This book contains fifteen sermons and fifteen hymns; and it is remarkable that the hymns are not given in his hymn-books published afterwards.

"Now let our souls on wings sublime."—No. 713.

This is the hymn given at the close of "Sermon IV.," in the volume just referred to. The title of the sermon is, "The Return of the Body to Earth, and the Return of the Soul to God, Practically Improved." The text is, "Then shall the dust return to the earth as it was; and the spirit shall return unto God who gave it."—Eccles. xii. 7. Verse 2 is omitted in the "New Congregational Hymn Book."

"Great God! the nations of the earth."—No. 908.

This is part of a piece of forty-six verses, which appeared in the first volume of hymns, 1769. It is the sixty-ninth in that collection, and is headed, "The Universal Diffusion of the Gospel Promised by God and Pleaded by His people," in seven parts. It is somewhat altered from the original. The collection gives the authors' names, and the preface explains that Dr. Gibbons' hymns were written at different times during many years of his ministry, as he had opportunity and inclination.

Other poetical works by Dr. Gibbons were the following:—
"The Christian Minister, in three Poetical Epistles to Philander, to which are added—1st. Poetical versions of several parts of Scripture; 2nd. Translations of poems from Greek and Latin writers; and 3rd. Original pieces on various occasions," 1772. And "An English Version of the Latin Epitaphs in the Nonconformists' Memorial, with a Poem to the Memory of the 2,000 Ministers Ejected by the Act of Uniformity," 1775.

JOHN BAKEWELL.
1721—1819.

JOHN BAKEWELL was born at Brailsford, in Derbyshire, in the year 1721. At about eighteen years of age he was converted, chiefly through reading "Boston's Fourfold State." With the warmth of his early zeal, he began to preach the Gospel in his own neighbourhood in 1744. From this good work he was not deterred by the violent opposition he met with; and at length, by the Divine blessing, he made converts and friends of some of his former opponents.

Afterwards he removed to London, where he became acquainted with the Wesleys, Toplady, Madan, and others. At one time he resided at Westminster, and at his house Thomas Olivers is said to have written his celebrated hymn,

"The God of Abraham praise."—No. 256.

For many years Mr. Bakewell carried on the Greenwich Royal Park Academy, and at his house he conducted a Wesleyan "class," until the chapel was opened. There also he received the preachers. So early as 1749 he had been appointed a local preacher, and when he had given up his academy to his son-in-law, Dr. James Egan, and had in consequence more leisure, he used to go wherever the Wesleyan ministry was interrupted, to supply lack of service. His long life was one of eminent piety, devotedness, and usefulness. Three or four years before his death he removed from Greenwich to Lewisham, where he died in March, 1819, in the ninety-eighth year of his age. His tomb, in the City Road Chapel ground, near to that of Mr. Wesley, records that "he adorned the doctrine of God our Saviour eighty years, and preached His glorious Gospel about seventy years."

Mr. Bakewell was the author of several hymns, and in the "Methodist Magazine" for July, 1816, there is a letter by him on brotherly love, written when he was more than ninety years of age. As a hymn-writer, he is chiefly known for his favourite hymn,—

"Hail! Thou once despised Jesus."—No. 335.

This is now introduced into almost all collections. It is believed to have first appeared in Madan's collection in 1760. Madan gave it in an abridged form. The entire hymn was given by the author to Toplady, who published it, with verbal alterations, to accommodate it to his own views, in his collection in 1776. It is sometimes given beginning with the second verse, and usually as it is in the "New Congregational Hymn Book," without the fifth stanza—

"Soon we shall, with those in glory,"

a verse scarcely equal to the preceding. There is no doubt of this hymn being by Bakewell. It has always been known as his by his family, who frequently conversed with him about it.

SAMUEL DAVIES, M.A.
1724—1761.

This eminent preacher and professor was born in the county of Newcastle, Delaware, America, November 3, 1724. He had pious parents, and was educated under the direction of the Rev. Samuel Blair, of Fog's Manor, Chester County, Pennsylvania.

About the year 1740, a religious movement began in the county of Hanover, chiefly through the reading, by a wealthy planter, of a few leaves of "Boston's Fourfold State." A Mr. Morris also was impressed with the claims of evangelical truth by reading "Luther on Galatians:" and, in consequence, called his friends together, and erected a meeting-house, which was called "Morris' Reading Room." To meet the spirit of enquiry that had been awakened amongst the people, the Rev. William Robinson, a minister belonging to the Presbytery of New Brunswick, paid a visit to the district; and his labours were so much valued that on his departure the people wished to make him a present of money. This he refused to receive, but they were so determined in their expression of gratitude that they put the money in his saddle-bags. At length he accepted the money, and determined to devote it to the training of young Davies; who, after receiving his education, went to labour in the same district.

He was licensed in 1745, by the Presbytery of Newcastle, as a probationer for the ministry of the Gospel, and in 1747, he went to pursue his work in Virginia. He preached in "Morris' Reading Room," and in several other licensed places. But the enemies of the good cause tried to stop a course of operations that they deemed irregular; and the important question whether the "Toleration Act" extended to Virginia had to be tried. Davies maintained his own case so successfully as to astonish his adversaries and to gain his cause. Notwithstanding his feeble state of health, he preached from place to place with great fervour; and he took a deep interest in the negroes, amongst whom he introduced religious books, and especially "Watts' Psalms," which they valued very much.

In 1753, Mr. Davies was appointed by the trustees of the College of New Jersey to visit England with Gilbert Tennent, to solicit donations for the college. He was absent from America about eighteen months, serving the college and making the acquaintance of some of the leading divines of that day in England. In the year 1753 he received the degree of M.A., and in the year 1759 he was appointed to succeed the celebrated President, Jonathan Edwards, as President of New Jersey (Presbyterian) College, Princetown. But he was not long spared to fill this responsible position. He died on the 4th of February, 1761, aged only thirty-six. He had commenced the year by preaching on the words, "This year thou shalt die." He was a very earnest and evangelical divine. His sermons were not only listened to with interest, but in print were exceedingly popular, and had a large sale. Some of them were published during his life. His "Sermons on Important Subjects" had reached a fifth edition in 1804. And so late as 1851, his collected sermons, in three volumes, were published, with a life by the Rev. Albert Barnes. In 1757, he published "Letters from S. D., showing the state of religion in Virginia, &c." There was a good deal of poetry in President Davies' prose, and he was also a poet. Three of his poems are given at the end of his collected sermons. One is on the birth of his third son. He also wrote some hymns.

There is one hymn by him in the "New Congregational Hymn Book,"—

"Great God of wonders, all thy ways,"—No. 295,

—a hymn admirable for its unity, comprehensiveness, simplicity, and force. This hymn is given in Dr. Thomas Gibbons' earlier collection, "Hymns adapted to Divine Worship," in two books, 1769. Dr. Gibbons says in the preface, that he took it and some others from President Davies' MSS., entrusted to him. The hymn is given in the "New Congregational Hymn Book," with the omission of the third verse, and with several alterations. It is the fifty-ninth in Dr. Gibbons' Collection, and is headed, "The Glories of God in pardoning Sinners." (Micah vii. 18.)

ANDREW KIPPIS, D.D., F.R.S.
1725—1795.

Not the least eminent amongst the pupils of Dr. Doddridge was Dr. Andrew Kippis, one of the most talented and laborious authors and ministers of the last century. He was born at Nottingham, where his father was a silk-hosier, March 28, 1725; his parents could trace their descent from the heroic men who had patiently suffered ejectment on the passing of the Act of Uniformity in 1662. Dr. Kippis was educated in the Academy at Northampton, when it was under the care of Dr. Doddridge; but he turned aside from the orthodox doctrine to the school of his friend Dr. Lardner.

After exercising his ministry for a few years at Boston, Lincolnshire, whither he went in 1746, and at Dorking, Surrey, from 1751-53, he undertook his life-work in London, in 1753, as pastor of a congregation of Presbyterian dissenters, who met in Prince's Street, Westminster. In this position he continued till his death, which took place on the 8th of October, 1795.

In 1763, Dr. Kippis became classical and philological tutor in Coward's Academy, an office he held till 1784, when his divergence of doctrine rendered it desirable that he should retire from his position. He was a man of great and varied learning. In 1771 he was elected a Fellow of the Society of Antiquaries, and in the following year a Fellow of the Royal Society. His degree of D.D., was from the University of Edinburgh.

Dr. Kippis was a most productive author. He was a principal contributor to the "Monthly Review," the leading periodical of that day. He also assisted in "The New Annual Register." He published a volume of sermons and several pamphlets, also "The ethical and theological lectures of Dr. Doddridge," in two volumes, with valuable notes; and the "Collected edition of the works of Dr. Lardner, with a life," 1788; also "A Vindication of the Protestant Dissenting Ministry in their application to Parliament, 1773."

But his greatest work as an author was the assistance he rendered in the production of the second edition of the "Biographia Britannica." (1777—1793), our first national biographical dictionary. Unfortunately this edition was not carried farther than the letter F. But this portion consisted of five folio volumes, and contained several lives by Kippis, and especially that of Captain Cook, which was also published separately.

Dr. Kippis also published a "Collection of Psalms and Hymns," 1795. He wrote a few himself.

"With grateful hearts, with joyful tongues."—No. 997.

This is the latter part of his hymn of four verses, beginning, in his Collection,—

"How rich Thy gifts, Almighty King."

It is headed there, "National Thanksgiving." It is given without name in the "New Congregational."

JOHN NEWTON.
1725—1807.

LONDON was the birth-place of this eminent servant of God, "once an infidel and libertine, a servant of slaves in Africa," as he wrote of himself in his epitaph. He was an only child, and had the misfortune to lose his mother in his seventh year; by this similarity being prepared to sympathize with Cowper, the companion of his later years. Newton's mother was a pious dissenter, and trained her son carefully, having it in her heart that he would be one day engaged in the Christian ministry—a work to which she had devoted him. Young Newton's father and step-mother did not carry on this good work, but he was "much left to himself, to mingle with idle and wicked boys, and soon learnt their ways."

As a young man, Newton passed through various religious experiences, but at length became an infidel in his notions, and a profligate in his conduct. Having been accustomed to take voyages with his father, he at last devoted himself entirely to a seafaring life. Before he was of age, he deserted his ship, and was brought back to Plymouth as a felon, kept in irons, degraded from his office as midshipman, and publicly whipped. But sin and severe punishment only hardened him more and more. While on a voyage, he obtained leave to exchange into a vessel bound for the African coast. His purpose was to be free to sin. Having reached the coast of Africa, he left the ship and lived on the Island of Plantains, where he was treated with severity by his master, a slave-trader, and by his master's wife, and suffered great hardships and afflictions. There, too, he sinned with the freedom he had purposed, and led others into sin; but, on writing to his father, arrangements were made for a vessel to call for him. In the beginning of the year 1748 the vessel, having received him on board, set out on a tedious homeward voyage. During this voyage he one day took up Stanhope's "Thomas à Kempis," and the thought struck him, "What if these things should be true?" That very night the vessel was almost wrecked in a terrible storm. On the following day, when exhausted with pumping, after resting a little, he steered the ship for some time. During those hours of solemn reflection, his whole former life passed in review before him, and especially his scoffing at Scripture, his vicious conduct, and the dangers he had been in. The ship outrode the storm, and the awakened sinner was saved to serve God in the world. On reaching Ireland, Newton heard from his father, who had gone to be Governor of York Fort, Hudson's Bay, but soon after received the painful news that his father had been drowned while bathing.

In his twenty-fifth year, Newton married Miss Catlett, whom he had loved from his boyhood with unfailing constancy, and whom he afterwards idolized. Up to the year 1754, we find him actively engaged in what he did not then regard as an unlawful occupation —the slave trade. As a captain, he did what he could for the religious benefit of the sailors under him. At the end of 1754, when about to set out on a voyage, he was seized with an apoplectic fit. In consequence of this, he rested for a time, and then obtained the office of tide-surveyor, at Liverpool. This position he held for eight years. His Christian life now became purified and strengthened by his experience, and he owed much to the religious influence of a captain whom he met with on one of his voyages.

Anxious to turn to good account for others the remarkable religious change he had experienced, he began, in the year 1758, to attempt to preach. His first efforts were so little successful, that he confined himself to a meeting on Sundays with his friends in his own house. He had all through life given some attention to mental improvement. Even amidst his privations in Africa he studied Euclid, and mastered six books, and during his voyages he pursued the study of Latin, though at first he had not even a dictionary to assist him. In the year 1764, and when in his thirty-ninth year, he entered upon a regular ministry. The Earl of Dartmouth presented him to the Vicarage of Olney. There he remained nearly sixteen years, faithfully serving in the Gospel, and at the same time daily consoling the suffering poet Cowper, and stimulating him to useful effort. Together they enjoyed the friendship of the eminent dissenting minister, the Rev. William Bull; together they dispensed the bounty of the benevolent John Thornton; and together they produced the "Olney Hymns." These hymns were written for the use of Newton's congregation, and contain those of Newton's and Cowper's which are so much in use in the Christian Church, and several of which are found in the "New Congregational Hymn Book."

On leaving Olney, Newton became rector of St. Mary Woolnoth, in London; there he became generally known, and his Christian usefulness was very great. His power was not merely in the pulpit, but in conversation and in his correspondence. Several of his works consist of letters: they are rich in Christian experience, and admirable for their clearness and simplicity. In this also Newton and Cowper were alike: both were eminent letter-writers.

His principal works were, besides the "Olney Hymns," a volume of Sermons, in 1760, before he took orders; "Forty-one Letters on Religious Subjects;" his "Narrative," published in 1764; a volume of Sermons in 1767; his "Review of Ecclesiastical History," in 1769; and in 1781 his "Cardiphonia, or Utterances of the Heart." He also published, in 1786, "Messiah," being fifty discourses on the Scripture passages in the Oratorio of that name.

One of the above works, his "Narrative," is intensely interesting. It traces minutely those remarkable special providences by which his life was spared just when it seemed about to be taken, and by which his course was diverted into the path of safety just when its persistency in the downward way seemed inevitable. At the venerable age of eighty-two, Newton laid down his life and labour together, and fell asleep in Jesus.

In the preface to the "Olney Hymns," which were published in 1779, and the greater number of which were written by Newton, he disclaims all pretensions to being a poet, and only claims the "mediocrity of talent which might qualify him for usefulness to the weak and poor of his flock;" and he further states, that his hymns are "the fruit and expression of his own experience." It is this that gives a personal interest and an evident reality to his hymns quite peculiar to them, and it is an important element in their value. We trace in them indications of his former wayward and miserable course; and, at the same time, we find in them the expression of the mind and heart of the matured Christian, and of the Christian minister in the midst of his activity, anxiety, and success: and Newton having to form a collection, was under the necessity of preparing hymns to meet the various requirements of public worship; hence, from him we obtain some of our most serviceable and most used hymns.

There are twenty-four hymns by Newton in the "New Congregational Hymn Book." Several of them are only parts of the originals. Almost all of them are from the "Olney Collection." Newton has stated his own views of what hymns should be, that are designed for use in public worship, in which the poor and unlearned join as well as the rich and cultivated. He says, "Perspicuity, simplicity, and ease, should be chiefly attended to; and the imagery and colouring of poetry, if admitted at all, should be indulged very sparingly, and with great judgment." His own hymns are in exact accordance with these views.

"How sweet the name of Jesus sounds."—No. 328.

It has been thought that this hymn was suggested by Bernard's "Jesu dulcis memoria," given in part in No. 329. No. 326, by Doddridge, and 327, by C. Wesley, are also similar, and may have sprung from the same ancient source.

"Day of judgment, day of wonders."—No. 419.

This is Newton's rendering of the "Dies iræ," by Thomas de Celano, about 1250.

"Though troubles assail."—No. 656.

This hymn appeared before the "Olney Collection," in the "Gospel Magazine," January, 1777.

"For a season called to part."—No. 848.

This is part of a parting hymn of seven verses given in the "Olney Collection," 1779, and beginning—

"As the sun's enlivening eye."

"Dear Shepherd of Thy people, hear."—No. 885.

This is part of a hymn of seven verses found in the "Olney Collection," 1779, beginning—

"O Lord, our languid souls inspire."

and headed "On Opening a Place for Social Prayer." It was one of two, of which Cowper wrote the other, written on the occasion of opening the Hall for prayer, near Olney, and of which some account is given in the sketch of Cowper.

"Bless, O Lord, the opening year."—No. 953.

This is part of one of Newton's hymns written to be sung "before Annual Sermons to young people on New Year's evenings." It consists of seven verses in the "Olney Collection," 1779, and begins with the verse given as the second in the "New Congregational,"—

"Now may fervent prayer arise."

LANGFORD.

"Now begin the heavenly theme."—No. 365.

This valued and beautiful hymn has had a place in the Christian Church for about a century. It is in Madan's collection, 1760, and in "A Collection of Hymns, by John Edwards, Minister of the Gospel, Leeds, Yorks. 2nd edition, 1769." It is said also to be in the first edition of that collection as early as 1756. It has long been usual to give the name "Langford" as that of the author of this hymn, but it is at present uncertain which Langford. The Rev. John Langford, a dissenting minister, who entered the ministry at Black's-fields, Southwark, 1766, and died 1790, published some Sermons and "Hymns and spiritual Songs," 1776; but this hymn is not in that collection, and is superior to those found there.

Some have thought that this hymn is by the celebrated divine, Dr. William Langford. He was born in 1704, at Westfield, near Battle, in Sussex. His father died when he was young, and he removed with his mother to Tenterden, in Kent, where he was educated. In 1721, he went to study at Glasgow University, where he graduated M.A. in 1727. He was distinguished for his early piety, and there is on record the covenant he made with God while at the University. On completing his studies, he became pastor of a church at Gravesend, and in 1734, co-pastor with the Rev. Thomas Bures, Silver Street, London. He also assisted Mr. Wood, at the Weigh-house Chapel, Eastcheap, from the year 1736, and in 1742 succeeded him in the pastorate, in which he continued with honour till his decease on April 23, 1775. In 1762, he received the diploma of D.D. from King's College, Aberdeen. He was the author of some published sermons. Dr. Thomas Gibbons, in his funeral sermon in memory of Dr. William Langford (of which there is a copy in Dr. Williams's library), gives a brief memoir of him, but does not speak of him as an author of hymns. This seems to be against his claim, because Dr. Gibbons, as himself a hymn-writer, would not have been likely to omit a fact of so much interest.

WILLIAM MASON, M.A.
1725—1797.

"Again returns the day of holy rest."—No. 760.

THIS is the first of a small number of hymns and select pieces given at the end of vol. i, of "The works of William Mason,

M.A., Precentor of York, and Rector of Aston," in four vols., 1811.

William Mason was a son of the vicar of St. Trinity Hall, in the East Riding of Yorkshire. He was born at Kingston-upon-Hull, in 1725. In 1742, he went to study at St. John's College, Cambridge, where he graduated; he was afterwards a fellow of Pembroke Hall. In 1754, he took orders, received the living of Aston, and became one of the chaplains of George III. In 1765, he married a lady, Miss Sherman, who died of consumption two years after.

Mr. Mason had early displayed poetical talent, and during his life he produced many odes, tragedies, and other poems. He enjoyed the friendship of the poet Gray, and published his memoirs and letters, in four vols., in 1775. His autobiographical style of memoir has had many imitators, from the time when Boswell successfully adopted his plan. Mr. Mason's tastes were not confined to poetry. He made, in 1783, a translation into English verse of "C. A. Du Fresnoy's Art of Painting," with notes full of information; and he published, in 1795, an " Essay, historical and critical, on English Church Music." The cause of his death was remarkable. In alighting from his carriage, he received a slight injury which was allowed to pass without notice, but at length mortification ensued, and he died, April 5th, 1797.

In addition to those named, he was the author of the following works. " Isis," a poem, 1748. Tragedies on the model of the ancients :—" Elfrida," 1751, and " Caractacus," 1759, which was afterwards given at Covent Garden Theatre. Other pieces were " Odes on Memory, Independency, Melancholy, and the Tale of Tyranny," 1756. Some excesses of style in this work exposed the author to ridicule. " Three elegies," 1762; his book of the " English Garden," four vols., in 1772, 1777, 1778, and, 1782; his "Ode to the Naval Officers of Great Britain;" his " Ode to Mr. Pitt," 1782; and his " Secular Ode in commemoration of the Glorious Revolution of 1688."

THOMAS OLIVERS.
1725—1799.

As the lark, ascending from the hidden depths of the grassy hollow, rises high and sings long and sweetly, so Olivers, coming of humble parentage, was at length known and honoured as a sweet singer in Israel. He was born at a village called Tregonan, in Montgomeryshire, in 1725. Both his parents died when he was four years old, and he was brought up by a farmer, Mr. Tudor, a distant relative, at Forden, in the same county. At eighteen, he was bound apprentice to a shoemaker; but owing to his bad conduct, of which he makes full confession in his "Autobiography," he was obliged to leave the neighbourhood. He went to Shrewsbury, then to Wrexham, and then to Bristol.

At Bristol, where he had gone to carry on his business, a sermon by Whitefield on the text, "Is not this a brand plucked out of the fire?" was the means of his spiritual quickening, and he became a true Christian. He says, that at that time he spent so many hours on his knees in prayer as to make him limp a little in walking.

As he had pursued a sinful course, and had left small sums owing in several places where he had lived, he went first to pay these sums, and to make what reparation he could. He removed to Bradford in Wiltshire, where he became a member of the Wesleyan Society, and was very zealous. He had scarcely set up in business, before Mr. Wesley sent for him to become one of his travelling preachers in Cornwall. He had preached before. He set out on the 1st of October, 1753, and preached in many parts of England and Ireland, accomplishing most of his journeys on a horse which he had for twenty-five years, and upon which he rode about 100,000 miles, often meeting with opposition and violence in his good work. He married Miss Green, a person of piety and good family in Scotland. He was a severe sufferer in himself and in his family, and died suddenly in London, in March,

1799. His educational advantages were small, yet he composed several hymns of very great excellence. Of these the most known are the two given in the "New Congregational Hymn Book."

"The God of Abraham praise,"—No. 256,

is part of a piece consisting of twelve stanzas. In the "New Congregational Hymn Book," seven stanzas are omitted between verses 4 and 5. Of the whole piece, Montgomery says, "This noble ode, though the essay of an unlettered man, claims special honour. There is not in our language a lyric of more majestic style, more elevated thought, or more glorious imagery: its structure, indeed, is unattractive; and, on account of the short lines, occasionally uncouth; but like a stately pile of architecture, severe and simple in design, it strikes less on the first view, than after deliberate examination, when its proportions become more graceful, its dimensions expand, and the mind itself grows greater in contemplating it." And Lord Henley mentions in his collection (1833) that this hymn was a source of great consolation to Henry Martyn, when with mingled feelings of regret and anxious hope he was bidding adieu to his native land, and setting out on his important missionary career. This hymn was written (1772) to a celebrated air, sung by Leoni at the Jews' Synagogue, in London. The hymn and tune reached their thirtieth edition in 1779.

The hymn—

"Lo! He comes, with clouds descending."—No. 418,

is erroneously attributed to Olivers. He composed the tune Helmsley for it, and several other tunes. It is by Cennick and C. Wesley, *vide* Cennick, p. 168.

Mr. Olivers wrote a "Descriptive and Plaintive Elegy on the death of the late Rev. John Wesley," 1791. He was also the author of some tracts on the Calvinistic controversy, written in defence of Wesley. In his later years he took the charge of Wesley's printing, and undertook the supervision of the "Arminian Magazine," but he desisted from this in 1789, as his literary accuracy and scholarship were found inadequate to the work.

HON. AND REV. WALTER SHIRLEY.

1725—1786.

"Lord, dismiss us with Thy blessing."—No. 702

The first appearance of this favourite hymn (in the "New Congregational Hymn Book," erroneously attributed to Madan) is believed to be in Dr. Conyers' Collection, 1774. A. C. Hobart Seymour, Esq., himself one of our hymn-writers, and one who has given, for many years, attention to hymnology, has assigned to this hymn the above-named authorship. Mr. Seymour is connected by marriage with Mr. Shirley's descendants, and has in his possession the manuscript of some of his hymns. He has informed the author of this work, that the late Rev. Walter Shirley, son of the poet, always stated that this hymn was by his father, and that it was so believed generally by the members of the family.

The Hon. and Rev. Walter Shirley was the friend of Whitefield and Wesley, and the brother-in-law and friend of the Countess of Huntingdon, in whose chapels he often preached. He was a successful Episcopal minister at Loughrea, in Ireland. He died of a painful disease, in his sixty-first year, in 1786. When he could no longer leave the house, he used to preach seated in his chair in his drawing-room to many who gladly assembled to hear. He took a deep interest in the modern missionary work, then in its infancy, and when, in 1772, the missionaries sent by Lady Huntingdon were about to embark for America, he wrote the hymn,—

"Go, destined vessel, heavenly freighted, go!
For lo! the Lord's ambassadors are there," &c.

About the year 1774, the Countess appointed Mr. Shirley to

revise her collection of hymns. That collection contained several beautiful hymns by him. He was the author of a volume of sermons, and of two poems, published in Dublin in 1761, entitled " Liberty, an Ode," and " The Judgment."

EDWARD PERRONET.
Died 1792.

About the year 1750, we find references in Charles Wesley's Diary to one in whom he took a deep interest, a Christian brother and companion in travel, whom he familiarly calls " Ned." This was his friend Edward Perronet, son of the Rev. Vincent Perronet, a well-known excellent evangelical clergyman, who was Vicar of Shoreham for fifty years; and we learn from Lady Huntingdon's Memoirs (Vol. II., page 135), that Charles and Edward Perronet were preachers in Mr. Wesley's Connexion for a short time. " The former desisted for want of health, and the latter from some change in his opinions. Charles Perronet died at Canterbury in 1776, but his brother survived him many years, and possessed equal powers with him, to which was superadded a large fund of wit." After assisting the preachers the Countess of Huntingdon sent to Canterbury, Mr. Perronet preached there and elsewhere by the direction of the Countess, and with great success. But his great hostility to the Church system at length gave offence to the Countess, and she ceased to avail herself of his services. For although the son of a clergyman, Edward Perronet was the author of an anonymous poem, called " The Mitre," which is believed to have been a very keen satire on the national Establishment. It was printed, but did not appear, because, it is said, of the intervention of Mr. Wesley. After ceasing his connection with Lady Huntingdon, Mr. Perronet preached to a small congregation of Dissenters till his death, in January, 1792. He died at Canterbury, and his dying words were,

"Glory to God in the height of His divinity: Glory to God in the depth of His humanity; Glory to God in His all-sufficiency; and into His hands I commend my spirit."

Edward Perronet wrote a number of small poems and hymns, chiefly on sacred subjects. They do not display much poetical talent, but the versification is smooth and pleasing, and the sentiment is always good. His pieces were not written for publication, but were published by request of his friends. They are entitled " Occasional Verses, Moral and Sacred, published for the Instruction and Amusement of the candidly serious and religious." 1785.

" All hail the power of Jesu's name!"—No. 414.

This well-known hymn, his sole contribution to the "New Congregational Hymn Book," is found in the above-mentioned book, page 22, and is headed, "On the Resurrection." It is altered from the original, which has eight verses. It had previously appeared, without signature, in the "Gospel Magazine," for 1780.

At his death, Perronet is said to have left a large sum of money to Shrubsole, who was organist at Spafields Chapel, London, from 1784 till his death, in 1806, and who had composed the tune, "Miles' Lane," for the above hymn. This tune was in former times usually sung to this hymn.

JOHN STOCKER.

1776.

IN the years 1776 and 1777 several hymns were published in the " Gospel Magazine," which are believed to be the productions of the above hymn-writer. All that is known of him is that he was of Honiton, Devon. Mr. Daniel Sedgwick has published the hymns given in the " Gospel Magazine," along with the poems and hymns of Job Hupton. There are nine hymns by Stocker; they are all earnest Gospel hymns. Two are superior to the rest—

"Gracious Spirit, Dove divine,"

a hymn not found in the "New Congregational Hymn Book," but given in some collections; and—

"Thy mercy, my God, is the theme of my song."—No. 297.

This is given in the "Gospel Magazine," March, 1776, with the initials "J. S." In the "New Congregational Hymn Book," four verses, similar in character to the rest, are omitted. As a genuine heart-utterance in praise of mercy, it will be admitted to have a charm peculiar to itself.

MADAN.

FOUR hymns in the "New Congregational" are attributed to the Rev. Martin Madan (1726—1790), the friend and relative of Cowper, and the popular preacher at the Lock Hospital, London. But as these hymns were not actually written by Madan, but only thought to be because they were in his collection, a sketch of him is not given. His collection was first published in 1760, and had reached its thirteenth edition in 1794. It might have been of great service to hymnology, but unfortunately the authors' names were not given.

For hymn 581—

"Lord, if Thou the grace impart,"

vide under "Charles Wesley," page 143.

For hymn 782—

"Come, Thou Almighty King,"

vide also under "Charles Wesley," page 144.

For hymn 703—

"Rise, my soul, and stretch thy wings,"

vide under "Robert Seagrave," page 102.

For hymn 792—
"Lord, dismiss us with Thy blessing,"
vide under "Hon. and Rev. Walter Shirley," page 193.

SAMUEL STENNETT, D.D.
1727—1795.

In the Baptist denomination Stennett is an honoured name. The most illustrious member of the family was the subject of this sketch. He was born at Exeter, where his father, Dr. Joseph Stennett, was pastor of the Baptist Church. In 1737 his father became pastor of the Baptist Church in Little Wild Street, London. Into this fellowship the poet was received while still young, and subsequently he became his father's assistant, and, at length, in 1758, his successor. Of this church he continued to be the pastor till his death. He was eminent as a scholar, and received his diploma of Doctor of Divinity from King's College, Aberdeen, in the year 1763. His style of writing was at once Addisonian and forcible, and his style of speaking accurate and classical. He enjoyed the friendship of his sovereign, George III., for whom he is said to have done some literary work; but, faithful to his convictions, he refused the preferment offered to him; and as a true friend of freedom, he used his utmost efforts to assist in the good work of getting the Test and Corporation Acts repealed, a work subsequently accomplished in 1828. Dr. Stennett felt severely the death of his wife, which happened in the year of his own death; but having strength to acquiesce in the Divine will, he patiently awaited his own departure. He died, with joyful confidence in Christ, August 24th, 1795.

John Howard, the eminent philanthropist, was an admiring hearer of Dr. Samuel Stennett, and wrote from Smyrna, August 11th, 1786, expressing the pleasure he had experienced in reviewing the notes of his sermons which he had with him.

Dr. Samuel Stennett was the author of a work, entitled "Remarks on the Christian Minister's Reasons for administering Baptism by Sprinkling, &c., 1772 ;" and about three years after he published a second volume, entitled, "An Answer to the Christian Minister's Reasons for Baptizing Infants, &c." His works have been published with a memoir by Mr. William Jones (1824); thirty-four hymns, written by Dr. S. Stennett, are given at the end. Five others, by him, have been found in " Rippon's Selection," for which he probably wrote his hymns.

Three hymns in the " New Congregational Hymn Book," Nos. 527, 741, and 804, are by Dr. Samuel Stennett ; they are given at the end of his works : without displaying special poetic genius, they are good and useful.

" On Jordan's stormy banks I stand."—No. 741.

Dr. Stennett, who was just arriving at manhood when Dr. Watts died, has evidently followed him in this hymn, which bears a close resemblance to Watts'—

" There is a land of pure delight."—No. 742.

But Dr. Stennett says less of fear, and is bolder in confidence. Compare the last verse of each hymn.

WILLIAM SHRUBSOLE.
1729—1797.

" Arm of the Lord, awake ! awake !"—No. 918.

THIS fine missionary hymn, which is found in many collections, is the work of the Rev. William Shrubsole, of Sheerness. It is the only hymn by him in the " New Congregational Hymn Book." It is given in " Dobell's Collection," 1806, from a " Missionary Collection." 1780 is the date assigned to it. Hymn 910, erroneously attributed to him, is by the Rev. Matthew Wilks. Charles Wesley has a hymn, founded on the same passage as Shrubsole's, Isaiah li. 9, and beginning with the same line.

Mr. Shrubsole's principal work was " Christian Memoirs ; or a review of the present state of religion in England, in the form of a new Pilgrimage to the Heavenly Jerusalem ; containing, by way of allegorical narrative, a great variety of dialogues and adventures of eminently religious persons," 1776, Rochester. This is a curious allegorical work—after the manner of Bunyan. It extends to 400 pages, and is very severe on religious errors. This work is prefaced by a letter of approval from W. Mason, author of " The Christian's Spiritual Treasury." The letter bears date Rotherhithe, September 24th, 1775. In the address to the reader, Mr. Shrubsole says, " The following narrative was first taken in hand to divert my mind from melancholy reflections, which arose from too great attention to what might be the fatal consequence of an accident that befel me in October, 1773." The congenial pursuit cheered his mind, and the work extended as he gave attention to it. The second edition of this work was published in 1790. To this edition, which contained some alterations, was appended an elegy by Mr. Shrubsole, on the death of Whitefield ; originally published in 1771, the year after Whitefield died. The elegy extends to thirty-five verses, and is vigorous and eulogistic. It maintains an average excellence without being marked by indications of poetic genius. The third edition of the same work was published in 1807, after the author's death, by his son, who has added a life of the author, from which we glean the following particulars :—

Mr. Shrubsole was born at Sandwich, on the 7th of April, 1729. After a few years' instruction in the Town School, he went to work with his father, and in February, 1743, he was apprenticed to Mr. George Cook, a shipwright, at Sheerness. His removal from home gave him more scope to indulge his vicious propensities ; but by providential circumstances his evil course was checked, and he was led to reflect on the uncertainty of life, and of all human things. At about the age of twenty, he took up casually a volume by Isaac Ambrose, and reading again and again in the same book, he was conscious, by the Divine blessing, of a great spiritual change. He derived benefit also from reading " Luther on the Galatians." Then he began to devote all his leisure to the reading of the Scriptures and of religious books. There were at Sheerness a few persons who used to meet on Sunday afternoon to read and pray, after the service of the Established Church was ended. Among them he found the Christian sympathy and help he required.

In the year 1752, when he was twenty-three years of age, the Society encouraged him to lead their devotions, and to read sermons to them; and as he ripened in his manhood, he found great encouragement to self improvement from his friendship with a bookseller at Rochester, Thomas Fisher, who obtained books for him, and encouraged him to learn languages, and to pursue theological studies. In 1768 the Society erected a meeting-house, and he continued to read sermons to them whenever ministers could not be obtained, (till 1766.) After that year he expounded to them, and at length undertook public preaching, though with great diffidence, and with some apprehension that by so public a procedure he should for ever forfeit the promotion which he expected in the dockyard. This fear proved to be groundless, and he received the promotion he desired. Subsequently, he preached on Sundays at Sheerness, and occasionally at other towns in Kent. In 1773 he was appointed master mastmaker at Woolwich, but later in the same year he received promotion at Sheerness, and returned to be with his old friends. This was the year in which he was bitten by a mad dog, and his life was thus put in jeopardy. It was to relieve his anxiety with respect to his family if a fatal result should follow, that he occupied his mind with his "Christian Memoirs."

In 1784, a great blessing having attended Mr. Shrubsole's ministry, it was found necessary to erect a new chapel, and this in its turn had three years after to be enlarged. In 1793 he had a paralytic stroke, and two years after, in consequence of his increasing infirmities, a co-pastor, the Rev. Mr. Buck, was appointed. On Sunday, the 5th of February, 1797, he preached with fervour in the afternoon, but on Monday he was taken with an alarming illness that terminated his life on Tuesday, the 7th. He had often expressed himself desirous of joining his numerous departed friends, and of being with his Saviour in heaven. Mr. Shrubsole had married Margaret Cook, the daughter of his worthy master and mistress at Sheerness, in October, 1757. He had four children, two of whom, with his widow, survived him. His ministerial services, which were both laborious and useful, were entirely gratuitous. While fulfilling his ministry, he maintained himself and his family by his salary in the dockyard.

Mr. Shrubsole was the author of several series of letters, which appeared in periodicals on the great religious controversies of his day, and of some pamphlets on the same subjects. He also wrote some lectures on edifying subjects in Scripture history, for distribution by the late benevolent John Thornton, Esq., of Clapham; and to assist his companions in their effort to get increased pay, he wrote an able pamphlet entitled, "A plea in favour of the Shipwrights belonging to the Royal Dockyard," 1770. He was also the author of "The plain Christian Shepherd's Defence of his Flock, being Five Letters in support of Infant Baptism," 1794.

WILLIAM COWPER.
1731—1800.

WILLIAM COWPER was the son of Dr. John Cowper, who was chaplain to George II., and rector of Berkhampstead, Hertfordshire, where the poet was born, on the 15th November, 1731. He was also cousin to Martin Madan, compiler of "Madan's Collection;" and his grandfather was a judge, and brother of the first Earl Cowper, the Lord Chancellor. At six years of age, Cowper experienced one of the greatest losses possible to any child, but inexpressibly great to him, in being deprived of a fond and faithful mother. Dear to every filial heart are the pathetic verses he wrote on receiving her portrait many years after her death. As a child, Cowper had delicate health, and suffered from a complaint in his eyes. But at nine years of age he was thought strong enough to be sent to a public

school. Westminster was fixed on, and there he enjoyed educational advantages, and formed friendships with some who were afterwards known as men of talent and position; but there he was to so great an extent the victim of the "fagging" system as to feel through life a strong dislike to public schools. Hence his severe exposure of their evils in his "Tirocinium, or a Review of Schools," written in 1784. Of this book, he says:—
"The business and purpose of it are to censure the want of discipline and the scandalous inattention to morals that obtain in them, especially in the largest, and to recommend private tuition as a mode of education preferable on all accounts."

At the age of eighteen, Cowper was articled for three years to an attorney; but, not liking the law and having good prospects in life, he was "constantly employed," as he says, "from morning to night in giggling and making giggle, instead of studying the law." His companion in the office was the future Lord Chancellor Thurlow. Up to the age of thirty-two, Cowper was engaged in the Temple, nominally preparing himself for the profession of a barrister, but really doing little more than cultivate literary acquaintance with his old Westminster companions, and occasionally compose a few verses, or contribute to the periodicals. But so unimportant were his literary productions at that period of his life, that when at the age of fifty he began to publish his works, they were regarded as those of a new writer.

After spending several years in this way without any special result, and when his resources began to be reduced, his influential relatives obtained for him the offices of Reading Clerk and Clerk of the Committees of the House of Lords. But as these appointments involved his frequent appearance before the House, his diffidence would not allow him to retain them. He was next appointed Clerk of the Journals, an office that did not require such public appearances. But, unfortunately, in consequence of the right of nomination having been disputed, it was necessary for Cowper to appear at the bar of the House before he could receive the office. This untoward circumstance quite overset his reason; and, after attempting suicide, he was placed under the care of Dr. Cotton, at St. Albans.

In 1765, on his recovery, Cowper went to reside at Huntingdon, in order to be near his brother, who was then studying at Cambridge. At Huntingdon the poet made the acquaintance of the Unwins, who became his companions and friends for life, and with whom he resided till Mrs. Unwin's death, many years after. In 1767, on the death of Mr. Unwin, Cowper and Mrs. Unwin removed to Olney, on the invitation of the Rev. John Newton, who was then curate there. The succeeding nine years were of the greatest importance to Cowper. His religious life was developed as they passed; he began to feel his power as a writer; he had many home blessings, and found himself in happy association with several persons of genius and piety: and what was still more to one tempted to gloomy seclusion and morbid melancholy, he met with friends who constantly made efforts to beguile him of those dreary thoughts that drove him to the brink of despair. Amongst his principal friends were the Rev. William Bull, of Newport Pagnel, and the Rev. John Newton, of Olney. Mrs. Unwin's house was close to the vicarage, and Newton and Cowper exchanged visits almost daily. Newton had passed through extraordinary experiences himself, and knew how to meet the case of his suffering friend. Cowper describes himself as a stricken deer, found by "one who had himself been hurt by th' archers," and how with gentle force,

> "The darts soliciting,
> He drew them forth, and heal'd and bade him live."

At that time Cowper had so far overcome his diffidence as occasionally to offer prayer at a religious meeting, established by Mr. Newton, at a mansion in the neighbourhood of Olney. One who was often present, said—"Of all the men I ever heard pray none equalled Mr. Cowper."

It was during this period that the "Olney Hymns" were prepared. Cowper had promised to share with his friend Newton in the labour of their production, but before he had contributed many hymns, he was visited with a second attack of insanity, and compelled to desist from his work. The " Olney Collection " was published in 1779, and before Cowper was known as a poet. To it Cowper contributed sixty-two hymns, and Newton 286.

In the year 1770, Cowper was distressed by the loss of his brother, to whom he was much attached, and in 1773 he sank into a state of despondency. For a long time the kindness of his friends was unavailing for his restoration. Ceasing from literary occupation, and amusing himself with his hares, whose memory he has immortalized by what he has written of them, he at length, in 1778, recovered. But it was not till 1780, and when he was nearly fifty years of age, that he began to write his poems. He says of himself:—"At fifty years of age I commenced as an author; it is a whim that has served me longest and best, and will probably be my last." He was urged to engage in the production of poetry, to occupy and amuse his mind, and to prevent it from despondency. His first volume, published in 1782, included "The Progress of Error," "Truth," "Expostulation," "Hope," "Charity," "Conversation," and "Retirement." On the departure of Newton to London, in 1780, his place had been supplied by the Rev. William Bull; and, in 1781, the poet's small circle was increased by the addition of Lady Austen—a lady whose vivacity and genius qualified her to cheer him in his melancholy gloom. The amusing poem, "John Gilpin," arose from a story Lady Austen related to Cowper, and at her suggestion he began, in 1784, his work, "The Task." It was at the request of Mr. Bull, that Cowper made, in 1782, his translations from the poems of Madame Guyon. Of her poetry, he says, "her verse is the only French verse I can read that I find agreeable, and there is a neatness in it equal to that which we applaud with so much reason in the composition of Prior." And on reading to his friends Pope's translation of Homer, and having often to complain of its deviations from the original, Lady Austen proposed that he should write another translation. This was begun in 1784, and occupied him, in its first production and subsequent revision, till the end of his days.

His second volume of poetry appeared in 1785, and his translation of Homer in 1791. In 1792 he published a translation of letters written in Latin by Mr. Vanleer, a minister in the Dutch colony at the Cape. The work is entitled "The Power of Grace Illustrated," and consists of an account of the writer's conversion from scepticism to Christianity. Other publishing plans he had thought of, but the failure of Mrs. Unwin's health increased his depression of mind, and prevented him from carrying out his projects. His cousin, Lady Hesketh, endeavoured to cheer and console him when Mrs. Unwin's state of health rendered her unequal to her former work of companionship and consolation. She also afforded him valuable pecuniary assistance, and, in 1795, a royal pension of £300 per annum was granted to him.

At this time, a relative, Mr. Johnson, having a living in Norfolk, induced Mrs. Unwin and Cowper to remove thither, where they resided, first at North Tuddenham, and then at Mundesley, on the coast. Mrs. Unwin died in 1796. The grateful poet continued to the last unceasing in his attentions to the faithful companion to whom he had at one time hoped to be united in marriage. Cowper's uncertain mental condition prevented this union, but the honourable friendship continued to the end. From the blow of separation he never recovered, though he was able afterwards to give some attention to the revision of his "Homer;" but after becoming surrounded again by the dark cloud of despondency that had so often encompassed him, he died of dropsy, April, 1800, in the sixty-ninth year of his age.

His poems were received coldly at first, partly from the uninviting form in which they at that time appeared; partly perhaps from their unpretending style, which carefully avoids the obscurity often mistaken for profundity; and partly because of the high tone of their religious character, which made them unpalatable to some. But they have now risen to their just place in the public estimation. They have a melancholy interest as the productions of the man Cowper. "He has invented," says Thomas Campbell, "no character in fable, nor in the drama; but he has left a record of his own character, which forms not only an object of deep sympathy, but a subject for the study of human nature." And his works have long been recognized as the poems of the philanthropist, they are not only pure from evil, but powerful for good. His invectives against slavery and other national wrongs, have left an indelible impression upon the public mind, the full results of which we are only now receiving.

And Cowper marks an era in the history of our poetry. Macaulay says: "The forerunner of the great restoration of our literature was Cowper." And a modern writer has well said of his poetry: "Its main charm, and that which is never wanting, is its earnestness. This is a quality which gives it a power over many minds not at all alive to the poetical; but it is also the source of some of its strongest attractions for those that are. Hence, its truth both of landscape-painting, and of the description of character and states of mind; hence its skilful expression of such emotions and passions as it allows itself to deal with; hence the force and fervour of its denunciatory eloquence, giving to some passages as fine an inspiration of the moral sublime as is perhaps anywhere to be found in didactic poetry. Hence, we may say, even the directness, simplicity, and manliness of Cowper's diction—all that is best in the form, as well as in the spirit of his verse. It was this quality, or temper of mind, in short, that principally made him an original poet; and if not the founder of a new school, the pioneer of a new era of English poetry. Instead of repeating the unmeaning conventionalities and faded affectations of his predecessors, it led him to turn to the actual nature within him and around him, and there to learn both the truths he should utter and the words in which he should utter them."

As a prose writer, Cowper left no important work, but his letters have been collected and published; and besides the value they possess because of the light they throw on his sad but intensely interesting character and career, they have their own intrinsic worth as models of correspondence. Their excellence made Southey describe Cowper as "the most popular poet of his generation, and the best of English letter-writers."

Cowper's hymns are part of the prized treasures of the Christian Church. Several of them give expression to the dark passages of religious experience through which he was passing.

"God moves in a mysterious way."—No. 281.

The title of this hymn is "Light shining out of darkness." It is said, that on one occasion Cowper thought it was the Divine will he should go to a particular part of the river Ouse and drown himself, but the driver of the postchaise missed his way, and on the poet's return he wrote this hymn. By others, it is said to have been written during a solitary walk in the fields, when he had a presentiment of the gloom that would soon fall on him again, but was still cleaving to God in whom he trusted. Montgomery says, "It is a lyric of high tone and character, and rendered awfully interesting by the circumstances under which it was written—in the twilight of departing reason." It was the last he composed for the "Olney Collection." And after studying his life, we are not surprised to find two hymns (Nos. 640 and 644) by Cowper, under the head of "Declensions in the Christian Life." It was a happy circumstance that having to contribute to a collection that was to meet the various wants of a public assembly, led Cowper to write on several great subjects; but those of his hymns are the most pathetic which give expression to his own inward fears and conflicts. Such are:—

"O for a closer walk with God,
A calm and heavenly frame."—No. 644.

And,

"O Lord, my best desire fulfil"—No. 598.

especially the last verse—

"But ah! mine inward spirit cries,
Still bind me to Thy sway:
Else the next cloud that veils my skies,
Drives all these thoughts away."

"Far from the world, O Lord, I flee."—No. 679.

This is said to have been the second hymn Cowper composed for the "Olney Collection." It deserves notice as containing the germ of the poem he afterwards wrote on "Retirement." This hymn has a history. On his journey to Huntingdon when recovering, the poet enjoyed communion with God. On reaching Huntingdon, he found himself left by his brother amongst strangers, and being depressed in mind he withdrew into a solitary place and prayed. God heard him and cheered his heart. The next day being Sunday, he greatly enjoyed the service at church, and was struck by the devotion of a fellow-worshipper. Full of joy, he retired from God's house to the same "calm retreat," and there, having seen God as it were "face to face," he poured out his heart in this hymn.

There are eighteen of Cowper's hymns in the "New Congregational Hymn Book." They are all taken from the "Olney Collection;" and admirable as they are, they are to be thought of as produced when the poet, though not young in years, was but trying his "'prentice hand," and had not yet composed those master pieces upon which his reputation as a poet rests.

"Jesus, where'er Thy people meet."—No. 883.

This is one of two hymns written, one by Cowper and the other by Newton, and headed "On opening a place for Social Prayer." The occasion is believed to have been the opening of a mansion, called the "Great House," in the neighbourhood of Olney, by Newton, for a religious meeting. There Cowper was amongst those who offered public prayer; and there Newton used to go for meditation and private prayer.

The much admired hymn—

"To Jesus, the crown of my hope"

was written after his contributions to the "Olney Collection." It was probably the last hymn Cowper wrote. It is not given in the "New Congregational Hymn Book."

Authors and publishers are sometimes tempted to regard each

other as natural enemies, and they are usually jealous of any interference with each others' domain. But it was otherwise with Cowper and his publisher, Joseph Johnson, of St. Paul's Churchyard. Johnson, who was a man of good taste, had printed the "Olney Hymns," and on Newton's recommendation, was appointed to publish Cowper's poems. Through Newton, the poetic publisher suggested that if Mr. Cowper would not be offended he could point out lines that might easily be much improved. Cowper's reply, July 7th, 1781, exhibits his character in a very pleasing light. He says: "I had rather submit to chastisement now than be obliged to undergo it hereafter. If Johnson therefore will mark with a marginal (qy), those lines that he or his object to, I will willingly retouch them, or give a reason for my refusal." Cowper afterwards acknowledged that these marked lines had been altered much to the improvement of his poems.

JAMES NEWTON, M.A.
1733—1790.

"Let plenteous grace descend on those."—No. 839.

This is hymn 469 in "Rippon's Selection," 1787, where it is headed "After Baptism." It begins there with another verse:—

"Proclaim, saith Christ, my wondrous grace."

James Newton was a native of Chenies, Bucks, where he was born in 1733. He was trained in piety. At seventeen years of age, he went to London, where he became a member of the church at Maze Pond, under the care of the Rev. Benjamin Wallin, M.A. Having received some preparation for the ministry under Dr. Llewelyn, he became, about the year 1757, assistant minister to Mr. Tommas, at the Pithay Chapel, Bristol. In 1770, he became classical tutor to the Bristol Education Society, along with Dr. Caleb Evans and the Rev. Hugh Evans, M.A. That office he filled with honour till his decease, April 8th, 1790, in the fifty-seventh year of his age. He was the author of some published sermons and pamphlets, and of a few useful hymns.

JAMES ALLEN.
1734—1804.

THIS preacher and poet, the son of Oswald Allen, was born at Gayle, in Wensleydale, Yorkshire, on the 24th of June, 1734. He was placed at first under the care of a clergyman to be trained for the Established Church; but as the conduct of that clergyman was not approved, he was removed, at the age of seventeen, to Scorton School, near Richmond, Yorkshire. This school was under the charge of a respected clergyman, the Rev. Mr. Noble. During this period of schooling, James Allen often heard the preachers connected with Mr. Ingham, or Mr. Ingham himself, and became attached to them and their doctrines. Mr. Benjamin Ingham had left the Church of England in 1732, and had at first joined the Methodists. He accompanied the Wesleys to Georgia, and on his return joined the Moravian Brethren. He afterwards became one of Lady Huntingdon's preachers, and married Lady Mary Hastings, her daughter. In 1760, he came under the influence of the writings of Glas and Sandeman, and incorporated some of their views with his own. His followers were called Inghamites. They were Independents in Church discipline, but insisted upon some minor peculiarities in doctrine and practice.

With Mr. Ingham, James Allen connected himself in 1752. He had previously spent a year at St. John's College, Cambridge. Mr. Allen soon became, like his leader, a zealous and useful itinerant preacher. It is recorded that on one occasion, being in danger from the mob at Kirkby-Lonsdale, he was delivered by the timely arrival of a magistrate who was an old college friend. In 1761, Mr. Allen went to Scotland, in company with the Messrs. Batty, to make inquiry concerning the character of the churches founded by Messrs. Glas and Sandeman. Impressed with what he had seen, Mr. Allen urged upon Mr. Ingham to adopt the new methods, but as Mr. Ingham was not prepared to adopt all that he wished, he retired, with many others, from his connexion. At first he joined the Sandemanians, but subsequently he left them and built a chapel on his own estate at Gayle, where he continued to minister until his death in 1804. His doctrine as well as his discipline, he says, had received some modification.

James Allen was the editor and principal contributor to what is called "The Kendal Hymn Book." The title of this book, taken from Charles Wesley's smaller collection, of ten years previous, was "A Collection of Hymns for the use of those that seek, and those that have found Redemption in the Blood of Christ. Kendal, 1757." The preface explains that the book is not intended to supersede others, but to aid in promoting the cause of the Redeemer. The preface is signed " J. A., C. B. &c."; and it is known that the contributors were James Allen, Christopher Batty, William Batty, Thomas Rawson, James Hartley, John Green, Alice Batty, Benjamin Ingham, and S. M. The number of hymns (second edition) was 142, of which James Allen contributed seventy-one, and C. Batty, thirty. The third edition contained a few additional hymns; and after his settlement at Gayle, Mr. Allen published seventeen hymns, entitled " Christian Songs :" these also have been reprinted.

"Glory to God on high."—No. 338.

This is erroneously attributed in the "New Congregational Hymn Book," to Boden. It is given with great variations from the original; the verses being transposed, and verses two and six substituted for those in the original. This hymn is found in the "Appendix" to the above-mentioned "Kendal Hymn Book." The appendix was not printed until 1761.

"Sweet the moments rich in blessing."—No. 871.

This is erroneously attributed in the "New Congregational Hymn Book" to Batty. On the authority of Allen's own marked copy of the " Kendal Hymn Book," we know that it is part of his piece of six stanzas given there, beginning—

" While my Jesus I'm possessing."

The form in which it is given in the "New Congregational Hymn Book" is that in which it is given in the Countess of Huntingdon's collection. It is the work of the Hon. and Rev. Walter Shirley, the editor of an edition of that collection, a relative of the Countess, and himself a hymn-writer. He had poetic feeling enough to recognize a true hymn in the original. He saw the diamond in the rough, and he had taste to remove what was superfluous, and to give the needed polish to the precious gem that remained. So that we owe this valued hymn scarcely less to Shirley than to Allen. Unaltered, the hymn would have been rejected as objectionable ; wisely and tastefully altered, it takes its place among the best.

THOMAS HAWEIS, LL.B., M.D.

1734—1820.

THIS poet-preacher, to whom we are indebted for two of our favourite hymns, was born at Truro, Cornwall, and educated at Christ's College, Cambridge. He was afterwards assistant-preacher to the Rev. M. Madan, at the Lock Hospital, London. Subsequently he became chaplain to the Countess of Huntingdon and entered upon the rectorship of All Saints, Aldwinkle, Northamptonshire. The rectorship was undertaken for a definite period, but when the time came for relinquishing it, Dr. Haweis was unwilling to do so. This involved him in a paper war with Mr. Madan ; but the matter was compromised by the Countess of Huntingdon, and Dr. Haweis retained his living till his death. He died at Bath, where he had gone to reside. He was popular preacher, and one of the founders' of the London Missionary Society. By reading Captain Cook's account of his voyages to the South Seas, his mind was much affected, and he desired that a missionary should be sent to Tahiti. Having brought the matter under the attention of the Countess of Huntingdon, two students from Trevecca, Messrs. Waugh and Price went to Dr. Haweis, at Bath, to prepare for the work. Dr. Haweis was the author of several prose works : " A Life of the Rev. W. Romaine ; " a work entitled " The Communicant's Spiritual Companion ; " " A History of the Church," in three vols, 1800 ; " A Translation of the New Testament ;" and " A Commentary on the Holy Bible."

"Enthroned on high, Almighty Lord,"—No. 426,

is by Dr. Haweis. In his own collection it is under the heading, " Day of Pentecost." He is also the author of No. 506, and of the favourite hymn, No. 649—

"O Thou, from whom all goodness flows."

These hymns are taken from his collection, " Carmina Christo ; or, Hymns to the Saviour : designed for the use and comfort of those who worship the Lamb that was slain. 1792." This collection consists of 256 hymns by the author : it has gone through several editions. In the preface, the author complains that, " Even in our public worship the voice of joy and gladness is too commonly silent, unless in that shameful mode of psalmody, now almost confined to the wretched solo of a parish clerk, or to a few persons huddled together in one corner of the church, who sing to the praise and glory of themselves, for the entertainment, or oftener for the weariness, of the rest of the congregation—an absurdity too glaring to be overlooked, and too shocking to be ridiculous ! "

And after recognizing the valuable labours of Watts, Doddridge, Cowper, Wesley, and others, he says, " I come with these offerers to cast my mite into the treasury. With what success or acceptance I know not ; but this I may venture to say, whether these hymns engage the attention or meet the neglect, suffer the censure or receive the approbation of the Christian world, they are such as my heart indited, and they speak the things which I have believed concerning my God and King. They all point to one object, and lead to one end—to a crucified Jesus!"

ROBERT ROBINSON.
1735—1790.

It may excite surprise to find the eccentric and talented Robinson, of Cambridge, among the hymn-writers, because he is so little known as a poet, but it will be found that he wrote at least two hymns that bear marks of his genius and power, and that have become favourites.

He was born at Swaffham, in Norfolk, but in his eighth year his parents removed to Scarning, in the same county. A few years after, Robinson's mother was left a widow, to struggle with poverty. Young Robinson was very promising as a boy, and there was an intention of training him for the Established Church, but the requisite means could not be obtained. At the age of fourteen, he was apprenticed to a hair-dresser in London, who often had to find fault with him for giving more attention to his books than to his business.

At the age of seventeen, he went on one occasion on Sunday with some companions to spend a day as a holiday. Their first sport was to render a fortune-telling old woman intoxicated, that they might amuse themselves with her predictions. While in this state, she predicted that Robinson would see his children and grandchildren. This prospect struck his active mind, and he determined to store his memory with what might interest his family in future years. To make a beginning, he determined to hear the celebrated George Whitefield that night. In a letter written to Whitefield six years after, he says, "I confess, it was to spy the *nakedness* of the land I came—to pity the folly of the preacher, the infatuation of the hearers, and to abhor the doctrine." He adds, " I went pitying the poor deluded Methodists, but came away envying their happiness." Whitefield was preaching on Matthew iii. 7, and his solemn words on " the wrath to come," produced a profound and lasting impression on the mind of young Robinson. For two years and seven months he remained in a state of perplexity and fear, but at length in 1755 he found, he believed, "full and free forgiveness through the precious blood of Jesus Christ." His own account of this momentous change in his life is interesting. It is as follows, and was written on a blank leaf of one of his books:—" Robertus, Michælis Mariæque Robinson Filius. Natus Swaffahmi, comitatu Norfolciæ, Saturni die Sept. 27, 1735. Renatus Sabbati die, Maii 24, 1752, per predicationem potentem Georgii Whitefield. Et gustatis doloribus Renovationis duos annos mensesque septem, absolutionem plenam gratuitamque, per sanguinem pretiosum Jesu Christi, inveni (Tuesday, Dec. 10, 1755), cui sit honor et gloria in secula seculorum. Amen." He remained in London a few years longer, often hearing Wesley, Whitefield, and others, associating with Christian men and gaining religious experience.

His Christian friends in London soon perceived in him the qualifications for a preacher, and urged him to develope and exercise his gifts. At length, in the beginning of 1758, he removed to Mildenhall, where he occasionally preached, and thence to Norwich, to be a pastor there. But, owing to his dissatisfaction with the character of some of the members of this church, he seceded with others to found another Christian church. In the following year he married, and began supplying a church at Cambridge, the scene of his future labours. This was a Baptist church, Robinson having then recently joined that denomination. The church there urged him, again and again, to the acceptance of the full pastoral office, but it was not till the year 1761, and when they had conceded the point of open communion, upon which he insisted, that he consented. At first his means were very small, and his church and congregation were few in number. But at the end of three years a good chapel was erected, and the congregation increased, often including in its number members of the University, some of whom, however, came to find sport and give annoyance.

It was while at Cambridge that Robinson added to his other pursuits that of farmer. From 1782 to 1785 he was in possession of a considerable extent of land, which he had under his own care, and he had previously farmed a little, his object being probably to supplement his means in order to supply the wants of his numerous children. It was there too that he wrote his able works. In 1770, he commenced as an author by publishing a translation of one of Saurin's sermons. He afterwards published others of Saurin's sermons, and in 1778-79, "Claude's Essay on the Composition of a Sermon," in two volumes. This was a translation with many notes, full of lively anecdotes and valuable suggestions, added by the translator. In 1774, Mr. Robinson took his place as a powerful writer by writing a masterly work, entitled "Arcana; or, the Principles of the late Petitioners to Parliament for Relief in the Matter of Subscription." The work was written when there was great excitement on the subject, and both Churchmen and Nonconformists were petitioning.

In 1781, he was invited by the Baptists of London to undertake to write a new "History of the Baptists." For this purpose he was to visit London, and preach in some of the principal chapels, while detained in London to pursue his historical researches. This plan proved too laborious, and he had to continue his researches at home, availing himself of the rich treasures of the University library. He spared no pains to master the different languages, in which various works on the subject were written, and with ceaseless industry traversed the whole of the wide field. But the toil was too severe, and the writer did not live to complete all that he had purposed. The result appeared in "The History of Baptism," quarto, published in 1790, and followed by another work—"Ecclesiastical Researches," in 1792, published after his death.

Robinson was also the author of "A Plea for the Divinity of our Lord Jesus Christ," of which several editions were published; and of "The History and the Mystery of Good Friday," 1777; and of "A Plan of Lectures on the Principles of Nonconformity," of which also several editions were sold; and of several sermons and pamphlets.

During his life, Robinson had passed through many changes of religious association; at first he was under parents without piety, who designed him for the Church; afterwards he was connected in turn, it is believed, with the Wesleyans, Independents, and Baptists; and at all times he was a man of great vehemence of character, and of intense, almost morbid, love of liberty. These considerations may perhaps account, in some degree, for the sad changes of doctrine that marked his later years. About the year 1780, he began to separate from his former religious associates, and to take pleasure in the society of such men as Paulus and Dr. Priestley. His biographer, the Rev. William Robinson, on a review of the evidence, concludes that "he was one of the most decided Unitarians of the age, but never a mere humanitarian." It was on a visit to Dr. Priestley, at Birmingham, to preach for him, in 1790, that Robinson was found dead in his bed. He had continued to preside over his church at Cambridge till the time of his death, but not without dissatisfaction, on the part of some, on account of his change of doctrine.

In a catalogue of his works up to 1781, Robinson thus describes his own contributions to Christian verse. "While R. was among the Methodists, the Rev. George Whitefield published eleven hymns composed by him for a fast-day (1757)." In an advertisement on the title-page of the work referred to, Mr. Whitefield speaks of these hymns as from "an unknown hand," and says that he prints them "for the use of the Tabernacle congregation, as they breathe a spirit of devotion and loyalty." These hymns were not marked by the excellencies that characterize the author's later productions. His own next note is, "Mr. Wheatley, of Norwich, published a hymn, beginning,

'Come, thou fount of every blessing!'

since reprinted in the hymn-books of Messrs. Madan, Wesley,

Gifford, &c., 1758." This is the well-known hymn (No. 666) in the "New Congregational Hymn Book." He also mentions that he " reprinted ' Barton's Psalms,' and wrote part of the preface, 1768." He thus refers to his other celebrated hymn, " A Christmas Hymn, set to music by Dr. Randall, and, with the notes, engraven on a copper-plate half-sheet. It begins,

'Mighty God, while angels bless Thee,' &c.

1774." This is the 311th hymn in the "New Congregational Hymn Book."

Both his well-known hymns express his adoration of Christ, as he felt it before his doctrinal difficulties had darkened the brightness of his view. And there is " a very current tradition, that on one occasion, when he was preaching from home, his two well-known hymns were sung, and that he afterwards expressed very strongly his wish that he could feel as he did when he wrote them."

A long controversy has recently been carried on with respect to the first-mentioned hymn,

" Come, thou fount of every blessing."

Mr. Daniel Sedgwick, the well-known hymn-book collector, claims it for the Countess of Huntingdon, because of the evidence afforded by a manuscript in his possession—which the writer of this sketch has examined—in which it is attributed to her by her friend Diana Vandeleur, afterwards Diana Bindon, and because the writing is thought to be of an earlier date than that at which Robinson wrote his hymn. Over against this we have the definite claim made to it by Robinson, in the church book as given above. It has been sought to invalidate this claim by producing a hymn of the same length and metre attributed to Robinson, and beginning,

"Hail! Thou source of every blessing."

And much has been made against Robinson of his words in a letter dated December 3, 1766. He writes: "Who could tell you I was an author? my works consist of II hymns, which Mr. Whitefield printed; besides these I have printed nothing." The

II is thought to be the old way of printing eleven, and the reference is supposed to be to the eleven hymns already spoken of. But a man might justly disclaim authorship and yet have written a hymn which others had put in print; and no negative evidence or theory, however plausible, can set aside the positive evidence in favour of Robinson's claim. Some doubt having been cast upon the entry in the church book, the writer of this sketch has corresponded with the Rev. William Robinson, Robert Robinson's biographer, who has the book in his possession, and is assured by him that this entry is in the same handwriting as that of the whole book, down very nearly to the end of Robinson's life, and that it is absolutely certain that it is his handwriting. And in confirmation of Robinson's claim, we have before us the letter of a venerable correspondent, who can speak of seventy years of his own experience, whose father has often given out the hymn as Robinson's, and whose grandfather was one of Robinson's deacons, and their family testimony is unequivocal in favour of Robinson.

The late Dr. Joseph Belcher, in his work, "Historical Sketches of Hymns," relates the following anecdotes about Robinson's celebrated hymns. The first with reference to the hymn,

"Come, thou fount of every blessing,"

was told Dr. Belcher by a descendant of one of the parties referred to in the narrative. It is as follows:—" In the latter part of his life, when Mr. Robinson seemed to have lost much of his devotional feeling, and when he indulged in habits of levity, he was travelling in a stage-coach with a lady, who soon perceived that he was well acquainted with religion. She had just before been reading the hymn of which we were writing, and asked his opinion of it,—as she might properly do, since neither of them knew who the other was. He waived the subject, and turned her attention to some other topic; but after a short period she contrived to return to it, and described the benefits she had often derived from the hymn, and her strong admiration of its sentiments. She observed that the gentleman was strongly agitated, but as he was dressed in coloured clothes, did not suspect the cause. This garb Robinson was compelled to assume in travelling, as wherever he was known he was pressed to stay to preach. At length, entirely overcome by the power of his feelings, he burst into tears, and said, 'Madam, I am the poor unhappy man who composed that hymn many years ago; and I would give a thousand worlds, if I had them, to enjoy the feelings I then had.'"

"The other hymn," says Dr. Belcher,

'Mighty God, while angels bless Thee,'

the second line of which was written by Mr. Robinson,

'May *an infant lisp* Thy name,'

was composed for the use of the late excellent Benjamin Williams, Esq., for many years senior deacon of the first Baptist church at Reading, a man of great influence and usefulness. When a little boy, Benjamin sat on Robinson's knee while he wrote this hymn, who, after having read it to him, placed it in his hand. Well do we remember the deep feeling with which the venerable man described to us the scene, as we sat with him at his own fireside."

In "Dobell's Collection," 1806, this hymn is printed in nine stanzas of four lines each, and to each is added,

"Hallelujah! Hallelujah! Amen."

The omitted seventh stanza is—

"Did archangels sing Thy coming?
Did the shepherds learn their lays?—
Shame would cover me ungrateful
Should my tongue refuse to praise."

SAMUEL MEDLEY.

1738—1799.

A BRIEF account of this hymn-writer is given in "The General Baptist Magazine" for August, 1799, the month after his death, and full details are given in the memoir published by his son in

1807. Samuel Medley was born at Cheshunt, Hertfordshire, on the 23rd of June, 1738. He was at first apprenticed to an oilman in London, but not liking this business, he claimed the privilege granted in that time of war of finishing the years of his apprenticeship in the navy. He was at first, in 1755, midshipman on board the "Buckingham," but he was transferred to the "Intrepid," and sailed under Admiral Boscawen. After serving in other actions, he was with his ship in a terrible conflict off Cape Lagos, on the 18th of August, 1759. Many fell, and Medley himself received a severe wound in the leg. On the return of the fleet, Mr. Medley was removed from it to the house of his grandfather, Mr. Tonge, who had trained him as a child at Enfield, and who now received him under his care in London, whither he had removed. Mr. Tonge was a pious man, and took every opportunity to endeavour to wean his grandson from the love of the world, and to lead him to pursue the better life. On one occasion, Mr. Tonge having remained in the house on Sunday evening to read a sermon to his grandson, the Word, though unwelcome, was with power. The sermon was Dr. Watts's, on Isaiah xlii. 6, 7. The seventh verse—"To open the blind eyes, to bring out the prisoners from the prison," &c., was felt to describe the hearer to himself. He saw his sinful condition, and cried for mercy. God soon granted the joys of His salvation. On his recovery, he often heard Whitefield, and in December, 1760, he joined Dr. Gifford's church, in Eagle-street, London. Having given up thoughts of the navy, though promotion was promised him, he opened a school near the Seven Dials. Afterwards, in 1762, he married, and removed his school to King-street, Soho. Encouraged by his pastor, Dr. Gifford, he began to preach in 1766. He had received a good education, and possessed natural talents. In 1767, he became the pastor of the Baptist church at Watford Herts, and in that position he remained till 1772, when he removed to Liverpool. His former life on the sea made him master of those maritime expressions which were specially pleasing and easy to be understood by many of his seafaring hearers. His congregation became very large, the meeting-house was enlarged, and, in 1790, the new and larger one in Byrom-street was erected. Mr. Medley was also very acceptable in his annual visits to the Tabernacle and Tottenham-court-road Chapel. It was on one of these journeys, in 1798, that sickness came upon him. His health had been impaired from the time of his receiving his wound in the naval action, but the immediate cause of his death was jaundice, terminating in dropsy. His mind was at first depressed by his affliction, but, regaining his composure, he gladly spent his remaining days in recounting God's providential arrangements for him, and in telling of the promises and blessings of the Gospel. Amongst his last words were—"I am now a poor shattered bark just about to gain the blissful harbour, and, oh! how sweet will be the port after the storm! But a point or two more, and I shall be at my heavenly Father's house." At another time, he said, "Dying is sweet work! sweet work. My heavenly Father! I am looking up to my dear Jesus, my God, my portion, my all in all," and then with a dying voice continued, "Glory! Glory! Home! Home!" Thus he departed in peace, and in Jesus, July 17th, 1799.

Mr. Medley's hymns appeared on broadsides as they were composed. Thirty-six of these were issued between 1786 and 1790, and in 1789 he published a small volume of his hymns. More hymns were added in later editions. The modest preface disclaims merit on the part of the author, but expresses a desire to comfort Christians and glorify Christ, and at the same time to comply with the wish of many friends who had requested the publication of these hymns. If we try Mr. Medley by his hymns we must pronounce him no poet, though there is nothing wanting in his piety and zeal.

"Mortals, awake, with angels join."—No. 344.

This is much above Mr. Medley's average, and borders closely on sacred poetry. It is taken from the third edition of the above-mentioned hymn-book, published 1800. Hymns 366 and 505 are from the second edition, 1789.

JOHN FAWCETT, D.D.
1739—1817.

For several hymns of average excellence we are indebted to this divine, who was chiefly remarkable for his laborious faithfulness to his people and his work during a long period of years. From his "Life and Letters," 1818, by the Rev. John Parker, and from other sources, we learn the following particulars :—He was born January 6th, 1739, at Lidget Green, near Bradford, Yorkshire. At the age of twelve he lost his father, to whom he was much attached, and was left one of a numerous family, with his widowed mother. The following year he was apprenticed at Bradford, where he remained six years. He had been brought up in connection with the Established Church; but during his apprenticeship, when, at the age of sixteen, he heard Mr. Whitefield preach on the words, "And as Moses lifted up the serpent in the wilderness, even so must the Son of man be lifted up." John iii. 14. "As long as life remains," he says, "I shall remember both the text and the sermon." Changed in heart, he felt himself at first drawn into sympathy with Whitefield's followers, at that time called Methodists; but three years after, in 1758, he joined the newly-formed Baptist Church at Bradford. At an early age he married Susannah, the daughter of John Skirrow, of Bingley.

After engaging in works of Christian usefulness, he was, in 1763, requested by the church at Bradford to go beyond private exhortation, and to stand forth and preach the Gospel. This he did, though at first discouraged by the seeming difficulties of the work. In May, 1764, he went to be the Baptist minister at Wainsgate, where he was ordained, July, 1765. At first the pressure of the work was so great on him that he seriously thought of resigning, and feared that he had undertaken a work for which he was not qualified; but, overcoming his fears, he remained faithfully at his post, and after a time undertook also the labours of authorship. In 1772, he went to London to preach for Dr. Gill, who was relinquishing his public duties on account of age and infirmities, and his services were so acceptable that he was invited to succeed the declining doctor. This was a great temptation to a man conscious of growing capacities, with a limited opportunity for their exercise, and with scarcely means to meet the wants of his increasing family. But he allowed love to prevail, and remained with his attached people.

In 1777, a new chapel was built at Hebden Bridge, not far from Wainsgate, and thither he removed his ministry; and the previous year he went to reside at Brearley Hall, a convenient home for his family and pupils. There he had a lecture on Sunday evenings for many years. After the death of Dr. Caleb Evans, in 1793, he was invited to succeed him as President of the Baptist Academy at Bristol, but this honour he declined. His life was one of suffering, but, notwithstanding, of incessant useful activity. From 1807 to 1811, he was occupied in storing the ripe fruits of his later years in a work called "The Devotional Family Bible." It consisted of comments on the Scriptures. In the year this was completed, 1811, he received his degree of D.D. from America. His sufferings increased towards the close of his life, but they were borne with patience. When near the end of his course, he said, "Come, Lord Jesus, come quickly!"

In addition to the commentary already mentioned, Dr. Fawcett was the author of several other works. In 1772, he sent out a pamphlet, entitled "The Christian's humble Plea for his God and Saviour." This was published under the assumed name of Christophilus. The following were some of his other works:— "The Sick Man's Employ," 1774; "Advice to Youth, on the Advantages of Early Piety," 1778 (of this several editions were sold); an "Essay on Anger," 1788; "The Cross of Christ— the Christian's Glory," 1793 (this was afterwards issued by the Tract Society); "The Life of the Rev. Oliver Heywood," 1796. He was also the author of "The History of John Wise,"—a book for children. Of this also there was a great sale.

Dr. Fawcett began authorship by publishing his "Poetic

Essays," 1767: they are pieces written mostly before he left Bradford. His hymn-book was not written till he was in the middle of life: it is entitled "Hymns adapted to the circumstances of Public Worship and Private Devotion." The preface bears date January 17th, 1782, Brearley Hall, near Halifax. It contains 166 pieces: some were written in early life and some during his ministry, many being intended to be sung after sermon. It was not intended to supplant Dr. Watts's Psalms and Hymns, but only to supplement it, and to provide suitable metres for new tunes. Without the highest excellence, the hymns are yet suitable for public worship, and eminently spiritual and experimental in their character.

"Praise to Thee, Thou great Creator."—No. 273.

This is part of a piece of his, No. 56, on "Spring."

"Infinite excellence is Thine."—No. 309.

This is part of his 42nd hymn, which consists of twelve verses. It is one of his most pleasing hymns.

"How precious is the Book divine."—No. 466.

This is part of his 41st, but the third verse here is not in his hymn of six verses as given in the first edition.

"Thus far my God hath led me on."—No. 633.

This is the last portion, slightly altered, of a hymn of twelve verses.

"Blest is the tie that binds."—No. 832.

This favourite hymn is said to have been written in 1772, to commemorate the determination of its author to remain with his attached people at Wainsgate. The farewell sermon was preached, the waggons were loaded, when love and tears prevailed, and Dr. Fawcett sacrificed the attractions of a London pulpit to the affection of his poor but devoted flock.

"O God, my helper, ever near."—No. 958.

This is his 108th, with a few lines omitted.

"Religion is the chief concern."—No. 968.

His 68th, with three verses omitted.

"With humble heart and tongue."—No. 970.

His 86th given in full.

AUGUSTUS MONTAGUE TOPLADY.
1740—1778.

"Toplady," says Montgomery, "evidently kindled his poetic torch at that of his contemporary, Charles Wesley." In opposition to the Wesleys, he stoutly maintained the Calvinistic doctrines, and sometimes indulged in the severe and scurrilous language that was tolerated in controversy in those times; but though differing in doctrine, the polemics were alike in the sweetness and spirituality of their songs.

Toplady was born at Farnham, in Surrey. His father, Richard Toplady, was a major in the army. He died at the siege of Carthagena, soon after the birth of his son. To his mother, Toplady owed very much for her maternal kindness, and for the wisely-directed plan she pursued in promoting his education and advancement. He retained a deep and lasting sense of his indebtedness to her. He studied at first at Westminster School, and during his stay there he accompanied his mother in a journey to Ireland to pursue her claims to an estate which she had in that kingdom. In the year 1755, he experienced some spiritual awakening, and in the following year, in August, while in Ireland, Providence directed his steps into a barn, at a place called Codymain. Mr. Morris, a layman, was preaching from the words, "Ye, who sometimes were afar off, are made nigh by the blood of Christ," and by this discourse Toplady was brought to religious decision. He says of that occasion, "Strange that I, who had so long sat under the means of grace in England, should be brought near to God in an obscure part of Ireland, amidst a handful of God's people met together in a barn, and under the ministry of one who could hardly spell his name. Surely it was the Lord's doing, and is marvellous!" Shortly before his death he said, in reference to the same part of his history, "Though awakened in 1755, I was not led into a full and clear view of the doctrines of grace till the year 1758, when, through the great goodness of God, my Arminian prejudices received an effectual shock in reading Dr. Manton's sermons on the 17th of St. John. I shall remember the years 1755 and 1758 with gratitude and joy, in the heaven of heavens, to all eternity."

Toplady, besides being a laborious student, early employed his talents in hymn-writing. Between the ages of fifteen and eighteen he wrote several pious pieces, which were published in Dublin in 1759. The work is entitled "Poems on Sacred Subjects, wherein the fundamental doctrines of Christianity, with many other interesting points, are occasionally introduced." The hymns in this volume gave the promise which was fulfilled in later years. In June, 1762, Toplady was ordained as a minister of the Church of England. His first living was at Blagdon, in Somersetshire. This he soon resigned. He afterwards held the living of New Ottery, and in 1768 he became vicar of Broad Hembury, Devonshire, a position he held till his death. It was at Broad Hembury that most of his writings and poems were produced.

Like Bruce, Kirke White, and McCheyne, Toplady was early called to join the heavenly choirs. The moist air of Devonshire was thought injurious to his weak lungs, and he endeavoured to exchange his living for one in some more favourable part, but did not succeed. At length, in 1775, he went, on the advice of his doctor, to London, where he at first preached occasionally; and in the following year he obtained, by an engagement with the trustees of the French Calvinist Reformed Church, in Orange Street, Leicester Fields, their chapel for Divine service, on Sunday and Wednesday evenings. With fast failing health he continued these services for two years and three months, preaching with the solemnity of a voice from the tomb, and the joy of one on the very verge of heaven. At all times an impressive preacher, his peculiar circumstances lent additional weight to his words.

During the first year of this ministry, in 1776, he published his collection of hymns, 419 in number. They were collected from forty or fifty volumes, and included some of his own. And in December, 1775, he became editor of the "Gospel Magazine," but was compelled by illness to relinquish his editorship in the following summer, 1776. Some of his articles are signed "Minimus," some "Concionator," and some with his initials. They appeared in several volumes of the "Gospel Magazine," from 1774. He was also the author of "The Church of England, vindicated from the charge of Arminianism, &c.," 1779, and of some sermons.

Toplady's end was as happy and triumphant as was to have been expected from his holy and devoted course. Upon his doctor informing him, in answer to his inquiry, that his pulse was becoming weaker and weaker, he replied, "Why, that is a good sign that my death is fast approaching, and, blessed be God, I can add that my heart beats every day stronger and stronger for glory." And after many other beautiful Christian words he said, when close to his end, bursting while he said it into tears of joy, "It will not be long before God takes me, for no mortal man can live after the glories which God has manifested to my soul." Thus he died in the 38th year of his age. His remains were brought from Knightsbridge to Tottenham Court Road Chapel, to be interred. Toplady had requested that the funeral should be as private as possible, and that there should be no funeral sermon; but thousands gathered together, and the Rev. Rowland Hill felt impelled by his feelings to address the multitude, prior to the burial, on the solemn interest of the occasion, and to express his ardent affection for the departed saint.

We are indebted to Mr. Daniel Sedgwick for a complete collection of Toplady's hymns. This was published in 1860, and consists of 133 hymns and poems, with a memoir. There is also given at the end a list of hymns that have been erroneously attributed to Toplady. The collection includes forty-five Petitionary Hymns, fifteen Hymns of Thanksgiving, twenty Select Paraphrases, eight Hymns of Invitation, nine pieces on the Death of Friends, eight miscellaneous pieces in an Appendix, and there are added twenty-eight Occasional Hymns and Poems, composed between the years 1760—1778. Montgomery has justly said of Toplady's hymns—"There is a peculiarly ethereal spirit in some of these, in which, whether mourning or rejoicing, praying or praising, the writer seems absorbed in the full triumph of faith, and ' whether in the body or out of the body, caught up into the third heaven and beholding unutterable things.' " And he adds, that though his poetic torch is inferior in breadth and volume of flame to Charles Wesley's, " yet the light which it sheds is not less vivid and sparkling, while it may be said to be more delicate to the eye and refreshing to the spirits than that prodigality of radiance which the rival luminary casts alike on everything it touched." The correctness of this criticism may be seen by examining Toplady's almost peerless hymn—

" Deathless principle, arise ! "—No. 724 ;

and especially verses four and five—

" See the haven full in view," &c.,

and

" Mount, their transports to improve," &c.,

and then comparing it with one of Charles Wesley's very bold flights: for instance—

" Come, let us join our friends above."—No. 708.

Toplady's hymns are full of great Scripture doctrines, and of the richest and deepest experience of the Christian in the use of them ; but they do not contain many references to his own special circumstances. There is, however, one, entitled " Praise for Conversion," which contains such verses as these :—

> "4. In sins and trespasses
> When more than dead I lay,
> Drew near my tomb the Prince of Peace
> And rolled the stone away;
> With me His spirit strove,
> Almighty to retrieve,
> He saw me in a time of love
> And said unto me, live."

And one of his later pieces, "written in illness," begins

> "When languor and disease invade
> This trembling house of clay,
> 'Tis sweet to look beyond the cage
> And long to fly away."

And after several verses descriptive of his sources of spiritual joy, he says, in verse 14—

> "If such the sweetness of the stream
> What must the fountain be,
> Where saints and angels draw their bliss
> Immediately from thee?"

"Holy Ghost! dispel our sadness."—No. 439.

This is a short extract from Toplady's piece beginning with these words. It was taken from a piece, translated by J. C. Jacobi, in the "Psalmodia Germanica," 1725—

> "O thou sweetest source of gladness."

Toplady altered it, and inserted it in the "Gospel Magazine" for 1776. The original is believed to be a piece by Paul Gerhard.

"Bowed with a sense of sin, I faint."—No. 526.

This is part of a piece of twenty-two verses, entitled "The Prayer of King Manasses, paraphrased," and beginning—

> "Author of all in earth or sky."

"Rock of ages, cleft for me."—No. 549.

This hymn, so justly prized by the Christian Church, was inserted in the "Gospel Magazine" for March, 1776, with the title, "A Living and Dying Prayer for the holiest Believer in the World."

The hymn is given at the end of an article in prose, which is a spiritual improvement of a preceding article, signed J. F., and entitled " Questions and Answers relative to the National Debt." By numerical calculations the number of a man's sins is shown to be very great, and that of all the redeemed therefore overwhelming, and hence the unspeakable value of Christ's atonement,— and then this hymn is introduced. It gave consolation to the late lamented Prince Consort in his dying hour. Dr. Pomeroy relates that a few years ago when in an Armenian Church, at Constantinople, he observed many weeping as they sang, and found on enquiry that they were singing this affecting hymn.

" Jesus, at thy command."—No. 609.

This hymn is wrongly attributed to Toplady : it is by Richard de Courcy, and is found in his collection, 1793.

" Your harps, ye trembling saints."—No. 632.

This is little more than one-third of the original piece.

"Deathless principle! arise."—No. 724.

The author entitled this hymn, " The Dying Believer to his Soul." The third verse is omitted in the " New Congregational Hymn Book."

" Now may the Spirit's holy fire."—No. 787.

This hymn, erroneously attributed to Toplady, is by Rev. Robert Seagrave, M.A., *vide* under his name, page 102.

" Shepherd divine, our wants relieve."—No. 811.

This is erroneously attributed to Toplady : it is by Charles Wesley, 1749.

" Inspirer and Hearer of prayer."—No. 937.

This is the latter part of a piece beginning—

" What tho' my frail eyelids refuse."

" We sing to thee, Thou Son of God."—No. 310.

This is erroneously attributed to Toplady : it is by Cennick ; *vide* under Cennick, p 167.

RICHARD DE COURCY.
1743—1803.

BORN in Ireland, in 1743, Richard de Courcy was of good family, and possessed of talents of a high order. He received his education at Trinity College, Dublin ; and, in 1767, having entered the Church, became curate to the Rev. Walter Shirley : but his evangelical doctrines made him enemies in those cold and formal times, and when on one occasion he was about to preach at St. Andrew's, Dublin, he received an inhibition from the Metropolitan, Dr. Smythe. Undismayed by this painful circumstance, he announced to the congregation that, not being allowed to address them in the church, he should deliver his discourse in the churchyard ; and the crowd soon gathered around him there.

But Mr. De Courcy found himself a marked man, and was refused a licence and priest's orders. At this juncture the Countess of Huntingdon invited Mr. De Courcy to England. On his arrival he met with encouragement from Mr. Whitefield and others, and preached with much success as a minister of the Countess's Connexion. He also obtained ordination from the Bishop of Lichfield, and he afterwards preached in Lady Glenorchy's chapel, in Edinburgh. In 1770, he became curate of Shawbury, near Hawkstone, Salop, and in 1774 received from Lord Dartmouth, the Lord Chancellor, the vicarage of Aldwinkle, near Shrewsbury. In 1776, during his absence, some of his congregation attended the Baptist chapel. In consequence, he wrote "A Letter to a Baptist Minister," which drew forth a spirited reply.

Mr. De Courcy suffered from a weakness in the chest, and as he approached his sixtieth year he was greatly affected by the loss of his youngest son. A cold, taken on the fast-day in 1803, aggravated his disorder, and he died on the following day, the 4th of November. Shortly before his death, he said, "I shall not recover; but Christ is mine: He is my foundation, He is the rock I build upon!"

Among Mr. De Courcy's works were, "Some Elegiac Lines on the Death of the Rev. G. Whitefield," 1771; "A Letter of Solemn Counsel to a Person in a Declining State of Health," 1778; and a large work in two volumes, a reply to Dr. Priestley, entitled "Christ Crucified," 1791. He was also the author of a pamphlet with the curious title, "Jehu's Looking-glass; or, a Treatise on True and False Zeal." He also published some sermons.

In 1775, Mr. De Courcy published "A Collection of Psalms and Hymns extracted from different Authors." In the preface he finds fault with Sternhold and Hopkins, with Tate and Brady, and even with Merrick, as well as with the Scotch paraphrases. He says that "in all these compositions we labour through great Old Testament obscurity, which is manifestly done away in Christ." His object was to produce a book full of Christ. The preface is dated December 6th, 1775, Shrewsbury. The third edition, which was much enlarged, appeared in 1784: it contained several hymns by Mr. De Courcy. Mr. John Nunn, of Manchester, marks ten as De Courcy's in his copy bearing date 1806, but there are only seven that remain his undisputed productions. They are Nos. 192, 204, 260, 261, 263, 311, 312—as the numbers are given in the fourth edition of 1793.

The first of these, No. 192—

"Jesus, at Thy command,"

is No. 609 in the "New Congregational Hymn Book," erroneously attributed to Toplady. It is said to have been written on the occasion of Mr. Whitefield sailing to America. If this is so, it must have been when he went on one of his later voyages, as Mr. Whitefield's first voyage to America was before Mr. De Courcy was born. In the original, the hymn has another verse—a second verse. Mr. de Courcy's hymns, though admirable in their Christian excellence, fell short of the high poetic standard he had desired to reach.

ANNA LÆTITIA BARBAULD.
1743—1825.

THIS accomplished poetess, born June 20th, 1743, was the daughter of Dr. John Aikin, who kept a school at Kibworth, Leicestershire; and afterwards, when his daughter Anna was fifteen years of age, removed to Warrington, Lancashire, to superintend the public academy there. The future poetess early became distinguished for her talents, and her acquirements included a knowledge of Latin and Greek, and she enjoyed the mental stimulus arising from associating with Dr. Doddridge and men of the same calibre. At the age of thirty-one, she married the Rev. Rochemont Barbauld, a Unitarian minister, who opened a school at Palgrave, near Diss, in Suffolk, where he also exercised his ministry. He had studied under Dr. Doddridge, and was ordained at Palgrave in 1775. They carried on the scholastic establishment for eleven years, Mrs. Barbauld assisting in the work of tuition. During this period, Lord Denman and some other persons afterwards eminent, were among their pupils.

In 1773, with the assistance of her brother, Mrs. Barbauld (who was then Miss Aikin) published some poems, of which four editions were sold in one year; and in the same year they sent forth " Miscellaneous Pieces in Prose," by J. and A. L. Aikin. Mrs. Barbauld's " Hymns in Prose," and her " Early Lessons," published in 1775, were written for her pupils. In the same year appeared her " Devotional Pieces compiled from the Psalms of David, &c."

When eleven years had been passed by the successful educators in their useful but arduous work, they found a change necessary, and went to travel on the Continent. On their return, in 1787, they resided at Hampstead; and in 1802, they went to live at Stoke Newington, as Mr. Barbauld was the minister of a Unitarian congregation in that neighbourhood. He died in 1808.

In 1790, Mrs. Barbauld began to write valuable political pamphlets on great questions of the time. She also assisted her brother, Dr. Aikin, in his work, " Evenings at Home." Her brother is known as the author of a " Biographical Dictionary," and of the " Works of British Poets." Later, she published some of the works of Addison, Collins, and Akenside, prefixing to each writer's works a valuable introductory essay. In addition to these literary undertakings, she edited the " British Novelists ; " and, at the age of sixty-eight, she published her largest and most highly finished poem, " Eighteen Hundred and Eleven." Besides the great talent displayed in her longer pieces in prose and verse, some of her shorter pieces have been justly admired, especially her " Address to the Deity."

Her sole contribution to the " New Congregational Hymn Book " is justly a favourite : —

" How blest the righteous when he dies ! "—No. 727.

It is a happy illustration of how much poetry a hymn may contain, without ceasing to be simple, easily intelligible, and adapted to public worship ; without, in fact, ceasing to be what we understand by a hymn. It is found at page 315 of Vol. I. of " The Works of A. L. Barbauld, with a Memoir," by Lucy Aikin, 1825. The hymn is headed, " The Death of the Virtuous," and begins in the original : —

" Sweet is the scene when Virtue dies !—
When sinks a righteous soul to rest."

Verse 3 is also different in the original. It is as follows : —

" Triumphant smiles the victor's brow,
Fanned by some angel's purple wing :—
Where is, O Grave, thy victory now ?
And where, insidious Death ! thy sting ?"

The other part of the hymn is given in the " New Congregational" almost exactly as in the original. The hymn stands in her works immediately before her twelve hymns.

OTTIWELL HEGINBOTHAM.
1744—1768.

"God of our life! Thy various praise."—No. 957.

This hymn is found in the "Protestant Dissenters' Magazine," for December, 1794. It is entitled, "A Hymn for New Year's Day." In the same Magazine, other hymns by the same author were published. The following two additional verses are given :—

> "This year, perhaps, the hand of death
> May snatch my soul away;
> That awful hand may stop my breath
> Before the opening day.

> "Father in heaven, Thy will be done,
> I cheerfully resign;
> Make me in life, in death, Thine own,
> This year, for ever Thine."

Mr. Heginbotham's hymns were privately printed in London, 1799. In Dr. Collyer's collection, 1812, ten are given. They are hymns of promise. If the talented author had been spared, he might have taken a prominent place amongst hymn-writers.

The librarian of Dr. Williams's library has kindly supplied the following account of Mr. Heginbotham, from "Walter Wilson's MS. Account of Various Congregations in England," which is preserved there. The name is spelt differently, and in order to understand the account it is necessary to bear in mind that there were two hostile parties in the church at Sudbury, to which Mr. Heginbotham was invited. The account is believed to be the fullest extant of the short career of its subject. It is as follows :—

" Ottiwell Heginbotham, a student of Daventry, was invited (in 1762 or 3) by the society at Sudbury, to preach as a candidate, and eventually chosen pastor; but his ordination was deferred till 1765, in the hope that his uncommon merit and abilities would have overcome all political and worldly prejudices. The neighbouring ministers who were assembled at Mr. Braybrook's ordination, at Rendham, were likewise applied to by the other party to judge between them. Those ministers unanimously determined that the majority had a right to fill up the vacancy in their assembly if they chose so to do; and also, that it seemed to be to no purpose to wait any longer with respect to Mr. Heginbotham, or to think of choosing any other person, since those secular Dissenters, there was reason to believe, would ever occasion an opposition. In consequence of these resolutions, they agreed to attend the ordination of Mr. Heginbotham, and concurred with the majority of the Church in their choice. Accordingly, he was solemnly ordained at Sudbury, November 20, 1765. Mr. Harmer gave the charge from 2 Tim. iv. 5. A separation immediately ensued, and the minority formed themselves into a distinct society, erected a new meeting-house, and chose Mr. John Lombard their pastor. Mr. Heginbotham fell a victim to their party disputes. The sensibility, gentleness, and tenderness of his disposition disqualified him for bearing so much contention. He fell into a consumption, which conveyed him to his grave in very early life, leaving a most amiable character behind him. He died in 1768, in the twenty-fourth year of his age. Fatal was the illustration given to him of that passage in James —' Where envying and strife is, there is confusion and every evil work.' "

ROWLAND HILL, M.A.

1744—1833.

This eccentric but eminently devoted and useful minister of the Gospel, was a son of Sir Rowland Hill, Bart. He was born at Hawkstone, near Shrewsbury, on the 23rd August, 1744. His earlier studies were pursued at the Grammar School at Shrewsbury. He afterwards studied at Eton. When a child, religious impressions had been produced by reading Dr. Watts's "Hymns for Children," and while at Eton, the reading to him by his brother of a sermon of Beveridge's, on the words, "Behold the Lamb of God who taketh away the sins of the world," was so blessed to him that he became decided for God. This was in 1762. He afterwards often attended the ministry of the Rev. John Beveridge, at Everton. After leaving Eton he went, in 1764, to study for the Church, at St. John's College, Cambridge; and, in 1769, he obtained his bachelor's degree with honours. Evangelical religion was at that time at a low ebb at Cambridge; and Mr. Hill having advocated it with all the ardour of his native zeal, soon brought upon himself opposition and persecution, such as he was often to meet with in his outspoken and earnest life. Subsequently, we find him coming to London to preach at the Tabernacle, for Whitefield, who was then exceedingly popular. Mr. Hill afterwards took his M.A. degree, and was, after overcoming some preliminary difficulties, ordained by Dr. Moss, Bishop of Bath and Wells.

Mr. Hill's first public position was that of a curate at Kingston, near Taunton. Afterwards he itinerated for about twelve years. He preached much in Wilts, Gloucestershire, and Somersetshire, as well as in various parts of London. He often addressed multitudes in the open air, and frequently met with the coarse ridicule and rude violence of the unchristianized masses of those days. He was alike happy in disarming their opposition and in gaining their attention. He was master of a humour that exposed, without exasperating, the wrong-doer; he had ready access to the fountains of human feeling; and all were struck with his disinterested devotedness to his Master's service, and his tender yearning for the souls of his perishing fellow-men.

At Wootton-under-Edge, he built a tabernacle and dwelling-house, and always took a deep interest in that place, preaching there usually a part of the year, and the other part at Surrey

Chapel, London. This latter edifice was opened in 1783. It was for about fifty years the principal scene of Rowland Hill's popularity and usefulness; and there he gathered one of the most numerous congregations in the Metropolis—a congregation ever since well maintained by his successful and devoted successors. His position as being in a sense neither in nor out of the Church of England, exposed him to the criticisms of friends and enemies. His Nonconformist friends could not understand how the author of the severe and humorous pamphlet on the "Sale of Curates" could be in any way complicated with the Episcopal system, and his Episcopalian friends thought it anomalous that he, an ordained clergyman, who had not formally seceded, should yet occupy what was practically a dissenting pulpit; but the course he took seemed to him to be justified by the circumstances.

Mr. Hill was united in marriage to Mary, sister of Clement Tudway, M.P. She died after a few years, leaving no family. Various benevolent and religious objects found in Mr. Hill an able advocate and supporter. He vindicated Sunday-schools when they had many enemies, and prepared hymns and catechisms for children. He was also one of the earliest advocates for the introduction of inoculation. In this he co-operated with Dr. Jenner, who resided near Wootton-under-Edge. Home and Foreign Missions also found in him a zealous friend. He travelled at his own cost thousands of miles, on behalf of the London Missionary Society, of which he was one of the founders. The Religious Tract Society also received help from him, and he was on its first committee. He also entered warmly into theological controversy in favour of Calvinism and Toplady, and against Wesley; and he was not free from the polemical asperity of those times. He was strong in his attachment to Calvinism, but as strong in his hatred of Antinomianism. In promoting religious objects he gave as well as laboured. Towards one work alone, the erection of a chapel at Leamington, Warwickshire, he is said to have given £2,000. As he approached the close of his disinterested course, he was heard saying—"Eye hath not seen nor ear heard, neither have entered into the heart of man, the things which God hath prepared for them that love him." And the favourite verse he quoted was that by the Rev. John Gambold (who died 1771)—

> "And when I'm to die,
> Receive me, I'll cry,
> For Jesus hath lov'd me, I cannot tell why;
> But this I can find,
> We two are so join'd,
> He'll not be in glory and leave me behind."

He died the 11th April, 1833, aged eighty-eight.

Rowland Hill was the author of the following prose works:—"An Account of his Journey in Scotland and the North of England, 1800." "Apology for Sunday Schools, 1801." This was to meet the remarks of the Bishop of Rochester against Sunday-schools. "Village Dialogues," first edition, 1802. This was his most popular work; many editions of it have been sold. It is full of wise sayings and useful religious instruction, and all is presented in a conversational form, and with such rusticity of manner as exactly to adapt it to the readers for whom it is designed. An improved edition was prepared about twenty years after the first. His pamphlet in favour of inoculation appeared in 1806. He also published "Instructions for Children," and a "Catechism for Children," and some sermons; he also published his controversy with Wesley. His "Spiritual Characteristics—A Sale of Curates by Auction," was published towards the close of his life. He also wrote for the Religious Tract Society the tracts, "The Four Dialogues in Prison," and "Thomas Steady and John Wild."

Rowland Hill also wrote a few hymns. One of the sermons preached at the founding of the London Missionary Society, 24th September, 1795, was by Dr. Bogue, who, rejoicing in the union of Christians of different denominations, said in his sermon, "Behold us here assembled with one accord to attend the funeral of bigotry." These words so struck Rowland Hill, and were so entirely in harmony with his sentiments, that he wrote his well-known epitaph on "Bigotry," to be sung at the close of the sermon:—

"Here lies old Bigotry, abhorr'd
By all that love our common Lord," &c.

In 1803, Rowland Hill preached a sermon to volunteers, at Surrey Chapel, and appended a hymn written by himself:—

"When Jesus first at heaven's command."

It was first composed for the use of the Missionary Society, and appeared in the "Evangelical Magazine," vol. v., p. 263. In 1774, he published a "Collection of Psalms and Hymns," chiefly intended for the use of the poor; and, in 1783, he published "A Collection of Psalms and Hymns," of which many editions were issued. Some of the hymns are believed to be by himself, as he remarks of some in the preface—"Some of them are by no means the better for being entirely new." A supplement appeared in 1796. He published "Divine Hymns for the Use of Children, 1790." This work had the advantage of the correction of the poet Cowper. He also published a "Collection of Hymns for Children, 1808;" and "Hymns for Schools, 1832."

"Ye that in these courts are found."—No. 504.

This is given without name in the "New Congregational Hymn Book." It is No. 29 in R. Hill's "Collection of Psalms and Hymns, chiefly intended for Public Worship, 1783," and is believed to be his. The hymn is headed, "Enjoyment of Christ in Worship." Its first appearance was in R. Hill's "Collection of Psalms and Hymns, chiefly intended for the Use of the Poor," first edition, 1774; third edition, 1780.

"We sing His love, who once was slain."—No. 740.

This also is given anonymously, but it is believed to be by Rowland Hill. It is in his Supplement to his Collection, containing Fourteen Hymns by various Authors, published in 1796.

MICHAEL BRUCE.
1746—1767.

The life of this poet was almost a counterpart of that of Henry Kirke White, who flourished a generation later. In both instances the light of genius shone forth for a time, and then it was all too suddenly put out.

Born of pious Scotch parents at Kinneswood, Kinross-shire, Michael Bruce enjoyed the advantages of a religious education, first at home, then at Kinross, and afterwards in Edinburgh. Two discerning friends, David Arnot and David Pearson, whose names should be held in honour, recognizing the taste and talent of the youth, supplied him with the works of the great poets, and encouraged him in his literary pursuits. On coming to Edinburgh, where he spent four sessions in the University, he made the acquaintance of the poet Logan, who became his companion, and, after his death, the editor and eulogist of his works, which, however, lost more by his plagiarisms than they gained by his patronage.

The educational advantages Bruce enjoyed were given to him by his father, an operative weaver, in the expectation that his son would thus be prepared to be a minister of the Gospel. He was a youth of piety and promise, and, when but a child, would sometimes lead the family devotion. But as the parents' means were limited, the son had to contend with poverty; and in order to maintain himself he kept a school during the summer, first at Gairney Bridge, and afterwards at Forrest Mill, near Alloa. This was too much for his frail constitution. Hard fare and mental effort, combined with the severity of the climate, at length brought on a rapid decline; and in 1766 he returned to his native village to die. He had previously spent a session in the Theological Hall, under Professor Swanston, of Kinross, a minister of the Associate Synod, to whose church he belonged. In the spring of 1767, as he approached his end, he gave expression to his own pensive feelings in his inimitable pathetic "Elegy on Spring," especially in verse sixteen :—

> "Now spring returns; but not to me returns
> The vernal joy my better years have known;
> Dim in my breast life's dying taper burns,
> And all the joys of life with health are flown."

He had purposed publishing his poems during his life, but finding his strength waning, he obtained a volume of paper, and daily occupied himself in transcribing his "Ode to the Cuckoo," "Hymns," and "Paraphrases," and "Elegy on Spring," and whatever he thought worthy of preservation. During the latter part of his illness he was confined to his bed. His constant companion was his little pocket Bible, from which he used to commit passages to memory, and repeat and comment upon them to visitors. After maintaining his Christian cheerfulness to the end, he was found dead on the morning of the 5th of July, 1767, having passed peacefully away in his sleep.

The manuscript volume he had prepared in his last illness was obtained from the poet's parents by Logan, that he might publish it for their benefit. But after waiting for its appearance for some time in vain, the family received no advantage, and the manuscript was not restored. In 1770, Logan published a small volume, entitled "Poems on Several Occasions," by Michael Bruce. In the preface, Logan professes to have added several poems to make up a miscellany. He says that these are by other authors, and that only seven of the seventeen poems are by Bruce. The omission from this book of the "Ode to the Cuckoo," and the well-known "Gospel Sonnets," excited the surprise and indignation of Bruce's former companions. His father went to Edinburgh to remonstrate with Logan, but could obtain no satisfaction. These "sonnets," as the villagers called them, had been prepared by Bruce to be used at a singing-class to which he belonged. Buchan, the leader of the class, had asked Bruce to prepare them in place of some unsuitable pieces they were using. The poet's successful hymns were well-known, because some of the members of the class had committed them to memory. Logan's shameless purpose was seen when, in 1781, he published as his own in a volume of " poems" the " Ode to the Cuckoo," and several of Bruce's hymns. The Rev. A. B. Grosart, in his " Works of Michael Bruce," 1865, has fully established these facts.

Some of Bruce's principal pieces were "Lochleven," written at Forrest Hill, in 1766; his " Ode to the Cuckoo," his " Elegy written on Spring," and his piece on " The Last Day." He also wrote twelve hymns. His " Ode to the Cuckoo" will always be valued as a gem of poesy. Its pleasing versification, its truthfulness to nature, and the touching reference to the writer with which it concludes, strike all readers. His other pieces are not wanting in sustained dignity of style and thought, pleasing and appropriate imagery, and just and noble sentiments; but they are valued most as earnests of what the author would have accomplished if his life had been spared.

His hymns are admirable for their faithfulness to the passages of scripture they render, for their poetic imagery, and for their style, which is dignified without being pretentious. Here and there they reveal a pensive tendency, resembling what is found in the author's letters, and suggestive of high purposes disappointed by life's early decay. Most of the hymns have rhymes only in the second and fourth lines, and not in the first and third, and thus, in versification, fall behind what some other hymn writers have accomplished.

" Almighty Father of mankind."—No. 104.

This is four verses of a hymn of eight verses, given by Logan as his own in his book of 1781. It is slightly altered from the original, which is believed to have been by Michael Bruce. The reasons are given above.

" Where high the heavenly temple stands."—No. 400.

This exceedingly touching and much prized hymn is erroneously attributed to Logan. It is by Michael Bruce. It is the fifty-eighth of the "Translations and Paraphrases," a book prepared by a Committee appointed by the General Assembly of the Church of Scotland. It was published in 1745, and these hymns were added in 1781. The hymn is given complete in the "New Congregational Hymn Book," but with slight verbal alterations.

"The hour of my departure's come."—No. 725.

This forms hymn five, of the five hymns appended to the "Translations and Paraphrases." It is evidently by the dying poet, Bruce, and not by the pleasure-seeking Logan. And there is the same external evidence that it is by Bruce, as in the other verses.

"Behold! the mountain of the Lord."—No. 925.

This is four verses of a piece of six verses, forming the eighteenth of the "Translations and Paraphrases."

Verse three—

"The beam that shines from Zion's hill," &c.,

is known to have been Bruce's. It lingered in the memories of his companions at Kinneswood. Probably the other part was felicitously altered by him from an older version. It is too late to determine what alterations Logan made in Bruce's pieces.

MATTHEW WILKS.
1746—1829.

This eccentric, but deservedly eminent Congregational minister, was born in 1746 at Gibraltar, where his father, an officer in the army, was stationed with his regiment. Soon after Matthew's birth, his father removed to Ireland, where he remained for many years, and subsequently on retiring on half-pay he settled down at Birmingham. Mr. Wilks's youth was marked by the display of talent, but was devoid of the fruits of personal piety. It was not till his twenty-fifth year that he became a convert to Christ.

"Early in the year 1771," he says, "I was born of God at West Bromwich, in Staffordshire." He had been drawn by curiosity to listen at the window of a cottage in which the Rev. W. Percy, curate of the parish, was preaching. Such power attended the preaching of the Gospel that, by the Divine blessing, Mr. Wilks's heart and life were changed. The Rev. W. Percy, recognizing the qualifications of the new convert, very strongly urged him to prepare for the ministry. To use his own language: "To the Countess of Huntingdon's college, at Trevecca, I *must* and *should* go; and though against my inclination, I went, and closely pursued my studies."

Towards the end of Mr. Wilks's college course at Trevecca, Mr. Robert Keene, one of the executors of Mr. Whitefield, and a manager of his London chapels, having paid Lady Huntingdon a visit, and heard Mr. Wilks preach, he was in consequence invited to preach in London, and in 1775 appointed minister of the Tabernacle, where he preached, in conjunction with his labours at Tottenham Court Chapel, more than fifty years. His ministry was very popular and very useful. His work was to preach. He had a natural talent for awakening interest and producing impression by public addresses and appeals. His sermons were full of weighty Scriptural truths, and rich in real Christian experience. His characteristic element was that he was *striking* —his pithy, pointed sayings remained in the memory as nails in a sure place. That he occasionally spoke words so quaint as to offend, and to be a cause of regret to himself, only showed that his excellence when exaggerated became a fault.

Mr. Wilks was the friend of the poor, and promoted the establishment of several benevolent institutions for their benefit. Brother ministers found in him a sympathizing and helpful friend; and several of the more important religious institutions received his effective support at the time of their origin. He was the father of the Irish Evangelical Society, and acted for twenty-five years as gratuitous secretary of the Society for Village Itinerancy. The Religious Tract Society, the British and Foreign

Bible Society, and the London Missionary Society, found in him one of their earliest and warmest supporters.

The "Evangelical Magazine" was originated by the Rev. John Eyre and Mr. Wilks; and the latter wrote several of the biographical articles in the earlier volumes of the magazine. In 1798, he published "Whitefield's Collection of Hymns, with a Life of Whitefield." In 1803, he edited "Secker's Nonsuch Professor," and, in 1819, he sent forth "Cennick's Discourses, with a Life." The Rev. T. Sharp, M.A., minister of Crown Street Chapel, Soho, published, in 1834, "Select Remains of the Rev. Matthew Wilks." This work contains a biography of Mr. Wilks, with outlines of twenty-four of his sermons, and at the end twenty-four of his hymns are given. It is not an uncharitable judgment to say that his hymns are only rhymed prose, without any sparks of poetic fire. Some of them were contributed to the "Evangelical Magazine."

Mr. Wilks's dying testimony was in harmony with that of his life. He said to his son, "*I know — know — know, yes, I know* my Saviour is Christ! He has all power. I have no concern, no alarm, no uneasiness, not the slightest anxiety about my soul;' and to his venerable fellow-labourer, Rowland Hill, "I shall be at home before you." He fell asleep in Jesus at the end of January, 1829.

"Bright as the sun's meridian blaze," —No. 910,

erroneously attributed to Shrubsole, is Mr. Wilks's sole contribution to the "New Congregational Hymn Book." It is given with one verse omitted. It is said to have first appeared in the "Evangelical Magazine."

JOHN LOGAN.
1748—1788.

It is doubtful whether Logan has any claim to a place in the biographies of our hymn-writers. The uncertainty he allowed to arise as to what were his own productions is believed to have been intentional, and with a view to conceal his plagiarisms. Recent investigations have shown that the hymns Logan claimed as his own were the work of Michael Bruce; but as Logan's name has been introduced, though erroneously, and as it appears in the controversy about the works of Michael Bruce, a brief sketch will be given:—

John Logan, who was the son of a farmer, was born at Fala, in the county of Mid-Lothian, Scotland. He pursued his studies in Edinburgh University, and became tutor to Sir John Sinclair. His parents had brought him up in connection with the United Presbyterian Church, but he preferred the Established Church of Scotland, and became one of its ministers, at Leith, in 1770. There he was popular as a preacher, and his sermons were published after his death. His other prose works were in 1781:— "Elements of the Philosophy of History," consisting of some of the lectures he had delivered in Edinburgh, and a "Dissertation on the Government, Manners, and Spirit of Asia."

In 1770, he published a small volume of Poems, by Michael Bruce, but according to the preface only a part are by him, and Logan left it to be inferred that some of the others were by himself. In 1781, he published a volume, entitled "Poems by the Rev. Mr. Logan, one of the ministers of Leith." This book had no preface, but those who knew Bruce's productions saw at once that in it there were several pieces which Logan had appropriated from a manuscript he possessed of Bruce's, and without acknowledgment. This unprincipled conduct towards a departed friend has been justly reprobated by all writers on the subject. In 1783, Logan printed and caused to be acted in Edinburgh a tragedy, called "Runnimede." This gave offence there, as it had been refused a license by the Lord Chamberlain, in London. Logan resorted to intoxication as a solace in his disappointment; and at length found it necessary to leave his parish. In 1785, he resigned his ministry, and went to London, where he supplemented his scanty resources by the rewards of his literary labours. The following pieces are attributed to him:—"The Braes of

Yarrow;" a dramatic poem, entitled " The Lovers;" " A Visit to the Country in Autumn;" and some hymns.

Hymns 104 and 400 in the "New Congregational Hymn Book" are erroneously attributed to Logan. They are by Michael Bruce, *vide* under his name; but Logan may have made some verbal alterations in them before appropriating them. Logan succeeded in throwing a mist of uncertainty around the claims of Bruce, but it is quite certain that in the case of Doddridge's hymn—

"O God of Bethel, by whose hand,"—No. 285,

Logan adopted it as his own without any acknowledgment. Doddridge's collection appeared in 1755. This hymn of his had been given in the Scotch "Paraphrases, &c.," in 1745, having been written by him, as his MS. shows, as early as 1736; and Logan claimed it, slightly altered either by Bruce or himself, in 1781.

FRANCIS.

Vide under the following name.

JONATHAN EVANS.
1749—1809.

"Come, Thou soul-transforming Spirit."—No. 788.

THIS hymn was written by the Rev. Jonathan Evans, an earnest evangelical minister of the Congregational body. He was a successful preacher in the villages of Warwickshire, and founded a Congregational church at Foleshill, near Coventry. He began preaching at Foleshill in 1782, and commenced his stated ministry there in 1795. He had been a member of the church at Coventry under the pastorate of the Rev. George Burder. He was ordained to the ministry, April 4th, 1799, and Mr. Burder gave the charge. The discourses preached on the occasion were afterwards published. He died, after a few days' illness, August 31st, 1809, aged sixty years. The above hymn is attributed to him in the Rev. George

Burder's "Supplement," 1784. A brief sketch of him in the "Evangelical Magazine," October, 1809, describes him as "a man of sense, piety, activity, and fortitude; a firm and generous friend; and a kind benefactor to the poor, both by his medical assistance and his ministerial labours."

From a sketch in the "Evangelical Magazine," March, 1847, by Dr. John Styles, who was then minister at Foleshill, we glean a few additional particulars of Mr. Evans. He was born of humble parents, at Coventry, in 1748 or 1749. He was employed in a ribbon manufactory, and as a youth went beyond his companions in gaiety and excesses. About the year 1778 he became a Christian convert, and a member of the church under the pastorate of the Rev. G. Burder, at Coventry. Circumstances did not at first admit of his leaving his secular pursuits to engage in the work of the ministry, but he gladly seized every opportunity to preach the Gospel, and often experienced the violent opposition Gospel preachers of those times were exposed to. In 1784, he purchased a building at Foleshill, and fitted it up for a chapel. This was enlarged, and in 1795 a new chapel was built. His last illness came upon him suddenly, and produced some anxiety in his mind for the future of his attached congregation. Dr. Styles has given several of Mr. Evans's hymns in the "Evangelical Magazine," and the people of Foleshill still remember them. He assigns to him there the authorship of hymn 384. Mr. Evans published a sermon on New Year's Day, 1800, called "A New Year's Gift," and he was the author of an able controversial pamphlet on the subjects and mode of baptism.

"Hark! the voice of love and mercy."—No. 384.

The authorship of this spirit-stirring noble Christian hymn is disputed. The late Dr. Joseph Belcher, in his "Historical Sketches of Hymns," 1859, assigns it without hesitation to the above-named author, and says that it is part of a much longer piece by him. The congregation at Foleshill have for a long time attributed it to him; and the late Rev. John Styles, D.D., who was their pastor from 1844 till the time of his death in 1848, held the same opinion. But the Rev. G. L. Withers, who has been their pastor nearly seventeen years, saw Mr. Evans's manuscript book about nineteen years ago, and it is his impression that this hymn was not in it. It is very much to be regretted that this MS. cannot now be found. An important element of negative evidence against Evans's authorship is, that in the Rev. George Burder's " Supplement " Evans's name is not put to this hymn, at least in the editions published during his life, although Mr. Burder was Mr. Evans's pastor, and when at Coventry knew him well as a neighbouring minister; and this evidence is strengthened by the fact that in Burder's collection (1784) the name Evans is given to

"Come, thou soul-transforming Spirit,"—No. 788,

but is not given to

"Hark! the voice of love and mercy."—No. 384.

In "Rippon's Selection" (fifth edition, 1794) this hymn is No. 71. It is given with an additional verse. For the author's name an "F——" is put. In a later edition the "F" is changed to "Francis." But not much weight belongs to this fact, because Dr. Rippon knew the hymns of Francis, who was a Baptist minister living at that time, and put his name to them in the early editions. Probably the "F" was a mistake, and the "Francis" a conjecture. It is thought that it is against Evans's claim that, for years during his life, he allowed the name "Francis" to stand against this hymn in "Rippon's Selection."

JOHN FELLOWS.
About 1770.

There is one hymn in the "New Congregational Hymn Book" by this author :—

"Great God! now condescend."—No. 858.

It is his 22nd hymn in a book, entitled "Infants Devoted to God, but not Baptized," 1773. There are seven verses in the original hymn, of which only two are here taken. The third verse here is by another writer. The same verse is given in the old "Congregational Hymn Book" (1833). The work from which this hymn is taken contains fifty-five hymns. Mr. Fellows was a Baptist, and most of his works date from Birmingham.

The following are some of his works:—"Grace Triumphant, a sacred poem in nine dialogues," 1770; "Bromsgrove Elegy, in blank verse, on the death of the Rev. G. Whitefield," 1771; also, "An Elegy on the death of Dr. Gill," 1771; "Hymns on Believers' Baptism," 1773; "Eloquent and Noble Defence of the Gospel, in his three celebrated speeches, paraphrased in blank verse," 1775; "Hymns, in a great variety of metres, on the Perfection of the Word of God and the Gospel of Jesus Christ," 1776; "The History of the Holy Bible, attempted in easy verse," 1777; also, "A Fair and Impartial Enquiry into the Rise, &c., of the Church of Rome, in a series of familiar dialogues," 1779; also, "A Protestant Catechism."

JOHN RIPPON, D.D.

1751—1836.

The well-known author of "Rippon's Selection" was born at Tiverton, Devon, April 29th, 1751. He received his education for the ministry at the Baptist Academy, Bristol. In 1772, he was invited to preach to the Baptist Church assembling in Carter Lane, Tooley Street, London, and, in 1773, he became their pastor. They had been under the pastoral care of Dr. Gill for fifty-four years, till the time of his death. On the erection of the present London Bridge, in 1833, the Church found it necessary to remove to a new site, and they erected a new chapel in New Park Street. There Dr. Rippon continued to be their pastor till his death in 1836, having presided over them for sixty-three years. He was one of the most popular preachers of the modern Calvinistic school. The Rev. C. H. Spurgeon was for a time one of his successors at New Park Street. Dr. Rippon died December 17th, 1836, and, along with many other departed saints, was buried in Bunhill Fields.

From 1790 till 1802 he issued the "Baptist Annual Register," containing accounts of all the Baptist churches and ministers in the kingdom.

He published a small work, entitled "Divine Aspirations," the hymns in which are believed to be his own. In 1787 appeared his "Selection of Hymns from the best Authors, with a great number of Originals." More than thirty editions of this work have been published. It gives the authors' names as far as he knew them. He also published "An Arrangement of the Psalms of I. Watts," 1805, and also, "An Index of all the lines in Watts's Hymns and Psalms," 1810.

"Great God, where'er we pitch our tent."—No. 990.

This is in the first edition of his "Collection," 1787, and is believed to be by him. He does not give any name.

TIMOTHY DWIGHT, S.T.D., LL.D.
1752—1817.

This celebrated American poet and divine, best known as the President of Yale College, was born at Northampton, in the county of Hampshire, Massachusetts. His family came from Dedham, in England, in the year 1637. Timothy Dwight's father was a wealthy merchant, a graduate of Yale College, a man of good education and fervent piety; and his mother, to whom he owed very much, was the third daughter of the celebrated Jonathan Edwards.

As a child, young Dwight displayed remarkable ardour in the

pursuit of knowledge. First, at home under his mother, then at the grammar-school, and afterwards at Middletown, he pursued his industrious and successful course regardless of the necessity for exercise and recreation. In his fourteenth year he became a member of Yale College, but for two years his progress was interrupted, and he was exposed to some dangers from the disorganized state of the college. Immediately after this period he resumed his habit of laborious study; and to accomplish as much as possible, he studied very early in the morning by candle-light, thus originating that disease in his eyes from which he suffered during the remainder of his life.

In the year 1769, his eighteenth year, he received the degree of Bachelor of Arts, and soon after took charge of a grammar-school at New Haven. This office he retained for two years, at the same time pursuing his own studies; and, in 1771, he was chosen tutor in Yale College, Connecticut, a position he retained for six years. During his period of office, he added new lustre to the institution, and in particular encouraged the study of rhetoric, till then in a great measure neglected. He also carried very far the severer study of mathematics. It was during the earlier years of this tutorship that Dwight wrote his "Conquest of Canaan," an epic poem, in eleven books. It is founded on the history as it is given in the Scriptures, and is the production of poetical powers of a high order. It was finished in 1774, but owing to the unsettled state of the country, it was not published till 1785. As a youth, the author had written some verses and taken a deep interest in sacred music. In the year 1772, he received the degree of Master of Arts. It was on that occasion that he delivered "A Dissertation on the History, Eloquence, and Poetry of the Bible." This was printed and republished in Europe, and became generally known. About this time, Dwight aggravated the disease in his eyes by close application to study after an attack of the small-pox; and in order to leave his mind as free as possible, he reduced his diet so low as to undermine his health and threaten his life. This led him to adopt a valetudinarian course of out-door exercise, to which he was indebted for his subsequent vigour and health.

In the year 1774, Dwight joined the college-church. He was at that time studying for the practice of the law; and, in 1777, he was married to Mary, the daughter of Benjamin Woolsey, of Long Island. Their family consisted of eight sons, of whom six survived their father. The same year he was licensed as a preacher, and became a chaplain in the United States' army. In this capacity he laboured for the spiritual good of the soldiers. He also wrote patriotic songs. These were popular, especially one, his "Columbia." But at the end of a year, the death of his father rendered it necessary that he should leave the army, and go to the comfort and assistance of his mother. He was the eldest of thirteen children, and the circumstances of the country rendered the maintenance and care of so large a family a matter of grave difficulty and responsibility; but Dwight did not shrink from it. Bringing his various talents to bear on the work, he, at the same time, carried on a school at Northampton, preached on Sunday to vacant congregations, and superintended the profitable cultivation of the family estate. He also represented his native town in the State Legislature, in the years 1781-2; and there was an intention of obtaining for him a seat in Congress, but he declined this in order to give himself to the Christian ministry.

In 1783, he became the pastor of the church at Greenfield, a parish in the town of Fairfield, in Connecticut. There he was regularly ordained, and continued his pastorate for twelve years. During that period he conducted an academy with great success, training, during the time, more than a thousand young men and women. In this way he supplemented his inadequate ministerial stipend. At the age of thirty-five, Dwight received the degree of Doctor of Divinity from the college at Princeton, New Jersey. In the year 1794, he published a poem, in seven parts, called "Greenfield Hill," from the place of his residence. In it he shows that he possessed an intimate knowledge of agriculture along with his other acquirements. In the following year, he was elected President of Yale College. This institution rose to the highest renown under his presidency. The number of students was more than doubled; the standard of education was maintained at a great height; infidelity, which had been gaining ground, was effectually checked; and the students felt that they had in their president a personal Christian friend, as well as a prince of preceptors.

In addition to his duties as president, Dr. Dwight held the office of Professor of Theology at Yale College, undertaking it for the first ten years annually, and afterwards to the end of his life holding it as a permanent appointment. The diseased state of his eyes did not allow of his writing his lectures, hence he had the assistance of an amanuensis. His theological lectures were in the form of sermons, and a large number were preached twice to his congregation at Greenfield, and twice at New Haven. Subsequently he adopted the plan of preaching one each Sunday morning in term-time, so that a student during his four years might hear them all. This manner of origin accounts for the practical and evangelical character of Dr. Dwight's theological course. It was written for the pulpit as well as for the class-room. The style is adapted to public impression, yet it is sometimes held in check lest it should interfere with the clearness and force of the various arguments. His work is entitled, "Theology Explained and Defended in a Series of Sermons." It was written out at the close of 1809, and consists of five volumes.

With a view to the restoration and preservation of his health, he made extensive journeys during the college vacations; and on the way he collected a great variety of information on various subjects. The fruit of this was his posthumous work, "Travels in New England and New York," in 4 vols., 1823. Several sermons and essays were published when they were written, and some additional volumes of sermons by him were published after his death. His "Discourses on the Nature and Danger of Infidel Philosophy" were republished in London, and much commended. His extraordinary industry was continued through his life, notwithstanding his occasional suffering in his eyes; and it was pursued till his death, in spite of his severe sufferings at the end. His service to Christ's Church was what he had said in his hymn (No. 828)—

> " For her my tears shall fall,
> For her my prayers ascend,
> To her my cares and toils be given,
> Till toils and cares shall end."

Dr. Dwight died as he had lived, faithful to Christ and safe and happy in Him. His day of peaceful departure was the 11th of January, 1817.

A man of large and generous sympathies, Dr. Dwight was accustomed to give a hearty welcome to strangers of many lands who came to see him in his hospitable home. He lived in communication with many persons of influence; and great literary and religious societies found in him one willing to lay their first foundations. Science, education, missions, and Bible-circulation were the objects he laboured to advance; and he did special service in promoting the union of the Presbyterian and Congregational Churches of his country. Dr. Dwight was equally celebrated for the variety of his attainments, the power of his genius, and the fervour of his piety, for his usefulness as a minister, his ability as a writer, his skill as a teacher, and his unwavering zeal for the cause of God.

Besides the larger poems already referred to, Dr. Dwight wrote verse for amusement from his boyhood to the time of his death. He was accustomed to dictate it in the evening to his amanuensis, and sometimes fifty or more lines at a time. It was the play of his fancy after the severer toils of the day. In the year 1797, he was asked to use his poetical talents for the service of the Church. The General Association of Connecticut wished him " to revise Dr. Watts's version of the Psalms, to versify such as he had omitted, and to make a selection of hymns suited to the general purposes of public worship. The work was completed in 1800, and laid before a joint committee of that body and of the General Assembly of the Presbyterian Church, by whom it was approved, and recommended to the use of the Congregational and Presbyterian Churches throughout the United States. In the performance of this difficult task, he made alterations of more or less consequence, in a considerable number of Dr. Watts's Psalms; and composed thirty-three entire psalms, containing about twelve hundred and fifty lines."

Dr. Dwight supplies two hymns to the "New Congregational Hymn Book:" No. 36, his rendering of the 28th Psalm. The second part of his version is given. Its date is 1800.

"I love Thy kingdom, Lord."—No. 828.

A favourite hymn given also in the "Lyra Americana," and in other collections. Two verses are omitted in the "New Congregational Hymn Book." This hymn also bears date 1800.

GEORGE BURDER.

1752—1832.

THE well-known author of the "Village Sermons" has added his name to the long list of hymn-writers. He was born in London, on the 5th of June, 1752. His father, Henry Burder, Esq., lived and died in Fair Street, Southwark. Young George had the misfortune to lose his mother in 1762, while he was still a child. He was educated in London, and distinguished himself at his school. The profession chosen for him was that of an artist, as he had shown a taste for drawing. He was put with Isaac Taylor, an artist, and studied at the Royal Academy. As a child he had received deep religious impressions. He speaks in his autobiography of retiring (June 5, 1762), after a pious conversation, and pouring out his soul to God, beseeching Him to give him an interest in Christ, and desiring above all things to be found in Him. These impressions were deepened by some dangerous accidents that happened to him when he was a young man, and by the preaching of Mr. Whitefield. He heard Mr. Whitefield's last two sermons in London, and reported and printed them.

At the age of twenty-three, he became a member of the Church at the Tabernacle in London, and having received some encouragement from the celebrated Mr. Fletcher, he began preaching, and at length relinquished his artistic pursuits to devote himself entirely to the ministry. After preaching at Ulverstone and Lancaster, he was ordained pastor of the Congregational Church at Lancaster, on the 29th of October, 1778. There his labours were useful, and he made journeys in the neighbourhood, and in various parts of England and Wales, in order to preach the Gospel. In 1781 he was united in marriage to Miss Harrison, of Newcastle-under-Lyne. In November, 1783, he removed to Coventry, where he became minister of the West Orchard Chapel, and maintained a useful ministry for twenty years.

Before leaving London, Mr. Burder had published, in 1776, a small book for children, called "Early Piety." This did much good, and its ready sale and acknowledged usefulness encouraged the author. In 1781 he published and circulated at Lancaster a tract, "The Good Old Way;" and afterwards others, called "Village Tracts." Seeing how the cause of Christ could be served by the press, he published editions of "Bunyan's Pilgrims' Progress," with the observations he had made thereon at his Monday evening prayer meetings, and the "Holy War," and an abridgment of Dr. Owen's work on the Holy Spirit, and other works. The failure of Mr. Burder's London bookseller pointed to the necessity for a society equal to the large undertakings requisite for the supply of the public. Hence, in 1799, Mr. Burder called together some influential ministers and others in London, and with their co-operation commenced the "Religious Tract Society," whose course has been continually progressive, and whose useful agencies extend to every quarter of the world.

Impressed with the moral necessities of our village populations, Mr. Burder prepared, in 1797, a volume of "Village Sermons." These were so well received that he was encouraged to prepare volume after volume, till he had, in 1820, completed eight volumes, including one hundred discourses. Simple, evangelical, and earnest, these sermons met a want, and were blessed by God to the salvation of many souls. They have been translated into Malay, Singalese, and other tongues. In 1821 he published twelve " Sea Sermons," the nautical phrases being corrected by a minister who had been in the navy; and in 1826, twelve " Cottage Sermons." And in 1828, when approaching his own end, he prepared twelve " Sermons for the Aged." These various sets of sermons have had a great sale—nearly a million copies before his death—and the author heard of many instances in which they had been useful, and in some cases by their occasional use the hearts of unconverted clergymen were changed and a regular gospel ministry was introduced. Mr. Burder was also the author of " Evangelical Truth defended," 1788; " Missionary Anecdotes," 1811; and several other works.

In the year 1803, he left Coventry to undertake important duties in London. He succeeded the Rev. John Eyre, who had died, in his offices as editor of the " Evangelical Magazine," and secretary of the London Missionary Society. This institution, founded in 1795, owed very much at its origin, if not that origin itself, to the zeal of the delegates sent to London by the " Warwickshire Association of Ministers for the spread of the Gospel both at home and abroad." In the formation of that association Mr. Burder had taken an active part. For twenty-four years, up to 1827, he continued to be the laborious but unpaid secretary of the London Missionary Society. Along with these onerous duties, Mr. Burder undertook the pastoral office at Fetter Lane, a charge he retained till his death. In 1804 he assisted in the formation of the British and Foreign Bible Society; and in 1806 he became one of the preachers of the ancient " Merchants' Lecture." During the last few years of his life, his failing sight and other infirmities rendered it necessary for him to give up his duties one by one; but he was able to preach occasionally till within three months of his departure. His second wife died March 6th, 1824. He peacefully departed on the 29th of May, 1832, having almost completed his eightieth year. His memoir was written in 1833, by the late Dr. Henry Forster Burder, also an eminent congregational minister, and his eldest son.

In 1784, soon after going to Coventry, Mr. Burder published "A Collection of Hymns, from Various Authors: intended as a Supplement to Dr. Watts's Hymns, and Imitations of the Psalms." The preface, bearing date November 20th, 1784, explains that the work had been prepared to take advantage of the labours of the authors who had sprung up since the time of Watts, and to introduce "a larger variety of musical measures and tunes." This collection has passed through many editions. It contains three hymns by Mr. Burder himself. The best of these is that given in the "New Congregational Hymn Book"—

"Great the joy when Christians meet."—No. 831.

It is given with the omission of one verse, and with a few verba alterations. It is the 66th in his collection, where it begins—

"Sweet the time, exceeding sweet."

"Lord, dismiss us with Thy blessing."—No. 793.

This is erroneously attributed to Burder in the "New Congregational Hymn Book." It first appeared in 1793, in Edward Smyth's collection, Manchester.

"Great God, impress our trifling minds."—No. 786.

This is No. 200 in George Burder's collection of 1784, where it begins—

"Lord, solemnize our trifling minds."

The author has claimed it as his own by putting "B" to it.

"Jesus, immortal King, arise."—No. 920.

In the "New Congregational Hymn Book," the name "Burder" is erroneously given to this hymn. It is by A. C. Hobart Seymour, *vide* under his name.

JOHN RYLAND, D.D.
1753—1825.

Few names are more honoured in the Baptist denomination than that of Ryland, the name of a family that produced in several generations men of the highest eminence. Not the least of these was the subject of this sketch, " J. R., Jun.," as he used to subscribe himself in the magazines. His father was the Rev. John Collett Ryland, pastor of the Baptist Church at Warwick, at the time of John's birth, January 29th, 1753. The elder Ryland was a fine scholar, and very early trained his son in the knowledge of Greek and Hebrew; and from his pious mother he received, as Doddridge had done, scriptural instruction from the Dutch tiles that adorned their fireplace. As a child, his feelings were very tender, and when about fourteen years of age he experienced a great spiritual change, and, in company with some pious youths in his father's school, made a profession of religion. At this early age, when but fourteen, he was baptised and received into the church over which his father presided.

Subsequently, for several years he increased his own knowledge, while assisting in his father's school at Northampton, whither he had removed in 1759. And after a time, with the approval of the Church at Northampton, he assisted his father in the ministry, and in 1781 was ordained and appointed his co-pastor. In 1786, on his father's removal to London, he succeeded him as sole pastor. Making Northampton a centre, he preached in many parts around, and by the pen as well as the living voice contended earnestly for the faith. In co-operation with Carey, Fuller, Sutcliffe, and others, he originated the Baptist Missionary Society, at Kettering, on the 2nd of October, 1792. His name is first on the committee of five, and his signature attests the first humble list of subscriptions, amounting in all to £13 2s. 6d.

In 1794 he left Northampton to undertake the presidency of the Baptist College, Bristol, and the pastorate at Broadmead

Chapel. He had not long before received the degree of Doctor of Divinity, from Brown University, in Rhode Island, America. His twofold duties at Bristol as pastor and president of the college he retained till his death, in 1825. And in 1815, on the death of the Rev. Andrew Fuller, he undertook the duties of secretary of the Baptist Missionary Society, a position he held for two or three years. In his sixty-ninth year, Dr. Ryland's laborious course began to wear down his constitution : and each year found him weaker, till on the 25th of May, 1825, after uttering the words "No more pain," he peacefully departed.

Dr. Ryland's memory was honoured by a sketch from John Foster in the "Eclectic Review," and by a funeral sermon by his celebrated successor at Broadmead, Robert Hall. Both writers pass a high eulogium upon Dr. Ryland as a pastor, preacher, tutor, and author.

Amongst Dr. Ryland's prose works were "Memoirs of the Rev. R. Hall, of Arnsby," second edition, 1852 ; and " A Candid Statement of the Reasons which induce the Baptists to differ from their Christian Brethren." He also published some sermons.

Dr. Ryland's earliest productions were poetical. We are indebted to Mr. Daniel Sedgwick for a reprint of Dr. Ryland's hymns, ninety-nine in number. Many of them are taken from the close of his "Pastoral Memorials," two vols., 1825. The dates are given, and the hymns are found to have been composed at different times, from the author's twentieth year to the year of his death. They never rise above an humble level as poetic productions, but some are useful. One of his hymns, "Lord, teach a little child to pray," was composed at the request of the Rev. Andrew Fuller for his dying daughter, who died May 30th, 1786, aged six years and six months. This hymn was often repeated to her, and her father elicited from her that she was accustomed to pray over it. And one of his well-known hymns—

"When Abraham's servant, to procure."

was composed in 1773, during the preaching of a sermon on

the words, "Hinder me not" (Gen. xxiv. 56), words that are repeated in every verse, except the first. The sermon was preached by a brother minister who was on his way through Northampton, and who was detained by Dr. Ryland somewhat against his will.

"Thou Son of God and Son of man."—No. 355.

This hymn, given without name in the "New Congregational Hymn Book," is also by Dr. John Ryland.

"Sovereign Ruler of the skies."—No. 595.

This is five verses of a hymn of nine verses, bearing date August, 1777.

"O Lord! I would delight in Thee."—No. 685.

This is four verses of a hymn (1777) of seven verses. In the original MS. the following interesting note is given :—" I recollect deeper feelings of mind in composing this hymn, than perhaps I ever felt in making any other."

THOMAS GREENE.

"It is the Lord—enthroned in light."—No. 602.

This hymn is found at page 52 in "Hymns and Poems on Various Subjects, chiefly sacred," by Thomas Greene, of Ware, Herts. Of this work the first edition appeared in 1780, and the second in 1802. The hymn admirably expresses the meaning of the passage upon which it is founded, "It is the Lord : let him do what seemeth him good," 1 Sam. iii. 18, and, although Mr. Greene's only contribution to the "New Congregational Hymn Book," is a valuable one. It is entitled in the original "Quieting considerations under afflicting dispensations," and consists of ten stanzas.

Mr. Greene was a gentleman of good means, residing at Ware, where he held some land. Previously to the year 1778, he was a member of a congregational church at Ware, that has for some years ceased to be. In the year 1778 the minority of that church, who had become favourable to Arian principles, obtained a renewal of the chapel lease in their own favour. In consequence of this, the majority withdrew and erected what is known as the old Independent Chapel. Mr. Greene belonged to this seceding majority. He contributed £100 to the new edifice; and he was for many years a member of the seceding Church, and contributed liberally towards meeting the expenses of public worship. Correspondence with the present minister and with the friends and relatives of Mr. Greene has not elicited more precise information than this. His poems include a large number of pleasing pious pieces on moral and religious subjects. The versification is good, but they do not possess sufficient merit to preserve them from the oblivion of mediocrity.

EDMUND BUTCHER.
1757—1822.

The Rev. Edmund Butcher was born in 1757, at Colchester, Essex. His family came from Feering, in the same county, of which place his ancestor, John Butcher, was rector in the previous century. Edmund's father, a carpenter and builder, was unable to afford him educational advantages. But Dr. Stanton, a dissenting minister at Colchester, gave him some instruction of which he made good use, and early gave proofs of the possession of talent.

When a little more than fourteen years of age, he was apprenticed to a linendraper in London. While in the metropolis he devoted his leisure hours to literary pursuits, and contributed to some periodicals, giving his early gains to his parents and only sister, who needed his help. In London also he found a friend in the Rev. Mr. Worthington, whose ministry he attended at Salters' Hall. Mr. Worthington encouraged him to enter the ministry, and assisted in preparing him for a college course. To study for the ministry he entered the Daventry Academy. This was the institution that had been under the care of Dr. Doddridge at Northampton. At the time when Mr. Butcher entered it, the Rev. Thomas Belsham was the theological tutor, a divine who during his tutorship forsook his former faith and openly avowed his adoption of Socinianism.

Mr. Butcher's first settlement was at Sowerby, in Yorkshire. After some time he removed to London, and preached occasionally at Monkwell Street and Carter Lane. But the principal scene of his labours was at a chapel in Leather Lane, Holborn, where he was minister of a congregation of Protestant Dissenters. There he was ordained in 1789; Messrs. Kippis, Worthington, Belsham, and others, taking part in the service. There he had a respectable audience, and might have been popular if the weakness of his voice had not prevented; and there he remained until the state of his health compelled him to leave London. And while in London he assisted in maintaining a course of Wednesday evening lectures at Salters' Hall during several winters.

In 1798, Mr. Butcher removed to Sidbury Vale, near Sidmouth, where the mildness of the Devonshire air speedily restored to him the use of his lungs. At Sidmouth he became the pastor of a small but appreciating congregation, and enjoyed in his family and pastoral circles those pleasures of home and friendship which he greatly prized. For a few years previous to his death he suffered from paralysis and great debility. In November, 1821, he removed to Bath, with the hope of gaining some relief; but soon after he fell down and dislocated his hip. He was, in consequence of this accident, confined to his bed, and grew worse until his peaceful departure on April 14th, 1822. He entered into rest on a Sabbath-day—a day of rest—as he had often wished.

He was the author of a useful work on an original plan, "A Family Bible." This was prepared in conjunction with the Rev. Mr. Worthington. His other works were his "Picture of Sidmouth," and a "Tour through Various Parts of England." As a boy, Edmund Butcher had felt poetical promptings, and had written, at the age of fourteen, a little poem, entitled "The Brutæis," founded on the fabled tradition of the peopling of Britain by the Trojans. And in 1798, on his removal to Sidbury, when he thought it right to publish for the use of his London congregation some of the sermons he had preached to them, he added hymns to the discourses, and called the work "Sermons: to which are added suitable Hymns." And he says in the preface that he had composed the hymns expressly to be sung when the sermon was read in the family, and he hoped that the hymn would be read where it could not be sung. He is said to have published three volumes of "Sermons for the Use of Families." His last work was a volume of "Prayers for the Use of Families and Individuals." These were adapted to each sermon in his volume, and there were forms suitable for particular occasions. After his death, Mrs. Butcher published a small volume of his "Discourses on our Lord's Sermon on the Mount." Mr. Butcher was also the editor of the later volumes of the "Protestant Dissenters' Magazine." Some of his hymns are in Kippis' and other collections.

"Great God, as seasons disappear."—No. 952.

This is, in a very much altered form, the hymn of six verses given after his sermon xvi., in his work of 1798, "Sermons, &c." The title of the sermon is "Harvest Reflections," and the text, Jeremiah viii. 20, "The harvest is past, the summer is ended, and we are not saved." There are twenty-one discourses in the volume. The author says in the preface : "I pray God, that these poetical epitomes may be instrumental in fixing upon the memory the leading ideas of the discourse to which each belongs." The writer had around him the harvest scene, and in his own frail condition a pre-intimation of the blow of the sickle of which he writes.

JAMES BODEN.
1757—1841.

In the house at Chester, where the eminent commentator Matthew Henry once resided, James Boden first saw the light, and in the garden where he played there was a summer-house, where it is said a large part of the commentary was written. The youth often heard of his great forerunner, and at length desired to tread in his steps. At the age of sixteen, he made a profession of his faith in Christ. Subsequently, he studied for the ministry at Homerton College. He commenced his ministry as pastor of the Congregational Church at Hanley, in Staffordshire, where he laboured for about fifteen years.

In the year 1795, he was one of the founders of the London Missionary Society, and he lived to be the last survivor of that noble band. In 1796, he succeeded the Rev. Jehoiada Brewer at Queen Street, Sheffield, where he retained the pastorate for nearly forty-three years. During his ministry he preached three times every Sunday, and was indefatigable in promoting the interests of local religious and benevolent institutions. Two years before the end of his long and laborious life, his growing infirmities made it necessary that he should retire from public life. During his last illness he gave full proof of his peaceful confidence in Christ. He died at Chesterfield, on the 4th of June, 1841, aged eighty-four years.

In the year 1801, Mr. Boden, with the assistance of Dr. Williams, theological tutor of Rotherham College, prepared a collection of hymns, entitled " A Collection of above Six Hundred Hymns, designed as a New Supplement to Dr. Watts's Psalms and Hymns. By the Rev. Edward Williams, D.D., and the Rev. James Boden." This was a carefully prepared collection. It had reached a fifth edition in 1812. It contained seven hymns by Mr. Boden, numbered in that collection 100, 130, 133, 167,

205, 464, and 526. His hymns had appeared in the "Gospel Magazine" for 1777, and the following years.

"Glory to God on high!"—No. 338.

This is erroneously attributed to Boden in the "New Congregational." It is by James Allen, *vide* "James Allen."

"Ye dying sons of men."—No. 513.

This hymn appeared in the "Gospel Magazine" for February, 1777. It is given in the "New Congregational" without abridgment, and with the alteration of only one word.

"Bright source of everlasting love."—No. 977.

This is No. 526 in the above collection. It was written to be sung after a charity sermon for the benefit of the sick poor. Two verses are omitted.

JOSEPH STRAPHAN.

"Blest work, the youthful mind to win."—No. 974.

THIS is part of hymn 523 in "Rippon's Selection." The original hymn has six verses, and begins—

"Blest is the man whose heart expands."

It appears in an altered form in the "New Congregational." There are three hymns by Straphan in "Rippon's Selection."

JOHN DOBELL.
1757—1840.

"Now is the accepted time."—No. 495.

THIS simple but useful hymn, given without name in the "New Congregational," is No. 360 in John Dobell's Collection, where his own name is put to it, and it is given with an additional verse. The full title of that collection is "A New

Selection of 700 Evangelical Hymns for Private, Family, and Public Worship (many original), from more than 200 of the best authors in England, Scotland, Ireland, and America; arranged in alphabetical order, intended as a Supplement to Dr. Watts's Psalms and Hymns." The preface is dated Poole, Dorset, March 1st, 1806. It explains that many of the hymns were taken from manuscripts which Mr. Dobell deemed too valuable to be suffered to remain in obscurity, and that some of the hymns were supplied by friends. He had laboured at his book for years, and selected from thousands of hymns. He had altered some of the hymns, sometimes omitting verses and sometimes adding new ones; and he contributed about twenty of his own hymns, which are plain and evangelical, and make no pretension to high poetic excellence. In his collection, Mr. Dobell did an important service by giving the names of the authors. He gives the complete list separately, at the beginning of his collection, and also adds the name to each hymn as far as he could, and in most instances correctly. He has thus become a valuable pioneer in this interesting branch of study, and has preserved some elements of information that might have now become irrecoverable. In its enlarged form, his collection included seven hundred hymns, fifteen choruses, and a long hymn on "Heaven," by Erskine. It passed through several editions.

Conspicuous in the congregation that assembled at Skinner Street Chapel, Poole, more than fifty years ago, was the tall form of Mr. Dobell, a somewhat eccentric and remarkable man. During the long pastorate of the Rev. Edward Ashburner, and during the greater part of that of his successor, the Rev. Thomas Durant, he attended there, his wife being a church member, though there is no record of his being in union with the church. There his collection was used, there many came to call him familiarly "Old Dobell," (pronouncing his name with the accent on the first syllable, as if it were spelt "Doble"); and there he was buried, June 1st, 1840, by Dr. A. Morton Brown, who was then co-pastor there.

Mr. Dobell's occupation was that of port-gauger, a situation under the Board of Excise. The nature of his duties left him a good deal of leisure, which he improved in the preparation of collections of hymns and in writing religious books. He was the author of "Baptism," 1807, and a work on "Humanity," 1812. He also published a fourth volume of Dr. Watts's "Psalms," and in 1828, he published another collection of hymns, containing many of his own. This work, in two volumes, was prepared at the suggestion of a pious lady, whom he visited in her sickness, in Cornwall. She said, "I wish I could see before I die a hymn book full of Christ and His Gospel, and without any mixture of free-will or merit." The first volume of this work contains one hundred and twenty-four hymns, and is entitled "The Christian's Golden Treasure; or, Gospel Comfort for Doubting Minds." The second volume is entitled "The Christian's Companion in his Journey to Heaven, &c." This work was reprinted, and much used in America.

JOSEPH SWAIN.
1761—1796.

THE brief life of this hymn-writer found suitable expression in earnest and successful Christian labours, and in sweet and spiritual Christian songs. He was born at Birmingham, and had the misfortune to lose his parents while he was young. After being apprenticed to an engraver he removed to London, where he was exposed to great moral dangers from his association with gay youthful companions.

But after experiencing deep religious convictions, and being agitated by distressing fears, he at length found peace in Jesus. To give utterance to his new life, he began to write hymns, which he took delight in singing. A friend having overheard him singing these Christian hymns, took him to hear Gospel preaching—a privilege he had not enjoyed before. This gave him great delight, and served to develope his spiritual life. He was baptized by Dr. Rippon in 1788, and in 1791 he became minister of a congregation in East Street, Walworth. There his success was great. It became necessary to enlarge the chapel, and the number of the members of the church increased from twenty-seven to two hundred. But his useful course was cut short, as he died in 1796.

He was the author of the "Walworth Hymns," published in 1792.

"How sweet, how heavenly is the sight,"—No. 584,

his only contribution to the "New Congregational Hymn Book," is an excellent hymn, and a favourable specimen of his poetical productions.

HELEN MARIA WILLIAMS.
1762—1827.

"While Thee I seek, Almighty Power."—No. 286.

This is the sole contribution of this authoress to the "New Congregational." It bears date 1786. The original contains another verse, and begins—

"While Thee I seek, protecting Power."

Helen Maria Williams was born in the north of England, in 1762. At the age of eighteen she came to London, where she was introduced to the literary world by Dr. Andrew Kippis. Her first work was a legendary tale in verse, entitled "Edwin and Eltruda," 1782. Two years after, she sent forth "Peru," a poem; and in 1786, "An Ode to Peace," and a collection of Miscellaneous Poems, in two volumes; and in 1788, a poem "On the Slave Trade."

In the year 1786 she visited France, and became known in literary circles. And in the year 1790, having settled in Paris, she published her "Letters from France," and a continuation of the same work in 1792. Her works courted the favour of the

Brissotines, and on their fall under Robespierre she was in danger, and she was actually imprisoned in the Temple in Paris. Other works by her were: "A Translation of Humboldt's Personal Narratives of his Travels," 1815; "A Narrative of the Events which have taken place in France, from the Landing of Napoleon Buonaparte till the Restoration of Louis XVIII.," &c., 1815; also, a work "On the Late Persecution of the Protestants in the South of France," 1816. She was also at one time a contributor to the "New Annual Register." She died in Paris, December, 1827.

THOMAS KELLY.
1769—1855.

THOMAS KELLY was the only son of Judge Kelly, of Kellyville, near Athy, Queen's County, Ireland. He was educated at Portarlington and Kilkenny, and afterwards passed with honours through the Dublin University. Being designed for the bar, he entered at the Temple, and while in London enjoyed the friendship of the celebrated Edmund Burke.

Before being called to the bar, his reading of Hutchinson's "Moses' Principia" led him to study Hebrew, and this led him to the use of Romaine's edition of Calasio's Hebrew Concordance, and subsequently to inquire about Romaine's evangelical doctrines. While studying the gospel doctrine he became convinced of sin, and was filled with great anxiety about his state before God. To remove his distress, he made attempts at self-reformation, practised asceticism, and put his life in jeopardy by fasting. But at length he had peace with God through the Lord Jesus Christ, by that way of "justification by faith" of which he became afterwards so firm and faithful an advocate.

In conjunction with several others as evangelical as himself, he was ordained a minister of the Established Church in 1792. The gospel was preached in few churches in Ireland at that time;

but Mr. Kelly was encouraged in his evangelistic purposes by the visit of Rowland Hill to Ireland in 1793. For a time the young evangelical clergymen gave the Sunday afternoon lectures at St. Luke's Church, in Dublin, till their success awakened the opposition of the rector. Then afterwards they preached on Sunday morning at the Episcopal Church, at Irishtown; but the Archbishop of Dublin, Dr. Fowler, on hearing of the new doctrine, summoned Mr. Kelly and his companions before him; and having reproved them, issued a decree, closing the Dublin pulpits against them. In consequence, the brethren betook themselves to two non-episcopal chapels in the city—Plunket Street and the Bethesda—where they preached with much fervour. Mr. Kelly also preached in the house of Alderman Hutton, in Luson Street. This meeting was kept up for many years, and issued in the erection of the chapel in York Street.

Soon after his ordination Mr. Kelly had felt scruples about his connection with the Established Church. These increased with his extended study of the Scriptures, until he was a dissenter, not from persecution, but on principle. Possessed of ample means, Mr. Kelly built churches at Athy, Portarlington, Wexford, Waterford, &c. They were not actually connected with the Congregational body, but they were really Independent, and were conducted on what was substantially a congregational plan. Besides preaching at other places, Mr. Kelly acted as pastor at Athy and Dublin.

Mr. Kelly was a man of great and varied learning, skilled in the Oriental tongues, and an excellent Bible critic. He was possessed also of musical talent, and composed and published a work that was received with favour, consisting of music adapted to every form of metre in his Hymn Book. Naturally of an amiable disposition, and thorough in his Christian piety, Mr. Kelly became the friend of good men, and the advocate of every worthy, benevolent, and religious cause. He was admired alike for his zeal and his humility; and his liberality found ample scope in Ireland, especially during the year of famine.

About his thirtieth year, Mr. Kelly was united in marriage to

Miss Tighe, of Rosanna, in the county of Wicklow, a member of a family remarkable for their wealth, rank, and piety.

In the year 1854, while preaching, at the age of eighty-five, he was smitten with a stroke, and in the following year he died, on the 14th of May, aged eighty-six years. His last words were, "Not my will, but thine be done."

He was the author of "Andrew Dunn," a narrative controversial work against Romanism, and of a pamphlet, "Thoughts on Imputed Righteousness," by T. K. But as a writer he is chiefly known as the author of "Hymns on various Passages of Scripture." The first edition, in 1804, contained only ninety-six hymns; but the subsequent editions were increased, until the seventh edition, published in Dublin, 1853, contained 767 hymns. In the preface, the author says: "It will be perceived by those who read these hymns, that though there is an interval between the first and last of near sixty years, both speak of the same great truths, and in the same way. In the course of that long period, the author has seen much and heard much; but nothing that he has seen or heard has made the least change in his mind, that he is conscious of, as to the grand truths of the gospel. What pacified the conscience then, does so now. What gave hope then, does so now. 'Other foundation can no man lay than that is laid, which is Jesus Christ.'"

Nine hymns in the "New Congregational Hymn Book" are by Kelly, and are taken from the above collection. They are somewhat altered and abridged. Like their author, they are all earnestly evangelical. They are Nos. 387, 410, 411, 709, 710, 766, 789, 833, and 919. Of these, 387, 709, 710, 789, and 833 were in the second edition, 1806. Without any great poetic merits, some of Kelly's hymns have taken their place as serviceable. This is true of such hymns as—

"In Thy name, O Lord, assembling."—No. 766,

"Now may the gospel's conquering power."—No. 789,

and the hymn No. 411—

"Look, ye saints, the sight is glorious,"

is a fine rendering of the passage, "We see Jesus—crowned with glory." Heb. ii. 9.

JAMES MONTGOMERY.
1771—1854.

Montgomery, whom we may describe as the Cowper of the 19th century, was born at Irvine, in Ayrshire, where his father was a Moravian minister. In his fifth year he accompanied his parents to Grace Hill, a settlement of the Moravians, near Ballymena, in Ireland. Two years after he was sent to the Moravian seminary at Fulneck, in Yorkshire. In the year 1783, and while he was still at Fulneck, his parents were sent as missionaries to the West Indies, where they both died.

Fulneck was the chief settlement of the Moravians in England. It was built in 1760, the year of Count Zinzendorf's death. There the young poet had offered to him the advantages of a liberal and religious education, and came under the beneficial influence of men of ardent piety. Montgomery was designed for a preacher, but his early devotion to the muses, which began in his tenth year, diverted his attention from severe study and altered the course of the current of his life. It was a happy element in his history that he early recognized his own bent, and saw that he was to serve the cause of Christ better as a poet than he could as a preacher.

Leaving Fulneck in 1787, he entered a retail shop at Mirfield, near Wakefield. There he continued to write poetry and cultivate music. But after remaining there a year and a half, being afflicted with that pensive melancholy which often returned upon him, he set out with a few shillings in his pocket to try his fortune in the world. But he soon repented of his rash undertaking, and gladly accepted a situation similar to that he had left, at the village of Wath, near Rotherham. After remaining there for a year, he went to London, carrying with him some of his early poems to offer to the publishers. But the cold caution of the London publishers destroyed his golden dream of sudden fame, and sent him back almost broken-hearted to his business routine at Wath.

From Wath, Montgomery went, in 1792, to Sheffield, to assist a Mr. Gales, an auctioneer and bookseller, and the printer of the "Sheffield Register." In 1794, when Mr. Gales left England to avoid persecution for the political principles he had advocated in his paper, Montgomery undertook it, and under the altered name of the "Iris," edited it for thirty-one years.

But as the principles of the paper continued to be too liberal for the government of that day, Montgomery was fined and imprisoned; in the first instance, for reprinting a song commemorating "The Fall of the Bastile," and in the second, in 1795, for the account he gave of a riot at Sheffield. The "Iris" was much read, and the state prosecution may be accepted as a tribute to the power of the pen it was intended to stop. During Montgomery's second imprisonment, John Pye Smith, then a village preacher, and afterwards one of the brightest ornaments of the congregational body, courageously undertook the editorship of the persecuted "Iris." Montgomery continued to advocate those liberal principles which he lived to see prevail, and he found his incarceration less irksome than he had feared, cheered as it was by the production of short poems, which appeared in 1797, with the title of "Prison Amusements."

Of his other works, the principal were: "The Wanderer of Switzerland," 1806—a denunciation of the war spirit of the French revolutionists, given in an account of the fortunes of a Swiss family, driven forth from their country in consequence of its subjugation by the French. This work, notwithstanding that it was met by the frown of the "Edinburgh Review," became very popular, and had a large sale. In the following year Montgomery published "The West Indies," a heroic poem, written in honour of the abolition of the African slave-trade by the British

Legislature, in 1807. This work was one of the agencies that have at length led to the entire abolition of slavery itself. "The World before the Flood" appeared in 1813. It is a highly imaginative work, describing the contests of the good and the evil, and the triumphs of the good in the antediluvian age. In 1819 he published "Greenland." This is an historical account of the Moravian missions in that country, but is not so complete as the author at first intended it to be. In 1828 Montgomery published the last of his longer poems, "The Pelican Island," a poetic description of the haunts of the pelican in the island of New Holland. Some of his smaller pieces were very striking, as for instance, "The Common Lot," a piece of ten stanzas, written during a country walk in the snow, on his thirty-fourth birthday. Other works by the poet were "Prose by a Poet," in 1824. This was a collection of his best prose contributions to the "Iris," with other original pieces; "A Poet's Portfolio," in 1835; and his collected works were afterwards published. He had been a contributor to the "Eclectic Review" in its palmiest days. In 1830-31 he delivered a course of "Lectures on Poetry and General Literature," at the Royal Institution. These were published in 1833, and about the same time he received a royal pension of £200 a year.

Montgomery lived for many years in an old house, the "Iris" office, in a central part of Sheffield, but in his later years he went to reside at the well-known "Mount," at the west end of Sheffield, where many eminent literary persons visited him. Like Cowper, Montgomery never married. Trained under the best religious influences, and never losing those influences, the poet, even up to his thirty-sixth year, speaks of his unbelief and religious despondency in affecting words that remind us of Cowper. And he delayed his formal public profession of religion till his forty-third year, when he became a member of the Moravian Church. The letters of Daniel Parkin, the editor of the "Eclectic Review," afforded him important assistance in arriving at religious decision. He was also indebted to the sermons of the hymn-writer Cennick, under whose ministry his father had been converted. As the Moravians had no chapel at Sheffield, the poet continued to worship with the Wesleyans. Treated as a martyr for principle, we might expect to find in Montgomery acerbity of disposition and severity of language, provoking such persecution and increased by it. But, on the contrary, he was peculiarly urbane and charitable in his disposition, and his writings are less marked for their assertion of dogmas than for their advocacy of Christianity as fruitful in whatsover is "pure, lovely, and of good report." Religious and benevolent objects found in him an earnest advocate, and he went on journeys to advocate the Bible and Moravian Missionary Societies. His hymns are valued as giving adequate expression to the best thoughts of believers, and even his secular pieces have a religious aim. He died in his sleep, April 30th, 1854, at the venerable age of eighty-two.

Willmott says of Montgomery that "he followed no leader in poetry, and belonged to no school, but appealed to universal principles, to imperishable affections, and to the elements of our common nature." Without being a Milton or a Shakspere, there are in his poems flights of fancy and flashes of genius that sustain his claim to the honoured name of poet. And in all his poems we mark his skill in versification, his purity of taste, and the excellence of his moral purpose.

Montgomery has laid the modern Christian church under great obligations by his hymns. In 1822 he published his "Songs of Zion, being Imitations of Psalms." This work consisted of sixty-seven pieces. The psalms are closely, as well as beautifully, rendered. Several of these are given in the "New Congregational Hymn Book." No. 206, his rendering of Psalm 122, may be taken as a favourable example. And in 1825 he published his "Christian Psalmist; or Hymns Selected and Original." This work consists of 562 hymns, of which 103, most of which are placed at the end, are by Montgomery, and the rest are by various authors. It is from this work that most of Montgomery's hymns in the "New Congregational Hymn Book" are taken. In 1853 he published "Original Hymns for Public, Private, and Social Devotion." In his "Introductory Essay" to his "Christian Psalmist," he has given an interesting sketch of some of the hymns-writers whose hymns he has included in his collection, and at the same time has given his account of what a hymn should be. He calls for unity in hymns, gradation in the thoughts, and their mutual dependence, a conscious progress, and at the end a sense of completeness; and he insists that hymns ought to be easy to understand. He says:—"The faults in ordinary hymns are vulgar phrases, low words, hard words, technical terms, inverted construction, broken syntax, barbarous abbreviations, that make our beautiful English horrid even to the eye, bad rhymes, or no rhymes where rhymes are expected; but, above all, numbers without cadence." As to the form and general character of his hymns, Montgomery has certainly been faithful to his own canons; but it is open to question whether some of his pieces are in the true sense hymns. This is especially applicable to the favourite piece—

"Prayer is the soul's sincere desire."—No. 800,

which consists almost entirely of definition and statement. It bears date 1819. Taken as a whole, Montgomery's hymns are the most valuable recent contribution to our collections. In a letter written in 1807, Montgomery informs us of the history of his hymn-writing. He says:—"When I was a boy I wrote a great many hymns; indeed, the first-fruits of my mind were all consecrated to Him who never despises the day of small things, even in the poorest of His creatures. But as I grew up and my heart degenerated, I directed my talents, such as they were, to other services, and seldom, indeed, since my fourteenth year, have they been employed in the delightful duties of the sanctuary. Many conspiring and adverse circumstances that have confounded, afflicted, and discouraged my mind, have also compelled me to forbear from composing hymns of prayer and praise, because I found that I could not enter into the spirit of such divine themes with that humble boldness, that earnest expectation, and ardent feeling of love to God and truth, which were wont to inspire me when I was an uncorrupted boy, full of tenderness, zeal, and simplicity." And with regard to his poems he says:—"I have not dared to assume a sacred subject as the theme of any whole piece that I have written, on account of the gloom and despondency that frequently hung over my prospects, and sometimes almost sunk my hopes into despair." Farther on he says:—" I compose very slowly, and only by fits, when I can arouse my indolent powers into exertion ;" and he promises to "lie in wait for his heart, and when he can, string it to the pitch of David's lyre, to set a psalm to the chief musician." With the experiences of the Christian life came their expression in Christian song. When Montgomery was advanced in years and seriously ill, he placed in the hands of his friend, Dr. Holland, transcripts of his original hymns to be read to him. But as the poet became much affected, the Doctor was about to desist, when Montgomery said, " Read on, I am glad to hear you. The words recall the feelings which first suggested them, and it is good for me to feel affected and humbled by the terms in which I have endeavoured to provide for the expression of similar religious experience in others. As all my hymns embody some portions of the history of the joys or sorrows, the hopes and the fears of this poor heart, so I cannot doubt but that they will be found an acceptable vehicle of expression of the experience of many of my fellow-creatures who may be similarly exercised during the pilgrimage of their Christian life."

Written, with a few exceptions, late in the author's life, Montgomery's hymns are the productions of a skilled hand, and bear traces of the writer's maturity as a poet and as a Christian. There is nothing in them to offend the taste, and much to gratify it. The most precious truths of Scripture, and the richest experiences of the Christian, find in them simple but poetic expression, and they are made suitable for the use of congregations, by a poet who was quite familiar with the requirements of an assembly of worshippers. " His hymns illustrate," says Wilson in his " Recreations," " the close connection there is between a pure heart and a fine fancy; the simplest feelings and thoughts he intertwines with the flowers of poetry, filling his readers with surprise that they are capable of such adornment, and with pleasure that the adornment becomes them—adding wonder to love." To this it may justly be added, that here and there we find in his hymns verses that we feel to be poetry of a high order. Take for instance his noble missionary hymn (1825)—

"O Spirit of the living God,"—No. 992,

and especially the Miltonic verse—

"O Spirit of the Lord, prepare
All the round earth her God to meet;
Breathe Thou abroad like morning air,
Till hearts of stone begin to beat."

Montgomery contributes forty-four hymns to the "New Congregational Hymn Book:" there were sixty-eight of his in the old "Congregational Hymn Book."

"Servants of God, in joyful lays." No. 177. (Psalm cxiii.)

This is said to have been written while the poet was at Mirfield, and but a youth.

"Angels, from the realms of glory."—No. 343.

This advent hymn (1825) for comprehensiveness, appropriateness of expression, force, and elevation of sentiment, may challenge comparison with any hymn that was ever written in any language or country.

"Father of eternal grace."—No. 359.

This hymn appeared in Gardiner's "Sacred Melodies," 1808, as we learn from a letter from W. Gardiner, given in "Montgomery's Memoirs, by Holland."

In this hymn we trace the influence of the author's Moravian training. It is marked for its simplicity and spirituality, and for its expression of readiness for suffering with Christ, if only there may be identification and fellowship with Him. In his other hymns we find less of this influence than we should have expected.

"When on Sinai's top I see."—No. 383.

This hymn (1825) on the three mountains may serve to illustrate Montgomery's concise comprehensiveness.

"Holy, holy, holy, Lord."—No. 454.

This is from his work of 1853.

"O, where shall rest be found?"—No. 704.

This is one of the author's fine pieces. He evidently had on his "singing-robes" when he wrote it. (1825.)

"According to Thy gracious word,"—No. 865,

a hymn for the Lord's Supper, is justly a favourite, and reminds of Bernard's most pious breathings.

Montgomery took a deep interest in the missionary cause. He has written some good missionary hymns: No. 922 has already been referred to. He also wrote No. 914, and—

"Hark! the song of Jubilee,"—No. 924,

a peculiarly noble and sublime pæan of missionary triumph. (1819.)

The pen of the poet was also sometimes put in requisition to provide Sunday-school hymns, and for this welcome task Montgomery's clearness and simplicity of style well qualified him.

"Glory to the Father give,"—No. 973,

may be taken as an example.

MRS. VOKE.

"Ye messengers of Christ."—No. 899.

Mrs. Voke's hymns appeared in "Dobell's Collection," 1806, where this hymn is No. 436, and has an additional verse.

"Behold the expected time draw near."—No. 909.

This is No. 428 in the same collection, where it has two additional verses. Dr. Collyer, in his "Collection, 1812," gives seven of Mrs. Voke's pleasing hymns, six of which are, like the above, missionary hymns. The conversion of the world was the sublime object that moved her Christian muse. One of her hymns is headed "The Taheite Mission." She seems to have watched with the deepest interest each anxious and difficult step of the early progress of that mission, and in that hymn the words occur—

"When Jesus on the cross was lifted high,
O, was there no Taheitean in His eye?"

JOHN BURTON.

"Holy Bible, book Divine."—No. 464.

There is an author now living at Stratford, Essex, whose hymns have been published by the Religious Tract Society, and who has often been supposed to have written this hymn. But he has informed the author of this work that he can lay no claim to this hymn, as it was written, it is believed, in 1800, three years before his own birth. "The Youths' Monitor," by John Burton, 1799, is by the author of the hymn.

KIRKHAM.

"How firm a foundation, ye saints of the Lord."—No. 664.

This is part of a hymn that appeared in "Rippon's Selection, 1787," with seven verses. Mr. Kirkham is said to have been one of the early Methodists, but there is no reference to him in Charles Wesley's Diary. This hymn is not in "Thomas Kirkham's Collection, 1788." Rippon gives to it and to some others in his "Collection," the letter "K," but there is no proof that they are Kirkham's. Dr. Alexander Fletcher, in his

"Collection,' (1822), gives the name "Keen" to this hymn. In other collections it is attributed to "Kennedy." It is probably a hymn given to Rippon for his collection, but without the author's name.

THOMAS PARK, F.S.A.
1760—1835.

"My soul, praise the Lord, speak good of His name."—No. 249.

This first appears in "Psalms and Hymns, selected from Various Authors, with Occasional Alterations, for the use of a Parochial Church. By a Country Clergyman. London, 1807." The hymn has this note—"At the moment of closing this little collection, I am favoured with the above hymn from my obliging friend. This almost *extemporaneous* effusion of his peculiarly neat and poetic pen was excited by my expressing (in a letter soliciting some psalmodic information) much regret that I had only one set of words for Handel's simple, sublime tune for the 104th Psalm." The third verse of the hymn is omitted in the "New Congregational Hymn Book."

Mr. Park was the author of "Nugæ Modernæ, &c., 1818," a work of prose and poetry on various subjects. He was employed in the editorship of various works, including the works of J. Hammond, 1805; the works of John Dryden, 1806; the works of T. Warton; a work called "Nugæ Antiquæ, by Sir J. Harrington;" and the works of the British Poets, in forty-two small volumes, 1808. The Harleian Miscellany was published under his direction in the same year. Mr. Park was brought up as an engraver, but gave his attention to literary pursuits. He died in 1835.

HARRIET AUBER.
1773—1862.

The Rev. H. Auber Harvey, rector of Tring, whose father edited the work by which Miss Auber is known, has kindly supplied the following particulars of the life and writings of his talented relative. Her work is entitled "The Spirit of the Psalms, or a Compressed Version of Select Portions of the Psalms of David, London, 1829." Owing to the similarity of title that work is liable to be confounded with "The Spirit of the Psalms," 1834, by the Rev. H. F. Lyte, M.A. The latter author required this title as exactly expressive of the nature of his work, and was probably unaware that it had been already appropriated. Miss Auber's work is not entirely original, it contains some pieces by other authors whose names are given, and some well-known hymns without names, such as Bishop Heber's for Easter-day, page 146. All the rest are her own. Her work was published anonymously in 1829, in her 56th year.

She was born on the 4th of October, 1773, and died in her 89th year, January 20th, 1862. She wrote a great deal of poetry both before and after the publication of her work, but it has never been seen by any but her own friends and relatives, never having been published; although it has been thought that amongst her MSS. there is much of equal or even superior merit to the contents of "The Spirit of the Psalms." She did not confine herself to devotional poetry, but often wrote, on various subjects, verses marked by their great beauty or clever playfulness.

Her life was a very quiet and secluded one. The greater part of it was spent at Broxbourne and Hoddesdon, Herts. In both these places the memory of her name and her sisters' is still cherished with affection and veneration, as it is amongst all their surviving friends and relatives. She had a valued friend in the authoress of a beautiful tale, called "Private Life," and of "Lectures on the Parables," and of "Lectures on the Miracles," Miss Mary Jane McKenzie, who lived with her during many of the latter years of her life. Miss Auber died at Hoddesdon, where she is buried beside her friend Miss McKenzie, whom she had survived a few years. They were "lovely and pleasant in their lives, and in their death they were not divided."

"That Thou, O Lord, art ever nigh."—No. 110.

This is Miss Auber's version of Psalm lxxv., given in her "Spirit of the Psalms," 1829. The second verse is altered from the original, which reads—lines 2 and 3—

"To Thee the monarch owes his crown,
The conqueror his wreath."

The word "beneath" being given in the last line of the stanza instead of "below." The other alterations are unimportant. This is the only piece by this authoress in the "New Congregational Hymn Book." It will be acknowledged to be an admirable psalm, presenting, with well-maintained dignity and simplicity, the grandeur and sublimity of the original by Asaph.

RICHARD MANT, D.D.
1776—1848.

This poet-bishop was born on the 12th February, 1776, at Southampton, where his father, of the same name, was master of the Grammar School. He studied at Winchester School, and afterwards at Trinity College, Oxford. He graduated at Oxford, B.A. in 1797, and M.A. in 1801. He received the Chancellor's prize for an English essay in 1799, and was a fellow of Oriel and a college tutor.

In 1802 he commenced his life-work as a curate with his father, at Southampton. Afterwards he entered upon the curacy of Buriton, near Petersfield, Hants, where he took pupils and wrote several works. There he married, in 1804, Miss Elizabeth Woods, and a son and daughter were born to him. From Buriton he removed to Crawley, and thence, in 1809, he went to assist his father again at Southampton. In 1810 he was presented to the vicarage of Coggeshall, Essex. In the following year he preached the Bampton Lecture. He was appointed domestic chaplain to the Archbishop of Canterbury in 1813, and in 1816 became rector of St. Botolph, Bishopsgate, London. He also received the rectory of East Horsley in 1818. By the patronage of Lord Liverpool he became Bishop of Killaloe in 1820, and in 1823 he was translated to the see of Down and Connor. This diocese he adorned with his learning and piety, till, full of years, he exchanged toil for rest on the 2nd of November, 1848.

Bishop Mant was a voluminous writer; his works are too numerous even to name. The following were his principal prose works:—in 1804, "A Familar and Easy Guide to the Church Catechism;" " Puritanism Revived, in a Series of Letters from a Curate to his Rector," 1809; "An Appeal to the Gospel; or, an Inquiry into the justice of the charge alleged by Methodists and other objectors that the Gospel is not preached by the National Clergy." This was his Bampton Lecture for 1811, and went through several editions. Between 1812 and 1814 he published three volumes of sermons. He was joint-editor with Dr. D'Oyley, rector of Lambeth, of a "Commentary on the Bible." He also wrote "Biographical Notices of the Apostles," 1828; "Scriptural Narratives of Passages in our Blessed Lord's life and ministry;" and "The Happiness of the Blessed, &c.," 1833. This was his most popular work. It had reached a sixth edition in 1848. In 1838 he published a volume of sermons, "The Church and her Ministrations," and in 1840 his great work, "The History of the Church of Ireland."

From his early years Bishop Mant courted the muses. One of his earliest pieces was a poem in honour of his father, to whose care in his education he was much indebted. In 1802 he wrote some verses in honour of his schoolmaster, Joseph Warton, and edited the poems of Thomas Warton the poet laureate. In 1804 he sent forth a poem called "The Country Curate." Even the reasons for his choice in marriage were put in verse and sent to the object of his choice; and, losing his fellowship in consequence of his marriage, he wrote his "Farewell to Oxford." In 1806 he published his "Poems in three parts." In 1807 "The Slave." In 1824 he sent forth "The Book of Psalms, in an English Metrical Version, with notes critical and illustrative." He wrote numerous hymns about the year 1828, and appended some of them to the chapters in his works on the Apostles and on Christ's life. In 1832 he sent forth "The Gospel Miracles, in a Series of Poetical Sketches, &c." This work consists of conversations and poems. In 1835 he published "The British Months," a poem in two volumes. He is also the author of "Ancient Hymns, from the Roman Breviary, with Original Hymns," 1837. Bishop Mant's hymns are not free from the defects that usually mark works produced in haste, in a life crowded with conflicting duties, and erring in excess of literary production.

"Praise the Lord, ye heavens adore Him."—No. 245.

This is his rendering of Psalm 148, and is a favourable specimen of his psalms. It first appeared in a Dublin collection during his episcopate in Ireland. His other hymns in the "New Congregational Hymn Book" are 322 and 637.

THOMAS COTTERILL, M.A.
1779—1823.

This excellent clergyman was born December 4th, 1779, at Cannock, in Staffordshire. After some previous education he studied at St. John's College, Cambridge, and graduated M.A. He was afterwards a fellow of the same college. In 1806 he was ordained, and entered upon his parochial work at Tutbury. After two years of useful labour there, he removed to Lane End, in the Staffordshire Potteries, where he remained for about nine years. He found the people in a morally dead condition, and was the means of reviving amongst them religious life. In 1817 Mr. Cotterill became perpetual curate of St. Paul's, Sheffield, where his evangelical zeal was still maintained, though not without opposition on the part of some of his congregation. While in the prime of life, and in the midst of his labours at Sheffield, he was cut down, after a short illness, on the 29th December, 1823, aged forty-four, leaving a wife and five children to lament his loss.

U

Mr. Cotterill was the author of a volume of Family Prayers, which had reached a sixth edition in 1824. But he is chiefly known as an author for his hymn-book: "A Selection of Psalms and Hymns for Public and Private Use, adapted to the Services of the Church of England." This is a compilation of evangelical hymns, and it includes a few by the compiler himself. It was first prepared for his congregation at Lane End; being favourably received, it had reached a fifth edition in 1812. The eighth edition was published, at Sheffield, in 1819. It contained 150 psalms and 367 hymns. In the preface, he vindicates the use of hymns in worship, not only on Scripture grounds, but also because "hymns have been annexed to the Prayer Book from the time of the Reformation without any legislative or royal sanction." In the preparation of this edition Mr. Cotterill had the assistance of Montgomery, many of whose hymns were introduced. Mr. Cotterill introduced his hymn-book to his congregation as a matter of course; but a few of its members, who did not work amicably with their pastor, opposed its introduction as irregular, and carried their opposition so far that the matter was taken into the Ecclesiastical Court at York, where it was tried in July, 1820, before Granville Venables Vernon, the commissary on the occasion, but the matter was settled by both parties agreeing to accept the mediation of the Archbishop. The course the Archbishop pursued was to pass in review the hymns submitted by Mr. Cotterill, and adopt or reject them. He also added some from the book he used at Bishopthorpe. The proofs were also read by Mr. Montgomery. Some of the hymns were much altered. "Good Mr. Cotterill and I," says Montgomery, "bestowed a great deal of labour and care on the compilation of that book; clipping, interlining, and remodelling hymns of all sorts as we thought we could correct the sentiment or improve the expression." Thus Montgomery was guilty of what he condemned. The hymn-book, as revised by the Archbishop, is used in the Sheffield churches and elsewhere in the diocese of York.

It is difficult to determine which hymns in his collection are by

Cotterill himself. They are few in number and are not characterized by any distinguishing excellence. Montgomery has fixed the authorship of two. In his "Christian Psalmist" he assigns to Cotterill the authorship of:—

"O'er the realms of pagan darkness."

And he also attributes to Cotterill:—

"Let songs of praises fill the sky."

It is hymn 291 in his "Christian Psalmist," seventh edition, 1832, 229 in Cotterill's eighth edition, 1819, and No. 428 in the "New Congregational Hymn Book;" but Montgomery gives it in a different metre, with these lines added to each verse:—

"All hail the day of Pentecost,
The coming of the Holy Ghost,"

and verse three is slightly altered from the original.

"Jesus, exalted far on high."—No. 352.

This is given without name in the "New Congregational." It is by T. Cotterill.

RALPH WARDLAW, D.D.
1779—1853.

This eminent nonconformist divine was born at Dalkeith. His father, who was a merchant, removed to Glasgow during his son's infancy, and was a magistrate there for some years. His mother was a descendant of the illustrious Ebenezer Erskine, the father of the Secession Church. Young Wardlaw, having studied from his boyhood in the university of Glasgow, entered the Theological Seminary of the Secession Church, intending to be a minister of that church; but when the Revs. Ewing and Innes left the Established Church to become Congregationalists, the young student entered into the controversy and resolved to join the seceders. He became a member of Mr. Ewing's church.

Subsequently he gathered a congregation, and, with the assistance of friends, erected a chapel in Albion Street, Glasgow. Eight years after, he added to his pastoral duties those of a Professor in the Theological Academy that was then founded by the Congregationalists. He filled both offices till his death, and for twenty-four years received no remuneration for his professorial work. In 1819 his increased congregation removed to a much larger chapel they had erected in West George Street, at a cost of more than £10,000. In the year 1853, ministers of all denominations joined to celebrate with every mark of respect the jubilee of Dr. Wardlaw's ministry. He had been invited to the presidency of Hoxton Academy, in 1817, to that of Spring Hill College, in 1837, and to Lancashire Independent College in 1842, but had declined each gratifying and honourable invitation. He received his diploma of D.D. from Yale College in 1818. Dr. Wardlaw married early, having been united to his cousin Jane, daughter of the Rev. Mr. Smith, of Dunfermline, in August, 1803. Of his numerous children one honourably represents his father in the Congregational ministry, the Rev. J. S. Wardlaw, M.A., formerly a missionary in Bellary, and now Principal of the Mission College, Highgate, London.

Dr. Wardlaw possessed a mind of great grasp and power. The bent of it was towards careful analysis and sound reasoning. He had skill to distinguish things that differed, and felt at home in polemics and philosophy; yet he was not without the play of wit and the graces of a refined taste. Every noble public object found in him an earnest advocate. In everything he was the divine; his philosophy as well as his religion being built on Bible truth. As an author, Dr. Wardlaw was widely known: one of his principal works was entitled "Discourses on the Principal Points of the Socinian Controversy." This work went through several editions. He was also the author of "Unitarianism Incapable of Vindication." His work on "Christian Ethics,"

1833, was the first of the Congregational Lectures. It had reached a fifth edition in 1852. He also wrote "Letters to the Society of Friends," "Lectures on Ecclesiastical Establishments," "Lectures on Ecclesiastes," on "Baptism," (this had reached a third edition in 1846,) on "Miracles," on "Female Prostitution," (this also had reached a third edition in 1846,) a "Memoir of Dr. McAll," "Memoirs of Rev. John Reid," besides other sermons, essays, and memoirs.

Dr. W. L. Alexander, of Edinburgh, in his interesting "Memoirs of Dr. Wardlaw," 1856, has shown the connection the subject of his memoir had with hymnology. As a youth, Dr. Wardlaw had attempted to write poetry, and when at college he wrote a satire, that was read, though not published, called "Porteousiana." It was on the Rev. Dr. Porteous, a Glasgow minister, who had published a pamphlet, "The New Light Examined;" criticising the proceedings of the Associate Synod. And at various times in his life Dr. Wardlaw showed a rhyming tendency, sometimes, when travelling, putting the whole account of his journey in his home-letter in rhyme.

In 1803, while he was awaiting the completion of his chapel at Glasgow, he prepared a selection of hymns to replace the inferior "Tabernacle Selection," then in use by Congregationalists in Scotland. He was assisted in this work of preparation by Dr. Charles Stuart. Some of the hymns were altered, and a Scripture arrangement was adopted. The first edition of the work in this revised form was published in May, 1803; it contained 322 hymns. Some years afterwards a supplement was added, containing 171 additional hymns; of these eleven were by the editor, Dr. Wardlaw. They were hymns of sterling excellence, and they have been inserted in several collections; two of the eleven had previously appeared in the "Missionary Magazine, volume eight, page forty-eight. Dr. Alexander has given all these hymns in his appendix to the "Memoirs."

"Lift up to God the voice of praise."—No. 288.

Those who maintain that hymns should be confined to the utterance of praise, will find their wishes fully met in this most comprehensive and soul-moving hymn of praise: it is one of the eleven.

"Hail! morning known among the blest."—No. 756.

This excellent Sabbath hymn is also one of the eleven. It is given with the omission of one verse.

JOHN CAWOOD, M.A.
1775—1852.

CAWOOD was one of those useful hymn-writers whose works maintain their place, even when poems, once welcomed with applause, are forgotten. In this respect his hymns are a type of his life, which perseveringly emerged from obscurity till it filled a useful place in the world. Cawood's parents were small farmers at Matlock, Derbyshire, where he was born, March 18th, 1775. He enjoyed small educational advantages, and, at eighteen years of age, went to occupy a menial position in the establishment of a clergyman named Carsham, at Sutton-in-Ashfield, Nottinghamshire. While in this position, he received religious convictions, and felt that it was his duty to prepare to engage in the work of the ministry.

He had previously sought to improve himself, and he now studied under the Rev. Edward Spencer, rector of Wingfield, Wilts. In 1797 he entered St. Edmund's Hall, Oxford, completing his course under the tutorship of the vice-principal, the Rev. Isaac Crouch. He was ordained in 1801, and the same year obtained his B.A. degree. He became M.A. in 1807. Under the Rev. W. Jesse, he held the adjacent curacies of Ribbesford and Dowles, and, in 1814, Mr. Jesse presented him to the perpetual curacy of St. Ann's Chapel of Ease, Bewdley, Worcestershire. At this place he spent the greater part of his life. He was twice married, and had five children. He died, at the age of seventy-seven, on November 7th, 1852.

His principal work was his " Sermons," in two volumes, published in 1842. He also published separate sermons; and a pamphlet, in 1831, enlarged from an article in the forty-eighth number of the "British Review," 1825, and entitled " The Church and Dissent." It is an attack on the Rev. J. A. James's " Church Member's Guide." Mr. Cawood did not publish any volume of hymns or poems, but he wrote a few hymns on various occasions. Some have found their way into collections: one is in the " New Congregational Hymn Book."

"Almighty God! Thy word is cast."—No. 790.

This is found in Montgomery's " Christian Psalmist," with an added fourth verse of less poetic merit, but useful as recognizing the sinner's responsibility in rejecting the Gospel. Montgomery's book was sent forth in 1825, so that this hymn must have been written before that date. Few hymns are more often used. I am indebted to the son of the poet, the Rev. John Cawood, rector of Pensax, Tenbury, Worcestershire, for a copy of the MS. The added verse is in the original. It is as follows :—

" Let not Thy word so kindly sent
To raise us to Thy throne,
Return to Thee, and sadly tell
That we reject Thy Son !"

The original differs also in a few words from the hymn as it is given in the " New Congregational Hymn Book." I am indebted also to the poet's son for the following information. He says :— " My father composed about thirteen hymns, which have one by one got into print, though never published by himself or any one representing him. I do not know the occasion of the hymn No. 790, further than that it was meant to be sung after sermon. I think it must have been written about 1815, but there is no date to it, though there is to several of his hymns in the MS. collection of them."

CARLISLE.

This name is given in the "New Congregational" to hymn 810, instead of the following:—

JOSEPH DACRE CARLYLE, B.D.

This learned and accomplished divine accompanied the Earl of Elgin, in 1799, when he went as ambassador to the Porte. The object of Mr. Carlyle's journey was to ascertain what literary treasures there were in the public library of Constantinople. He extended his journey to Asia Minor, and the islands and shores of the Archipelago. The scenes of his travels awakened his muse, and he published, in 1805, "Poems, suggested chiefly by Scenes in Asia Minor, Syria, &c." Illness prevented him from revising his poems, and they were edited by Susanna Maria Carlyle. The volume includes some miscellaneous pieces and three religious pieces at the end. One is Hymn No. 810 in the "New Congregational Hymn Book:— "

"Lord, when we bend before Thy Throne."

It is headed "A Hymn before Public Worship." It is given in the original in stanzas of eight lines, of which, one is omitted in the "New Congregational Hymn Book," and the others are a little altered.

Mr. Carlyle was a clergyman of the Established Church, Chancellor of Carlisle, vicar of Newcastle-on-Tyne, and professor of Arabic in the University of Cambridge. He was the author of "Specimens of Arabian Poetry, &c., with some account of the Authors," 1796; and he edited, "The Old and New Testaments, in Arabic," 1811.

THOMAS MORELL.

1781—1840.

The Rev. Thomas Morell, who was best known as the theological and resident tutor of Coward College, was born at Maldon, Essex. He studied for the ministry at Homerton College, and afterwards became pastor of a Congregational Church at St. Neot's, Huntingdonshire, in which position he continued for twenty years. In 1821 he became the divinity tutor of Wymondley Academy, and removed to London with that institution in 1833 when it took the name of its munificent supporter, Mr. Coward, and was stationed in the metropolis in order that its students might attend the literary course at University College. Mr. Morell filled with honour to the end of his life the professorial chair of his great predecessor, Dr. Doddridge, being like him a hymn-writer as well as a theologian and a preacher. He published at various times a series of volumes entitled "Studies in History," together with a poem called "The Christian Pastor," 1809,—a poem in three books, in its manner resembling Cowper's works, and containing many excellent passages,—and a few occasional sermons. He is the author of only one hymn in the "New Congregational Hymn Book:"—

"Father of mercies, condescend."—No. 900.

A better missionary hymn of his is No. 495 in the "Old Congregational:"—

"Go, and the Saviour's grace proclaim."

The Rev. Thomas Morell, of Little Baddow, has kindly given the occasion when his uncle's hymn, No. 900, was first used. Most likely the hymn was written for that occasion. It was at the ordination of the Rev. Charles Mault, who was a member of Mr. Morell's church at St. Neot's, and who was then (1818) being set apart for the work of a missionary of the London Missionary Society in India. Mr. Morell also wrote a hymn on the death of the Princess Charlotte, some lines on the removal of the College from Wymondley to London, and some hymns and pieces which were in a MS. now unfortunately lost, but which was for a long time in the possession of his relative, Mrs. Metcalf, of Roxton Park.

GERARD THOMAS NOEL, M.A.
1782—1851.
"If human kindness meets return."—No. 877.

THIS favourite hymn is found with a few others of like excellence at the end of a work, entitled "Arvendel, or Sketches in Italy and Switzerland," by the author whose name is at the head of this sketch. The work consists of accounts of travels, with poems and hymns. Second edition, 1813.

The Hon. and Rev. Gerard T. Noel was the second son of Sir Gerard Noel, Bart., and the Baroness Barham, and elder brother of the excellent Rev Baptist W. Noel. He was born on the 2nd December, 1782. His studies were pursued at the Universities of Edinburgh and Cambridge. At Cambridge he studied at Trinity College, and graduated M.A. As a clergyman of the Established Church, he was at first curate of Radwell, Hertfordshire; then vicar of Rainham, Kent, and curate of Richmond, Surrey. In 1834, he was canon of Winchester, and in 1840 he became vicar of Romsey, where he died on the 24th of February, 1851.

Besides the above-mentioned work, Mr. Noel was the author of "A Selection of Psalms and Hymns from the new version of the Church of England, and others, corrected and revised for public worship," 1820. This consists of forty-five pieces. He published separate sermons, and after his death his "Sermons preached in Romsey" appeared with "A Preface by the Bishop of Oxford," 1853.

WILLIAM BENGO COLLYER, D.D., LL.D., F.A.S.
1782—1854.

THIS most popular London preacher was born at Blackheath, and studied at Homerton College under Dr. J. Pye Smith. Before completing his twentieth year he became pastor of a

Congregational Church at Peckham, and he continued to occupy that position to the end of his long and useful life.

At his ordination in December, 1801, the church at Peckham consisted of only ten members. But it soon increased, and at length his popularity rendered a larger chapel necessary, and in 1817 Hanover Chapel was built. For about twelve years from 1814, Dr. Collyer was also pastor of the church assembling in Salters' Hall. Both at Peckham and at Salters' Hall he was the means of reviving the spiritual life of the people, and of gathering in converts, and of restoring sound doctrine when it was giving place to serious error.

For half a century Dr. Collyer was one of the most popular dissenting ministers in London, attracting sometimes even the royal dukes within the walls of his crowded chapel. He was also much beloved by his brethren in the ministry, and by a large circle of admiring friends, and most of all by the members of his own attached family. His fidelity to the great truths of the Gospel was marked by all, and his works on theology remain as a testimony to the truths he taught. They are in the form of lectures on "Parables," "Doctrines," "Duties," "Comparisons," and "Facts."

Within a month of his death he preached his last sermon from the words, "How wilt thou do in the swellings of Jordan?"

In 1812 Dr. Collyer published a collection of hymns for the use of his congregation. Some of the hymns are original, and others are by various authors. All the hymns by each author are arranged together, and the author's name is given. There are 979 hymns in the collection, and the last 57 are by Dr. Collyer himself. Several of them, though not without traces of genius, are of a stilted, sensational character, and are therefore wisely omitted from our collections.

In the "New Congregational Hymn Book," hymns 520, 846, 857, and 913 are by Dr. Collyer. All but No. 846 are found in his collection of 1812. They are given with verses omitted. Without displaying any high poetical talent, they are of the useful character we might expect from one who as a minister knew the requirements of public worship, and who, as a compiler of a collection, found it necessary to supply some hymns suitable for special occasions. Like some of the early nonconformist preachers, Dr. Collyer prepared some of his hymns to be sung after his sermons, and they were founded on the texts.

To Dr. Collyer also is attributed a share in the production of Ringwaldt's well-known hymn :—

"Great God, what do I see and hear?"—No. 420.

J. C. Jacobi, in his "Psalmodia Germanica," 1722, had translated Ringwaldt's hymn written in 1585 in seven verses.

"Es ist gewisslich an der Zeit."

"'Tis sure that awful time will come."

Dr. Collyer saw one verse, probably given as the words of an anthem, and attributed to Luther. It is not known who put Jacobi's verse in the form Collyer saw, or whether it was a verse translated by some other poet immediately from the German. Taking this, he composed these additional verses and put the following note in his collection, 1812, page 545 :—"This hymn, which is adapted to Luther's celebrated tune, is universally ascribed to that great man. As I never saw more than this first verse, I was obliged to lengthen it for the completion of the subject, and am responsible for the verses which follow." The compilers of the "New Congregational Hymn Book" have adopted Dr. Collyer's second verse with slight alterations, omitted his third verse, and adopted the latter half of his fourth verse, combining with it half of Ringwaldt's first verse. *Vide* also under Ringwaldt, page 24.

JOHN BOWDLER.

1783—1815.

"Lord, before Thy throne we bend."—No. 207.

THIS psalm is found at page 215 of the first volume of "Select

Pieces in verse and prose by the late John Bowdler, jun., Esq., of Lincoln's Inn, barrister-at-law. Third edition. 1818. Two vols." In the "New Congregational" it is slightly altered and improved, and the last two verses are compressed into one. This third edition of Mr. Bowdler's works, published after his death, contains a brief account of his history.

He was born in London, February 4, 1783. After receiving some training at the grammar school at Sevenoaks, he went to study at the school and college at Winchester. As a youth he was pious and showed the possession of talent. At the age of seventeen he was articled to a solicitor in London. He was exceedingly studious, and his studies were guided by a gentleman of eminence in the Court of Chancery. In 1807 he was called to the bar; but signs of consumption having appeared, it was thought necessary that he should leave England for the south of Europe. He set out in October, 1810, and returned in the August of the following year, and the year after that he wintered abroad. On his return his health seemed re-established, and he resumed the duties of his profession. But the weakness remained, and at length he broke a bloodvessel, and died on the 1st of February, 1815.

The third edition of his works includes the journal kept while on his travels, and some letters showing the intelligent piety of the writer. It contains also some very pleasing poetical pieces on various subjects. The main portion of it consists of reviews, theological tracts, and carefully elaborated essays on important subjects. That one so pious and promising should fall so soon—when but thirty-one years of age—awakens regret, and lends a peculiar interest to his literary remains.

ANNE FLOWERDEW.
About 1800.

"Fountain of mercy, God of love."—No. 950.

In the "New Congregational" this hymn has the name

"Needham," probably it was altered from a hymn by John Needham, 1768. By comparing it with the following hymn, which is Needham's, it will be seen to be superior, especially in form, Needham's rhymes being deficient or imperfect. Mrs. Flowerdew's hymn, which is given in the "New Congregational" with the fifth verse altered, and the sixth omitted, bears date 1811. It appeared in a later edition of her "Poems on Moral and Religious Subjects." It is not found in the first edition, 1803. Her poems are pleasing and pious, but do not show the possession of genius. In the preface, dated May 24, 1803, she says they were "written at different periods of life; some indeed at a very early age, and others under the very severe pressure of misfortune, when my pen has frequently given that relief which could not be derived from other employments."

Mrs. Flowerdew kept a ladies' boarding-school in High-street, Islington. She is said to have been a member of the Baptist Church in Worship-street, under the pastorate of the Rev. Dr. John Evans, the author of "A Sketch of the Several Religious Denominations, 1795," and of several other works.

REGINALD HEBER, D.D.

1783—1826.

This poet-bishop belonged to an ancient Yorkshire family, and was the son of a father of the same name, who was rector of Malpas, in Cheshire. After displaying unusual talent in childhood, he commenced his collegiate career at Brazenose College, Oxford, in November, 1800. In the following year he gained the Chancellor's prize for a Latin poem on "The Commencement of the New Century." During his brilliant University course he produced, in 1803, his prize poem on "Palestine;" and later, his English prose essay on the "Sense of Honour." Soon after, he made an extended tour in Germany, Russia, and the Crimea, making valuable notes, and familiarizing himself with men and manners in foreign lands.

On his return, he entered upon the living of Hodnet, in Shropshire. He was the Bampton Lecturer for 1815, and in 1822 he wrote a life of Jeremy Taylor. In the same year he was appointed to the preachership of Lincoln's Inn, and urged to accept the bishopric of Calcutta. This latter appointment he at first refused, for the sake of his wife and child, but at length, impelled by missionary zeal, he accepted it, and embarked for the East Indies on the 16th of June, 1823. The extraordinary extent of his diocese, which included more than the whole of India, laid so heavy a burden of toil upon him that in three short years it sunk him to the grave. His published journal of his travels shows his remarkable assiduity and his devotedness to his work. He died at Tirutchinopoli, of apoplexy, while on a visitation, on the 2nd April, 1826. In addition to the above-mentioned works, he contributed to the "Quarterly Review," and commenced a "Dictionary of the Bible."

His hymns are dear to every section of the Christian Church; elegant in structure, flowing in rhythm, and charged with Christian sentiment. It has been objected to them that some of them are odes, rather than hymns, and that they are built on natural, rather than on Christian religion. Thus, it is said, that in—

"From Greenland's icy mountains,—No. 912."

the appeal is to the winds, and waters—

"Waft, waft ye winds," &c., verse 4;

and that his hymn—

"Brightest and best," &c.,

is an apostrophe to a star. But this is a form of hyper-criticism from which many of his thoroughly Christian hymns sufficiently defend him. Yet it is felt by all, however much they may approve his hymns, that they carry the poetic element to its utmost point, and have a marked character of their own. They are usually distinguished by a rhetorical flow and an elevation of manner and imagery that threaten to take them out of the class of hymns, and rob them of the pious moderation we ordinarily expect to meet with in such productions.

While at Hodnet, Heber was dissuaded by the Archbishop of Canterbury from the project of publishing a Hymn Book for the use of the Church at large. But some of his hymns appeared in the " Christian Observer" for 1811, with the initials " D. R."

In 1812 he published a small volume of " Poems and Translations for Weekly Church Service," which has gone through many editions; and even amid the toils of India he found time to carry out his favourite poetical pursuits.

It is to be regretted that one of his best-known hymns, an Epiphany hymn :—

"Brightest and best of the sons of the morning,"

is not in the " New Congregational Hymn Book."

" From Greenland's icy mountains."—No. 912.

This hymn was written at Hodnet, in 1820, to be sung by his people with a sermon appealing to them on behalf of missions. The MS. used to be in the possession of Dr. Raffles, of Liverpool. This hymn explains Heber's devoted course in India.

Obliged to say " No!" to his own question—

"Can we to men benighted,
The lamp of life deny?"

he willingly became a sacrifice to his noble Christian self-dedication, and found a too early grave in the land of his adoption.

"Hosanna to the living Lord."—No. 312.

"The Lord shall come! the earth shall quake."—No. 417.

These were two of four hymns sent by Heber to the " Christian Observer," in October, 1811. They were accompanied by a letter, having the signature "D. R.," complaining of the defects in existing Church Hymns, such as the too familiar epithets applied to the Divine Being, and similar blemishes, and asking suggestions for improvement. Hymn 417 is not given in the "New Congregational" as Heber wrote it, but in the altered form in which it appeared in Cottcrill's Collection, fifth edition, 1815. In November of the same year others were sent to the same periodical, including—

"Lord of mercy and of might,"—No. 332,

and some others were sent in the year 1812. After Bishop Heber's death, his widow, Mrs. Amelia Heber, published, in 1827, "Hymns written and adapted to the Weekly Church Service of the Year." This was intended for general adoption, and was to have been published in India, but the Bishop's early death prevented. It included hymns by Jeremy Taylor, Addison, Sir Walter Scott, Dean Milman, and others, and several by Heber himself, composed at different intervals of leisure, during his parochial ministry in Shropshire. This book includes the four hymns already mentioned, and the other three given in the "New Congregational Hymn Book."

"The Lord of might from Sinai's brow."—No. 416.

This is his second hymn for the "Sixth Sunday in Lent."

"Holy, holy, holy, Lord God Almighty."—No. 455.

This is his "Hymn for Trinity Sunday."

"Thou art gone to the grave! but we will not deplore thee."—No. 733.

This justly admired piece is found on page 150 of the last-mentioned Hymn Book, and is written to be sung "At a Funeral."

In Heber's Works, 1842, there are fifty-seven hymns by him. There are two or three others that were published on broadsides that are not given.

x

GEORGE CLAYTON.
1783—1862.

The subject of this sketch was the son and brother of distinguished Congregational ministers, and himself not less eminent in that capacity. He was born in London, and after pious training, early became a decided Christian. Having enjoyed considerable educational advantages, the young student went to Hoxton Academy, to prepare for the ministry. At the age of nineteen he became co-pastor with Mr. Kingsbury, at Southampton, and two years after entered upon the pastorate of a Congregational Church at Walworth. In that position he continued for more than half a century, labouring with continued and growing usefulness and success. He gave himself wholly to his popular and evangelical ministry, and at the same time used his talents and position for the advocacy of those Institutions that are for the furtherance of the Gospel in the world.

Full of years he at length departed in peace and in Jesus. On his last Sabbath he said, "I know the hand of the Lord is upon me, but I would not wish to raise my little finger to alter any of His dispensations, for I feel that it is love, and I know I have a home prepared for me above."

There is one hymn by Mr. Clayton in the "New Congregational Hymn Book"—

"From yon delusive scene."—No. 969.

It is in T. Russell's Selection. Twelfth Edition, 1827; where it is No. 153.

BERNARD BARTON.
1784—1849.

This hymn-writer is known as the "Quaker poet." His parents and himself lived and died faithful members of the Society of

Friends. His ancestors had been manufacturers at Carlisle, but shortly before his birth his father removed to London, where Bernard was born, January 31st, 1784. He was educated in a Quaker school at Ipswich. At the age of fourteen he was apprenticed to Mr. Samuel Jesup, a shopkeeper at Halstead, in Essex, where he remained eight years. In 1806 he went to Woodbridge, Suffolk, and a year after married Lucy Jesup, the niece of his former master, and entered into partnership with her brother as a coal and corn merchant. But his happy married life was cut short by death, a year after he had entered upon it, and he left Woodbridge and became private tutor in a family at Liverpool. After a year at Liverpool, he returned in 1810 to Woodbridge, and became a clerk in Messrs. Alexander's bank, where he continued for about forty years, till his death. He did not marry again, but found a life companion in his only daughter Lucy, who edited his "Poems and Letters, with a Memoir," in the year of his death, 1849.

Some idea of Mr. Barton's life may be formed from what he says in a letter, dated "11 mo. 16, 1843." Some of his words are these:—"I took my seat on the identical stool I now occupy at the desk, to the wood of which I have now well-nigh grown, in the third month of the year 1810; and there I have sat on for three-and-thirty years, beside the odd eight months, without one month's respite in all that time. I often wonder that my health has stood this sedentary probation as it has, and that my mental faculties have survived three-and-thirty years of putting down figures in three rows, casting them up, and carrying them forward, *ad infinitum*. Nor is this all—for during that time, I think, I have put forth some half-dozen volumes of verse; to say nothing of scores and scores of odd bits of verse contributed to annuals, periodicals, albums, and what not; and a correspondence implying a hundred times the writing of all these put together." His life had two different elements, the daily routine, and the evenings, too often prolonged into the night, devoted to poetical efforts, the excitement of launching new books, and the variety of a correspondence generally literary and sometimes religious. Amongst his correspondents with whom he often communicated were Robert Southey and Charles Lamb, and he had occasional communications with Mrs. Hemans, the Howitts, Sir John Bowring, Byron, and Sir Walter Scott. In 1824, the poet's moderate income received a little addition from the interest of £1,200, a sum presented to him, as a mark of esteem, by Joseph John Gurney and a few other members of the Society of Friends; and, in 1846, he received from the Queen an annual pension of £100, on the recommendation of Sir Robert Peel. After some indications of failing health, he died, almost suddenly, on the 19th of February, 1849.

In 1812, Bernard Barton published his first volume of poems, called "Metrical Effusions." In 1818, he published by subscription, "Poems by an Amateur." A volume of his "Poems," published shortly after in London, having gained the approval of the "Edinburgh Review," reached a fourth edition in 1825. In 1822 he sent forth his "Napoleon," which he dedicated and presented to George the Fourth.

Between 1822 and 1828 he published five volumes of verse, and during this period injured his health by his excessive application. His "Poetic Vigils" appeared in 1824, and his "Devotional Verses, founded on Select Texts of Scripture," in 1827.

After that period he wrote less, but continued to contribute to annuals. In 1836 he published a volume of collected fragments, and in 1845 came out his last volume, "Household Verses," which he got permission to dedicate to the Queen.

Bernard Barton's versification is easy and good, his diction tasteful and refined, his sentiment high in its moral tone, and he is not without pathos and beauty. He follows, though at a distance, his admired model, Cowper. Jeffrey justly pronounced him "a man of a fine and cultivated, rather than of a bold and original mind."

He contributes two good hymns to the "New Congregational Hymn Book."

"Lamp of our feet, whereby we trace."—No. 468.

This is taken from a piece of eleven verses on "The Bible," bearing date 1827, and in it several appropriate images are gathered together, without being crowded or confused; and—

"Walk in the light, so shalt thou know,"—No. 682,

a hymn to be commended for its simplicity and comprehensiveness; its unity of idea, happily retained along with variety in the aspects of that idea presented to view.

THOMAS HASTINGS, Mus. Doc.

Born 1784.

This writer is better known as a musician than as a poet; but he deserves an honourable place as a hymn-writer. Without equalling the productions of men of decided genius, his hymns are pleasing and tasteful in conception and diction, and rich in scripture teaching and Christian sentiment. Their strong point is, as we might have expected from the special mission of the author, their adaptation for use in church psalmody. As musical, Milton remembered in his poetry "the pealing organ," and the "full-voiced quire"—

"In service high and anthems clear;"

and as Shakespeare often refers to the stage on which he acted, and writes with it in view, so this humbler bard writes not to be read but to be sung. Thus his book of hymns begins—

"Attune the heart to praise,
In melody of song,
The hallowed anthem sweetly raise
Amid the choral throng."

Thomas Hastings, the son of a physician, was born in Washington, Litchfield County, Connecticut, on the 15th of October, 1784. At twelve years of age he removed with his father to Clinton, Oneida County, New York. A natural taste for music led him to give much attention to his favourite pursuit. On attaining manhood he became a trainer of church choirs, and began to publish books of instruction in music, and collections of musical pieces. From 1824 to 1832 he conducted a religious journal in Utica, and availed himself of his position to advocate his own views of church psalmody. It was during this period that he published his "Union Minstrel, for the use of Sabbath Schools, &c." 1830. At length, in 1832, a committee of twelve churches in New York invited him to come and make their psalmody what he had taught it should be. He accepted the invitation, and has been since that time residing there and successfully carrying out his great work in the improvement of the psalmody of the Church. We omit the titles of his musical works, only mentioning one as suggestive of what his life-work is—"The History of Forty Choirs," published in 1854.

In 1832, he published his "Spiritual Songs;" in 1836, his "Christian Psalmist: a book of Psalms and Hymns for the Use of Churches." In 1849, "The Mother's Hymn Book: compiled from various Authors and Private Manuscripts, for the use of Maternal Associations, &c." And in 1850, "Devotional Hymns and Religious Poems." It consists of 199 hymns and three poems. One of the poems, "The Reign of Heaven," extends to thirty-five pages. This poem is not equal to the author's hymns. The author explains in the preface that the reception of his earliest efforts had encouraged him in his habits of versification; that some of his pieces published anonymously had been widely circulated, and that some were written to enable him to make use of foreign pieces of music for which they had not hymns of suitable metre. In 1864, he published his "Church Melodies," including some additional hymns.

Dr. Hastings is the author of several favourite hymns besides those given in the "New Congregational Hymn Book." One of the best known is the hymn—

"Why that look of sadness?"

the 107th in his "Devotional Hymns," 1850.

"To-day the Saviour calls."—No. 494.

This is given in "The Sabbath Hymn Book," 1858.

"Return, O wanderer, to thy home."—No. 521.

This is the 61st in his "Devotional Hymns," 1850. It had appeared in 1834.

"O Lord, Thy work revive."—No. 812.

This is erroneously attributed to "Browne" in the "New Congregational Hymn Book." It is by Thomas Hastings. It is also given in "Hymns and Devotional Poetry, collected by C. W. Andrews, New York," 1857.

JOHN BULMER.

1784—1857.

Mr Bulmer was a useful Congregational minister during a long life, and the author of some works. He was born in Yorkshire, and, after a pious youth, entered upon his studies for the ministry at Rotherham College. His longest pastorate was for twenty-seven years at Haverfordwest. He was afterwards pastor at Rugely, Staffordshire, and subsequently engaged in useful ministerial work at Bristol and Newbury, and finally at Langrove, near Ross.

He wrote several good hymns. There are two by him in the "New Congregational Hymn Book," Nos. 770 and 778. They are found in his "Hymns Original and Select," 1835, a work containing a few hymns by himself.

"Lord of the vast creation."—No. 770.

This is his 40th hymn. It has a fourth stanza which has been omitted.

"To Thee, in ages past."—No. 778.

If a hymn ought to be simple so that a congregation can at once understand it, yet full of thought in contrast with a succession of platitudes; and if it ought to be perfect in form and yet easy and natural in manner; and if it ought to have remembrances that touch the heart, and humble aspirations that lift it to heaven, then this piece, without pretending to be a poem, is good as a hymn. It is the first in the above-mentioned collection.

Mr. Bulmer was the author of "Hymns and Evangelical Songs for the use of Sunday Schools"—this reached a sixth edition: and of "Beauties of the Vicar of Llandovery; Light from the Welshman's Candle." These are poems by Rees Prichard, who died 1644—they are translated from the Welsh. Also of "The Christian Catechist," and of "A Concise Statement of the Nature, Design, &c., of a Christian Church." Haverfordwest, 1813.

SAMUEL FLETCHER.
1785—1863.

"Father of life and light."—No. 980.

"Lord, as a family we meet."—No. 982.

These family hymns were given to the Rev. Henry Allon for the "New Congregational Hymn Book," (1855) by Samuel Fletcher, Esq., of Broomfield, near Manchester, a "merchant prince" of cultivated mind, who occasionally wrote in verse, and who about that time was improving the leisure supplied by an attack of illness, in preparing a collection of hymns for the use of his family. His collection was called "Family Praise." It was published in 1850, and contained a small number of hymns by himself, including the two above.

Samuel Fletcher was born at Compton, near Wolverhampton,

in Staffordshire, where his forefathers had lived for some generations on their own land. This property, which his grandfather had diminished by extravagance, Samuel's father saved from further diminution and brought up on it a family of ten, of whom the subject of this sketch was the youngest but one. His mother, the daughter of a Dissenting minister at Dudley, was a woman of great activity, strong sense, and earnest piety; and in each of these respects she found a faithful imitator in the son, of whom we are writing. At ten years of age he went to the grammar school at Wolverhampton, accomplishing his walk of two miles thither before seven in the morning, in all weathers, and filling up his evening with work for his industry-loving mother.

At the age of fourteen, he was apprenticed at Wolverhampton, where he continued his work of mental improvement concurrently with the fulfilment of his business duties. In 1805, when twenty years of age, he came to Manchester, and after some years of experience in a Manchester house he entered upon business for himself, and soon rose by his talents and integrity to a first place among the merchants of that city.

During his whole course, Mr. Fletcher continually gave attention to his own mental improvement, to the happiness and culture of his family, and to the service of Christ in the world. He did not admit that the man of business must renounce letters, and be stunted in mind for the sake of the growth of his material prosperity. It was his constant aim to supply his mind with invigorating pabulum, and to keep its energies well exercised, and he urged the same course upon others. To him, it is believed, is due the formation of Owens' College, Manchester, which was opened in 1851. It was his wish that there should be in Manchester an institution where men of business might in their opening manhood have the opportunity of carrying on their education; and the liberality of Mr. Owens made it possible to carry out this wish. In Owens' College Mr. Fletcher took the liveliest interest. He founded a scholarship in it, and contributed largely to its other funds.

Mr. Fletcher's character, attainments, and wealth, opened

before him a path to the highest honours, but he preferred to be useful in an humbler circle. He was a county magistrate for many years, but declined to be a candidate for a place in Parliament. Possessed of great wealth, he gratefully acted as a steward of God, and freely gave what he had freely received. The writer of an interesting sketch in "Good Words," July, 1864, says, "the present writer speaks from knowledge, and strictly within the limits, in saying, that for a series of years Mr. Fletcher's annual benefactions amounted to nearly thirty or forty per cent. of his income." To the Bible and Missionary Societies he contributed very largely, and also to the Manchester City Mission, paying the annual stipend of one missionary. To the various institutions of the Congregational Church, Grosvernor Street, he was also for more than half a century a very liberal contributor. He had begun his membership there in 1806, under the Rev. W. Roby, during whose ministry he was also a deacon of the church. In all his benefactions, Mr. Fletcher exercised a careful discrimination; not unfrequently surpassing the expectation of those who needed his help by the munificence of his gifts, and sometimes seeking out for help ministers and others who were sorrowing in secret over their pecuniary embarrassments: and his munificence was without pride as it was without ostentation. A sentence in his diary, penned when he moved to Broomfield, is characteristic of his humble Christian "walk with God." "This day I removed with my family to Cheetham Hill, and took possession of a house more spacious and costly than I ever expected. I pray to God that my heart may not be lifted up on this account, and that I may not be permitted to indulge proud and vain thoughts of my own sufficiency and stability; and disposed to be less earnest in seeking 'a building of God, a house not made with hands, eternal in the heavens.'" He died, October 13th, 1863, in his seventy-ninth year.

JOHN PIERPONT.

BORN 1785.

"O Thou, to whom in ancient time."—No. 779.

This hymn is found as early as 1824. It is given as the "Hymn for the Occasion, by the Rev. John Pierpont," at the close of "A Discourse on the proper character of Religious Institutions, delivered at the opening of the Independent Congregational Church, in Barton Square, Salem, Tuesday, December 7th, 1824, by Henry Colman." An additional verse is given. This sermon was reprinted from the American edition in 1825.

The Rev. James Martineau more recently took the same hymn from a Boston (U.S.) collection, on which he knew he could rely, for his "Hymns for the Christian Church and Home," 1852. Thence it was taken for the "Leeds Hymn Book," 1853, by Professor Reynolds, now of Cheshunt. And, in 1859, it was inserted in the "New Congregational Hymn Book." Mr. Martineau was inclined to look with a favourable eye on Mr. Pierpont's hymns, even if their intrinsic excellence had not deserved it: for as a boy he was appointed by his schoolmaster, Dr. Lant Carpenter, to show the accomplished author through Clifton and parts of Bristol, and he says Mr. Pierpont's " graceful kindness and scholarly dignity left a deep impression u him."

John Pierpont was a native of Litchfield, Connecticut, and was born in 1785. He continued in business till 1816, and then entered upon literary pursuits. He studied theology at Baltimore, and then in the Theological School connected with Harvard College, Boston. In 1819 he became the minister of the Unitarian Church, Hollis Street, Boston. In 1835 and 1836 he travelled for his health in England, France, Italy, Asia Minor, and Greece. Some account of his journey appeared in letters written from Rome in the "Evening Gazette," in 1835. And in the "Knickerbocker," February 14th, 1836, he published a poem written behind Cape Matapan, and called " A Sunday Night at Sea."

In 1840, Mr. Pierpont suffered from an unhappy controversy with a number of his congregation at Hollis Street. He was requested by a committee of the congregation to resign, which he, in his own defence, refused to do. After ineffectual attempts at mediation, the whole matter came before an Ecclesiastical Council. Various charges were investigated, and there was much discussion as to whether Mr. Pierpont wrote a prologue at the opening of a new theatre, and as to whether his earnest advocacy of various public movements interfered with his pastoral work. After a long trial, the Council decided, in 1841, that some of the charges were not proved, and that those that were proved, were not such as to necessitate his resignation of his pulpit. The whole account of this tedious and unhappy controversy is given in a volume, entitled " Proceedings of an Ecclesiastical Council in the case of the Hollis Street Meeting and the Rev. J. Pierpont," by Samuel K. Lothrop.

Mr. Pierpont is the author of " Airs of Palestine, and other Poems and Hymns," Boston, 1840. He also published a very remarkable sermon on Acts xix. 19, 20, called " The Burning of the Ephesian Letters," 1834, directed against the trade in wines and spirits; a production both ingenious and courageous, and attended with a good deal of inconvenience in its effects upon himself. Other popular works by him are " The American First Class Book," 26th edition, 1835 ; " The National Reader," 29th edition, 1835; "An Introduction to the National Reader," 1831 ; and some sermons. He is still living (1866), and a daughter of his is the wife of Mr. Morgan, one of the Peabody Trustees, and partner in the great house of Peabody, in London.

SIR ROBERT GRANT.
1785—1838.

Sir Robert Grant, who belonged to an ancient Scotch family, was the second son of Charles Grant, an esteemed philanthropist. He was born in 1785. He studied at Cambridge, where he graduated in 1806. In the year 1807 he became a member of the English bar, and in 1826 entered parliament as member for the Inverness Burghs. He was sworn a privy councillor in 1831, and was appointed Governor of Bombay in 1834. He died in India, in December, 1838. While in India he published several works.

In the year after his death his elder brother, Lord Glenelg, published in London, in a volume entitled "Sacred Poems," twelve of his poetical pieces. In the preface, he explains that they had been written by his brother at different periods of his life, and some had already appeared in periodicals. These hymns show that there was in the heart of their author a rich vein of spiritual life. Three of these pieces are given in full in the "New Congregational Hymn Book." They are in the less-used metres.

"O, worship the King,"—No. 162,

is No. 11 in the above-named collection.

"Saviour, when in dust to Thee."—No. 367.

This is No. 2 of the same collection. It had appeared in the "Christian Observer," 1815. If prayers may properly be turned into hymns, this will be accepted as one of the best of that class of hymns.

"When gathering clouds around I view."—No. 369.

This affecting Christian hymn had appeared in the "Christian Observer" for February, 1806, and again in the same magazine, February, 1812, with a letter explaining that it is sent in an altered form. The letter is signed "E—y. D. R."

ANDREW REED, D.D.

1787—1862.

The subject of this sketch was born in London, and trained for the ministry at Hackney College. He owed much to the piety and earnest Christian activity of his parents. They trained him up in the way he should go, and when he was old he did not depart from it, but continued for fifty years the devoted and successful pastor of the Congregational Church of which he himself and his parents before him were members. It assembled first at the New Road Chapel, St. George's-in-the-East, and afterwards at Wycliffe Chapel, which was built in 1830 by Dr. Reed's exertions.

The sameness of his long pastoral course was broken by the visit he paid to America in 1834. He went in company with Dr. Matheson as a deputation from the Congregational Union of England to the churches in America. There he saw the work of the religious revival; and on his return a similar spiritual quickening was experienced in his own congregation. This subject is treated in his works—a "Narrative of the Revival of Religion in Wycliffe Chapel," and the "Advancement of Religion the Claim of the Times," 1843; and a "Narrative of the Visit to the American Churches," of which Dr. Reed wrote the greater part, was also published in two volumes, 1835. His writings on the subject of religious revivals were of great spiritual service, not only to his own congregation, but also to other churches in different parts of the country. Dr. Reed was also the author of a very popular book, entitled "No Fiction." It was written in the author's thirty-second year, 1819, and long before his theological works were produced. It had reached an eighth edition in 1835. The affecting facts upon which it is founded produced so deep an impression on the mind of Dr. Reed, that he felt almost compelled to put them on record for the benefit of others; and several of his sermons and charges were published: in 1861 they were published in a collected form. During his stay in America, he received the diploma of D.D. from Yale College.

But Dr. Reed will always be best known to posterity as the philanthropic founder of no less than five of our great national benevolent institutions, viz.:—the London Orphan Asylum, the Asylum for Fatherless Children, the Asylum for Idiots, the Infant Orphan Asylum, and the Hospital for Incurables. By consummate ability and extraordinary industry, he succeeded in inaugurating these noble institutions, and in forcing them into public notice, until they obtained adequate funds, suitable buildings, and a permanent place in the country. This he accomplished, regardless of the personal sacrifices he had to make of property and time, and along with the conscientious discharge of the duties devolving on a London pastor with a numerous church and congregation; and he was at the same time the friend and advocate of every good cause.

Dr. Reed made a collection of hymns, called "The Hymn Book." It was designed to include all that was necessary in one volume; and especially to provide a collection containing more hymns of praise, and more hymns bearing on the revival of religion, than were to be found in former collections. As early as 1817 he began preparing this work, and some of his original hymns were written while strolling in the woods of Beaconsfield, where he was then stopping. He first prepared, in 1817, a supplement, with some originals, to be used by his congregation along with Dr. Watts's Psalms and Hymns; and afterwards, in 1841, his complete collection, to take the place of both. In the work of hymn-writing he received assistance from Mrs. Reed, who is an authoress, and survives him. His collection is on the same plan as the "New Congregational Hymn Book," but with fewer hymns, and a less extensive list of authors. It is used by a large number of congregations in England and in the colonies. It contains twenty-seven hymns written by himself. None of them display any special poetic talent, but some are distinguished for their excellence of diction, their clearness, comprehensiveness, and force.

One of the best is his sole contribution to the "New Congregational Hymn Book:"—

"Spirit Divine, attend our prayers."—No. 441.

Another that is deservedly commended is the hymn beginning—

"There is an hour when I must part."

It is not found in the "New Congregational Hymn Book." This hymn was read to Dr. Reed, at his own request, when he was approaching his end. After hearing it, he said, "That hymn I wrote at Geneva: it has brought comfort to many, and now it brings comfort to me."

HENRY KIRKE WHITE.
1785—1806.

This poet of promise, who has been named "The Crichton of Nottingham," averts the arrows of criticism by the melancholy brevity of his career. We think more of what he would have accomplished than of the works he had actually produced. Before the critic with searching eye has had time to find spots in the sun, he weeps because that sun has set to rise no more. But there is compensation. That departure can scarcely be called untimely which gained for Kirke White an apotheosis from the fathers of song, giving him Southey for his enthusiastic biographer, and Byron for his brilliant eulogist.

Kirke White's father was a butcher at Nottingham, and at first the son is said to have followed his father's business. Southey says that the youth was, at the age of fourteen, placed in a stocking loom, with the view at some future period of getting a situation in a hosier's warehouse. But in his fifteenth year the young poet was removed from his uncongenial toil to enter an attorney's office, Messrs. Coldham and Enfield's, at Nottingham, where, after two years' service as the price of his articles, he was articled in 1802. At this time he made acquisitions in knowledge with extraordinary rapidity, and distinguished himself in a local literary society. As early as the age of fifteen he had obtained from the "Monthly Preceptor" a silver medal and a pair of globes for a translation from Horace; and when but seventeen years of age he became known as a contributor to periodicals, and he was encouraged to prepare a volume of poems for the press. This was published in 1802.

At first inclined to scepticism, Kirke White at length acknowledged himself subdued by the holy loving voice of God in His word. As a poet-philosopher panting for a life of noble sentiment, and yearning after a noble ideal which had not entered into the thoughts of the multitude, Christianity not only showed him his dream realized and surpassed, but at the same time convinced him that that realization could not become his possession apart from the faith in Christ which the Gospel required. In his progress towards full Christian faith, Kirke White was much assisted by the companionship of a young friend, who at first shrank from him as a scoffer, but afterwards sympathized with him in his spiritual conflicts, and introduced to his notice "Scott's Force of Truth," a work from which he derived benefit, though its statements at first provoked in him some opposition. His course from scepticism to Christian faith is recorded in his "Star of Bethlehem." His letters give proof of his amiability and piety.

His companion, Almond, from whom he had received so much benefit, having gone to Cambridge to study for the Church, Kirke White was seized with a strong desire to follow him thither for the same purpose; but at first it was beyond his power. At length, assisted by generous and appreciating friends, he quitted the attorney's office, in 1804, and repaired to Cambridge to carry out his cherished purpose. By the advice of Mr. Simeon, he studied a year at Winteringham, in Lincolnshire, under the tuition of the Rev. — Grainger. In 1806 he returned to Cambridge, for the great mathematical examination in June. His excessive studies, pursued too often by the light of the midnight lamp, gave him a first place in the University; but alas! wasted his too frail body, and he died before completing his twenty-third year.

From amidst the severe satire of his "English Bards and Scotch Reviewers," Byron turns aside thus adequately to celebrate in song this affecting event:

> "Unhappy White, when life was in its spring,
> And thy young muse just waved her joyous wing,
> The spoiler swept that soaring lyre away,
> Which else had sounded an immortal lay!
> Oh, what a noble heart was here undone,
> When science' self destroyed her favourite son.
> * * * *
> "'Twas thine own genius gave the final blow,
> And helped to plant the wound that laid thee low:
> So the struck eagle stretched upon the plain,
> No more through rolling clouds to soar again,
> Viewed his own feather on the fatal dart,
> And winged the shaft that quivered to his heart."

Kirke White's poems, published in 1804, did not receive much attention, but served to introduce him to Southey, whose work, "The Remains of Henry Kirke White," has become a favourite with the public. Besides the "Clifton Grove," 1802, dedicated to the Duchess of Devonshire, Kirke White's most important production is the "Christiad," an unfinished epic. The ten hymns of Kirke White, given by Dr. Collyer in his collection, 1812, are believed to be all that he wrote. There are two of his hymns in the "New Congregational Hymn Book," Nos. 627 and 984. They are not distinguished by any marks of great poetic genius.

"Oft in sorrow, oft in woe."—No. 627.

Dr. Collyer gives this hymn of the same length, but differently, in his "Hymns," 1812, with the following note:—"The mutilated state of this hymn, which was written on the back of one of the mathematical papers of this excellent young man, and which came into my hands a mere fragment, rendered it necessary for something to be added, and I am answerable for the last six lines." Ten lines of the original were by Kirke White. The hymn as it appears in the "New Congregational" retains only four of these, and in an altered form. The other three verses are not Dr. Collyer's, but are verses added by Fanny Fuller Maitland, in her "Hymns for Private Devotion, selected and original," 1827.

"O Lord, another day is flown."—No. 984.

Four verses of the original are here given with little alteration, but verse three is substituted for Kirke White's second and third verses, and is different from them. The substituted verse is, however, better than the two omitted, and the whole hymn gains by the substitution. Sir Roundell Palmer gives 1803 as the date of this hymn. The former, 627, bears date 1806.

JOHN MARRIOTT.
1780—1825.

"Thou, whose almighty word."—No. 917.

THE Rev. J. Marriott dates this hymn 1813. It is in a MS. of his father's, between two pieces, dated 1813 and 1814. His father did not publish any of his numerous pieces, but two volumes of his sermons were published in 1818 and 1838. He was a son of the Rev. R. Marriott, D.D., and was educated at Rugby and Oxford. After being private tutor in the family of the Duke of Buccleuch, he received from him the living of Church Lawford, in Warwickshire, but his wife's health compelled him to live in Devonshire, where he held curacies, and died at Broad Alyst, near Exeter.

WILLIAM GOODE, M.A.
1762—1816.

EACH new author of a work attempted before must give some reason for his fresh attempt, and to make good his claim, he is in some danger of undervaluing his predecessors. The Rev. W. Goode, in his preface to his " New Version of the Psalms," speaks truly of the older versions as obsolete and defective. But he seems unduly to undervalue the labours of other later writers, and especially of Watts, whose object seems to have been the same as his own, since he professes it as his purpose to make a version simple enough for the people generally, and Christian so as to be adapted to our dispensation. And this was the very work Dr. Watts undertook and successfully accomplished.

Mr. Goode's work is entitled, " A New Version of the Book of Psalms, with Original Prefaces and Notes, Critical and Explanatory." Two vols., 1811. It had reached a third edition in 1816. John Holland, in " The Psalmists of Britain" (1843) describes Mr. Goode as rector of St. Antholme's, London, " the very first church in which psalm-singing began in connexion with the Protestant worship."

On the title page of the above work he is described as " rector of St. Andrew Wardrobe, and St. Ann, Blackfriars, lecturer of St. John, of Wapping," &c.

"Thou, gracious God, and kind."—No. 114.

This is part of Mr. Goode's version of Psalm 79. His psalm consists of four verses in long metre and nine in short metre. In the " New Congregational," four of the latter verses are given without alteration.

The Rev. William Goode, D.D., dean of Ripon, who is the son of this psalm-writer, has supplied the following particulars of his father's life in a memoir first published with his father's " Essays" in 1822, and afterwards in a separate form in 1828.

William Goode was born on the 2nd of April, 1762, of pious parents, in the town of Buckingham. His first studies were pursued at his native place, but at the age of thirteen he went to be educated by the Rev. T. Bull, a dissenting minister at Newport Pagnell. Young Goode's parents had been driven from their parish church by the unsatisfactory state of the preaching therein, to seek the gospel they needed amongst dissenters. Their work in training their son was happily furthered by the education and ministry of Mr. Bull, and the youth was found carrying on prayer meetings with his schoolfellows, and early desiring to prepare for the ministry.

After a time he left Newport Pagnell, and returned home to assist his father in his business. But the desire for the ministry continued to burn within him, and he improved his leisure by preparative studies in Hebrew and theology, and in 1778 he began to read with the Rev. Thomas Clarke, a clergyman at Chesham Bois. In 1780 he entered Magdalen Hall, Oxford, where he graduated B.A. in 1784. The same year he became curate of Abbott's Langley, Herts. In 1786 he married Rebecca, daughter of Abraham Coles, of St. Albans. He graduated M.A. in 1787. Very earnest in his piety, wide in his sympathies, and thorough in his attainments, he at length found, in 1786, a suitable sphere in London as curate to the celebrated Romaine, whom he succeeded nine years after in the living of St. Ann's, Blackfriars. Mr. Goode also held lectureships in other parishes in London, and from 1791 engaged in useful literary work. He took a deep interest in the missionary societies, and was one of the founders of the Church Missionary Society. It was while on a journey to advocate its claims that he contracted a disease which, in its effects, terminated his life. He died on the 15th April, 1816. Amongst his last words were: "Dear Jesus," "Precious Jesus."

Besides the version of the Psalms, Mr. Goode published a volume of sermons in 1812, and ten essays on the Scripture titles of Christ in the "Christian Guardian," 1813—1816. These, with numerous other essays by him, were published posthumously in six volumes, edited by his son, in 1822, with the title, "Essays on all the Scriptural Names and Titles of Christ; or, the Economy of the Gospel Dispensation, as exhibited in the Person, Character, and Offices of the Redeemer."

WILLIAM HURN.

1754—1829.

"The God of truth His church has blest."—No. 826.

In the original this hymn is headed—

"The Church loved with an everlasting love."

It is the 316th hymn in a collection, entitled "Hymns and Spiritual Songs, with metrical versions from the Psalms. Second edition. (1824). By the Rev. William Hurn." This is an original work. The first edition (1813) in which this hymn is No. 307, was not entirely original. The second edition contains 150 hymns not printed before, and consists in all of 430 pieces. In the preface, dated Woodbridge, 1824, Mr. Hurn gives a history of his experience as a hymnbook maker and hymnwriter. He had not at first fully recognized the responsibility of preparing a book to guide the religious thoughts and devotions of congregations; but when he felt how great that responsibility was, he gave himself to the work with care and thought. He had consulted existing collections, and found them wanting in hymns on practical subjects, and rendered unfit for public worship by incautious expressions, such as those expressing a strong desire to depart out of this world, and by exaggerated statements of individual experience, which the congregation as a whole could not truthfully employ. In these criticisms, in which the author borders on hypercriticism, he has undoubtedly hit a blot in some of our best hymns. But, unfortunately, his own productions, while free from the defects of the masters, are at the same time without their unrivalled excellencies. They are close to the original in rendering the Scriptures, careful in their versification, but without the charm and moving power of sanctified genius. Hymn 826, an excellent and useful one, is a very favourable specimen of Mr. Hurn's productions. It is given in full, but with alterations.

Mr. Hurn was vicar of Debenham, and afterwards minister

at the Chapel, Woodbridge. In 1790 he published a discourse, "The Fundamental Principles of the Established Church proved to be the Doctrine of the Scripture." But in 1823 he published "A Farewell Testimony, containing the substance of Two Discourses (Acts xx. 32), preached in the parish church of Debenham, October 13, 1822, after a public notice given to take leave of the people, and secede from the Established Church." The sermons have no personal references, and do not give the reasons for secession. Besides the work already named, Mr. Hurn was the author of "Heath Hill; a Descriptive Poem," 1777, and of several published sermons.

In 1831 there was published a work of 326 pages, entitled "Brief Memorials of William Hurn, late minister at the Chapel, Woodbridge, formerly vicar of Debenham, Suffolk, and chaplain to the late Duchess Dowager of Chandos. By Esther Cooke and Ellen Rouse." Unfortunately this work is not in the British Museum, nor in Dr. Williams' Library.

William Hurn was born at Breccles Hall, Norfolk, December 21st, 1754. In 1777 he was appointed classical tutor in the Free Grammar School, Dedham, Essex. Two years after, he entered the army, but at the end of a year of military service he resigned his commission. In 1781 he was ordained by Bishop Yonge as a clergyman of the Church of England; but it was not till five years after that he experienced the great saving change which was necessary before he could be fitted for the life of earnest Christian usefulness he afterwards lived.

His marriage to Sarah, daughter of Thomas Wharrie, Esq., of Hull, took place in 1789. After a union of twenty-eight years his wife died in 1817. He adopted his nieces, who wrote his obituary. In 1788 he received the appointment of chaplain to the Duchess Dowager of Chandos, and in 1790 he was presented to the vicarage of Debenham, Suffolk.

In October, 1822, he seceded from the Established Church, and in the following year accepted an invitation to become pastor of the Congregational Church, Woodbridge. In that position he remained till his death, October 9, 1829, at the age of seventy-five. He was an eminently devoted, conscientious, and useful minister of the gospel. His work, " Reasons for Secession," was published posthumously, 1830, with a short memoir by his nieces.

ADONIRAM JUDSON, D.D.
1788—1850.

" Our Father, God, who art in heaven."—No. 558.

This hymn was written at the most critical time in the history of one of the most useful of American missionaries, Dr. Judson, whose course excited so deep an interest that his memoir is said to have sold in America twenty-five thousand copies in sixty days. The hymn is signed " Prison, Ava, March, 1825." It was written during the author's twenty-one months' imprisonment at Ava, at a time when his sufferings were very severe and his life was in peril from day to day. It is found at page 308 in Vol. I. of " A Memoir of the Life and Labours of Dr. A. Judson, by Francis Wayland, D.D., President of Brown University, in two vols., 1853." After some beautiful " Lines Addressed to an Infant Daughter, twenty days old, in the condemned prison at Ava," a child born January 26th, 1825, we read with regard to this hymn : " The following versification of the Lord's Prayer was composed a few weeks later. It illustrates the nature of the subjects which occupied the thoughts of the missionary during his long-protracted agony. It is said by the author to be comprised in fewer words than the original Greek, and in two more only than the common translation."

Adoniram Judson was born August 9th, 1788, at Maldon, Massachusetts. His father, of the same name, was a minister, and lived till 1826. In the year 1804, at the age of sixteen, young Adoniram entered Providence College, now called Brown University. He graduated B.A. in 1807, and commenced a private school at Plymouth. He also published a work on " English

Grammar," and "The Young Lady's Arithmetic." In 1808 he gave up his school and entered Andover Theological Seminary. He was not yet decidedly religious, but he was an earnest inquirer. At length, on the 28th of May, 1809, he became a member of the third congregational church, Plymouth.

In the year 1809, the reading of Buchanan's "Star in the East" stirred his whole soul with the thought of entering upon the missionary work; and, meeting with others likeminded, he decided in February, 1810, to begin to prepare for it. In 1811, he went with others to confer with the directors of the London Missionary Society in London, and to offer themselves to them, but they wisely remitted the enterprise to their American cousins, who were well able to undertake it. At length Mr. Judson and his first wife and others were sent forth to India by the American Board of Commissioners. On their way they became Baptists, and after meeting with much opposition from the East India Company, they at length, to avoid reshipment to England, sailed from Madras in a vessel bound to Rangoon. Thus they reached Burmah, where it was found that Providence had a great work for them to do. Their mission was commenced about the year 1815. They worked in connection with the American Baptists, and by the time the British war broke out in 1824, the mission had been already attended with some success.

On the 8th June, 1824, Rangoon having been taken by the British, Dr. Judson was seized with violence by the natives, cruelly bound, and cast into prison, and it was not till April, 1826, when the Burmese were obliged to capitulate, that he obtained his release. During his term of incarceration, he was removed from prison to prison, exposed to privations that brought on dangerous fever, and sometimes threatened with immediate death; but, like Paul and Silas, he cheered himself in his prison with Christian songs. It was during this period that he wrote the hymn referred to at the beginning of this sketch. His faithful wife soon after fell a sacrifice to her fatigue and anxiety. She died 24th October, 1826, aged thirty-seven.

Coming out of the furnace of affliction, Dr. Judson pursued his mission work with extraordinary devotion and success, and while labouring for others, carefully cultivated his own spiritual nature, and became a "vessel of gold" meet for the Master's use. In the memoir the man pleases us as much as his mission. On the 10th April, 1834, he married at Tavoy his second wife, Mrs. Sarah H., the widow of his companion in labour, the Rev. George D. Boardman. In 1845 he returned to America, and on the passage he suffered the loss of his second wife, who had taken a deep interest in the mission work, and had written Burmese hymns. It has been remarked that each of the three wives of Dr. Judson was an authoress. In the following year he married his third wife, Miss Emily Chubbuck, at Hamilton, New York. And soon after he again set out for the mission field in Burmah; but as his years increased, his absorbing duties began to tell upon his strength, and at length in 1850 he approached his end. At his own request he went on a voyage in a French barque, the "Aristide Marie," bound for the Isle of Bourbon, but the sea air came too late, and he sank peacefully in death on the 12th of April, 1850, and was committed to the deep. As death approached he had enjoyed the happy fruit of a life of habitual and elevated Christian godliness.

Dr. Judson was a scholar and an author as well as a missionary. In 1823 he received the degree of D.D. from Brown University, where he had once declined a tutorship. He wrote a work on "Christian Baptism," and two hymns on the same subject. He translated the Bible into Burmese in 1835 (three volumes), and he produced Burmese tracts and other works; and after his death, in 1852, a Burmese and English Dictionary was compiled from his papers.

THOMAS RAFFLES, D.D., LL.D.
1788—1863.

This eminent Congregational minister was born in London, on

the 17th of May, 1788, and, after enjoying a liberal education in his earlier years, was sent, at the age of seventeen, to study at Homerton for the ministry. After three years of collegiate study, he commenced his first pastorate at Hammersmith in 1809; but after a brief but successful ministry of three years there, he removed to Liverpool to succeed the lamented Thomas Spencer, of whose life he soon after published an eloquent memoir.

For fifty years Dr. Raffles continued his ministry at Liverpool with extraordinary success. Nor were his labours confined to his own numerous congregation. In every part of the country his services as a preacher were sought and valued; and in his own county, local missionary and other associations found in him a most efficient secretary and advocate. The Lancashire Independent College owed its origin and success mainly to his efforts; of which its Raffles' Library remains as a lasting memorial. Dr. Raffles' closing days were very happy and peaceful. He often gratefully passed in review his long and successful life, and gave all the glory to God. He died August 18th, 1863. Besides the popular memoir already referred to, Dr. Raffles was one of the authors of "Poems by the Rev. T. Raffles, of Liverpool, J. Baldwin Brown, Esq., of the Inner Temple, and Jeremiah Holmes Wiffen," 1815—this was originally published under the title of "Poems by Three Friends." He was also the author of "A Tour on the Continent in 1817," and of a work entitled, "Lectures on Christian Faith and Practice." He was also for a few years joint editor with Dr. Collyer and Dr. J. Baldwin Brown, of a London Quarterly. His degree of LL.D. was from the University of Aberdeen, and his diploma as Doctor of Divinity from a College in America.

As a man of literary tastes he was widely known, and he held no mean place as a religious poet. His original religious pieces were numerous and highly finished, and "some of the most finished classical lyrics have been rendered gracefully into English by his hand;" and some of his hymns have taken their place among the hymns of the Christian Church. For many years he addressed a poem to his congregation on New Year's day.

When the old " Congregational Hymn Book " appeared, it contained no hymns by Dr. Raffles, though they were found in other collections. In consequence of this omission he prepared a supplement to be used by his congregation along with " Watts's Psalms and Hymns." This was published in 1853. But when the " New Congregational Hymn Book " was being prepared, Dr. Raffles readily consented to contribute. Four of its hymns are by him—Nos. 531, 747, 979, 988.

Thomas Stamford Raffles, Esq., B.A., stipendiary magistrate of Liverpool, who has written a very interesting memoir of his lamented father, has kindly given the dates and occasions of three of these hymns from the original MSS.

"Lord, like the publican, I stand.'"—No. 531.

Dr. Raffles, being an exceedingly popular and eloquent preacher of the Gospel, had no doubt once and again preached from the favourite text that forms the subject of this hymn, " God be merciful to me a sinner." This is pre-eminently a minister's hymn, bringing out the meaning of the text, and just the hymn he would wish those impressed with a discourse on this text to sing. It bears date, " Seacombe, October 4th, 1831."

" High in yonder realms of light."—No. 747.

This is not in Dr. Raffles' MSS., but it is found with six stanzas in Dr. Collyer's collection of 1812. There are eight hymns by Dr. Raffles in that collection. They must have been written before he was twenty-four years of age, and they have the warmth, and eloquence, and pathos that marked his early style, as we see it in the memoir of Spencer, written at the same time.

" O God of families, we own."—No. 979.

This bears date January 15th, 1823.

" Saviour, let Thy sanction rest."—No. 988.

This is dated November 3rd, 1852, " On the marriage of the

Rev. J. F. Guenett." The original has two more stanzas, as follows—

> " Happy they who reach that place—
> In those regions find their home;
> Tears are wiped from every face,
> Toil and danger never come;
> They no pain nor sorrow know,
> Ransomed from this world of woe.
>
> " To that festival on high,
> To that banquet of the skies,
> To that glorious company,
> May we all at length arise;
> Mingle with the joyful throng,
> Join the everlasting song."

JOSIAH CONDER.
1789—1855.

It is sufficient praise for this most productive writer of prose and poetry, to say that he added lustre to a name rendered honourable amongst Nonconformists alike by those who bore it before him, and by those who bear it now. The opening genius of young Josiah Conder was encouraged by the stimulus of the great metropolis in which he was born; and, as his father was a bookseller, his mind early met with the pabulum it needed. While still young he displayed much literary taste, and wrote articles in the "Athenæum;" and at the age of twenty-one he produced, with the assistance of a few poetical friends, a volume of poems entitled, "The Associate Minstrels." This was published in 1810 and reprinted in 1812.

In 1814, in his capacity as a publisher, he purchased the "Eclectic Review." He also became its editor, and continued in that position till the year 1837, having retired from the bookselling business in 1819. During this brilliant period in the history of the " Eclectic," its pages were enriched by contributions from his friends, Robert Hall, John Foster, Dr. Chalmers, and others scarcely less eminent. In 1832 he started the "Patriot" weekly newspaper, which he continued to edit till the end of his life. He was also the author of several prose works, some of a general literary character, others having a special religious aim. His largest work was the "Modern Traveller," in thirty volumes, 1830, and "Italy," three volumes, 1831. In this he had assistance, but several of the volumes were written entirely by himself. He also wrote a "History of Italy," and a "Dictionary of Ancient and Modern Geography," 1834, and a "Life of Bunyan," 1835. Amongst his religious works were "Protestant Nonconformity," two volumes, 1818, and one volume, 1819. "The Village Lecturer, Original Discourses for Village Congregations," 1822. "The Law of the Sabbath," 1830; the "Epistle to the Hebrews," a new translation in 1834; a "View of all Religions;" an "Exposition of the Apocalypse;" and a "Literary History of the New Testament" in 1845. And along with these exhausting literary labours he was found taking his part as a lay preacher, and ready to render hearty co-operation in every useful religious or benevolent enterprise.

Modern hymnology owes much to Josiah Conder. Like his friend, James Montgomery, he cultivated it as an art, aided its promoters, and added to its riches. It was he who in 1836 produced the first "Congregational Hymn Book." This work was produced in accordance with a resolution of the Congregational Union, passed in 1833. It was designed to be used along with Dr. Watts's Psalms and Hymns. It was to include the valuable contributions of modern hymn-writers; to contain more hymns of direct praise to God than are found in some modern collections; and more of an experimentally religious character, and more suited to missionary services than are found in Watts's collection. The work consists of 620 hymns, by eighty writers. The preparation of it was confided to a sub-committee, by whom the task of collecting and revising the materials was ultimately devolved upon the single editor, Mr. Conder. The work, which appeared in 1836, met with general favour, and several hundred thousand copies have been sold.* In the year 1824, Mr. Conder sent forth his "Sacred Poems, Domestic Poems, and Miscellaneous Poems," and in 1837 he produced his third volume of poems, entitled "The Choir and the Oratory; or, Praise and Prayer." And in 1850 he read before the Congregational Union, at their meeting at Southampton, a valuable essay on Dr. Watts. This was afterwards published with the title, "The Poet of the Sanctuary." In the following year he produced a revised edition of Dr. Watts's Psalms and Hymns. His hope was that by omitting the less serviceable hymns, by modernising obsolete expressions, and by arranging the whole in convenient order, he might preserve Dr. Watts' Psalms and Hymns in use in our congregations as a separate collection—a hope that seems likely to be disappointed, now that the practice of using but one book seems to be everywhere gaining ground. But he had the satisfaction of seeing his alterations adopted in the psalms and hymns that were introduced into the "New Congregational." Mr. Conder died in peace, December 27th, 1855.

There are thirty-one hymns by him in the "New Congregational Hymn Book." There were fifty-six of his in the old "Congregational." Some that are omitted from the "New" we give up with regret, especially—

"O say not, think not in thy heart."—No. 388.

and—

"Oh! the hour when this material."—No. 620.

And it is an interesting fact in the history of his authorship that this hymn (No. 620) was one of three given by him to Dr. Collyer for his collection in 1812, when Mr. Conder was but twenty-three years of age. None of the three are in the "New Congregational." His hymns do not usually refer to his own personal history; but

---

* Many alterations of hymns introduced in that collection, approved by some, disapproved by others, have been attributed to Mr. Conder. We are informed that he has not left manuscript evidence of the precise nature of those alterations, nor of the extent to which they were made by himself or were due to other correctors.

there is one that contains a personal reference, No. 590 in the old "Congregational Hymn Book"—

"O thou God who hearest prayer."

It was written in the year 1820, when he was suffering severely, in consequence of a fall from a horse. He says in it—

"Listen to my feeble breath,
Now I touch the gates of death."

Most of his hymns were written after he had passed through many of the trials and vicissitudes of life. They are evidently the productions of one very familiar with Christian doctrine, rich in Christian experience, and well acquainted with the various requirements of public Christian worship. In diction tasteful and correct, and in sentiment and doctrine spiritual and devout, they yet cannot lay claim to more than the commendation of useful mediocrity; but the following will be familiar as favourites to many—

"How honoured, how dear."—No. 121.
"O give thanks to Him who made."—No. 277.
"How shall I follow Him I serve?"—No. 357.
"The Lord is King, lift up thy voice."—No. 407.
"Heavenly Father, to whose eye."—No. 636.
"Head of the church, our risen Lord."—No. 818.

Five of the hymns in the "New Congregational" are parts of a piece, in six parts, "On the Lord's Prayer," that appeared in "The Choir and the Oratory."

"Holy, holy, holy Lord."—No. 559.

This is the first part of the hymn to the words, "Our Father which art in heaven, hallowed be thy name." The second part is not given.

"Father of eternal grace."—No. 915.

This is the third part, for the words, "Thy will be done in earth, as it is in heaven."

"Day by day the manna fell."—No. 591.

This is the fourth part, for the words, "Give us this day our daily bread."

"Father, to Thy sinful child."—No. 535.

This is the fifth part, for the words, " Forgive us our trespasses as we forgive them that trespass against us."

"Heavenly Father, to whose eye."—No. 636.

This is the sixth part, for the words, "And lead us not into temptation, but deliver us from evil."

JOHN KEBLE, M.A.
1792—1866.

THE author of the "Christian Year" was educated at Corpus Christi College, Oxford, where he graduated B.A. in honours in 1810. He was M.A. in 1813. After receiving a fellowship at Oriel College, where he numbered Dr. Arnold amongst his friends, he was appointed public examiner and afterwards professor of poetry; and after some time he became vicar of Hursley, near Winchester. This living he held till his death, March 29th, 1866. He died at Bournemouth, in his seventy-fourth year, his end having been hastened by his assiduous attention to his afflicted wife.

He has published sermons and pamphlets on ecclesiastical subjects, and is the author of No. 78 of "Tracts for the Times," 1837; and along with Drs. Pusey and Newman, he edited the "Library of the Fathers" and the "Anglo-Catholic Library." He has been an active member of the "Church Union" movement. He is also the author of "Prælectiones Academicæ," two volumes, 1844; "Hooker's Works," 1836; and "Bishop Wilson's Life," 1863. In 1813 he gained the Chancellor's prize for an essay on "Translation from the Dead Languages."

As a poet, he is the author of "Lyra Innocentium; Thoughts in Verse on Children, their Ways and their Privileges," 1847; and of "The Psalter; or, Psalms of David in English Verse, by a member of the University of Oxford," 1839; and of poems in the "Lyra Apostolica." But his best known work is "The Christian

Year; Thoughts in Verse for the Sundays and Holydays throughout the Year," published in 1827. This work has gone through eighty editions, and his church at Hursley is said to have been rebuilt out of the profits of it. Several hymns in the "New Congregational Hymn Book" are parts of hymns in the "Christian Year." Keble's hymns are distinguished for their great refinement of taste, their word-painting, and graceful allusions to the charms of nature, and for a pleasing sentiment, which only offends when it threatens to degenerate into a mere sentimentalism; and the spiritual find in some of his verses a happy vein of piety and the highest doctrines applied to the duties of daily life. Members of other Christian communities find here and there verses in which the Church to which the author belongs, and its festivals, are made more prominent than they approve; but all Christians find much in Keble's hymns to enjoy and commend.

"There is a book who runs may read."—No. 276.

This is six verses of a hymn of twelve verses in the "Christian Year," on "The Invisible things of Him," &c., Romans i. 20.

"O God of mercy, God of might."—No. 874.

This is five verses of a hymn of seventeen verses in the "Christian Year," for the "Holy Communion."

"The livelong night we've toil'd in vain."—No. 888.

This is part of a hymn of fifteen verses in the "Christian Year," upon "Master, we have toiled all the Night, &c.," Luke v. 5, 6.

"Spirit of Light and Truth, to Thee."—No. 901.

This is part of an "Ordination" hymn, given in the "Christian Year," beginning thus—

"'Twas silence in Thy temple, Lord,"

and consisting of thirteen verses.

"O timely happy, timely wise."—No. 933.

This is part of his much-admired "Morning" hymn. It has sixteen verses, and begins thus—

"Hues of the rich, unfolding morn."

"Sun of my soul, Thou Saviour dear."—No. 946.

This is part of his "Evening" hymn, beginning—

"'Tis gone, that bright and orbèd blaze,"

a piece of fourteen verses.

Hymns 354 and 593 in the "New Congregational Hymn Book" are erroneously attributed to Keble. They are by his friend, Professor Joseph Anstice, M.A., whose hymns were published by his widow in 1836; *vide* under his name.

AARON CROSSLEY HOBART SEYMOUR.
Born 1789.

The following particulars of the history of this eminent literary character we have taken from a MS. autobiography with which he has favoured us, and which we regret our space does not allow us to give in full.

Mr. Seymour was born in the county of Limerick, December 19th, 1789. He was the eldest son of the late Rev. John Crossley Seymour, M.A., Vicar of Cahirelly, in the diocese of Cashel, a scion of the Seymour family, which had in former days its ducal and royal alliances. Mr. Seymour's mother was eldest daughter of the Rev. Edward Wight, M.A., rector of Meelick, Limerick, a descendant of an ancient family residing near Guildford, Surrey; and the name Hobart has been taken by the subject of this sketch because he is, along with the Rev. Sir John Hobart C. Seymour, Bart., a representative of the family arising from the alliance of the Hobarts and Seymours. Favoured with intellectual parents and a thorough education, Mr. Seymour was early distinguished. He early wrote in verse, and all his numerous compositions of that period were exclusively of a religious character. "When quite a youth he was providentially led to a chapel, which had formerly belonged to the Countess of Huntingdon, and there for the first time heard an unvarnished tale of Him who died upon the cross to save the chief of sinners."

When just arriving at manhood, Mr. Seymour was seriously afflicted by the bursting of a vessel in the lungs. While thus afflicted, and obliged to lie on his back, he composed a work which contains some of his hymns and poetical compositions. It is entitled, "Vital Christianity exhibited in a Series of Letters on the most Important Subjects of Religion, addressed to Young Persons," 1810. This work was followed by the publication of Dr. Gillies' "Life of Whitefield." This was an improved and enlarged edition, with the addition of sketches of Whitefield's eminent contemporaries. It did good service in Ireland, where at that time earnest ministers of the Gospel scarcely dared to declare themselves. In 1816, Mr. Seymour prefixed a memoir to the "Reliques of Ancient Irish Poetry, by Miss Charlotte Brooke." In preparing this work he was assisted by Miss Edgeworth and some other eminent writers, and by it he was introduced to Mrs. Hannah More and other literary celebrities.

"In conjunction with a younger brother, long since deceased, and another young friend, graduates in the University of Dublin, he was instrumental in collecting a band of the students to meet together for the purpose of 'praying, reading, and expounding the Scriptures, and singing hymns.' In a very short time the number amounted to nearly forty, nearly all of whom entered the ministry in the Established Church, and filled posts of usefulness in various parts of the kingdom." Mr. Seymour is the venerable survivor of that useful band.

His last, but most laborious work, was the "Life and Times of Selina, Countess of Huntingdon," two volumes, 1839, which has been pronounced one of the most industrious and remarkable pieces of religious biography that has issued from the press in modern times—combining more information about the Calvinistic Methodists, within and without the National Church, than has ever been brought together. It was undertaken with the sanction of the only surviving daughter of the venerable Countess, the well-known Countess of Moira (great grandmother of the present Marquis of Hastings), a great political character, a woman of exquisite taste, of extensive literary acquirements, and the patroness of all the literary geniuses of her day. Her Ladyship took great interest in his labours, and afforded him most valuable and important information. The late venerable Dr. Haweis was the first who inspired him with the desire to embark in such an undertaking, and kindly extended to him every facility for acquiring information. For more than thirty years he was engaged in collecting and arranging the numerous papers, documents, and voluminous correspondence, which he had easy and continued access to; and he has succeeded in producing such a view of the life and times of the noble Countess, so clear and so simple, as to render superfluous all future or collateral efforts at illustration. Mr. Seymour is also the author of numerous contributions to the periodicals and papers, and his pen is still being wielded with vigour on behalf of Evangelical Christianity.

About sixteen years ago, his failing health rendered it necessary that he should seek a warmer climate, and he resided for many years at Naples, doing what was possible to hasten on those happier days of political and religious freedom which the once down-trodden people of that kingdom now at length enjoy. In 1839 he was chosen a member of the Italian Scientific and Literary Congress, whose meetings he attended in several of the Italian cities till its final dissolution in Venice, in 1847, occasioned by the breaking out of the revolution. Mr. Seymour is at present residing in Bristol; he is an elder brother of the Rev. M. Hobart Seymour, of Bath, author of works on the Papacy.

The subject of this sketch has for many years taken a deep

interest in hymnology, and he has most promptly and kindly given the benefit of his reminiscences and researches to the author of this work.

"Jesus, immortal King, arise."—No. 920.

This hymn, erroneously attributed in the "New Congregational" to Burder, appears in Mr. Seymour's "Vital Christianity," 1810, with three more verses. "It was written more than sixty years ago," says its author. At that period the mind of the writer was much perplexed and agitated on the subject of missions to the heathen, principally owing to a very intimate correspondence with a female relative, the wife of a missionary who had been dedicated to the work at Spafields Chapel, London, and was captured on board the missionary ship "Duff," in 1798. It was sent with another, commencing—

"Awake! all conquering arm, awake!"

to the editor of the "Evangelical Magazine" some years after, when a younger brother, who had just then taken his degree in the University of Dublin, was accepted by the Directors of the London Missionary Society as a suitable person to send to Calcutta; but the obstinate refusal of the East India Company at that time to the landing of missionaries in India caused a very considerable delay, and in the interval he was taken to his eternal reward. Mr. G. Burder inserted this hymn (920) in the small collection published by the Missionary Society, and hence the mistake in attributing the hymn to him. In 1813, Mr. Seymour heard this hymn given out at a monthly missionary prayer meeting at Lady Henrietta Hope's Chapel, at the Hotwells, Bristol, and recognized it as his own.

JOHN PYER.
1790—1859.

THIS earnest minister began his labours as a tent missionary, and will always be remembered for his usefulness in that capacity. In the year 1814, the desire for increased Christian effort and for religious revival found one expression in the erection of a tent for religious services at Whitchurch, near Bristol. The tent was taken from place to place, and numerous services were held in it at times when the masses could be gathered together. John Pyer saw in the tent-work just the opening for religious usefulness he had long been desiring. Having lost his father while in childhood, he had been, to the grief of his mother, a wayward youth; but at length had been brought to religious decision by the labours of the Wesleyans, who had made him a local preacher. Having preached often in the tent, he at length gave up his business, to devote himself entirely to tent-preaching and the connected evangelistic work.

After six years' successful itinerancy the tent ceased to be the property of the Methodist body, and the work was carried on separately. In 1820, the tent was being used amongst the masses of London; and, in 1821, it was removed to Manchester. In Manchester, Mr. Pyer remained nine years, built a chapel, and had his doctrinal views so far modified, as to lead him to join the Congregational denomination. After this, Mr. Pyer was for four years an agent of the London Christian Instruction Society, and the tent was often put in requisition.

His surviving daughter, Mrs. Kate Russell, has written an interesting memoir of her father, 1865. Mr. Pyer was the subject of a life-long trial in the mental affliction of his wife. He married at the age of twenty-three, and his wife's affliction came on a few years after. Trial and exhausting labour rendered it at length necessary for Mr. Pyer to seek a less laborious position. In 1834, he became the Congregational pastor at South Molton; in 1838, he removed to Cork, and, in 1839, to Devonport, where he remained during a pastorate of twenty years, and where he died. Labouring to the very last day of his life, he was found by the servant lifeless, sitting in a peaceful attitude in his study, having literally fallen asleep in Jesus. This was on the 7th of April, 1859. Mr. Pyer wrote a few useful hymns. There is one by him in the " New Congregational Hymn Book."

"Met again in Jesus' name."—No. 803.

HENRY MARCH.

Born about 1790.

From materials kindly supplied by this venerable servant of God, we are able to give a few particulars of his useful course.

The Rev. Henry March was born about the year 1790, and received his education for the ministry among the Congregationalists at Homerton College. In 1818, he left Homerton to enter upon his ministry at Bungay, in Suffolk. There the attendance was so good as to induce the people to build a new and large chapel about twelve months after his settlement amongst them. But at the end of a pastorate of eight years, Mr. March was prevailed upon to leave Bungay in order to undertake the chaplaincy of Mill Hill School. This was at the request of his tutor, Dr. Pye Smith, who had persuaded the committee of that institution to separate the chaplaincy from the headmastership, and who thought Mr. March especially adapted to fill the former office.

After retaining his position at Mill Hill for about two years and a half, Mr. March resigned it, and soon after became pastor of the old Independent Church at Colchester. In this place he remained for more than ten years, till 1839; but finding the neighbourhood unfriendly to his health, and desiring another sphere of labour, pastor and people parted with mutual regret.

In the autumn of the year 1839, he accepted the call of the

Church at Newbury, Berks, where the climate was better suited to his health, and where he had " a path of peace and comforting success, so that he remained there for twenty years, at the end of which he retired from the ministry, having arrived at his sixty-ninth year." Mr. March afterwards resided for family reasons for a time at Rochdale, and more recently at Southampton, to be near his son, the Rev. Septimus March, B.A., minister of Albion Chapel. " At the close of a long life," says Mr. March, " my confession of faith you will find in Watts's hymn—

'No more, my God, I boast no more.' "—No. 543.

Mr. March is the author of several works. While at Bungay, he published, " Sabbaths at Home ; or, Help to their Right Improvement, founded on the 42nd and 43rd Psalms ; Contemplations and Reflections ; with a few Hymns." The proceeds of the first edition were given towards the cost of erecting the new chapel. This work had reached a third edition in 1826. To use the words of the author, " the hymn at the close of each chapter in that book is a kind of ' collect ' of the contents of the chapter." The one hymn contributed by Mr. March to the " New Congregational Hymn Book"—

" O send Thy light, Thy truth, my God,"—No. 771,

is on page 227 of this work, and first appeared there.

While at Mill Hill, Mr. March published, " The Early Life of Christ an Example to the Young." He has also printed several sermons at different times ; and he is the author of " Hymns for the Closet of the Christian Minister :" London, 1839.

HENRY HART MILMAN, D.D.

Born 1791.

Dean Milman is the youngest son of Sir Francis Milman, physician to George III. He was born in London, February

10th, 1791. After being educated at Dr. Burney's academy at Greenwich, then at Eton, and subsequently at Brazenose College, Oxford, he was ordained in 1817, and appointed vicar of St. Mary's, Reading, where he continued till 1835. He was B.A., 1813; M.A., 1816; B.D. and D.D., 1849. From 1821 to 1831 he was professor of poetry in the University of Oxford. From 1835 to 1849 he was rector of St. Margaret's, Westminster, and canon of Westminster, and he became dean of St. Paul's in 1849.

His principal prose works are a "History of Latin Christianity," six vols., 1854; "A History of the Jews," 1843; and a "Life of Keats." He also edited "Gibbon's Decline and Fall of the Roman Empire," which he enriched with his learned notes. He has also contributed many articles to the "Quarterly Review." In Macaulay's "History of England" he wrote a memoir of the author in 1858. This was republished separately in 1862. He also published the Bampton Lecture delivered by him in 1827.

As a poet, he published, in 1817, the tragedy of "Fazio," which was represented on the stage. Among his other poetical works are "Samor, Lord of the Bright City," 1818; "The Fall of Jerusalem," 1820; "Belshazzar;" the "Martyr of Antioch;" and "Anne Boleyn." He published the poetical works of MM. Bowles, Wilson, and A. Cornwall, 1829, and his own poetical works, in three vols., 1839. His poems are distinguished by their scholarly taste and skill rather than by the fire and genius of the true poet. Dean Milman published a "Selection of Psalms and Hymns for the use of St. Margaret's, Westminster, 1837;" he has also translated some poems from Sanscrit, and he is the author of an illustrated edition of "Horace, with a Life of the Poet, 1849;" and of "The Agamemnon of Æschylus and the Bacchanals of Euripides, with passages from the lyric and later Poets of Greece," translated by Dean Milman, 1865.

His hymns are good, without reaching the highest point of excellence. Some of them happily combine the Christian's experience of himself with his experience of Christ. This is true of Nos. 648 and 808, two of the three given in the "New Congregational Hymn Book."

"When our heads are bowed with woe,"—No. 648,

a very beautiful and affecting Christian hymn. This is the Second Hymn for the Sixteenth Sunday after Trinity. A verse is omitted. And—

"O help us, Lord, each hour of need."—No. 808.

This is the hymn for the Second Sunday in Lent. Two verses are omitted. The other is No. 809—

"Lord, have mercy when we pray,"

his hymn for the Sixth Sunday after Trinity. It is much altered. The original begins—

" Lord, have mercy when we *strive*."

These hymns appeared in a hymn book by Bishop Heber, entitled, " Hymns adapted to the Weekly Church Service of the Year," published by Heber's widow, in 1827.

JAMES EDMESTON.
Born 1791.

One of the largest contributors to our recent religious hymnology is James Edmeston, a London architect. We are much indebted to the venerable bard for a letter, dated 10th February, 1866, containing, in addition to a correct list of his poetical works, the following autobiographical information :—

" I was born 10th of September, 1791. My parents were Independents; my maternal grandfather was the well-known Rev. Samuel Brewer, for fifty years minister of the ancient Independent congregation at Stepney ; but, from early years, I had a strong leaning towards the Church of England, the service of which I always found more congenial to my own feelings ; and after many years of occasional conformity, became a member thereof, and joined the congregation of Ram's Episcopal Chapel at Homerton (where I then resided, and reside still), the incumbent of which was and is the Rev. Thomas Griffith, prebend of St. Paul's."

The embryo poet was educated at Hackney, whither his parents had removed in 1803. At the age of sixteen he was articled to an architect and surveyor. He continued in the office where he had learned his profession till 1816, and then commenced on his own account. Mr. Edmeston removed from Hackney to Homerton in 1822, and was married in the following year. His wife, after being the mother of a numerous family, died in 1850. In 1851 Mr. Edmeston became a churchwarden of St. Barnabas, Homerton, a new church erected in 1847. He also became secretary of the parochial schools, and took an active interest in promoting the erection of the new and costly school premises.

At the age of eighteen, Mr. Edmeston began to write for the press, and in 1817 he published a small volume, " The Search, and other Poems." This was dedicated to his friend, the Rev. F. A. Cox, better known afterwards as Dr. Cox. Then followed " Anston Park," a tale; and " The World of Spirits." In 1820 he published a small volume of " Sacred Lyrics," and in the two following years two other sets of " Sacred Lyrics ;" and in 1821, the " Home Missionary Society" published " The Cottage Minstrel; or, Hymns for the Assistance of Cottagers in their Domestic Worship." These were fifty hymns composed for the Society by Mr. Edmeston, at the request of one of the friends of the Institution. The same year he published " One Hundred Hymns for Sunday Schools." In the year 1822, Mr. Edmeston published fifty hymns on missionary subjects, for use in united missionary prayer-meetings ; and the same year, " One Hundred Sunday School Hymns for Particular Occasions." And in 1829, a small volume containing a dramatic sketch, " The Woman of Shunam, and other Poems ;" also, " Patmos, a Fragment, and other Poems," in 1824. More recently, the

Religious Tract Society have published his "Hymns for the Chamber of Sickness," 1844; and in the same year his "Closet Hymns and Poems." Mr. Edmeston is also the author of "Sacred Poetry," 1847; and of a small book for children, containing fifty hymns, and entitled "Infant Breathings: being Hymns for the Young," 1846; of which there was an improved edition in 1861. Mr. Edmeston has been very successful in his Hymns for Children, some of which are scarcely inferior in merit to those by Jane Taylor. Some were written at the suggestion of his friend, Mrs. Luke, an authoress, and the wife of the Rev. Samuel Luke. In all his productions this pious poet has made it his aim to glorify God and benefit men. Some of his hymns were written, week after week, to be read on Sunday at family prayer; and at all times hymn-writing has been to him a sacred and solemn work.

"Welcome! brethren, enter in."—No. 840.

This is No. 1 of five hymns supplied by Mr. Edmeston, at the request of a friend, for insertion in a provincial hymn book, on the subject of admitting members. The third verse is not in Mr. Edmeston's original MS. It has been added by some other hand.

"Saviour, breathe an evening blessing."—No. 985.

This was written many years ago, after reading in "Salte's Travels in Abyssinia," the following words:—"At night, their short Evening Hymn, 'Jesus, forgive us!' stole through the Camp." It has been sung for years at the close of the service at the church at Homerton, where Mr. Edmeston worships. It was given in "Sacred Lyrics," 1820.

SIR JOHN BOWRING, LL.D., F.R.S.
Born 1792.

THIS eminent living celebrity can almost claim for himself the name of a universal genius, having distinguished himself in many and various departments. He was born at Exeter, October 17th, 1792. His family belonged to Devonshire, where they gave their name to their estate, Bowringsleigh, in the parish of West Alvington. In early life young Bowring came under the influence of Jeremy Bentham, whose principles he adopted, and maintained in the "Westminster Review," of which he was, from 1825, for some years the editor. He was also Bentham's executor, and published his works, in twenty-three volumes, with a biography.

To two branches of knowledge Mr. Bowring gave special attention, languages and commerce. He sat in Parliament for the Clyde Boroughs from 1835 to 1837, and for Bolton from 1841 to 1849. He has carried several useful measures through Parliament, and filled several important offices under Government, especially in connection with foreign commerce, and with the public accounts. He is a strong advocate of "the decimal system," and we owe to him the introduction of the florin. In 1849, he was appointed British Consul at Canton, and in 1854, Governor of Hong Kong. In the year 1855, he undertook a special mission to Siam; and in 1859, he retired from the public service with a pension. Numerous honours have deservedly been conferred on him. The University of Groningen, in Holland, conferred on him the degree of LL.D. While in China, he was made a Fellow of the Royal Society, and he was knighted in 1854. He belongs to several learned societies, and foreign princes and peoples have recognized his services to commerce and literature, by sending him testimonials, presents, and orders. In religion, he is one of the most distinguished members of the Unitarian denomination, and he aids the movement for providing secular lectures on Sunday.

Sir John Bowring is a voluminous writer. Amongst his works are—"Minor Morals for Young People," 1834. "The Commercial Relations between England and France," 1836. "The Decimal System," 1854. "The Kingdom and People of Siam," 1857. "A Visit to the Philippine Islands," 1859. And many of his works reveal his extraordinary knowledge of languages. Amongst others we find—" Specimens of Russian Poets," 1831. " Ancient Poetry and Romances of Spain," 1824. " Specimens of Dutch Poets," 1824. " Specimens of Polish Poets," 1827. " Poetry of the Magyars," 1830. " History of the Poetical Literature of Bohemia," 1832. Sir John Bowring has also published works translated from the German and French, and while in Madrid he published, in Spanish, a work on " African Slavery."

To all this we must add, that Sir John Bowring is no mean poet. Many of the works already named consist of translations made from poets in different languages, and they show the translator's poetic taste and skill. But besides these, Sir John is the author of original poems and volumes of hymns. His " Matins and Vespers, with Hymns and Devotional Pieces," appeared in 1823; and several editions of it have been published. In 1825, " Hymns : as a Sequel to the Matins" were published.

"How sweetly flowed the gospel's sound."—No. 349.

This pleasing hymn is in the fourth edition of " Matins and Vespers," 1851.

" In the cross of Christ I glory."—No. 372.

This is found in " Hymns," as a Sequel to the " Matins." 1825.

WILLIAM BARTHOLOMEW.
Born 1793.

This venerable and talented author has kindly supplied the following particulars of his history :—He was born in London, September 6th, 1793. From the year 1822, he devoted much of his time to writing lyric versions for foreign music, till 1841, when he became acquainted with Dr. Felix Mendelssohn Bartholdy, who, on seeing some of his productions, made him his collaborator; which he continued to be until Mendelssohn's lamented death in 1847.

Among the works written by Mr. Bartholomew for Mendelssohn are:—the "Elijah," "Athalie," "Praise Jehovah," "Œdipus Coloneus," "Antigone," &c.; for the last-named, he was presented with the gold medal of merit by the late King of Prussia. Mr. Bartholomew has also written for Mr. Costa the libretti, or words to be sung, of the Oratorios "Eli" and "Naaman."

"Praise Jehovah! bow before Him."—No. 148.

This fine psalm is from a sacred cantata, written at the express desire of Mendelssohn, the composer of the music, to supersede the words of the Romish "Lauda Sion." This psalm was written in 1847.

"Lord, from my bed again I rise."—No. 931.

And—

"This night I lift my heart to Thee."—No. 910.

These hymns for morning and evening are the beautiful and appropriate words put by Mr. Bartholomew into the mouth of Samuel in the Oratorio of "Eli," for which Mr. Costa has written music as devotional as it is beautiful and simple. They were written in 1854.

HENRY FRANCIS LYTE, M.A.
1793—1847.

THIS hymn-writer of our own time was born at Kelso, June the 1st, 1793. After receiving some schooling at Protoro, he entered Trinity College, Dublin, in 1812. There he was successful on three occasions in competing for the English prize poem; and as his means were limited, he found the money thus obtained useful in assisting him to pursue his studies.

He had at first intended to follow the medical profession, but altering his purpose, he entered the Church. He was episcopally ordained in 1815, and entered upon a curacy in the neighbourhood of Wexford. In 1817 he removed to Marazion. Although a Christian minister, Lyte was up to this time worldly in his manner of life, and a stranger to vital religion; but in the year 1818 he was sent for by a neighbouring clergyman, who felt that he was dying, and who felt also, to his great distress, that he was unpardoned and unprepared. Together they pored over the Scriptures, and especially the writings of Paul, and together they came to the knowledge of Christian doctrine, and to the possession of Christian peace. "He died," says Lyte, "happy under the belief, that though he had deeply erred, there was *One* whose death and sufferings would atone for his delinquencies, and be accepted for all that he had incurred." And he adds, "I was greatly affected by the whole matter, and brought to look at life and its issue with a different eye than before; and I began to study my Bible, and preach in another manner than I had previously done." Having taken charge of the family of his departed friend, his increased anxieties proved too much for his feeble constitution, and he found it necessary to commence those travels in search of health, which had afterwards often to be repeated.

In 1819 he removed to Lymington, Hants. During his stay there he composed many "Tales on the Lord's Prayer," but these were not published till the year 1826. In the year 1823 he entered upon the perpetual curacy of Lower Brixham, Devon, which he held till his death, labouring faithfully, for nearly a quarter of a century, amongst its rough seafaring population. He was zealous in his parochial duties, and took special pains to train a band of seventy or eighty voluntary teachers, who taught several hundred children in the Sunday-school. Nor were his labours in vain, the rough material was wrought upon, and many of the hardy children of the deep became his sons in the faith.

In 1833 he published his "Poems chiefly Religious," and in 1834 a metrical version of the Psalms, entitled "The Spirit of the Psalms;" and in 1846 he published the "Poems of Henry Vaughan, with a Memoir." Increasing weakness of constitution having rendered rest and change necessary, he travelled for some time on the Continent; recreating himself by the production of some poems on his way. It was while thus travelling that he was overtaken by death, at Nice, in 1847. He is buried in the English cemetery there. His end was that of the happy Christian poet,—singing while strength lasted, and then waiting quiescently till, rising from the sleep of death, he should with renewed energies join in the hallelujahs of heaven.

His sole cause of regret was, that weakness and early death prevented him from accomplishing more for Christ. To this he thus pensively refers, in a piece entitled "Declining Days:"—

> "Might verse of mine inspire
>   One virtuous aim, one high resolve impart;
> Light in one drooping soul a hallowed fire,
>   Or bind one broken heart.
>
> "Death would be sweeter then,
>   More calm my slumber 'neath the silent sod;
> Might I thus live to bless my fellowmen,
>   Or glorify my God.
>
>   *   *   *   *   *
>
> "O Thou! whose touch can lend
>   Life to the dead, Thy quickening grace supply;
> And grant me, swanlike, my last breath to spend
>   In song that may not die!"

For several of these particulars we are indebted to an interesting narrative by A. M. M. H., published in 1850, whence we also learn that the poet was united in marriage to Anne, only daughter of Rev. W. Maxwell, D.D., of Bath.

In his "Spirit of the Psalms," 1834, Lyte says, "he endeavoured to give the *spirit* of each psalm in such a compass as the public taste would tolerate, and to furnish sometimes, when the length of the original would admit of it, an almost literal translation, sometimes a kind of spiritual paraphrase, at others even a brief commentary on the whole psalm."

In illustration of this we may point to

"My trust is in the Lord"—No. 10,

his version of Psalm 11. In it he keeps close to the original, and at the same time gives its spirit.

"Whom should we love like Thee,"—No. 15,

his version of the long eighteenth Psalm, gives effectively in the compass of a few verses the spirit of that Psalm. And

"Praise, Lord, for Thee in Zion waits,"—No. 89,

is a "spiritual paraphrase" of Psalm lxv., and a song of praise very suitable for public worship.

Lyte's hymns are free from harshness, correct in their versification, and always full of Scriptural thought and spiritual meaning. Some of them are of a high order. There were eleven of his hymns in the old "Congregational Hymn Book;" there are twenty in the new.

"Awake ye saints, awake!"—No. 758,

deserves notice as very good.

"O how blest the congregation!—No. 768,

is a general favourite; and

"Abide with me, fast falls the eventide,"—No. 941,

has at once taken its place as a universal favourite. We find in it an impassioned earnestness, and a familiarity with the Master, tender yet free from presumption, that reminds us of the best productions of St. Bernard and Gerhard. It was written when the author was approaching his end. It is the true utterance of a heart deeply feeling the need of Christ's presence, and strong in the confidence that it will not be denied.

HENRY USTICK ONDERDONK, D.D.

"The Spirit to our hearts."—No. 519.

This hymn, given anonymously in the "New Congregational," is by the above-named American prelate of the Protestant Episcopalian Church. It is the 131st in "Selections from the Psalms of David, in metre, with Hymns suited to the Feasts and Fasts of the Church, &c. New York. First edition, 1833." This work contains 124 selections of psalms and 212 hymns, with doxologies. This hymn is said to have been written as early as 1826.

Bishop Onderdonk is the author of several hymns. Before his consecration he was rector of St. Ann's Church, Brooklyn, New York. He was consecrated bishop, at Philadelphia, on the 25th October, 1827, and was at first assistant bishop to Bishop White, in Pennsylvania, so long as that prelate survived. A remonstrance against the appointment of Bishop Onderdonk, in 1827, was presented by some clergy and other persons, chiefly on the ground that the nomination of another minister had been improperly passed over; but the remonstrance was not regarded. An account of the whole matter is in the British Museum. Bishop Onderdonk is the author of "Episcopacy Examined and Re-examined," 1835, and of some published sermons.

FELICIA DOROTHEA HEMANS.
1794—1835.

This accomplished poetess was born at Liverpool, where her father, whose name was Browne, was engaged in mercantile pursuits. During her childhood, the family removed to the neighbourhood of Abergele, in North Wales. As a child, Miss Browne was encouraged to exercise her poetical talent by her mother, who was of Venetian descent, her father having been the commercial representative of Venice, at Liverpool. Mrs. Browne was a woman of taste and education, and the young poetess having such encouragement, published her first volume of poems as early as 1808.

In 1812, Miss Browne became the wife of Captain Hemans, and in the same year she published her second volume, "The Domestic Affections." Some years after, Captain Hemans, whose health had suffered in his military campaigns, went to reside in Italy, to have the advantage of its milder climate, leaving Mrs. Hemans, with her five sons, in North Wales, where she lived with her mother in the neighbourhood of St. Asaph.

Mrs. Hemans excelled as much in her linguistic acquirements as in her poetical productions, and she made poetical translations from the works of several of the most eminent of the continental writers. Of her earlier works may be mentioned "The Restoration of the Works of Art to Italy," 1815; "Tales and Historic Scenes," 1819; and about the same time, two poems, called "The Sceptic," and "Modern Greece." Her poem of "Dartmoor" obtained the prize from the Royal Society of Literature, in 1821. In 1823, she published "The Siege of Valencia, &c;" and in the same year appeared her first dramatic work, "The Vespers of Palermo." This piece was written at the suggestion of her friend, Bishop Heber, another of our well-known hymn-writers, but it met with little success. In 1827, she published a volume consisting of her "Lays of many Lands," and her "Forest Sanctuary." This last is said to be her best long poem. The following year appeared her "Records of Women." During the latter months of 1833 she was occupied in arranging and preparing for publication the three collections of her poems, which were published in the spring and summer of 1834— "Hymns for Childhood," "National Lyrics and Songs for Music," and "Scenes and Hymns of Life."

It was remarked that her religious impressions became stronger, and her poems more tinctured with religious thought and sentiment as she increased in years; and a tinge of melancholy was given to her life by the difficulty she experienced in obtaining a suitable training for her sons, and by the other difficulties she met with during the prolonged absence of the natural protector of her family. She died in Dublin, May 12th, 1835. Her too anxious life, weighed down by accumulated cares, being at length attacked by severe illness, prematurely succumbed in the unequal strife. A volume of "Poetical Remains" was published after her death.

Unsuccessful in tragedy, her short pieces, such as "The Better Land," and "The Pilgrim Fathers," are well-known, and in their own order are of great excellence. Without much profundity or force, she is yet not wanting in poetical feeling and good taste; and where she avoids her one defect, monotony, she is sure to please by the justness of her sentiment and the ease and beauty of her expression.

There is one hymn by Mrs. Hemans in the "New Congregational Hymn Book," a touching piece in an unusual and difficult metre:—

"Lowly and solemn be."—No. 721.

It is given at page 470, volume 2, of Mrs. Hemans' collected works, edited by her sister, 1847. It forms part of a funeral dirge given at the close of a poem in blank verse, and headed, "The Funeral-day of Sir Walter Scott." (He died on the 21st September, 1832.) The poem begins—

"A glorious voice hath ceased!"

The funeral song consists of nine stanzas, of which four are given in the "New Congregational" without alteration.

EDWARD SWAINE.
1795—1862.

THE larger proportion of our hymns have been written by Christian ministers of different denominations, and for some we are indebted to those who have held less prominent offices in the Christian Church. The subject of this sketch filled, with efficiency, for forty years, the office of deacon of a Congregational Church. He was born of pious parents, in the city of London, September 21st, 1795. He was an only son, but had two sisters who survived him. While very young his parents removed to Piccadilly, where they carried on their business, and where he continued it, and spent his life. He was a delicate child, and long remembered the painful effect of the unsympathizing manner of his treatment at the school at Peckham, to which he was sent. His education was defective in the length of time devoted to it, as well as in its character. He was removed from school in his fourteenth year, but having good natural abilities and great perseverance, he made amends for his early disadvantages by subsequent study.

His parents were originally Episcopalians, but being unable to obtain sittings at St. James's Church, which was near to their place of business, they went to Orange Street Chapel, where the Liturgy was read and the Gospel preached. Edward Swaine's pious mother, to whom he was much attached, exercised a most salutary influence over her only son; so that he attended the preaching of the Gospel with the advantage of home preparation. In the course of his attendance at Orange Street Chapel, he heard a preacher who was only a temporary supply, and whose name even is now forgotten. Casting the seed without knowledge of the soil, this sower was honoured to sow one germ that "lived and abode for ever," and, at the age of twenty, Mr. Swaine became a communicant in Orange Street Chapel. He had previously been a teacher in the Sunday-school; and when, in 1823, the Christian Church was formed for which Craven Chapel was erected, Mr. Swaine was one of its first members, and elected one of its first deacons—an office he filled with honour for about forty years, including the period of the long and successful pastorate of Dr. Leifchild, from 1831 to 1854, and a portion of the pastorate of the Rev. John Graham, who attended him in his dying moments and preached his funeral sermon.

Mr. Swaine was a man of clear and strong intellect, decided in his own views and zealous in maintaining them, and he used his talents diligently in the Master's service, giving time and thought and money to those benevolent and Christian objects that enlisted his generous sympathies. He was also a man of public spirit, and not backward in wielding his pen against any manifest national or social wrongs. As a deacon of one of the largest and most active Churches in London, his official duties were very onerous, and, in addition, he was one of the directors of the London Missionary Society, and the founder and chairman of the "Pastors' Insurance Aid Society;" and whatever office he undertook he discharged fully, whatever demands it might make on his time and means.

As a prose writer Mr. Swaine wrote tractates on "Church-rates" and on "Free Schools," and a work entitled "No Popery: the Cry Examined," which had reached a fifth edition in 1850; and "Objections to the Doctrine of Israel's Future Restoration to Palestine," &c., second edition, 1850.

His dying testimony was in harmony with the devoutness of his life. He was patient in suffering, and calm and grateful, though feeling the pain of separation from his wife and children and grandchildren, and many others who were very dear to him. To the Rev. J. Graham he said:—" My dear pastor, I have had a speculative mind; but I now rest in Jesus, *Jesus*, JESUS, who came into the world to save His people from their sins. I wish to be true. May God save me from entering into His presence with insincerity or sham. Nothing but the blood of Jesus Christ and the infinite compassion of God could save such a sinner as I." And shortly before death, on awaking, he murmured the words, " Salvation—grace." Without a struggle, he passed peacefully away on the 22nd of April, 1862.

Mr. Swaine printed, in 1839, a work entitled "The Hand of God, a Fragment, with Poems, Hymns, and Versions of Psalms." This was not published, but was printed for private circulation. He also wrote, at different times, during many years, some very pleasing family and sacred pieces, and occasionally a piece on political matters for the newspapers.

"Lord Jesus, let Thy watchful care."—No. 902.

This is the last four verses of a hymn written for emigrants and colonists, at the suggestion of the committee who were preparing the "New Congregational Hymn Book," 1855.

"Hail! blessed communion of love."—No. 906.

This also was written for the same committee as a Sacramental Hymn.

WILLIAM HILEY BATHURST, M.A.

Born 1796.

THE subject of this brief sketch is a son of Earl Bathurst, known before as the Hon. Charles Bragge, M.P. for Bristol. At Cleve Dale, near Bristol, young William was born, August 28, 1796. He was educated first at Winchester School and afterwards at Christchurch College, Oxford. He was successful at the University, and in 1818 graduated B.A. In the following year he entered the Church, and in 1820 he was presented to the rectory of Barwick-in-Elmet, a valuable living, about eight miles from Leeds, Yorkshire, and there was attached to it the perpetual curacy of Roundhay, also near Leeds. From 1820 to 1852 he continued to fulfil his parochial duties and to grow in the affections of his parishioners; but at that time the public attention given to the unsatisfactory condition of the Prayer Book, and especially the difficulty of conscientiously using the Baptismal and Burial Services, so impressed his mind that he resigned his valuable living rather than do what he could not fully approve. Mr. Bathurst resided from 1852 to 1863 at Darleydale, near Matlock, Derbyshire, and since then he has removed to Lydney Park, Gloucestershire, having come into possession of the estates of his father the Earl.

In 1827, Mr. Bathurst published "An Essay on the Limits of Human Knowledge," and in 1831, his "Psalms and Hymns for Public and Private Use." All the hymns, 206 in number, are original, and the greater number of the psalms are also original. In the year 1849, and before leaving Barwick, he published "The Georgics of Virgil: Translated by W. H. B." And in the same year, "Metrical Musings; or, Thoughts on Sacred Subjects in Verse." He also published a sermon in 1863. A second edition of his "Psalms and Hymns" appeared in 1842, and several of his hymns have been introduced into collections. We cannot assign to his hymns more than the praise of careful versification and pious sentiment. Where they do not greatly please they never offend, and some have taken their place as useful hymns for public worship. There are four hymns attributed to Bathurst in the "New Congregational Hymn Book," Nos. 432, 440, 836, and 927.

"Eternal Spirit, by whose power,"—No. 432,

will be acknowledged by all to be a good and valuable hymn. And—

"O Lord, defend us, as of old,"—No. 109,

given without name in the "New Congregational Hymn Book," is by him, and bears date 1830.

MRS. JOSIAH CONDER.

THERE is one beautiful Saturday Evening Hymn in the "New Congregational Hymn Book" by this authoress, the widow of the well-known author, Josiah Conder.

"The hours of evening close."—No. 949.

This is hymn 522 in the "Old Congregational" (where there are three others from her pen), and it is believed to have been written about the year 1833, when that collection was being compiled by her husband. This hymn, valuable from any author, has a new beauty when we accept it from a Christian mother, who from principle applied herself to home duties, when her talents invited her to an easier and more brilliant course. The "forms of outward care" and the "thought for many things" over which the Sabbath calm was to prevail were realities to her as they will be to many who will sing this hymn, and she had a mother's love, as they will have for the flock which the "guardian Shepherd" would "fold to sleep."

Mrs. Conder shrank from publicity, and refrained from publishing any separate work; but she wrote pieces for the

"Annuals" that were so much in fashion some years ago, and she contributed some pieces to her husband's volumes of poems, and there are seven hymns by her (of which the above is one) at the close of a work edited by her son, the Rev. E. R. Conder, M.A., of Leeds, and entitled "Hymns of Praise, Prayer, and Devout Meditation, by Josiah Conder," 1856. Mrs. Conder, whose maiden name was Eliza Thomas, is the daughter of Mr. Roger Thomas, of Southgate, and granddaughter on the mother's side of Roubiliac, the sculptor. She was united in marriage to the late Mr. Josiah Conder in 1815.

COOPER.

"Father of heaven! whose love profound."—No. 447.

This is the first hymn in "Cotterill's Selection of Psalms and Hymns," of which several editions were published between 1810 and 1819, and of which there is a further account under "Thomas Cotterill, M.A." The name Cooper has been given to this hymn in MS. in some collections, but it is not known on what authority. The hymn is without name in the "New Congregational."

CORNELIUS ELVEN.

Born 1797.

"With broken heart and contrite sigh."—No. 530.

We are indebted to the author of this excellent hymn for information of its date and occasion. It was written by him in January, 1852, along with other hymns to be used with the Revival Sermons, then being preached to his own congregation.

The Rev. Cornelius Elven is pastor of a Baptist Church at Bury St. Edmund's, Suffolk. He has held that position for forty-five years, and is now in his seventieth year. His devoted labours have been crowned with a very great blessing. During the forty-five years of his pastorate, the Church under his care has increased from forty members to over six hundred. Mr.

Elven has not published any works in prose or poetry, but has contributed numerous articles to periodicals.

THOMAS BINNEY.

Born about 1798.

This eminent city minister, who is a prince amongst thinkers, and who is not unknown to the general public, is an influential Congregational minister, and a conspicuous ornament of the denomination to which he belongs. For nearly forty years he has drawn around him, at his well-known chapel in the metropolis, many of the most earnest and thoughtful amongst the opening minds of the time ; and not a few Christian ministers and other men of influence attribute to Mr. Binney, under God, their first spiritual impulse and their subsequent moral moulding and nurture, and the denomination to which he belongs has found in him an able and willing friend of its institutions. Especially in the Colonial Missionary Society, and in the Congregational Union, have his advocacy and assistance been found most valuable. In the latter movement, he took a deep interest at its commencement in 1831, and he was chairman for the year in 1848.

Thomas Binney was born of humble parentage, about the year 1798, at Newcastle-on-Tyne, where he was in his youth occupied in a shop. He received his education for the ministry at Wymondley College. His first pastorate was at Newport, Isle of Wight, where he commenced his labours as a Congregational minister in 1823. Thence he removed in 1829 to undertake his life-work as pastor of the "King's Weigh House Chapel," then in Eastcheap. The new King's Weigh House, Fish-street-hill, was erected in 1834. Mr. Binney's life has been diversified by two important visits. In 1845 he paid a visit to America and the Canadas, and in 1857 he went for a visit of nearly two years to Australia, being attracted thither in part by the settlement of his sons there. While there, the clergy of the Episcopal Church wished to welcome him to their pulpits. This led to an important correspondence between Mr. Binney and the Bishop of Adelaide, and during his visit Mr. Binney published a work on "The Bishop of Adelaide's Idea of the Church of the Future." This work was afterwards published, with additions, in London, with the title, "Lights and Shadows of Church Life in Australia, including Thoughts on some Things at Home," 1860. On his return, Mr. Binney resumed his pastorate at the Weigh House, where he still continues it. In 1866, the growing demand for space for railway purposes necessitated the purchase of the honoured pile for removal. Mr. Binney has received from Aberdeen a degree of LL.D., which he does not use. He takes an active interest in several benevolent and religious institutions, and especially in New College, London. He has been for many years one of the preachers of the Merchants' Lecture.

Especially eminent as a powerful and eloquent preacher, Mr. Binney is scarcely less eminent as a writer. Without seeking to be an author, and without adequate time for authorship in his crowded life, he has in spite of himself become an extensive book producer. His lectures and sermons have been asked for in print, and have sometimes on revision grown into books.

The following are some of his works:—"Life of the Rev. Stephen Morell," 1826; a discourse on the "Ultimate Design of the Christian Ministry," 1827; pamphlets discussing religious questions, and signed "Fiat Justitia," about 1830.

An address on the laying of the first stone of his new chapel, Dec. 12, 1834, attracted much attention, and he subsequently published it, entitled, "Dissent not Schism," and similar forcible productions, explaining and vindicating the position of Congregational dissenters. One of the best known of these is his "Conscientious Clerical Nonconformity." 1848; fifth edition, 1860. He is also the author of papers on "The Great Gorham Case," and of "An Argument on the Levitical Law, touching the Marriage of a Deceased Wife's

Sister;" also of "The Closet and the Church," 1849, and of "Preface and Conclusion to a Chapter on Liturgies, by C. W. Baird," 1853. He has taken a deep interest in the improvement of public worship. In his own chapel, whither many go to hear the great sermon, the other portions of the service are conducted in a masterly manner. There chanting was introduced before it was practised in other Congregational churches, and without the aid of music. The "Service of Song" is of a high order. Mr. Binney is the author of "Service of Song in the House of the Lord," 1848. Two of the lectures delivered by Mr. Binney to the "Young Men's Christian Association," at Exeter Hall, have been expanded by him into books—the first, on "Sir Thomas Fowell Buxton, Bart., a Study for Young Men," delivered in 1849; and the other, on "Is it Possible to Make the Best of both Worlds?" delivered in 1852. Numerous editions of this latter work have been sold. Mr. Binney is also author of discourses on the eleventh chapter of Hebrews, entitled, "The Practical Power of Faith," 1830. This the author justly regards as one of his principal works. It has reached a third edition. He also edited the "Tower Church Sermons." They were preached by Monod, Krummacher, and himself, at Belvidere, Erith.

His later works are, "Money: a Popular Exposition in Rough Notes," 1864; "Life of St. Paul," 1866, and several of his sermons have been published separately. Two sermons, occasioned by the death and funeral of the late Rev. T. Guyer, of Ryde, and entitled "The Spirit admitted to the Heavenly House; the Body denied a Grave," published in 1846, excited much interest at the time of their publication.

"Eternal Light! eternal Light!"—No. 261.

This is Mr. Binney's only contribution to the "New Congregational Hymn Book," where the correct text is given. The hymn is in an unusual metre, and has in it traces of the sublimity and force of mind which characterize the author's discourses. Mr. Binney has kindly supplied the following information:

"It was written about forty years ago, and was set to music and published by Power, of the Strand, on behalf of some charitable object to which the profits went. It was some little time since set to music also by Mr. Burnett, of Highgate. It has appeared, I believe, in one or two books of sacred poetry, and in a mutilated state in a hymn-book in America." Mr. Binney has not written many hymns, but there is one by him in "The New Hymn Book" (General Baptist, 1851). It is a Sabbath evening hymn (No. 99 in that collection), and begins—

"Holy Father! whom we praise."

CHARLES BRADLEY.

"Jesus, and didst Thou condescend."—No. 351.

THIS is the forty-second hymn in a collection by the above author, entitled, "Psalms and Hymns, selected and arranged for Public Worship," Clapham, 1830. At that time, the Rev. C. Bradley was rector of St. James's Church, Clapham, where this hymn-book was used. The collection consists of 252 Hymns and the Psalms. The names of the authors are not given, but Mr. Bradley has kindly informed the writer of this work that the hymn is not by himself. The text given in his collection is Luke xviii. 35—43—the "Restoring of the Blind Beggar," and the last verse of the hymn begins—

"And didst Thou save a trembling frame."

The hymn is taken from J. Curtis's "Union Collection," 1827, where it is signed " Am—a," probably " Amelia."

JOHN REYNELL WREFORD, D.D., F.S.A.

A PLEASING national hymn, the last in the "New Congregational Hymn Book"—

"Lord, while for all mankind we pray,"—No. 1000,

is by this author, who contributed fifty-five hymns, including this one, to the Unitarian collection by Dr. J. R. Beard, entitled, "A Collection of Hymns for Public and Private Worship," 1837; and who is the author of numerous hymns and poetical pieces, which have appeared in periodicals in England and America. Hymn 1000 was written in the year 1837, about the time of the Queen's Accession to the Throne, and published with other loyal and patriotic pieces drawn from the author by that joyful occasion.

Dr. Wreford was educated for the ministry at Manchester College, York, and on leaving that institution in 1825, entered upon his public duties as co-pastor with the Rev. John Kentish, minister of the New Meeting House, Birmingham. In consequence of the failure of his voice, Dr. Wreford was obliged to retire from the active duties of the ministry in 1831. He then devoted himself to the work of tuition, in which he has been very successful for many years. He has now given up that profession, and lives in comparative retirement near Bristol; still, however, employing his productive pen in literary pursuits. Dr. Wreford does not, and never did, belong to the modern school of Unitarians, with whom he has no sympathy, but considers himself as connected with the good old body of "English Presbyterians, who always carefully repudiated all sectarian names and doctrinal distinctions."

Among his prose works are a "Sketch of the History of Presbyterian Nonconformity in Birmingham," and a translation from the French of "A Discourse on the Authenticity and Divine Origin of the Old Testament, with Notes and Illustrations by J. E. Cellérier." He is also one of the editors of the "Sermons by the late Rev. Henry Acton, of Exeter; with a Memoir of his Life:" and the author of some archæological papers and some sermons; and in poetry he has published "Lays of Loyalty;" "Songs of the Sea;" "Songs descriptive of the Christian Graces;" "Lays of Devotion," 1851; "A Memorial of Song," 1855; and he has in preparation (1866) his "Poems: including Hymns, Sonnets, and Lyrics."

CHARLOTTE ELLIOTT.

"O Thou, the contrite sinner's Friend."—No. 399.
"Just as I am—without one plea."—No. 517.
"My God, my Father, while I stray."—No. 599.

It is to be regretted that of the last of these (No. 599), an inaccurate or altered text is given in the "New Congregational," and a verse is omitted. The talented and excellent authoress has informed the writer of this work that Sir Roundell Palmer's text, as given in "The Book of Praise," is the correct one; yet the text in the "New Congregational" is the same as that given in her brother's collection. The hymn was written in 1834. No. 547, with its rich evangelical doctrine, its candour and simplicity, its personal confession of sin and expressions of trust, has taken a great hold upon the public mind. It bears date 1836. No. 399, bearing date 1837, appeared in 1843, in the collection of the late Rev. Henry Venn Elliott, an elder brother of Miss Elliott's, and himself a hymn-writer. In that collection it was by mistake attributed to Wesley, and the error followed it into other collections. Miss Elliott is sister to the Rev. E. B. Elliott, author of the "Horæ Apocalypticæ." She formerly resided at Torquay, where the neighbourhood benefited by her piety and benefactions, and is now residing, at an advanced age and in infirm health, at Brighton. She is the author of several hymns. Her aim in hymn-writing has been usefulness in Christ's service, and God has greatly blessed her labours.

JOHN HARRIS, D.D.
1802—1856.

The subject of this sketch rose from an humble origin to the highest eminence as an author, preacher, and college tutor. He was born on the 8th of March, 1802, in the village of Ugborough, Devon. He was the eldest of eight children, and being a delicate child he was left at liberty to follow the bent of his early taste for reading and contemplation. His father carried on a small business as a tailor and draper. To his pious mother the contemplative boy was much attached and much indebted. She died when he was about fourteen years of age.

About a year before her death his parents removed to Bristol. They attended at first at the cathedral, but on one Sunday, owing to a heavy fall of rain, they went to the Tabernacle, where a few months after both parents became members of the Church, and the children became scholars in the Sunday-school. Young Harris's first public duty was to take part in a prayer-meeting conducted by the boys of this school, and he soon after gave an address at Baptist Mills, on occasion of the death of one of the scholars. Towards the close of the year 1816 he was brought under the notice of the late Mr. Wills, the manager of the Tabernacle, by composing a poem on the perfections of God, after hearing a lecture on astronomy. Mr. Wills got the lines inserted in Felix Farley's *Bristol Journal*, on the 11th January, 1817, and became the friend and helper of the young poet. In his sixteenth or seventeenth year, young Harris became a member of the Church at the Tabernacle.

At this time he assisted his father in the shop, but spent much of the night in mental improvement. While still young he preached in the villages round the city, in connection with the Bristol Itinerant Society, and became exceedingly popular as the "boy preacher." Mr. Wills introduced him to the late Mr. Thomas Wilson, and after passing a year in preparatory study under the Rev. Walter Scott, at Rowell, he was admitted to Hoxton Academy. There he pursued his academic studies in such a way as to awaken high expectations in those who marked his course.

In 1825 he left college, and became the pastor of the Congregational Church at Epsom, over which he presided for twelve years. The healthful neighbourhood suited his delicate constitution, and the limited character of his position left him room to prepare for the greater work of his later years.

At length the time came when he was to take the place for which he had prepared. In the year 1838, he became the Theological Tutor and President of Cheshunt College, and in the same year he received the degree of Doctor of Divinity from Brown University, America. In the year 1843, he suffered from a partial failure of sight, which was relieved by a winter spent in Italy. In 1850, he left Cheshunt to become the Theological Tutor and Principal of New College, London. After continuing his duties there, along with the fulfilment of many public services, he was tempted by the return of robust health, at the close of 1856, to be more venturesome than usual, and in consequence he took a severe cold, which was soon followed by dangerous and at length fatal symptoms. In the closing hours of his life the fifty-first Psalm was on his lips, and he uttered also, "Lord Jesus, receive my spirit!" "O God, be merciful to me!" He died on the afternoon of Sunday, December the 21st, 1856, in the fifty-fifth year of his age.

Dr. Harris was eminent as a preacher and author. He was possessed of great refinement of taste, devoutness of feeling, and eloquence of expression. In society none were more condescending, gracious, and urbane than he. In the pulpit he was a great preacher, and the delivery of his principal sermons, ordinarily read with eloquence, was looked forward to as an event. Without the strength of Chalmers, he possessed a refinement and skill of diction, and sometimes an elevation and sublimity of sentiment and thought, all his own; and with the pen he not unfrequently outstripped all competitors, gaining prizes where many other able writers entered into the contest without success. His taste enabled him to avoid whatever would offend; he had talent to use the best thoughts, and to interweave the best words of others; he was a master of happy expressions and pleasing turns of thought; and, where it was necessary, he could bear all before him with an avalanche of argument and appeal.

Dr. Harris was a voluminous as well as a very able writer. He was one of the editors of the "Biblical Review," and contributed to the "Congregational" and "Evangelical" Magazines. Besides numerous essays and sermons, his principal works were— "The Great Teacher," 1835 : it had reached a tenth edition in 1849; "Mammon," a prize essay, second thousand, 1836; "The Great Commission," third thousand, 1842, and of which four editions were published; "Britannia : or, The Condition and Claims of Sailors," a prize essay, fourth thousand, 1837; "Union : or, the Divided Church made One," second thousand, 1837. He was also the author of a series of theological works —"The Pre-Adamite Earth," 1846 ; "Man Primeval," 1849; "Patriarchy," 1855; and another volume was in preparation, entitled "Theocracy."

Dr. Harris was also a hymn-writer. We have spoken of his early productions. He also published a volume, entitled "The Incarnate One," besides other minor poems.

"Light up this house with glory, Lord."—No. 882.

This was the hymn selected from several supplied by Dr. Harris to the Rev. Henry Allon, for insertion in the "New Congregational Hymn Book," 1855. It is given in the Hymn Book without the name.

JOHN HAMPDEN GURNEY, M.A.
1802—1862.

"Lord, as to Thy dear cross we flee."—No. 353.

THIS is part of a pleasing practical Christian hymn, bearing date 1838. It is found with Mr. Gurney's name in "Psalms and Hymns for Public Worship, selected for some of the Churches in Marylebone," a collection made by him, and which contains twelve other hymns. Mr. Gurney was born in Serjeant's Inn, Fleet Street, August 15th, 1802. He was the eldest son of Sir John Gurney, one of the Barons of the Exchequer.

He studied at Trinity College, Cambridge, where he graduated B.A. 1824, and M.A. 1828. He was admitted to deacon's orders in 1827, and a priest in 1828. He studied law for a time, but at length gave the preference to the Christian ministry. He was from 1827 to 1844, curate at Lutterworth. While there several incumbencies were offered to him, but he refused out of regard to what he believed was the interest of that place. In 1847, he was appointed to the district rectory of St. Mary's, Marylebone, an appointment he held till his death in 1862. He declined the offer of the rectory of the mother church. He was also a prebend of St. Paul's. He took a deep interest in the early progress of the Religious Tract Society, and is mentioned in their "Jubilee Memorial" as having "edited and paid for the stereotype plates of 'Baxter's Family Book.'" He was also an active member of the committee of the Society for the Promotion of Christian Knowledge. He was a man of great public spirit, very active and useful in his public labours, and unstinted in his munificence, though simple and self-denying in his own private life. Dr. Meyrick Goulburn, in his funeral sermon, pays a very high tribute to his memory. He died in London, March 8, 1862.

He was the author of numerous lectures and sermons, and of "Church Psalmody: Hints for the Improvement of a Collection of Hymns, published by the Society for Promoting Christian Knowledge," 1853. He also wrote several "Series of Historical Sketches," 1852—1858; "Chapters from French History, &c.," 1862; and "The Pastor's Last Words, being the last four sermons preached by J. H. G.," 1862, &c.

MATTHEW BRIDGES.

"Crown Him with many crowns."—No. 413.

This is part of a hymn called the "Song of the Seraphs." It is found at page 62 of a small book of hymns, entitled "The Passion of Jesus," 1852. Mr. Bridges had at that time become a Roman Catholic. In the preface to a small work, entitled "Hymns of the Heart, for the use of Catholics," 1848, and containing twenty-two hymns by himself, he expresses regret for having ever used his feeble pen against that Holy Apostolic Church, which by Divine grace he has latterly been able to join, after eight years spent in investigating her claims.

Mr. Bridges' hymns are very beautiful, and often give expression to sentiments dear to the hearts of Christians of all denominations. He is the author of several works: "Jerusalem Regained, a Poem," 1825 ; "The Roman Empire under Constantine the Great," 1828 ; "Babbicombe ; or, Visions of Memory, with other Poems," 1842 ; "Popular Ancient and Modern Histories in 1855-6 ;" "Report of the Discussion between J. Baylee and Matthew Bridges," 1856 ; "An Earnest Appeal to Evangelical Episcopalians, &c., on the State of Parties in the Anglican Establishment," 1864 ; and other works.

DARBY.

Vide under the following name—

JAMES GEORGE DECK.

"It is Thy hand, my God."—No. 600.

This hymn, erroneously attributed in the "New Congregational Hymn Book" to "Darby," is found at page 34 of "Joy in Departing : a Memoir of the Conversion and Last Days of Augustus James Clarke, who fell asleep in Jesus, May 2nd, 1845. By J. G. Deck. London. Second edition, 1847." This little book is a very interesting account of the last days of the son of a brother-officer, Lieutenant-Colonel A. Clarke, who was entrusted to Mr. Deck when he came to England for his health, in 1835, to be educated with his own children. At ten years of age this lovely child was a decided Christian, and in his fourteenth year, after being ten years under Mr. Deck's care, his dying testimony combined the simplicity of childhood with the ripe experience of the matured Christian. Hymn 600 was a favourite with the child during his last illness, and he had marked the first and last verses. It is given in the narrative with the following note:—" It was written originally to comfort a bereaved mother and widow in her hour of sorrow, and the Lord made it a comfort to the soul of this young disciple." It was the seventieth, second part in "Psalms and Hymns and Spiritual Songs," a collection without date. We believe the hymn was written in 1843 or 4, as a correspondent has informed us it was written at Wellington, whither Mr. Deck went in 1843.

In the year 1829, Mr. Deck was an officer in the Indian army on field service at Bangalore, where he met with the parents of the child already referred to. In 1835, he was obliged to return to England on account of the failure of his health. In 1843, he went to Wellington, Somerset, where he was the minister of the Brethren's congregation. He was afterwards for a time at Weymouth, and about the year 1852, he went out to New Zealand, where he is now residing.

In 1845, Mr. Deck published the second edition of "A Word of Warning to all who love the Lord Jesus: the Heresy of Mr. Prince, with Extracts from his Letters." In 1850, he published a letter, "On Receiving and Rejecting Brethren from the Table of the Lord." Two years after, he published another letter on the same subject, in which he explained that he had so far altered his views as to admit that scripture justified the corporate rejection of Churches that were not only evil but that refused to repent. A new edition of "Joy in Departing" appeared in 1855.

Mr. Deck has written a considerable number of good Christian hymns. In some, the versification is pleasing, but they do not rise to the level of Montgomery or Cowper. "The Wellington Hymn Book," 1857: a collection of 505 hymns, edited by D. C. Fox, contains twenty-seven hymns by Mr. Deck, of which the above-mentioned hymn (600) is No. 481: and in "Hymns and Spiritual Songs for the Children of God," 1860, edited by John Usticke Scobell, Esq., there are seventeen hymns by him.

HENRY ADDISCOTT.
1806—1860.

This useful Congregational minister was born, at Devonport, in 1806. Favoured by the teaching and influence of pious parents, and led to thoughtfulness by a severe affliction, he was brought to religious decision, and early joined the church at Mount Street, Devonport.

In 1832, he sought admission to the Western College, as a student for the ministry, but renewed illness threatened to prevent his entrance. At this juncture, the secretary of the College, the Rev. J. Bounsall, kindly arranged for the young candidate to reside with him till his strength was sufficient to enable him to enter on his college duties. In 1837, Mr. Addiscott commenced his first pastorate at Torquay. In the following year, he removed to Maidenhead. and in 1843, to Taunton, the town where he remained till his death, and with which his name was usually connected, and where his indefatigable labours were, by the Divine blessing, attended with much success; so that the Christian Church over which he presided was consolidated and built up. Mr. Addiscott was a man of much public spirit, and the warm advocate of every good cause. In particular, the Dissenters' Proprietary School, Taunton, owes its origin mainly to his advocacy. It was while on a journey in the North for the purpose of advocating the interests of the Western College, that this excellent minister was overtaken by his fatal attack. Walking in the streets of Liverpool on October 2, 1860, the hemorrhage he had previously suffered from returned upon him, and before he could reach his hotel his spirit had departed.

Mr. Addiscott was not known as an author, but he contributed one good hymn—admirable for its unity—to the " New Congregational Hymn Book "—

" And is there, Lord, a cross for me ? "—No. 650.

JOSEPH ANSTICE, M.A.
1808—1836.

"In all things like Thy brethen Thou."—No. 354.

THIS is No. 21 in "Hymns by the Rev. Joseph Anstice, M.A. London, 1836"—a selection containing fifty-four hymns, published by his widow after his death, and privately printed. In the original it begins thus—

"Lord, Thou in all things like wert made
To us, yet free from sin."

and there are two more verses.

"O Lord, how happy should we be."—No. 593.

This is hymn 44 in Mr. Anstice's collection, where two more verses are given. These beautiful spiritual hymns are erroneously attributed to Keble in the "New Congregational." Probably the mistake arose from the fact that twenty-seven of Professor Anstice's hymns were, in 1841, printed in "The Child's Christian Year," which was recommended by Keble, and sometimes supposed to be his, though in fact it was edited by Miss Yonge, of Winchester, and these hymns supposed to be by Keble had been in print as Professor Anstice's, in 1836. We are deeply indebted to the widow of Professor Anstice for the following interesting and affecting account of his brief but brilliant course :—"Professor Anstice was born in 1808. He was the second son of William Anstice, Esq., of Madeley Wood, Shropshire, but received all his early education at Enmore, near Bridgewater, in Somersetshire, of which village his uncle, the Rev. John Poole, formerly fellow of Oriel College, Oxford, was rector. Mr. Poole had great talent for teaching, and had obtained considerable local celebrity by the admirable way in which he had organized his village school. At that time he was unmarried, and his mother and several maiden sisters lived with him. In this parsonage Professor Anstice passed a very happy and profitable childhood. At thirteen years of age he was sent to Westminster, where he was elected a King's Scholar, and after the usual school course, he became a student of Christ Church, Oxford. There his academical course was very successful as he gained the two English prizes, and a double first-class. He also greatly enjoyed the social advantages of the place, the Debating and Essay Societies, and the friendship of many young men of his own age, who have since distinguished themselves in their several careers. When only twenty-two he was named Professor of Classical Literature, at King's College, London, then just established; and he soon after married. In 1835 he was obliged to give up his appointment on account of failing health. He took a house at Torquay in the autumn of that year, and died on the 29th of the next February, 1836. His only daughter, born a few months after his death, is married to Col. the Honourable H. H. Clifford, third son of the late Lord Clifford, of Chudleigh.

"The hymns were all dictated to his wife during the last few weeks of his life, and were composed just at the period of the day (the afternoon) when he most felt the oppression of his illness, all his brighter morning hours being given to pupils up to the very day of his death."

Professor Anstice was the author of "Richard Cœur de Lion," a prize poem recited in the Theatre, Oxford, June 18th, 1828; and of the Oxford English Prize Essay on "The Influence of the Roman Conquests upon Literature and the Arts in Rome." He also published "An Introductory Lecture," delivered at King's College, London, October 17th, 1831. His principal work was "Selections from the Choice Poetry of the Greek Dramatic Writers, translated into English Verse, 1832."

WILLIAM LINDSAY ALEXANDER, D.D.

Born 1808.

This eminent divine, the greatest ornament of Independency in Scotland, was born at Leith, August 24th, 1808. After being educated under Dr. Jamieson, at East Linton, he spent three sessions at the University of Edinburgh, and two at St. Andrews. He also had the advantage of coming under the powerful influence of Dr. Chalmers, whose lectures he attended. At an early age, Mr. Alexander began to distinguish himself as a writer, and obtained prizes for essays on subjects in moral philosophy. After finishing his University course, he was for four years classical tutor in the Independent College, Blackburn. He first pursued his ministry at Newington Chapel, Liverpool, but in 1835 he went to Argyle Chapel, Edinburgh, to undertake the important pastorate, which he still carries on. His labours were so successful, and his Church and congregation increased so much, that it was found necessary to erect a new church. In 1861, a more eligible site having been obtained, Augustine Church was erected at a cost of nearly £15,000. Since the death of Dr. Wardlaw, in 1853, Dr. Alexander has held, in addition to his pastorate, the Professorship of Theology and Church History in the Theological Hall of the Congregational Churches of Scotland.

Dr. Alexander is a man of extensive and various learning. He is especially skilled in languages, and in Biblical literature, and he is one of the most voluminous and scholarly of living writers. The following are some of his principal works:—" The Connection and Harmony of the Old and New Testaments," being his "Congregational Lecture." It was published in 1841, and the second edition, 1853. "Lectures to Young Men," 1842. "Anglo-catholicism," &c., in reply to "Tracts for the Times," 1843. "Memoir of the Rev. J. Watson," 1845. "Switzerland and the Swiss Churches," notes of a tour, 1846. "The Ancient British Church," 1852. "Christ and Christianity," 1854. "Memoir of Life and Writings of Dr. Wardlaw," 1856. "St. Paul at Athens," 1865. Dr. Alexander has also contributed numerous articles to magazines. He was at one time editor of the "Scottish Congregational Magazine." He was one of the contributors to "Kitto's Cyclopædia of Biblical Literature," in 1847, and he is now editing a new and greatly improved edition of the same valuable work. He also contributed articles to the " Encyclopædia Britannica."

Recently Dr. Alexander has contributed some hymns to the magazines, and some to the " United Presbyterian Hymn Book." He has also written some brief religious poems. There is one good hymn by him in the " New Congregational Hymn Book "—

"From distant corners of our land."—No. 886.

He has kindly supplied its history. It was written some years ago for the annual meeting of the Congregational Union of Scotland, and it is generally printed on the programme of the anniversary meeting, and sung on that occasion. It is a hymn exactly adapted for a meeting of ministers gathered from remote parts, but one in purpose and heart.

Dr. Alexander has printed no volume of poetry; but he prepared a collection of hymns some years ago, known from the name of his church as "The Augustine Hymn Book." This collection contains several of his hymns.

HORATIUS BONAR, D.D.
Born 1808.

This voluminous religious author, best known as Dr. Bonar of Kelso, is a native of Edinburgh, where he studied at the High School, and afterwards at the University. He was ordained to the ministry, at Kelso, in 1837, and has since continued his pastoral labours there. He joined the Free Church of Scotland in 1843. Several of his religious works have become popular, and command a large sale. Amongst his works are :—" The Night of Weeping; or, Words for the Suffering Family of God." This had reached its 45th thousand in 1853. And a sequel volume, " The Morning of Joy," 1850. Also " The Blood of the Cross," 7th edition, 1849. " The Coming and Kingdom of the Lord Jesus Christ," 1849. " Truth and Error," 1846. " Man : his Religion and his World," 1854. " The Desert of Sinai," notes of a journey,

1857. "The Land of Promise," notes of a journey, 1858. "Earth's Thirst and Heaven's Water-springs," 1860. "God's Way of Peace," 1862. "God's Way of Holiness," 1864. "The Word of Promise," 1864. Dr. Bonar is also the editor of several works by other writers, and of numerous useful tracts. He is a contributor to magazines, and is known as editor of the "Journal of Prophecy," and of the "Christian Treasury."

Dr. Bonar is also very favourably known as a religious poet and hymn-writer. He has contributed to hymnology, "The New Jerusalem; a Hymn of the Olden Time," 1852. An account of the various poetical renderings of the well-known hymn, "O mother, dear Jerusalem." His "Hymns of Faith and Hope" appeared in 1857. The preface is dated, "Kelso, December 19th, 1856." It explains that many of the pieces had appeared in journals and elsewhere during the previous twelve years. This work had reached an eighth edition in 1862. The second series of "Hymns of Faith and Hope" was published in 1861. His three hymns in the "New Congregational Hymn Book," Nos. 574, 814, and 928, are taken from the first series of "Hymns of Faith and Hope;" the last mentioned—

"Come, Lord, and tarry not,"—No. 928,

is only part of the original hymn, which consists of fourteen verses. It is suggestive of the author's views on the subject of the second coming of Christ, upon which he has written much.

RAY PALMER, D.D.
Born 1808.

This favourite American sacred poet is an eminent Congregational minister at Albany, New York. Born in Rhode Island, he went at the age of thirteen to Boston, where he spent part of his time at school, and part as a clerk in a draper's shop. After a time he was brought under religious impressions, and became a member of the Park Street Congregational Church, at that time under the care of Dr. S. E. Dwight, son of President Dwight. Having become a Christian, he decided that it was his duty to be a Christian minister. To qualify himself for this, he went first to Philips' Academy, Andover, Massachusetts, and after three years there, to Yale College, New Haven, where he graduated in 1830. After a year's study in New York, he returned to New Haven to spend three years in theological studies. He also assisted at the same time Dr. E. A. Andrews, the author of the well-known Latin Dictionary, in his Young Ladies' Institute.

From 1835 to 1850, Dr. Palmer was pastor of the Central Congregational Church, Bath, State of Maine. And in 1847, to recruit his health, he made a European tour, and on his return published his notes of travel in the "Christian Mirror," at Portland. In 1850 he became pastor of the first Congregational church at Albany, New York, a position he still occupies.

Dr. Palmer is a review writer, and has published sermons and pamphlets. He is also the author of "Spiritual Improvement; or, Aids to Growth in Grace:" and of "Meditations Preparatory to the Communion Service:" and of a work that has had a wide sale, "What is truth; or, Hints on the Formation of Religious Opinions," 1861.

As a translator of hymns from the Latin, Dr. Palmer has been very successful, and for many years his occasional hymns found an appreciative welcome; but it was not till 1865 that he published a volume of "Hymns and Sacred Poems." His hymns are justly prized on both sides of the Atlantic.

There is one hymn by Dr. Palmer in the "New Congregational Hymn Book," a hymn of acknowledged excellence—

"My faith looks up to Thee."—No. 544.

Dr. Belcher relates that Lowell Mason, having applied to Dr. Palmer for a hymn to set to music, he drew this from his pocket. It had been written a few weeks before. The words and music were shortly after published. It appeared in Dr. Andrew Reed's collection in 1841. In a modern American collection it is dated 1830.

HENRY ALFORD, D.D.
Born 1810.

DEAN ALFORD, better known for his *magnum opus*, "The Greek Testament, with Notes," and as an able preacher than as a sacred poet, was born in London, in the year 1810. He was educated at first at Ilminster Grammar School, Somerset, and afterwards studied at Trinity College, Cambridge. He was first-class wrangler and Bell's University scholar B.A. 1832, M.A. 1835, B.D. 1849. His first production was "Poems and Poetical Fragments," published at Cambridge in 1831; "The School of the Heart," in two volumes, published in 1835, went through several editions, and was also published in America.

In 1834, Henry Alford became fellow of Trinity College, Cambridge, and from 1835 to 1853 he held the living of Wymeswold, Leicestershire. In 1841 he published "Chapters on the Poets of Greece." He was Hulsean Lecturer in 1841—2, and was appointed Examiner in Logic and Moral Philosophy in the University of London. The first volume of the first edition of his work on the Greek Testament was published in 1849, and the whole work was completed in 1861. The different volumes of which it consists have gone through several editions, and notwithstanding the drawback to the value of the whole work arising from some modifications of method on the part of the author during the progress of the work, its value as a scholarly production is generally recognized. Dean Alford is also the author of several volumes of sermons, and of several series of elaborate magazine articles on "The Queen's English," on "Journeys in Italy," on "The Right Use of the Gospels," &c.

From 1853 to 1857 Dean Alford was known as the eloquent minister of Quebec-street Chapel, London, and in 1854-55, he published two volumes of "Quebec Chapel Sermons." In 1857 he succeeded Dean Lyall in the deanery of Canterbury. A fourth edition of his poetical works appeared in 1865, containing many pieces then first collected. He has written in various metres and on various subjects. Excessive occupation in other pursuits seems to have prevented his muse from fulfilling all its early promise. Some of his sonnets are very felicitous, but his later works are not in advance of his earlier, and he has produced no great poem that will live, and bear his name to posterity.

"Lo! the storms of life are breaking."—No. 607.

This hymn, his sole contribution to the "New Congregational" is No. 23 of a small collection, entitled, "Psalms and Hymns adapted to the Sundays and holydays throughout the year." The collection was made by Dean Alford in 1844. It contains thirty-four pieces by himself; the rest are by various authors. This is the hymn for the Fourth Sunday in Epiphany.

GEORGE DUFFIELD.
Born 1818.

We are indebted to Dr. Joseph Belcher's recent work for a brief account of this hymn-writer, who is a living American clergyman.

He is the son of the Rev. Dr. Duffield, a Presbyterian clergyman of Detroit. The poet was born at Carlisle, in 1818, graduated at Yale College in 1837, was ordained to the ministry in 1840, and removed to Philadelphia in 1852. He is a useful minister, a prose writer, and the author of several hymns.

"Stand up! stand up for Jesus!"—No. 890,

a heart-stirring hymn, is that by which Mr. Duffield is best known. It is his sole contribution to the "New Congregational Hymn Book." It was composed to be sung after a sermon delivered by its writer the Sabbath following the mournfully sudden death of the Rev. Dudley A. Tyng, who was called from earth in 1858, and whose dying counsel to his brethren in the ministry was, "Stand up for Jesus."

JOHN S. DWIGHT.

"God bless our native land."—No. 998.

This adaptation of the English national anthem to American ideas, in which "God save the State!" takes the place of "God save the Queen," bears date 1844. It is by the Rev. John S. Dwight, a son of the celebrated President of Yale College, Dr. Timothy Dwight. This son is the author of several hymns, and a translator, in conjunction with others, of select minor poems from the German of Goethe and Schiller, with notes, in Ripley's "Specimens of Foreign Standard Literature."

SAMUEL SIMPSON ENGLAND.

The Rev. S. S. England was for three years one of the committee who laboriously engaged in the compilation of the "New Congregational Hymn Book." Some of the members of the committee wished to have a version of *every* psalm, and Mr. England made this very faithful rendering of Psalm vi.—

"In anger, Lord, rebuke me not,"—No. 6,

as a contribution towards supplying those that were wanting. It was subsequently found that some of the psalms could not conveniently be adapted to public worship, and the purpose was abandoned, but this psalm was adopted.

Mr. England was born in London, and numbers amongst his ancestors the Rev. Peter Du Bourdieu, a Huguenot refugee and a clergyman of the Church of England. He was introduced to the ministry by the lamented Caleb Morris, the minister of Fetter-lane Chapel, and for five years enjoyed the tuition of the late revered Dr. J. Pye Smith, at Homerton College. His first charge as a Congregational minister was at Royston, Cambs, where he commenced his pastorate in 1838. In the year 1847 he became chaplain of Mill Hill Grammar School. At the end of 1853 he removed to Walthamstow, to be the pastor of the church formerly under the care of the Rev. George Collison, and subsequently he became pastor of the Church assembling at the Old Meeting, Halstead, Essex, which charge he was compelled to resign in March, 1865, in consequence of indisposition. He is not the author of any volume of poems, but has contributed some fugitive pieces to magazines.

ROBERT MURRAY McCHEYNE.
1813—1843.

Like the course of the falling star that after delighting us for a moment, seems to hasten quickly away to some more congenial sphere, so was the brief but beautiful career of this eminent servant of God. Born in Edinburgh, McCheyne studied with great success in the University there, and was adjudged the prize for a poem on the "Covenanters." Favoured by the good influence of Dr. Chalmers, and devoting himself to works of Christian usefulness, his piety ripened and his Christian character was developed.

In 1836, he was ordained a minister of the Presbyterian Church, and became pastor of St. Peter's, Dundee. There he became a popular preacher and a beloved pastor, and amidst the various engagements of his laborious pastorate he found time to write tracts and hymns.

In 1839, in consequence of the failure of his health, he joined with several eminent ministers in taking an extended tour in the East. The special object of this journey was to investigate the condition of the Jews. After his return, his labours soon terminated in a triumphant death. His eminent piety, great usefulness, and early death have encircled his name with a lasting halo.

His sole contribution to the "New Congregational Hymn Book" is hymn No. 575—

"When this passing world is done."

It is an appropriate expression, as it is a memorial of the heavenly mindedness in which he lived on earth preparing for heaven, and by which he encouraged many to follow him.

FREDERICK WILLIAM FABER, D.D.
1815—1863.

The hymns and poems of this eminent sacred poet are second to none in sentiment and beauty. Many of his verses express the best thoughts and feelings of Christians of all denominations; but Protestants will regret to meet with lines such as these—

> "For Mary's smiles each day convert
> The hardest hearts on earth."

F. W. Faber, who is a nephew of the Rev. George Stanley Faber, the well-known writer on prophecy, was born in 1815. He was educated at Harrow, graduated B.A. at Oxford in 1836, and became a college tutor and fellow. Subsequently, in 1843, he entered upon the living of Elton, Huntingdonshire; but in 1846, he became a Roman Catholic, and went to reside at St. Wilfrid's, Staffordshire. In 1849 he came to London, and established the brotherhood of the London "Oratorians," or "Priests of the Congregation of St. Philip Neri," in King William-street, Strand. The Oratory removed in 1854 to Brompton. To it Dr. Faber gave his energies till his death on Sept. 26th, 1863.

In 1840 he gained a reputation as a poet by his work, "The Cherwell Water-lily, and other poems." He is also the author of a work entitled, "Scenes in Foreign Churches," dedicated to his friend Wordsworth. In this, and in an earlier work, "The Ancient Things of the Church of England," 1838, he had vindicated the Protestant Church. Just before his change of religion he wrote his poems, "Lives of the Saints," and after that change, he sent forth several theological works in favour of his new views. His mind seems to have been influenced in favour of his new course by the persuasion of Pope Gregory, with whom he had an interview in 1843; but his secession was a sudden act arising from a feeling that he lacked priestly efficacy in the community to which he belonged. In his preface to his hymns, published in 1862, Dr. Faber explains that they were first published at Derby in 1848, and sold largely in England and Ireland ; that ten thousand copies of an edition published in London in 1849 were sold ; that a selection with additions was published in 1854, and sold largely, and also that some of the hymns were published as a penny book, "Hymns for the People." The edition of 1862 is complete, with fifty-six new hymns. It contains 150 pieces, some of them extending to more than twenty verses, and consists of hymns on the Divine attributes ; hymns for festivals, hymns addressed to Christ, and some to saints and angels ; hymns on the sacraments, on the spiritual life, on death, &c." Many of the pieces are of great beauty, and some have been gladly taken to enrich the new collections recently made by Christians of different denominations.

In the conclusion of his preface, the author says, " It is an immense mercy of God to allow any one to do the least thing which brings souls nearer to Him. Each man feels for himself the peculiar wonder of that mercy in his own case." In this devout and grateful spirit his poems are written.

"My God, how wonderful Thou art!"—No. 263.

This is part of No. 9 in Faber's collection of 1862. It had appeared in 1849 ; it is entitled, " Our Heavenly Father." In the "New Congregational Hymn Book," verses 6, 7, and 8 are omitted, and verse 9, given as a sixth verse, is slightly altered. The omitted verses are of the same character, and equal in beauty.

"Dear Jesus, ever at my side,"—No. 965,

is Faber's 69th hymn. It is entitled " The Guardian Angel," and was written for the school children. In the original it is—

" Dear Angel, ever at my side."

It had appeared in his " Jesus and Mary, or Catholic Hymns," 1849. In the "New Congregational Hymn Book," verses 7 to 13, containing Roman Catholic doctrine, are omitted, and a doxology is given as a seventh verse.

THOMAS WILLIAM BAXTER AVELING.
Born 1815.

Mr. Aveling, of Kingsland—for after a successful pastorate there of nearly thirty years the names naturally go together—was born at Castletown, in the Isle of Man, on the 11th of May, 1815. On the maternal side he is of Irish descent, a fact not to be overlooked, as accounting in part for his glowing words and moving pathos. Mr. Aveling was brought up at Wisbeach, Cambridgeshire. He did not enjoy the advantage of pious parentage, nor were his parents Dissenters, but having casually attended the Independent Chapel, he was encouraged to assist in the Sunday-school, and at length joined the church under the care of the Rev. W. Holmes. Mr. Aveling was trained in the school of Mr. James Smith, in which he became an usher, and his book of early poems he dedicated to Mr. Smith. After receiving some educational training from Mr. Holmes, he entered Highbury College to study for the Congregational ministry. To this step he was encouraged by the assistance of Thomas Wilson, the estimable founder of the college. After spending four years at Highbury, Mr. Aveling was ordained at Kingsland, on the 11th of October, 1838. He was at first co-pastor with the Rev. John Campbell, the celebrated African traveller, but on his death, at the end of two years, he succeeded him. The congregation at first worshipped at a small chapel, but in 1852 an elegant Gothic edifice was erected by them at a cost of £8,000. Mr. Aveling's earnest ministry has been attended with continual and growing success, and notwithstanding the demands of the pastorate and the pulpit, he has written some works and rendered good service to several religious and benevolent institutions. Prior to the year 1853, he was for several years the editor of the "Jewish Herald.' He also edited and contributed to the "Missionary Souvenir." In association with Dr. Andrew Reed, and since his death, he has also laboured indefatigably as the honorary secretary of the "Asylum for Fatherless Children." He is also honorary secretary of the Irish Evangelical Society. Besides several sermons and lectures, Mr. Aveling is the author of "The Irish Scholar, a narrative, 1841:" "Naaman; or, Life's Shadows and Sunshine, 1853:" "Voices of Many Waters; or, Travels in the Lands of the Tiber, the Jordan, and the Nile, 1855," written after a tour in the East: and "The Service of the Sanctuary, &c, 1859."

Before reaching the age of nineteen, Mr. Aveling had published, in 1834, a small volume of poems containing some of his hymns. During his ministry, he has for many years written annually hymns to be sung with the New Year's sermon to the young; and on other occasions he has written hymns that have been printed in magazines and annuals, but which have not been published in a collected form. They were not of sufficient merit to demand it, but some of them justly take a place in our collection. There are three hymns by him in the "New Congregational Hymn Book."

"On! towards Zion, on!"—No. 626.

This hymn was first published in the "Evangelical Magazine," and copied into the "Sunday at Home."

"Hail! Thou God of grace and glory!"—No. 816.

This was one of four hymns given on the occasion of the jubilee of the Old Congregational Chapel, Kingsland, which was held on June 16, 1844.

"Lord of the lofty and the low."—No. 976.

This was written for a ragged school anniversary held in Kingsland Congregational Church, under the presidency of the Earl of Shaftesbury, in the year 1856 or 1857.

BENJAMIN GUEST.

"Heavenly Father, may Thy love."—No. 851.

This hymn is given with this name in "Psalms and Hymns for Public, Private, and Social Worship, by the late Rev. Henry Venn Elliott, M.A.," (sixth thousand, 1843), a collection of 431 pieces.

The Rev. E. B. Elliott, M.A., author of "Horæ Apocalypticæ," and other works, and who is a brother of the late Rev. H. Venn Elliott, has kindly supplied the following information about Mr. Guest:—At the time when the Rev. H. Venn Elliott was preparing his collection, the Rev. Benjamin Guest had a school at Kemp's Town, Brighton, and constantly attended his ministry. There is no doubt that it was he who contributed this hymn to that collection. The Rev. B. Guest afterwards held a living in Rutlandshire for some years.

H. MAYO GUNN.

"To realms beyond the sounding sea."—No. 903.

The author of this hymn is the Rev. H. Mayo Gunn, a Congregational minister, who has been for many years fulfilling his ministry at Warminster, in Wilts. He studied at Coward College, and entered upon his ministry in 1839. The above hymn was written for the "New Congregational Hymn Book" (1855). Mr. Gunn has taken an interest in hymnology. He is the author of several hymns, and he has been very happy in some of his translations of ancient hymns. One of his best pieces is a hymn, which has been printed as a handbill and in other forms: it is entitled "The Cross of Christ." It consists of six verses, and commences—

"Higher, higher, to the cross."

This hymn so happily combining variety with unity, so simple and striking in form, and so thoroughly evangelical in doctrine, deserves a place in the collection of the denomination to which the author belongs.

Mr. Gunn is the author of "History of Nonconformity in Warminster; including an Account of the Oldest Chapel in England," 1853; "Congregational Psalmody," a Tract published by the Congregational Union in 1860; "A Memorial of the Nonconforming Clergy of Wilts and East Somerset in 1662," published by request of the Wilts and East Somerset Union, in 1862; "Church Efficiency," published by request of a conference of ministers, &c., held at Bristol in 1863; "Church Principles," 1863, and of some sermons published separately.

G. N. ALLEN.

"Must Jesus bear the cross alone?"—No. 652.

In the American "Plymouth Collection," 1855, by Rev. Henry Ward Beecher, this hymn is divided into two parts after verse three, the name is inserted there, and the numbering of the verses begins afresh. Inquiries on both sides of the Atlantic have up to this time failed to elicit any information concerning the author of this pleasing and impassioned hymn.

ANNE BRÖNTÉ.
1820—1849.

"Oppressed with sin and woe."—No. 525.

This simple and expressive Christian hymn is found at page 494 of "Wuthering Heights and Agnes Grey, by Ellis and Acton Bell. A new edition revised, with a biographical notice of the authors, a selection from their literary remains, and a preface by Currer Bell, 1850." It is now well known that these names were pseudonyms for Emily, Anne, and Charlotte Brönté, the talented authoresses who have so soon passed away from us. In giving a brief sketch of her sisters after their death, Charlotte has also supplied this and several other beautiful spiritual hymns by Anne. This hymn is headed " Confidence." It is given in the " New Congregational Hymn Book " with the omission of a fourth verse. Charlotte has added the following note to it :—" My sister had to taste the cup of life as it is mixed for the class termed ' Governesses.' "

Charlotte, with all her psychological discernment, does not seem to have appreciated the real and affecting elements of the Christian history of her sister. Of her, she says, " She was a very sincere and practical Christian, but the tinge of religious melancholy communicated a sad shade to her brief blameless life. She wanted the power, the fun, the originality of her sister Emily, but was well-endowed with quiet virtues of her own. Long-suffering, self-denying, reflective and intelligent, a constitutional reserve and taciturnity placed and kept her in the shade and covered her mind, and especially her feelings, with a sort of nun-like veil, which was rarely lifted."

Anne Brönté was the youngest daughter of the Rev. Patrick Brönté, B.A. She was born at Thornton, near Bradford, not long before her father removed, in 1820, to enter upon the living of Haworth. Her mother, whose maiden name was Maria Branwell, died September 15th, 1821, in her thirty-ninth year, leaving her children in helpless infancy and childhood. Their father was a recluse man, partly on account of his health and partly from choice—even taking some of his meals alone. And when at length his children's powers expanded, they found themselves treated by him rather as adults than as children, and he discoursed to them earnestly upon the leading persons and politics of the time. Such training of persons endowed as they were, and left usually to one another's company in the solitudes of a lonely northern parsonage, produced characters unique in the age. A strange contest was long carried on between their sense of capacity for public service through the press, and the modesty that shrank from the public gaze. At length, in the year 1846, the three sisters, under the assumed names of Currer, Ellis, and Acton Bell, sent forth a small volume of poems on secular and religious subjects. The pieces were contributed about equally by each of the three sisters, and have never excited any special attention. Soon after, they each wrote a tale. These, after meeting with neglect at first, took their place as works of fiction of the highest talent, and were followed by others, and especially by the works of Charlotte, "Jane Eyre," &c., which have achieved a great name. Anne's works were, in addition to her poems, "Agnes Grey," 1847, and in the same year, "The Tenant of Wildfell Hall," a work of intense truthfulness, but too sad to please the public mind.

The circumstances of the Brontë family rendered it necessary that the daughters should contribute something to the common support, and in April, 1839, Anne went out as a governess. In this capacity she bore with Christian fortitude much that was very painful to a nature so sensitive as hers. After a few years, the family disease made its appearance, and she began to sink by a gradual decline. In a letter written April 5th, 1849, about a month before her death, she writes, " I wish it would please God to spare me, not only for papa's and Charlotte's sake, but because I long to do some good in the world before I leave it. I have many schemes in my head for future practice—humble and limited indeed—but still I should not like them all to come to nothing, and myself to have lived to so little purpose ; but God's will be done." Shortly before her departure, she was removed to Scarborough, where she died, May 28th, 1849, aged twenty-nine.

When near her end, she was asked whether she felt easier, and she replied, "It is not you who can give me ease, but soon all will be well, through the merits of our Redeemer." Her poems and hymns are very beautiful and spiritual. One especially, because of its connection with her brief career as well as because of its intrinsic excellence, cannot fail to awaken interest. It begins—

"I hoped that with the brave and strong."

W. BROWN.

"Welcome, sacred day of rest."—No. 762.

This hymn, given anonymously in the "Old" and "New Congregational," and in other collections, has the above name given to it in "A Selection of Hymns for Congregational Worship," &c., by Thomas Russell, A.M., 20th edition, 1843. It is not in the tenth edition of "Russell's Selection, 1826." Of the author there is no known record.

S. F. SMITH, D.D.

"Spirit of holiness, descend."—No. 813.

This admirable hymn is by Dr. S. F. Smith, an eminent American Baptist minister. It is given without name in the "New Congregational." It is No. 384 in an American Hymn Book of which Dr. Smith was one of the editors. The work is entitled "The Psalmist: a New Collection of Hymns for the Use of the Baptist Churches," by Baron Stow and S. F. Smith, 1843. Dr. Smith was one of a committee appointed by the American Baptist Churches of New York to prepare this work. It is a large and valuable collection, containing 1,180 hymns, by 161 writers. Twenty-six of the hymns were contributed by Dr. Smith, and eight of the hymns in the "American Sabbath Hymn Book" are by him. He was editor, from 1843 to 1849, of "The Christian Review," an able work, published at Boston, America, and to which he contributed many extended and powerful articles on the great religious books and questions of the day.

DYER.

"Time is earnest, passing by."—No. 490.

This is part of a hymn of eight verses which was inserted by the editor in "The Bible Class Magazine," 1851, with the signature "Independent." It was an extract from an American paper of that name. It was subsequently re-inserted in the same magazine, with music by Mr. Joseph Dyer, the schoolmaster of the Wesleyan School, Pocklington. It also appeared in "Select Music for the Young," Sunday School Union, where it is headed, "All Things Earnest: Composed by Joseph Dyer." In this way probably the mistake arose in the "New Congregational," the name of the composer of the music being put for the author of the words. The hymn has been erroneously attributed to George Dyer, author of the "Poetics," 1795. It is evidently a modern hymn. The words "Life is earnest," verse 2, are also found in Longfellow's "Psalm of Life." It is probably an American hymn, but we have not yet learnt the name of the author.

G—— R——.

There are three hymns in the "New Congregational Hymn Book," by a writer, G. R., who wishes to continue to be anonymous, as he was when the hymns were contributed, in order that they might stand or fall by their own merits. The hymns are the following:—

"Come to our poor nature's night."—No. 438.
"Soul, thy week of toil is ended."—No. 948.
"Father of love and power."—No. 987.

The writer wishes to be known as "A Leeds Layman." He was residing at Leeds when these three and twelve other hymns were contributed by him to the "Leeds Hymn Book," 1853. In the formation of that collection he took an active, though anonymous, part. Besides the hymns he contributed, he re-wrote eight others, and altered two. To the "Psalms and Hymns for the Baptist Denomination," 1858, he also rendered important assistance, altering some of the hymns and re-writing others, and he contributed to that collection twenty-seven new hymns, including some already in the "Leeds Hymn Book." His hymns, as they appear in the "Psalms and Hymns," contain his latest corrections.

The productions of this writer are of varied excellence. Some do not rise beyond the rhymed prose that almost any intelligent Christian could produce, but here and there we find a hymn by him that makes us ask whether we have found another Newton or Montgomery. The hymn—

"Soul, thy week of toil is ended,"—No. 948,

will be recognized by all as of great excellence. It will be admitted to be the best Saturday Evening Hymn in the "New Congregational Hymn Book." It is admirable for its unity; for the ease of its manner, as if by a practised hand; for the appropriateness of its sentiments and illustrations, and for its reach of thought. And there is one Psalm in the "Leeds Hymn Book" which we miss from the "New Congregational" with regret, No. 200, G. R.'s rendering of Psalm 148—

"Praise ye the Lord, immortal choir."

We are impatient that the author of that psalm should refuse his honours by persisting in continuing to be anonymous.

GEORGE SMITH, D.D.

"Thou art, O Christ, the Way."—No. 333.
"Come in, ye chosen of the Lord."—No. 842.

THESE hymns are by the Rev. George Smith, D.D., best known as the indefatigable secretary of the Congregational Union, which office he has held since the year 1851, having as his colleague in office the Rev. Robert Ashton. Dr. Smith entered upon his ministry in 1827. It was while pastor of a Congregational Church at Plymouth that he prepared for his congregation a supplement to Dr. Watts'. In that work the above hymns appeared for the first time, and hymn 333 has also been inserted in the "American Sabbath Hymn Book." Dr. Smith has also contributed some poetical pieces to the "Evangelical Magazine."

In May, 1842, Dr. Smith removed to London, to become the minister of Trinity Chapel, Poplar, a commodious edifice, erected in the previous year at the sole expense of George Green, Esq., of Blackwall. A church was formed there in July, 1842, of which Dr. Smith has been the pastor ever since. In addition to the fulfilment of his arduous pastoral duties, Dr. Smith has taken an active part in maintaining several denominational and general religious and benevolent institutions of the day. Dr. Smith received his degree of Doctor of Divinity from the Glasgow University in 1864. In 1865, he went, in company with the Rev. J. L. Poore, as a deputation from the Congregational Union to the Churches of Canada and the adjacent Colonies.

Dr. Smith is the author of several prose works, including the following:—"The Domestic Prayer Book," 1848; second edition, 1852; "Sermons," 1851; "Life Spiritual," 1855; "Lectures on the Pentateuch," 1863; besides several lectures, sermons, tracts, and contributions to periodicals.

JAMES SPENCE, D.D.

THERE is one hymn in the "New Congregational Hymn Book" by Dr. Spence, pastor of the Church meeting in the Poultry Chapel, City, one of the largest and most ancient Congregational Churches in London. Dr. Spence disclaims all pretension to the name of poet, and has published no poetical works. This hymn—

"What means the water in this font?"—No. 850,

was supplied anonymously to the committee for preparing the "New Congregational Hymn Book." The author felt that there was a lack of hymns expressing what appear to Congregationalists to be right and scriptural views on the subject of baptism, and made this useful contribution. The hymn after passing the criticism of the London Committee, and then of the far more numerous country Corresponding Committee, was adopted.

Dr. Spence was born in 1821. He pursued his literary studies at the University of Aberdeen, where he took first class honours in classics and mental philosophy, and graduated M.A. After remaining five years at Aberdeen, he removed to Highbury College, to make special preparation for the ministry. In July, 1845, he was ordained, and entered upon his first pastorate as a Congregational minister at Oxford. Thence he removed, in 1848, to Preston, Lancashire, to be minister of Cannon Street Chapel. There his ministry was very successful amongst an attached and increasing congregation. In 1854, Dr. Spence left Preston to enter upon his important charge in London. Dr. Spence received his diploma of Doctor of Divinity from the University of Aberdeen, where he had graduated. Recently, on his return in ill-health from a tour in the East, he was requested by the Congregational Union to undertake the office of Chairman for 1866, but the honour was at that time declined.

The following prose works are by Dr. Spence:—" The Tractarian Heresy; a Voice from Oxford," 1847; "The Religion for Mankind: Christianity adapted to all the Aspects of Humanity," 1852; " The Pastor's Prayer for the People's Weal: a Practical Exposition of St. Paul's Prayer for the Ephesians; " Martha Dryland, &c.," 1862; " Scenes in the Life of St. Peter, a Biography and an Exposition," (Religious Tract Society)—1863.

ANNA LÆTITIA WARING.

" Father, I know that all my life"—No. 590.

THIS is the first piece in a volume, entitled, "Hymns and Meditations," 1850. The fourth edition, with considerable additions, appeared in 1854, the fifth in 1855, and the seventh in 1858. The seventh edition included thirty pieces. In the year 1858, the same writer published "Additional Hymns." She has kindly informed the author of this work that the earliest appearance of the above hymn was in the first edition of "Hymns and Meditations." It is given in the "New Congregational" with the omission of a fifth verse.

This talented authoress wishes to be known only as A. L. Waring, but many sympathizing and benefited readers will feel, that in the absence of dates and names, they know more of her through her beautiful spiritual hymns, than they do of some others whose life-story has long been written. Her hymns cannot be mingled and lost amongst the numerous productions of ordinary writers. Their intrinsic excellence as Christian hymns has given them a hold upon the public religious mind. They have a character of their own. They recall to our memories the effusions of Madame Guyon and her favourite doctrine of "Spiritual Union," but they are free from what was exceptional and extravagant in her religious verses. They are rich in personal experience, an experience not much varied in its aspects, but of the most thorough and fruitful nature. Each Christian reader feels that what the writer describes he experiences in his best hours, and that it will be so with him more and more in proportion as he is "crucified with Christ." Without attempt at word-painting or splendid descriptions of scenery, the writer is content to make her hymns the vehicle for conveying the impression of the power of Christianity within the domain of the soul to comfort and bless man in his daily life; and the devout reader, as he reads, finds his Christian life strengthened and developed.

HARRIET PARR.

"Hear my prayer, O heavenly Father."—No. 915.

This pleasing Christian hymn appeared in "The Wreck of the Golden Mary," which was the tale in the extra number of "Household Words," for Christmas, 1856. The "New Congregational Hymn Book" was at that time in course of collection; and the Rev. Henry Allon, one of the principal compilers, being struck with the excellence of this hymn, applied to Mr. Charles Dickens for permission to use it in the new hymn-book. Mr. Dickens referred him to the authoress, who was then residing at York, and she gave her consent.

The story runs that the ship "Golden Mary" struck on an iceberg, and the passengers and crew had to take to the boats, in which they remained suffering great privations for some days. To beguile the time they told stories. This hymn was repeated by one Dick Tarrant, a youth who had given himself up to dissipation on being disappointed in love. Having become a burden to his friends they had sent him off in the "Golden Mary" to California, to get him out of the way. After telling in touching terms some of his experience, he continues :—

"What can it be that brings all these old things over my mind? There's a child's hymn I and Tom used to say at my mother's knee when we were little ones, keeps running through my thoughts. It's the stars, maybe; there was a little window by my bed that I used to watch them at—a window in my room at home in Cheshire—and if I was ever afraid, as boys will be after reading a good ghost-story, I would keep on saying it till I fell asleep."

"That was a good mother of yours, Dick; could you say that hymn now, do you think? Some of us might like to hear it."

"It's as clear in my mind at this minute as if my mother was here listening to me," said Dick. And he repeated :—

"Hear my prayer, O heavenly Father," &c.

Miss Harriet Parr has kindly informed the author of this work that the hymn, and the story of "Poor Dick" in which it occurs, are both her own, that the hymn had not appeared before, and that she is not the author of other hymns.

Several works of fiction written under the *nom de plume* of "Holme Lee," are by Miss Parr. She is the author of "Kattie Brande," "Sylvan Holt's Daughter," "Against Wind and Tide," "In the Silver Age," and "The Life and Death of Jeanne d'Arc."

ELIZA FANNY MORRIS.
Born 1821.

"God of pity, God of grace."—No 533.

This hymn is found at page 63 of a work entitled "The Voice and the Reply." Worcester, 1858. The work consists of two parts. The first, "The Voice," consists of eighteen pieces, giving expression to God's utterances, whether in the "still small voice" of conscience, or in invitation, warning, or pity. The second part, "The Reply," consists of sixty-eight pieces, and gives expression to man's reply. This hymn is found in the second part; it is entitled "The Prayer in the Temple." The author of it says—"There is a regular progression of Christian experience running through the volume. 'The Prayer in the Temple' came in due course, as one of the noblest circumstances of the godly life; it was written on the 4th September, 1857." In the "New Congregational" one verse of this is omitted, and another is changed in position. The pieces in this volume are easy in versification, and pious in sentiment, and the first piece, "The Voice," especially strikes the reader as having a pleasing vein of poetry running through it.

Mrs. Morris, whose maiden name was Goffe, was born in London, in 1821. Owing to delicate health she was brought up in the country. Familiarity with the works of nature produced in her an enthusiastic interest therein, and early called forth her latent poetic talent. Before publishing "The Voice" and "The Reply" in 1858, she had received a prize from the "Band of Hope" for a poem on "Kindness to Animals." This recognition of ability encouraged her muse. She has since prepared by request a "Bible Class Hymn Book," which is not yet published, but has gained the approval of the Sunday School Union. Mrs. Morris also wrote the words for "School Harmonies, by J. Morris." She has contributed to the periodicals, and is at the present time (1866) sending out her "Life Lyrics," consisting of pieces on secular subjects treated religiously. Her husband, to whom she was united in 1849, is sub-editor of a provincial paper. She has for a time borne with a city life, and has now again returned to the country, and is courting the muses, favoured by the natural advantages of Malvern.

ANONYMOUS HYMNS.

In the "New Congregational Hymn Book," thirty-seven hymns were given without the authors' names. Most of these names we are able to supply, and where they could not be found, we have in most cases given the name of the collection in which the hymn is believed to have first appeared. The full particulars are given under the names to which the reader is referred.

"O Lord, defend us, as of old."—No. 109.

Vide William Hiley Bathurst, M.A., page 362.

"That Thou, O Lord, art ever nigh."—No. 110.

Vide Harriet Auber, page 287.

"All hail, victorious Lord."—No. 172.

This is Psalm 110 in "Psalms and Hymns for Public Worship, selected for the use of the Parish Churches of Islington," 1852.

"My God, when dangers press me round."—No. 235.

This is found in "Hall's Collection," 1836.

"We praise, we worship Thee, O God."—No. 252.

This is a modern rendering of the "Te Deum Laudamus." The fourth verse is given differently.

"Jesus, exalted far on high."—No. 352.

Vide Thomas Cotterill, M.A., page 291.

"Thou Son of God, and Son of man."—No. 355.

Vide John Ryland, D.D., page 264.

"Lo! on the inglorious tree."—No. 376.

An ancient hymn, the date and author not yet ascertained.

"All hail, triumphant Lord."—No. 392.

A correspondent has pointed out that the second stanza of this hymn closely resembles a stanza in one of Charles Wesley's "Family Hymns," as follows:—

> "Jesus to us impart
> Thy resurrection's power,
> And teach our quickened heart
> Its living Lord to adore.
> To vie with the redeemed above,
> Rejoicing in thy pardoning love."

"O thou, the contrite sinner's Friend."—No. 399.

Vide Charlotte Elliott, page 369.

"O Christ, our hope, our heart's desire."—No. 404.

This rendering of the ancient "Jesu, nostra Redemptio," is by the Rev. John Chandler, M.A., 1837.

"When Thou, my righteous Judge, shalt come."—No. 423.

Vide the Countess of Huntingdon, page 130.

"Come to our poor nature's night."—No. 438.

Vide G. R., page 396.

"Father of heaven! whose love profound."—No. 447.

Vide Cooper, page 363.

"While all the angel throng."—No. 452.

This is by C. Wesley, from "Hymns for those that seek, &c.," 1746.

"Now is the accepted time."—No. 495.

Vide John Dobell, page 269.

"Ye that in these courts are found."—No. 504.

Vide Rowland Hill, M.A., page 241.

"The Spirit to our hearts."—No. 519.

Vide H. U. Onderdonk, D.D., page 355.

"To Thee, Thou bleeding Lamb, to Thee."—No. 552.

This hymn is given without name in H. V. Elliott's Collection, 4th thousand, 1840.

"Hallelujah! song of gladness."—No. 714.

A hymn of the thirteenth century. Dr. J. Mason Neale in his "Mediæval Hymns and Sequences Translated," has given a similar rendering of this "Alleluia, dulce carmen," with his opinion that "various reasons render it probable that it is not of earlier date than the thirteenth century."

"We sing His love, who once was slain."—No. 740.

Vide Rowland Hill, M.A., page 241.

"How bright these glorious spirits shine."—No. 750.

Vide Isaac Watts, D.D., page 97.

"Welcome sacred day of rest."—No. 762.

Vide W. Brown, page 395.

"Spirit of holiness descend."—No. 813.

Vide S. F. Smith, D.D., page 395.

"Lord cause Thy face on us to shine."—No. 821.

This is by Thomas Cotterill, M.A., 1819, altered from Doddridge.

"Brother in Christ, and well-beloved."—No. 811.

Vide Charles Wesley, page 144.

"Light up this house with glory, Lord."—No. 882.

Vide John Harris, D.D., page 372.

"With heavenly power, O Lord, defend."—No. 897.

This is found in Dr. Conyers' Collection.

"Shall science distant lands explore."—No. 904.

This is taken from "Jay's Appendix to Dr. Watts, Bath." 1833. It is thought to be by the late Rev. William Jay.

"Ere I sleep, for every favour."—No. 942.

Vide John Cennick, page 169.

"Soul, thy week of toil is ended."—No. 948.

Vide G. R., page 396.

"Great God, as seasons disappear."—952.

Vide Edmund Butcher, page 267.

"Father of love and power."—No. 987.

Vide G. R., page 396.

"Thou sovereign Lord of earth and skies."—No. 989.

This is found in the "Old Congregational," 1836. We have not yet been able to ascertain who is the author of this hymn.

"Great God, where'er we pitch our tent."—No. 990.

Vide John Rippon, D.D., page 253.

"Happy the home when God is there."—No. 991.

This is No. 1087 in the "Sabbath Hymn Book." New York, 1858. A correspondent has pointed out that it closely resembles in form—

"Happy the clime where lives and reigns,"

by Thomas Hastings.

"With grateful hearts, with joyful tongues."—No. 997.

Vide Andrew Kippis, D.D., page 183.

"Swell the anthem, raise the song."—No. 999.

This is found in Dr. William Allen's "Psalms and Hymns," Boston, America, 1835, and it is there given from a "Presbyterian Collection." One verse is omitted in the "New Congregational."

INDEX OF PSALMS AND HYMNS
ILLUSTRATED.

	PAGE
Abide with me, fast falls the eventide	355
Absent from flesh, O blissful thought	97
According to Thy gracious word	283
Again returns the day of holy rest	189
All hail, incarnate God	148
All hail the power of Jesus' name	195
All hail, triumphant Lord	404
All hail, victorious Lord	403
All people that on earth do dwell	23
All scenes alike engaging prove	62
All ye that pass by	140
Almighty Father of mankind	244
Almighty God, Thy word is cast	295
Almighty Maker, God	91
Almighty Maker of my frame	163
And is there, Lord, a cross for me	376
And is this life prolonged to me	93
And will the great eternal God	121
Angels, from the realms of glory	282
Another six days' work is done	66
Are we the soldiers of the cross	95
Arise, my tenderest thoughts, arise	118
Arm of the Lord, awake, awake	198
Author of faith, eternal Word	143
Awake, and sing the song	152
Awake, my soul, and with the sun	57
Awake, my zeal; awake, my love	94
Awake, ye saints, awake	355
Before Jehovah's awful throne	90
Behold a stranger at the door	151
Behold how glorious is yon sky	26
Behold the amazing sight	120
Behold the expected time draw near	284
Behold the glories of the Lamb	79

Behold the mountain of the Lord		245
Behold the Saviour of mankind		67
Beyond the glittering starry skies	147	151
Bless, O Lord, the opening year		188
Blessèd are the sons of God		169
Blessed Redeemer, how divine		94
Blest be the dear uniting love		145
Blest be the wisdom and the power		91
Blest is the man, for ever blest		89
Blest is the tie that binds		225
Blest morning, whose young dawning rays		138
Blest work, the youthful mind to win		269
Blow ye the trumpet, blow		145
Bowed with a sense of sin, I faint		230
Brethren, let us join to bless		167
Bright as the sun's meridian blaze		247
Bright source of everlasting love		269
Brother in Christ, and well-beloved	144	405
Children of the heavenly King		168
Come, Father, Son, and Holy Ghost		145
Come, gracious Spirit, heavenly dove		73
Come, Holy Ghost, our hearts inspire		142
Come, Holy Spirit, come		156
Come in, ye chosen of the Lord		397
Come, let us join our friends above	144	229
Come, Lord, and tarry not		381
Come, O come, with sacred lays		32
Come, O Thou all-victorious Lord		142
Come on, my partners in distress		137
Come, Thou Almighty King	144	196
Come, Thou fount of every blessing	131	217
Come, Thou soul-transforming Spirit		249
Come to our poor nature's night	396	404
Come, ye sinners, poor and wretched		156
Creator Spirit, by whose aid		55
Crown Him with many crowns		373
Day by day the manna fell		336
Day of judgment, day of wonders		188
Dear Jesus, ever at my side		388
Dear Shepherd of Thy people, hear		188
Deathless principle, arise	229	231
Depth of mercy, can there be		142
Did Christ o'er sinners weep		175
Do flesh and nature dread to die		96
Do I believe what Jesus saith		95
Each other we have owned		175
Enthroned on high, Almighty Lord		213
Ere I sleep, for every favour	169	406

		PAGE
Eternal God, we look to Thee		176
Eternal Light, eternal Light		366
Eternal Power, whose high abode		91
Eternal Spirit, by whose power		362
Eternal Wisdom, Thee we praise		91
Faith, 'tis a precious grace		175
Far from the world, O Lord, I flee		208
Father, how wide Thy glories shine		92
Father, I know that all my life		399
Father of all, in whom alone		142
Father of eternal grace	282	336
Father of heaven, whose love profound	363	404
Father of life and light		312
Father of love and power	396	406
Father of mercies, bow Thine ear		175
Father of mercies, condescend		297
Father, to Thy sinful child		337
Father, whate'er of earthly bliss		163
For a season called to part		188
For ever here my rest shall be		145
Fountain of mercy, God of love	149	301
From distant corners of our land		380
From Greenland's icy mountains	303	304
From yon delusive scene		306
Give me the faith which can remove		145
Give me the wings of faith to rise		98
Give to the winds thy fears		35
Glory to God on high	211	269
Glory to the Father give		283
Glory to Thee, my God, this night		58
God bless our native land		385
God is gone up on high		139
God is our refuge in distress		20
God is the refuge of His saints		88
God moves in a mysterious way		207
God of my life, through all its days		119
God of my life, whose gracious power		143
God of our life, Thy various praise		236
God of pity, God of grace		402
Grace, 'tis a charming sound		119
Great God, as seasons disappear	267	406
Great God, impress our trifling minds		261
Great God, now condescend		251
Great God of heaven and earth, arise		122
Great God of wonders, all Thy ways		182
Great God, the nations of the earth		178
Great God, what do I see and hear	24	300
Great God, where'er we pitch our tent	253	406

Great God, with wonder and with praise	93
Great the joy when Christians meet	261
Guide me, O Thou great Jehovah	172
Hail! blessed communion of love	360
Hail! morning known among the blest	294
Hail! Thou God of grace and glory	390
Hail! Thou once despiséd Jesus	180
Hallelujah! song of gladness	405
Happy the heart where graces reign	94
Happy the home when God is there	406
Hark the glad sound, the Saviour comes	120
Hark! the herald angels sing	140
Hark! the song of Jubilee	283
Hark! the voice of love and mercy	251
Hasten, O sinner, to be wise	146
Head of the Church, our risen Lord	336
Head of the Church triumphant	139
Hear my prayer, O heavenly Father	401
Heavenly Father, may Thy love	391
Heavenly Father, to whose eye	336 337
He dies, the Friend of sinners dies	92
High in yonder realms of light	332
Ho, every one that thirsts draw nigh	126
Holy Bible, book divine	284
Holy Ghost dispel our sadness	230
Holy, holy, holy, Lord	283 336
Holy, holy, holy, Lord God Almighty	305
Holy Lamb, who Thee receive	35 156
Hosanna to the living God	304
How are Thy servants blest, O Lord	70
How blest the righteous when he dies	235
How bright these glorious spirits shine	97 405
How firm a foundation, ye saints of the Lord	284
How glorious is our heavenly King	98
How honoured, how dear	336
How is our nature spoiled by sin	93
How precious is the book divine	225
How shall I follow Him I serve	336
How sweet, how heavenly is the sight	272
How sweet the name of Jesus sounds	187
How sweetly flowed the gospel's sound	351
How vast the treasure we possess	95
I love Thy kingdom, Lord	258
I'll praise my Maker with my breath	91
If human kindness meets return	298
Immortal principles forbid	95
In all my ways, O God	174
In all things like Thy brethren Thou	377

		PAGE
In anger, Lord, rebuke me not		385
In the cross of Christ I glory		351
In Thy name, O Lord, assembling		275
Infinite excellence is Thine		225
Inspirer and hearer of prayer		231
Interval of grateful shade		121
It is the Lord enthroned in light		264
It is Thy hand, my God		374
Jerusalem, my happy home		5
Jesus, and can it ever be		151
Jesus, and didst Thou condescend		367
Jesus, at Thy command	231	233
Jesus, exalted far on high	291	404
Jesus, full of all compassion		147
Jesus, I love Thy charming name		120
Jesus, immortal King, arise	261	342
Jesus lives, no longer now		162
Jesus, my all, to heaven is gone		168
Jesus, refuge of my soul		143
Jesus, still lead on		112
Jesus, the name to sinners dear		140
Jesus, the very thought of Thee		8
Jesus, Thou everlasting King		92
Jesus, Thy boundless love to me		35
Jesus, Thy robe of righteousness		113
Jesus, where'er Thy people meet		208
Just as I am—without one plea		369
Keep silence, all created things		91
Lamb of God, whose bleeding love		145
Lamp of our feet, whereby we trace		309
Let all men praise the Lord		29
Let bitter words no more be known		94
Let God arise, and let His foes		20
Let party names no more		175
Let plenteous grace descend on those		209
Let songs of praises fill the sky		291
Let us, with a gladsome mind	41	151
Let Zion's watchmen all awake		121
Lift up to God the voice of praise		293
Light of those whose dreary dwelling		139
Light up this house with glory, Lord	372	405
Lo, God is here, let us adore		105
Lo, He comes with clouds descending	141, 168	192
Lo, on the inglorious tree		404
Lo! the storms of life are breaking		384
Look, ye saints, the sight is glorious		276
Lord, as a family we meet		312
Lord, as to Thy dear cross we flee		372

412 PSALMS AND HYMNS

	PAGE
Lord, at Thy feet we sinners lie ...	73
Lord, before Thy throne we bend	300
Lord, cause thy face on us to shine	405
Lord, dismiss us with Thy blessing ... 193, 197	261
Lord, from my bed again I rise ...	352
Lord, have mercy when we pray ...	347
Lord, how delightful 'tis to see ...	98
Lord, I believe a rest remains	144
Lord, if Thou the grace impart ... 143	196
Lord, it belongs not to my care ...	45
Lord Jesus, let Thy watchful care	360
Lord, like the publican I stand	332
Lord, look on all assembled here ...	156
Lord of mercy and of might	305
Lord of the lofty and the low	390
Lord of the Sabbath, hear our vows ... 118	120
Lord of the vast creation ...	311
Lord, we come before Thee now ...	152
Lord, when we bend before Thy throne ...	296
Lord, while for all mankind we pray	367
Lowly and solemn be	358
Man of sorrows, and acquainted ...	32
Met again in Jesus' name ...	344
Mighty God, while angels bless Thee ... 218	220
Mighty Redeemer, set me free	94
Mortals, awake, with angels join ...	222
Must friends and kindred droop and die ...	96
Must Jesus bear the cross alone ...	392
My faith looks up to Thee ...	382
My God, and is Thy table spread	121
My God, how wonderful Thou art	388
My God, my Father, while I stray	369
My God, the spring of all my joys	96
My God, when dangers press me round ...	403
My soul, praise the Lord, speak good of His name	285
My soul, Thy great Creator praise	90
My trust is in the Lord	354
No more, my God, I boast no more	345
Not all the blood of beasts	94
Now begin the heavenly theme	188
Now from the altar of our hearts ...	49
Now I have found the ground wherein ... 75	113
Now is the accepted time ... 269	404
Now let our cheerful eyes survey	120
Now let our mourning hearts revive	120
Now let our souls on wings sublime	178
Now let the children of the saints	98
Now let the feeble all be strong ...	120

		PAGE
Now may the gospel's conquering power	...	275
Now may the Spirit's holy fire	102	231
Now to the hands of Christ our King	...	95
O Christ, our hope, our heart's desire	...	404
O for a closer walk with God	...	207
O for a thousand tongues to sing	...	140
O give thanks to Him who made	...	336
O God, my Helper, ever near	...	225
O God, my strength and fortitude	...	22
O God of Bethel, by whose hand	119	249
O God of families, we own	...	332
O God of mercy, God of might	...	338
O God, we praise Thee, and confess	...	59
O happy day that fixed my choice	...	120
O happy soul that lives on high	...	96
O help us, Lord, each hour of need	...	347
O how blest the congregation	...	355
O! Jesus, King most wonderful	...	8
O Lord, another day is flown	...	323
O Lord, defend us as of old	362	403
O Lord, how happy we should be	...	377
O Lord, I would delight in Thee	...	264
O Lord, my best desire fulfil	...	207
O Lord, Thy work revive	73	311
O Love divine, how sweet Thou art	...	137
O sacred Head, once wounded	9	35
O send Thy light, Thy truth, my God	...	345
O Spirit of the living God	...	282
O that I knew the secret place	...	95
O Thou from whom all goodness flows	...	213
O Thou, the contrite sinner's Friend	369	404
O Thou, to whom in ancient time	...	315
O Thou, who camest from above	...	137
O timely happy, timely wise	...	339
O where shall rest be found	...	283
O worship the King	...	317
O Zion, afflicted with wave upon wave	...	154
O'er the gloomy hills of darkness	...	173
Oft in sorrow, oft in woe	...	322
On Jordan's stormy banks I stand	...	198
On, towards Zion on	...	390
Oppressed with sin and woe	...	392
Our Father, God, who art in heaven	...	328
Our God, our help in ages past	...	92
Our journey is a thorny maze	...	97
Out of the depths I cry to Thee	...	20
Praise God, from whom all blessings flow	...	58
Praise Jehovah, bow before Him	...	352

PSALMS AND HYMNS

	PAGE
Praise, Lord, for Thee in Zion waits	355
Praise the Lord, ye heavens, adore Him	289
Praise to Thee, Thou great Creator	225
Prayer is the soul's sincere desire	280
Questions and doubts be heard no more	92
Rejoice, the Lord is King	140
Religion is the chief concern	226
Return, O wanderer, to thy home	311
Rise, my soul, and stretch Thy wings ... 102	196
Rock of Ages, cleft for me	230
Saviour, breathe an evening blessing	349
Saviour, let Thy sanction rest	332
Saviour, when in dust to Thee	317
See how great a flame aspires	144
Servants of God, in joyful lays	282
Shall science distant lands explore	406
Shepherd divine, our wants relieve	231
Shepherd of Israel, bend Thine ear	121
Shepherd of tender youth	4
Show pity, Lord : O Lord, forgive	89
Since all the downward tracks of time	159
Sing, my tongue, the Saviour's glory	11
Sing the great Jehovah's praise	28
Sinner, O why so thoughtless grown	93
Soldiers of Christ, arise	143
Soul, thy week of toil is ended ... 396 397	406
Sovereign Ruler of the skies	264
Spirit Divine, attend our prayers	320
Spirit of holiness, descend... ... 395	405
Spirit of light and truth, to Thee	338
Stand up! stand up for Jesus	384
Stay, Thou insulted Spirit, stay	143
Sun of my soul, Thou Saviour dear	339
Sweet the moments rich in blessing	211
Swell the anthem, raise the song	406
That Thou, O Lord, art ever nigh ... 287	403
The festal morn, my God, has come	176
The God of Abraham praise ... 179	192
The God of truth His Church has blest	326
The heavens declare Thy glory, Lord ... 88	138
The hour of my departure's come	245
The hours of evening close	362
The livelong night we've toiled in vain	338
The Lord— how fearful is His name	91
The Lord is King, and weareth	32
The Lord is King, lift up Thy voice	336
The Lord my pasture shall prepare	70
The Lord of earth and sky	145

					PAGE
The Lord of might from Sinai's brow	...	...	...	...	305
The Lord of Sabbath let us praise	...	...	...	...	99
The Lord shall come, the earth shall quake	...	...	...	304
The Lord will come, and not be slow	...	...	...	...	40
The praises of my tongue ...	...	...	...	...	99
The spacious firmament on high ...	...	...	...	...	70
The Spirit to our hearts	...	...	...	...	355	405
There is a book, who runs may read	...	...	...	...	338
There is a land of pure delight	...	...	...	88	96	198
This God is the God we adore	...	...	...	...	156
This is the day when Christ arose	...	...	...	...	98
This night I lift my heart to Thee	...	...	...	...	352
Thou art gone to the grave, but we will not	...	...	...	305
Thou art, O Christ, the Way	...	...	...	...	397
Thou Glorious Sovereign of the skies	...	...	...	...	121
Thou God of glorious majesty	...	...	...	...	141
Thou gracious God, and kind	...	...	...	...	324
Thou hidden love of God, whose height...	...	...	...	105
Thou Son of God, and Son of man	...	...	...	264	404
Thou sovereign Lord of earth and skies...	...	...	...	406
Thou who art enthroned above	...	...	...	...	28
Thou whose Almighty word	...	...	...	...	323
Though troubles assail	...	...	...	...	...	188
Thrice happy souls, who, born from heaven	...	...	...	122
Thus far my God hath led me on...	...	...	...	225
Thy mercy, my God, is the theme of my song	...	...	...	196
Time is earnest, passing by	...	...	...	...	395
To-day the Saviour calls ...	...	...	...	...	311
To God be glory, peace on earth	...	...	...	1	64
To God on high be thanks and praise	...	...	...	...	12
To praise the ever-bounteous Lord	...	...	...	...	149
To realms beyond the sounding sea	...	...	...	...	391
To Thee in ages past	...	...	...	...	312
To thee, O dear, dear country	...	...	...	...	9
To Thee, O Lord, I yield my spirit	...	...	...	...	51
To Thee, Thou bleeding Lamb, to Thee...	...	...	...	405
Unveil thy bosom, faithful tomb ...	...	...	...	...	97
Vital spark of heavenly flame	...	...	...	...	77
Walk in the light, so shalt thou know	...	...	...	309
We praise, we worship Thee, O God	...	...	...	403
We sing His love, who once was slain	...	...	...	241	405
We sing to Thee, Thou Son of God	...	...	...	167	231
Welcome, brethren, enter in	...	...	...	...	349
Welcome, sacred day of rest	...	...	...	...	395	405
What means the water in this font	...	...	...	398
What shall the dying sinner do	...	...	...	...	93
What sinners value, I resign	...	...	...	...	88
When all Thy mercies, O my God	...	...	...	...	71

		PAGE
When gathering clouds around I view		317
When I can read my title clear		97
When I survey the wondrous cross		92
When Israel, freed from Pharaoh's hand		90
When on Sinai's top I see		283
When our heads are bowed with woe		347
When rising from the bed of death		71
When this passing world is done		386
When Thou, my righteous Judge, shalt come	130	404
Where high the heavenly temple stands		244
While all the angel throng		404
While Thee I seek, Almighty Power	172	272
Whom should we love like Thee		355
With broken heart and contrite sigh		363
With grateful hearts, with joyful tongues	183	406
With heavenly power, O Lord, defend		406
With heavenly weapons I have fought		95
With humble heart and tongue		226
Witness, ye men and angels now		175
Would Jesus have the sinner die		139
Ye dying sons of men		269
Ye hearts, with youthful vigour warm		118
Ye messengers of Christ		283
Ye servants of God		139
Ye servants of the Lord		120
Ye that in these courts are found	241	405
Ye virgin souls arise		141
Your harps, ye trembling saints		231

www.ingramcontent.com/pod-product-compliance
Lightning Source LLC
Chambersburg PA
CBHW051733300426
44115CB00007B/549